EUROPEAN STUDIES ON CHRISTIAN ORIGINS

Editor
Michael Labahn

Editorial Board
Tom Holmén, Bert Jan Lietaert Peerbolte, Loren T. Stuckenbruck,
Tom T. Thatcher

Published under

Library of New Testament Studies

374

formerly the Journal for the Study of the New Testament Supplement series

Editor
Mark Goodacre

THE NORDIC PAUL

Finnish Approaches to Pauline Theology

EDITED BY

LARS AEJMELAEUS
ANTTI MUSTAKALLIO

t&t clark

Copyright © Lars Aejmelaeus, Antti Mustakallio and contributors, 2008

Published by T&T Clark
A Continuum imprint
The Tower Building, 11 York Road, London SE1 7NX
80 Maiden Lane, Ste 704, New York, NY 10038

www.continuumbooks.com

British Library Cataloguing-in-Publication Data
A catalogue record for this book is available from the British Library

ISBN 10: HB: 0567033104
ISBN 13: HB: 9780567033109

Typeset by Data Standards Ltd, Frome, Somerset
Printed on acid-free paper in Great Britain by Biddles Ltd, King's Lynn, Norfolk

CONTENTS

LIST OF ABBREVIATIONS

AASF	Annales Academiae scientiarum fennicae
AB	Anchor Bible
AGTL	Arbeiten zur Geschichte und Theologie des Luthertums
AnBib	Analecta Biblica
ANRW	Hildegard Temporini and Wolfgang Haase (eds), *Aufstieg und Niedergang der römischen Welt: Geschichte und Kultur Roms im Spiegel der neueren Forschung* (Berlin: W. de Gruyter, 1972–)
ANTC	Abingdon New Testament Commentaries
BBR	*Bulletin for Biblical Research*
BECNT	Baker Exegetical Commentary on the New Testament
BETL	Bibliotheca Ephemeridum Theologicarum Lovaniensium
BEvT	Beiträge zur evangelischen Theologie
Bib	*Biblica*
BibInt	*Biblical Interpretation: A Journal of Contemporary Approaches*
BIS	Biblical Interpretation Series
BNTC	Black's New Testament Commentaries
BSac	*Bibliotheca Sacra*
BZAW	Beihefte zur *ZAW*
BZNW	Beihefte zur *ZNW*
CBET	Contributions to Biblical Exegesis and Theology
CBQ	*Catholic Biblical Quarterly*
CEV	Contemporary English Version
CNT	Commentaire du Nouveau Testament
ConBNT	Coniectanea biblica, New Testament
CRBS	*Currents in Research: Biblical Studies*
EKKNT	Evangelisch-Katholischer Kommentar zum Neuen Testament
ESCJ	Études sur le Christianisme et le Judaïsme
ESCO	European Studies on Christian Origins
ETS	Erfurter Theologische Studien
ExpT	*Expository Times*
FRLANT	Forschungen zur Religion und Literatur des Alten und Neuen Testaments
FSÖT	Forschungen zur systematischen und ökumenischen Theologie
GNB	Good News Bible

GNS	*Good News Studies*
GTA	Göttinger theologischer Arbeiten
HNT	Handbuch Zum Neuen Testament
HTKNT	Herders theologischer Kommentar zum Neuen Testament
HTR	*Harvard Theological Review*
ICC	International Critical Commentary
JBL	*Journal of Biblical Literature*
JR	*Journal of Religion*
JSNT	*Journal for the Study of the New Testament*
JSNTSup	*Journal for the Study of the New Testament*, Supplement Series
KTNT	Kommentar till Nya Testamentet
KNT	Kommentar zum Neuen Testament
LNTS	Library of New Testament Studies
LuthBei	*Lutherische Beiträge*
MeyerK	H.A.W. Meyer (ed.), Kritisch-exegetischer Kommentar über das Neue Testament
MNTC	Moffatt NT Commentary
NCB	New Century Bible
NCBC	New Century Bible Commentary
NEchtB	Die Neue Echter Bibel
Neot	*Neotestamentica*
NICNT	New International Commentary on the New Testament
NIGTC	The New International Greek Testament Commentary
NovT	*Novum Testamentum*
NovTSup	*Novum Testamentum*, Supplements
NRSV	New Revised Standard Version
NSBT	New Studies in Biblical Theology
NTAbh	Neutestamentliche Abhandlungen
NTS	*New Testament Studies*
NZST	*Neue Zeitschrift für systematische Theologie und Religionsphilosophie*
ÖTK	Ökumenischer Taschenbuch-Kommentar zum Neuen Testament
PDA	Studies of Argumentation in Pragmatics and Discourse Analysis
PFES	Publications of the Finnish Exegetical Society
RAC	*Reallexikon für Antike und Christentum*
RBL	*Review of Biblical Literature*
RNT	Regensburger Neues Testament
SBL	Society of Biblical Literature
SBLDS	SBL Dissertation Series
SBS	Stuttgarter Bibelstudien
SJS	*Scandinavian Jewish Studies*
SNTSMS	Society for New Testament Studies Monograph Series

SNTU	Studien zum Neuen Testament und seiner Umwelt
STGMA	Studien und Texte zur Geistesgeschichte des Mittelalters
SVF	*Stoicorum veterum fragmenta* (H. Von Arnim; 4 vols; Leipzig, 1903–1924)
TBü	Theologische Bücherei
TDNT	Gerhard Kittel and Gerhard Friedrich (ed), *Theological Dictionary of the New Testament* (trans. Geoffrey W. Bromiley; 10 vols; Grand Rapids: Eerdmans, 1964–)
THKNT	Theologischer Handkommentar zum Neuen Testament
TNT	Tolkning av Nya Testamentet
TRE	*Theologische Realenzyklopädie*
TU	Texte und Untersuchungen
UNT	Untersuchungen zum Neuen Testament
WA	*Weimarer Ausgabe, D. Martin Luthers Werke* (Weimar: Böhlau, 1883–)
WBC	Word Biblical Commentary
VIEG	Veröffentlichungen des Instituts für Europäische Geschichte
WUNT	Wissenschaftliche Untersuchungen zum Neuen Testament
ZAW	*Zeitschrift für die alttestamentliche Wissenschaft*
ZBK	Zürcher Bibelkommentare
ZNW	*Zeitschrift für neutestamentliche Wissenschaft*
ZTK	*Zeitschrift für Theologie und Kirche*
ZWT	*Zeitschrift für wissenschaftliche Theologie*

LIST OF CONTRIBUTORS

Lars Aejmelaeus (Professor of Biblical Studies, University of Helsinki)

Mika Hietanen (Researcher, Åbo Akademi University in Turku)

Niko Huttunen (Researcher, University of Helsinki)

Timo Laato (Associate Professor of New Testament, The Lutheran Theological Seminary in Gothenburg, Sweden)

Kenneth Liljeström (Researcher, University of Helsinki)

Jaakko Linko (Reverend Minister, Lapua)

Antti Mustakallio (Theological Secretary to the Bishop of Helsinki)

Nina Pehkonen (Researcher, University of Helsinki)

Heikki Räisänen (Professor Emeritus of New Testament Studies, University of Helsinki)

Risto Saarinen (Professor of Ecumenics, University of Helsinki)

Lauri Thurén (Professor of Biblical Studies, University of Joensuu)

Stephen Westerholm (Professor of Biblical Studies, McMaster University, Canada)

ACKNOWLEDGMENTS

The editors wish to thank warmly all the contributors for engaging in this project. We are grateful to the editors at Continuum for accepting this volume into their fine series. Especially, we would like to name Drs Tom Holmén and Michael Labahn who have been more than helpful before and during the editing process. The same holds true for the members of the T&T Clark staff, with whom it has been a pleasure to work. Finally, we are indebted to Ms Susanna Asikainen, who skilfully compiled the indices.

The Editors

PREFACE

The idea for this collection of essays by Finnish Pauline scholars originated from a Finnish national seminar on Paul and his theology held at the University of Helsinki in January 2007. Being the first of its kind, the seminar, which gathered virtually every Finnish Pauline scholar and many other exegetes together, proved successful. The organizers (who also happen to be the editors of the present volume) soon realised that the contents of several seminar papers might be of interest to a larger non-Finnish scholarly audience. In this book, the vision has materialized: many of the essays – namely those by Räisänen, Laato, Aejmelaeus, Pehkonen, Linko, Liljeström and Thurén – are reworked English versions of the original Finnish texts.

The opening essay, a contribution by Stephen Westerholm, the only non-Finnish writer in this volume, introduces the reader to the Finnish contributions to the debate on Paul and the law. Westerholm summarizes the views of five scholars: Heikki Räisänen, Kari Kuula, Timo Laato, Timo Eskola, and Lauri Thurén, and concludes with observations based on his own reading of Paul. It becomes clear that the discussion is polarized. In many respects, Räisänen and Kuula are sympathetically disposed towards E.P. Sanders' position and share the view of Paul as a confused thinker whose view on the Mosaic law remained incoherent. Laato and Eskola, on the other hand, consider Paul's thinking much more sound. Both emphasize the apostle's pessimistic anthropology. For Paul, sin is a mighty power in the bonds of which humanity suffers. Therefore, redemption must be the sole act of God with no human involvement. The contemporary Jewish view of man was more optimistic and thus different: salvation required active human co-operation. Thurén also thinks that one can find a 'fairly clear and solid' view of the law in Paul's letters, thus paralleling Laato and Eskola. His special emphasis is rhetoric: only when the nature of the letters as rhetorical documents is taken seriously into account can one hope to reach reliable results. Finally, Westerholm concludes that 'different positions in the current debate have strong advocates among contemporary Finnish scholars'.

In his contribution to the present book, Heikki Räisänen finds a number of features in Paul's discussion of Israel's fate in Romans 9–11 problematic. In those chapters, Paul, according to Räisänen, clings to three distinctive lines of thought which remain irreconcilable. In his opinion, the tensions manifest the seriousness of the difficulties which Paul came across when dealing with questions central to him on identity and continuity. Räisänen thinks that religious anxiety looms behind much of the criticism levelled against the thesis that Paul was inconsistent. The contradictions, however, only show that Paul was a real human, of flesh and blood. Taking Paul more as a discussion partner than an authority may assuage the religious problem, believes Räisänen.

In his essay, Timo Laato deals with the meaning of 'God's righteousness' in Paul – once again. Beginning with Romans, Laato examines the background and meaning of the concept in Paul's letters. After this, three different interpretations of Paul's understanding of righteousness are reviewed: those of Ernst Käsemann, the 'New Perspective', and, concentrating mainly on the work of Mark A. Seifrid, 'the Old Testament perspective on Paul', as Laato calls it. Finally, the traditional question is asked: what was the place of the doctrine of justification in Paul's overall theology? According to Laato, it forms 'without doubt the centre of Paul's theology': the apostle's theology is 'intertwined' with the doctrine and the key to his thinking. The essay culminates in a 'homiletic application' in which Laato deliberates the relation between the concept of 'God's righteousness' and the modern-day proclamation of the church.

According to Niko Huttunen's essay, Paul's teaching on law contained features that originate from Greco-Roman philosophy. Huttunen compares Epictetus, a gentile Stoic philosopher, and Paul, and concludes that the latter's teaching on law in 1 Corinthians 7 and Romans 1 and 2 incorporates Stoic elements. These elements cannot be found in Romans 13, where Paul is shown to differ from Epictetus' Stoic views. The comparison between the two attests, however, that the apostle was not ignorant of philosophical theories on the state and law. These parallels of thought between Epictetus and Paul lead Huttunen to encourage 'a fresh approach from the ancient philosophical point of view in order to exhibit the philosophical components of Paul's teaching'.

In his contribution (which is a slightly modified version of an article that appeared in *Pro Ecclesia* 15 [2006]), Risto Saarinen asks whether contemporary interpreters that compare the theological thought worlds of Paul and Martin Luther have managed to do justice to the reformer. Advocates of the 'New Perspective' have laboured to liberate Pauline studies from the bonds of Lutheranism. But does this 'Lutheranism' accord with the theological thought Luther himself represented? Saarinen answers negatively. Focusing on Romans 7, he demonstrates that, in contrast to the prevailing understanding, Luther's interpretation of the chapter 'does not entail the view that the apostle Paul, or the paradigmatic Christian, would remain unable to produce good actions'. Christians, with

Christ present in faith, can produce them, but in an imperfect manner, and *in this sense* sin continues. Hence the axiom *simul iustus et peccator*. In the end, Luther's theology proves to be much closer to the 'New Perspective' than is usually considered.

Lars Aejmelaeus' essay focuses on two verses in Second Corinthians, 13.3-4, in which 'an essential part of the Pauline theology is concentrated'. Explaining the verses with his overall view of the situation in which Paul wrote the 'Letter of Tears' (2 Cor. 10–13), Aejmelaeus notes that the apostle makes use of a Corinthian slander, 'Christ is weak in Paul, but mighty in us', and other criticism levelled against him by the letter recipients. In 13.4b, Paul declares that in his forthcoming visit he will punish Corinthian believers with the eschatological power of God. This will show that he can also be strong in the present, not only through his letters, thus disclosing the unfounded nature of Corinthian criticism.

Nina Pehkonen aims to solve the identity of Paul's opponents in Philippians 1.15-18a and to assess their relationship to the Judaisers in ch. 3. In her essay, the commonly held view that the opponents in ch. 1 cannot be the Judaisers is questioned. Could Paul say that he rejoices in the work of the Judaisers (1.18)? Pehkonen's answer is positive: in 1.15ff. the apostle refers to their 'genuine evangelism' and remains silent on the more inflammatory issues. Paul's motive is to show his joyous and noble attitude and he thus appear as having a higher ethos than his opponents, the Judaisers. He also aims to deny that he feels threatened by them. In ch. 3, Paul chooses to use strong language on the Judaisers, but he does this explicitly for the safety of the Philippians (3.1).

Despite the fact that today the majority of scholars consider Philippians as a unified letter, Jaakko Linko is of the opinion that the case is not closed yet. His essay claims that 'the new unity theories are no more convincing than most old division theories'. Examining the major arguments for and against the unity of Philippians, Linko ends up defending a two-letter hypothesis (Letter A: 1.1–3.1; 4.1-23; Letter B: 3.2-21). The biggest obstacle to regarding the letter as unified turns out to be that the style and contents of ch. 3 are out of line with the rest of Philippians. This change of tone needs to be sufficiently explained by the advocates of unity, concludes Linko.

Kenneth Liljeström's essay relates the historical events behind 2 Thessalonians. Considering the letter a pseudepigraph, Liljeström examines the 'hermeneutical battle' into the midst of which the author was forced when it was imperative to prove, against the belief held by his opponents (2 Thess. 2.2), that the day of the Lord had not yet come. Because the crux of the matter was the correct interpretation of Paul, the author of the letter decided to create new Pauline material, 2 Thessalonians, in order to establish the validity of his position. Liljeström focuses largely on the key verse 2.2 and shows that its most common readings are problematic. Appealing to the variations allowed by Greek grammar, he offers a fresh and unconventional exegesis of the verse.

Lauri Thurén emphasizes that many research results in Pauline studies are biased because the nature of the apostle's letters as rhetorical documents to the core has been neglected. Paul's primary aim with these texts was to influence the addressees. Thurén deals with three cases that serve as examples: (1) Heikki Räisänen's essay in the present volume suffers from too little attention to the persuasive nature of Romans 9–11, which results in random conclusions; (2) focusing on the rhetorical function of the account of Paul's conversion in Galatians leads us to regard the Damascus road incident more as the outcome of long theological pondering than an out-of-the-blue experience which completely changed the apostle's theology, as traditionally viewed; and (3) it may be that many of Paul's claims about his antagonists were not presented in order to convey historical information. Instead, their aim was to formulate his theological ideas and present them to his addressees. Following contemporary conventions, blaming the opponents in his letters is stereotypical in nature. Therefore, reliable historical information is scarcely to be attained. Thurén concludes that what we find in Romans and Galatians may well be straw men, which originated with the apostle.

Paul's letters bristle with arguments that are difficult to comprehend, but only very seldom have expositors sought help from argumentation theory, Mika Hietanen remarks. His essay introduces the reader to the Amsterdam-originated Pragma-Dialectical method, which is one of the most comprehensive methods for argumentation analysis. The method provides a framework for understanding and evaluating argumentation in the context of a dialogue, and is thus suitable for the purposes of Pauline scholars. Hietanen explains how the method works in theory and practice. The latter is done through an analysis of Galatians 3.6-9. Hietanen estimates that the argumentative quality of Paul's analogy of Abraham is not very high: the different arguments are only loosely connected to each other and several problems render the argumentation unconvincing. The quotations from the Old Testament only seemingly support Paul's claims and are therefore better regarded as rhetorical moves than as rational argumentation. Paul seems to rely on the rhetorical effect of cumulative 'evidence': he stacks different arguments in the hope that their combined impact will be persuasive.

Of whom were the very first audiences of Paul's letters composed? In his essay, Antti Mustakallio aims to find out whether epistolographical study of the form of end greetings in the letters could shed some light on the question. He concentrates mainly on the so-called second-person type of greetings which suggest that the persons greeted did not belong to the primary audience. Thus, their occurrence has an interesting bearing on the audience question. According to the results the examination yields, the first audiences of 1 Thessalonians and Philippians were probably church leaders whose responsibility it was to convey the letter's message to a wider audience, believers in the congregations. The case of Romans was similar: it seems that the letter was initially received by church leaders who transmitted Paul's greetings. However, the notorious problem of the (eventual) audience of Romans cannot be solved by this means.

The Editors

Part I

Chapter 1

FINNISH CONTRIBUTIONS TO THE DEBATE ON PAUL AND THE LAW

Stephen Westerholm

Let it be stated clearly at the outset: my participation in this project is a matter of grace, not merit. My own links to Finland are too weak[1] to allow anything I write to be itself considered a Finnish contribution. I have, however, had occasion elsewhere[2] to note the important part played by a number of Finnish scholars in the debate over the 'new perspective on Paul'. Those remarks led to an invitation to comment on these contributions in this volume. I am happy to do so, convinced as I am that Finnish scholarship in this area merits wider attention.

Any controversy related to Paul and the law is bound to attract scholarly attention in a land with Lutheran roots as strong as those in Finland. The particular debate under discussion here was launched by E. P. Sanders, whose *Paul and Palestinian Judaism*[3] called for a new view of Judaism as well as a rethinking of what Paul says about the law. Sanders opposed the notion that, according to Judaism, God awarded salvation to individuals who merited it by their good works. Those who understood Judaism in this way then read Paul as attacking the legalistic soteriology, self-righteousness and boasting of Jews. Paul's doctrine of justification was taken to mean that human beings cannot be approved ('justified') by God on the basis of deeds they have done, but only by divine grace,

---

1 Not nonexistent, however. If family traditions are correct, my grandmother was born Hilma Lindbeck in Finland (Vasa? Helsinki? On 1 June 1886? or 10 June 1888?) before emigrating to the United States (1911) and marrying my grandfather (1918); she died in 1923. Exhaustive research has revealed, however, that this connection is not sufficient to enable me to participate in the Olympics as a member of Finland's national baseball team. Assuming that similar regulations apply in other contexts, I can only attribute my part in this project to a special dispensation of grace.

2 Stephen Westerholm, *Perspectives Old and New on Paul: The 'Lutheran' Paul and His Critics* (Grand Rapids: Eerdmans, 2004), pp. 226–27; 'The "New Perspective" at Twenty-Five', in D.A Carson, Peter T. O'Brien, and Mark A. Seifrid (eds), *Justification and Variegated Nomism: The Paradoxes of Paul*, vol. 2 (WUNT, 2/181; Tübingen: Mohr Siebeck, 2004), pp. 1–38, (1–2, n. 1).

3 Philadelphia: Fortress, 1977.

appropriated by faith. Sanders countered such views by insisting that
Judaism, no less than Pauline Christianity, was based on grace: Jews
attributed their standing before God to God's gracious election of Israel
as his covenant people. To be sure, Jews were expected to *respond* (as Paul
expected his converts to respond) to God's grace by obeying God's
commands. But deeds of obedience merely served (for Judaism and Paul
alike) to *maintain* one's status as a member of God's people. Sanders
labelled this understanding of Judaism 'covenantal nomism'.

If the Judaism of Paul's day was not the legalistic religion that many
Pauline scholars had portrayed it as being, then the reason for which Paul
rejected it needed reconsideration as well: a Paul who faulted Judaism for
its legalism would have missed the target with his critique. Sanders himself
believes that Paul's ('Lutheran') interpreters introduced the distortion by
reading Luther's attacks on Catholic legalism back into Paul's rejection of
Judaism. For Sanders, Paul found Judaism wrong simply because it
sought salvation apart from Christ. After all, if salvation is through
Christ, then any other proposed path, including Judaism, *must* be wrong.

In what follows I will summarize the views of five Finnish contributors
to the debate, then offer some concluding observations based on my own
reading of Paul.

Heikki Räisänen

Undoubtedly the most influential Finnish contribution to the debate
provoked by Sanders' work is that of Heikki Räisänen. Sanders found
evidence for his proposal that Paul's thought moved 'from solution to
plight' in the inconsistencies he perceived in Paul's statements about the
human dilemma: it is apparent, Sanders maintained, that Paul did not
begin with a clear understanding of what was wrong with humanity, then
see Christ as the solution to the problem; rather, beginning with the
conviction that Christ is the solution, he attempted in various, and
mutually incompatible, ways to depict a plight that suited the solution.
Räisänen goes still further: contradictions and tensions mark *all* of Paul's
thinking about the law.[4] To that argument we must turn in a minute, but
first I would like to draw attention to three points on related matters
where Räisänen has shed significant light.

1. The ambiguity of the term 'legalism' has dogged the debate from the
start. A number of scholars (myself included) have found helpful
Räisänen's proposed distinction between 'hard' and 'soft' legalism: for

---

4 The thrust of Räisänen's argument is thus similar to that found in his article on
Romans 9–11 in this volume.

soft legalists, 'salvation consists of the observance of precepts';[5] *hard* legalists share this conviction but add to it the vices of smugness, boasting and self-righteousness. Räisänen's point – and it is well taken – is that the belief that one must observe God's commands if one is to gain salvation need not lead to the latter vices.

2. Rudolf Bultmann does not figure largely in recent discussions of Paul and the law; but he once did, and the Bultmannian dictum was well represented that 'according to Paul the person who fulfils the law needs grace as much as the one who trespasses against it – indeed it is he most of all who needs it! For in seeking to establish his own righteousness, he is acting *fundamentally* against God'.[6] Support for this position was found in the belief that, when Paul cited the commandment 'You shall not covet [or "desire"]' from the Decalogue (Rom. 7.7), he understood it to prohibit Jewish zeal ('desire') for fulfilling the law as well as acts of covetousness in the usual sense. Without retracing his argumentation here, I will simply say that Räisänen's article on Paul's terminology for 'desire'[7] decisively refutes what was not seen then (though it appears so now) as a bizarre interpretation.

3. Those who regard Judaism as 'legalistic' are wont to see in Judaism a distortion of what the Mosaic law is all about: Jews have perverted a law that fundamentally requires faith into one that demands 'works'. Starting in the 1950s, certain scholars found in Paul's expressions 'law of faith' (Rom. 3.27) and 'law of the spirit of life' (Rom. 8.2) support for this understanding. Though hitherto 'law' in these expressions had always been taken to mean something like 'principle', these interpreters saw Paul referring specifically to the Mosaic law and defining its essence as a 'law [which, rightly understood, is a law] of faith', or 'a law [which, rightly understood, is a law] of the spirit of life'. In two important articles,[8] Räisänen demonstrated (successfully, I believe) both that Greek usage of νόμος allows for the translation 'principle' in these verses, and that Paul's progression of thought requires it.

Numerous other points of detail could be mentioned; but undoubtedly what Räisänen is best known for is the position that inconsistencies should be accepted as constant features of Paul's thinking. Given the focus of this essay, I will here summarize briefly Räisänen's earlier work

---

5   Heikki Räisänen, 'Legalism and salvation by the law', in S. Pedersen (ed.), *Die paulinische Literatur und Theologie* (Aarhus: Aros, 1980), pp. 63–83 (64).

6   Rudolf Bultmann, 'Christ the end of the law', in *Essays, Philosophical and Theological* (London: SCM, 1955), pp. 36–66 (46).

7   Heikki Räisänen, 'The use of ἐπιθυμία and ἐπιθυμεῖν in Paul', in *Jesus, Paul and Torah: Collected Essays* (trans. David E. Orton; Sheffield: Sheffield Academic Press, 1992), pp. 95–111.

8   'The "law" of faith and spirit' and 'Paul's word-play on νόμος: a linguistic study', in *Jesus, Paul and Torah*, pp. 48–68 and 69–94, respectively.

on the law rather than his treatment (in this volume, and elsewhere) of Romans 9–11.[9]

In *Paul and the Law*,[10] Räisänen suggests that Paul's thinking on the law proves problematic in five different areas.

1. What Paul means by the law seems to shift from text to text. At times he speaks of the Mosaic law as given solely to Jews (e.g., 1 Cor. 9.20-21), at other times as though Gentiles, too, are subject to its demands (e.g., Gal. 3.13-14; 4.5-6; Rom. 7.4-6). At times he effectively reduces the law to its moral requirements (e.g., Rom. 2.14, 26-27; 8.4), though without noting the reduction.

2. At times Paul speaks of the law as though its period of validity has passed (e.g., 2 Corinthians 3; Galatians 3) and believers are not subject to its demands; elsewhere he cites demands of Torah as still binding (e.g., 1 Cor. 9.9; 2 Cor. 8.15) and sees the task of Christians as that of fulfilling the law (Gal. 5.14; Rom. 8.4; 13.8-10).

3. At times Paul indicates that human beings are incapable of fulfilling the law (e.g., Gal. 3.10); elsewhere such fulfillment seems unproblematic (e.g., Rom. 2.14-15, 26-27; Phil. 3.6).

4. Paul generally indicates that God gave the law, but in Gal. 3.19 he at least toys with the idea that it came from angels. Nor is he consistent in his explanations of God's purpose in giving the law: it was meant to give life to those who observe it (so, e.g., Rom. 7.10), or it never had that purpose (Gal. 3.21); it rendered sin culpable (Rom. 5.13; cf. 4.15), or God punishes sin even where there is no law (Rom. 2.12-16); it provokes sin (Rom. 5.20; 7.5, 7-13), though Paul is not clear whether sin itself does (Rom. 5.20; 7.13-14) or does not (7.7-11) exist apart from law.

5. Like Sanders, Räisänen believes that Judaism attributed salvation to divine grace. Unlike Sanders, Räisänen believes that Paul nonetheless portrays law observance as Judaism's path to salvation. In fact (Sanders and Räisänen both maintain), the relationship between grace and works is the same in Judaism as in Pauline thought: salvation (i.e., one's status as a member of God's people) is by grace, but judgement will be based on deeds, and grievous sins will lead to condemnation.

All of this suggests a Paul who was something less than the great theologian he is often made out to be. But Räisänen believes the root of the problem lies not with Paul's intelligence quotient, but with a dilemma at the very heart of Christian theology: Christians want to justify doing away with a law that they nonetheless believe to be divinely instituted. That Paul struggled vainly to resolve an insoluble dilemma does not in

---

9   Professor Räisänen and I have exchanged views on Romans 9–11 in James D.G. Dunn (ed.), *Paul and the Mosaic Law* (WUNT, 89; Tübingen: J.C.B. Mohr [Paul Siebeck], 1996), pp. 215–49.

10   WUNT, 29; Tübingen: Mohr (Siebeck), 2nd edn, 1987.

itself reflect poorly on Paul. But it does call for a reevaluation of his thought.

Kari Kuula

Three questions lie at the centre of Kuula's study of the law and the covenant in Paul's writings:[11] 1. Does Paul's thinking on the law and the covenant remain within the framework of Jewish covenantal nomism, or does it represent a fundamental break with his ancestral religion? 2. How do Paul's different statements on the law and the covenant relate to each other? Can we identify the starting-point of Paul's thought, then show how other claims derive from these beginnings? 3. Are the various claims Paul makes about the law and the covenant compatible with each other, or (as Räisänen suggests) mutually contradictory?

On the third question, Kuula's work emphatically reaffirms Räisänen's results in each area where the latter found Paul's arguments about the law problematic. These have been listed above and need not be repeated here.

On the second question, it is primarily the work of E.P. Sanders that Kuula reaffirms. Like Sanders, Kuula identifies participationist soteriology (i.e., the notion that one attains salvation through participation in Christ and in the Spirit) as the centre of Paul's thought. Other important starting-points for Paul's thinking are the convictions that God is the God of Israel, and that the Jewish scriptures are sacred and authoritative. Once these starting-points have been identified, Kuula believes that the problems posed by Pauline inconsistencies become at least explicable. Since salvation is based on participation in Christ, it follows that salvation *cannot* come from the Jewish law and covenant; that, with the coming of Christ, the latter have lost whatever validity they once had; and that Christians are not bound by (at least) the law's ritual and cultic requirements. From these conclusions Paul never wavered. Still, when he attempted to formulate arguments to support these conclusions, tensions and contradictions inevitably emerged: inevitably, because (and here Kuula repeats Räisänen's thesis) a profound dilemma lies at the heart of Paul's theology. Faith in (the faithfulness of) the God of Israel simply cannot be combined with Paul's christocentric soteriology.

On the question of continuity, Kuula believes that Paul has decisively broken with Jewish covenantal nomism. Admittedly, Paul uses scriptural language to describe his soteriology and claims that the 'law' (here meaning *scripture*) foretells it. But neither covenantal nomism nor Paul's christocentric soteriology can accommodate the other; and Paul, realizing

---

11   Kari Kuula, *The Law, the Covenant and God's Plan: Paul's Polemical Treatment of the Law in Galatians*, vol. 1 and *Paul's Treatment of the Law and Israel in Romans*, vol. 2 (PFES, 72 and 85; Helsinki: The Finnish Exegetical Society, 1999 and 2003).

this, insists that Jews no less than Gentiles need salvation in Christ. For Paul, then, Judaism and Christianity are separate religions. And he is left defending the indefensible position that God reveals his righteousness in the very gospel that represents his breaking of the covenant with Israel.

Timo Laato and Timo Eskola

Long before E.P. Sanders set the agenda for much of Pauline scholarship with his *Paul and Palestinian Judaism* (1977), the Jewish scholar Claude G. Montefiore articulated his thoughts on the relationship between the apostle and his ancestral faith.[12] One difference he noted was that Paul's thinking was consistently more pessimistic than that of the rabbis. The latter were certainly aware of human sin, but they also believed there was much human goodness in the world. While granting the need for divine help, they never 'supposed that human efforts count for nothing', or that human beings were incapable of coping with a sinful 'flesh'. 'Man could receive salvation, and get the better of sin (for God was always helping and forgiving), even without so strange and wonderful a device [as the cross of Christ].'[13] Paul, on the other hand, thought human beings ('in the flesh') could do no good.

Timo Laato[14] believes that this fundamental distinction between Paul and his Jewish contemporaries has been obscured in Sanders' work. Jewish texts (he notes) repeatedly affirm human freedom of will and the human capacity to keep God's commandments. The propensity to sin that lies within each human being falls far short of a compulsion. Adam's sin, far from determining the basic sinfulness of his descendants, was deemed merely a (bad) example that human beings may or may not choose to follow. From such views Paul's theology of sin is separated by an unbridgeable gulf. Humanity's problem, for Paul, is not simply the individual, concrete transgressions (plural) that human beings commit, but the (singular) *sin* that represents their total incapacity to do, or even choose, the good. For Paul, Adam's disobedience allowed sin not only to enter the world but also to gain dominion over it. Indeed, interpreting the latter half of Romans 7 as a depiction of Christian existence, Laato concludes that even Christians, for Paul, are at best able to overcome the *deeds* of the flesh; as long as they live in 'this body of death', they never escape its *desires*. In short, 'the anthropological presuppositions of the Jewish and the Pauline pattern of religion clearly differ from one another. The former is based on human free will, while the latter is founded on

---

12   Claude G. Montefiore, *Judaism and St Paul* (London: Max Goschen, 1914).
13   Montefiore, *Judaism*, p. 78.
14   Timo Laato, *Paul and Judaism: An Anthropological Approach* (trans. T. McElwain; South Florida Studies in the History of Judaism, 115; Atlanta: Scholars Press, 1995).

human depravity. Paul seems never to have given up [his] pessimistic anthropology.'[15]

This difference in anthropology, according to Laato, corresponds to a difference in soteriology. Jewish texts speak of the willingness of the exodus generation to accept the commandments revealed at Mount Sinai. Like that generation, proselytes to Judaism must freely submit to the laws of Torah. Even born Jews, though belonging to the covenant by birth, must later consciously take up the 'yoke' of God's rule. Thus non-Jew and Jew alike must acquire or renew entrance into the covenant by an act of their own free will; their salvation requires their active co-operation. By way of contrast, Paul's more pessimistic anthropology requires a soteriology in which God alone is the agent of salvation. Indeed, Paul can speak of the event by which a person comes to faith as an act of divine creation (2 Cor. 4.6; cf. 1 Cor. 1.28), and faith itself is repeatedly portrayed as a divine gift (Phil. 1.29; cf. Rom. 10.17; 1 Cor. 4.15).[16]

A somewhat similar line is taken in Timo Eskola's *Theodicy and Predestination in Pauline Soteriology*.[17] Eskola first questions Sanders' claim that Jews attributed their salvation to God's gracious election of Israel, then (like Laato) draws attention to the more radically pessimistic anthropology of Paul.[18] The theology of Second Temple Judaism, Eskola believes, was preoccupied with issues of theodicy – and necessarily so, in view of the series of disasters that had overtaken the Jewish people. The result was that for most Jewish groups, the covenant was no longer believed to secure their standing as God's people. In different categories of Jewish literature from the time, Eskola traces what he describes as a 'soteriological dualism' and a growing individualism: no longer able simply to rely on their Jewishness, Jews came to believe that virtuous conduct was required for salvation, and that Jews who did not show such conduct would be eternally damned. The divine 'service' imposed upon Israel required wholehearted obedience to the whole law of Moses, an obedience that was a matter of life and death. On the other hand, Eskola (like Laato) believes that repentance and virtuous conduct were always thought to be within the grasp of individual Jews.

The resulting theology, Eskola claims, should not be considered legalistic: though human actions affected salvation, both the reality of the temple cult and Jewish covenantal theology served to guarantee that

---

15 Laato, *Paul*, p. 146.

16 Note as well, in Laato's contribution to the present volume, the perfect 'fit' he sees between Paul's anthropology and his use of righteousness language – to indicate God's saving activity and the righteousness God grants to sinners.

17 WUNT, 2/100; Tübingen: Mohr (Siebeck), 1998.

18 In the discussion that follows, I avoid using the term 'predestination' even though it figures largely in Eskola's discussion. I have myself found his idiosyncratic use of the term confusing, and assume that, in a short summary, it would confuse others as well.

God was assigned a prominent role as well. Salvation was thought to be dependent on God's mercy, but it came with a condition: repentance and a commitment to observing Moses' law. Such a soteriology is best labelled 'synergistic'.

Pauline soteriology, on the other hand, cannot be synergistic, since Paul believed all human beings live under the power of sin: as godless sinners, human beings are utterly incapable of contributing to their own salvation. Like contemporary Jewish theology, Paul believed that God's eschatological judgment would fall on the godless; but his radical concept of sin meant that all human beings are susceptible to such wrath. Salvation can only be based on God's justifying activity, shown to those who respond to the divine call with faith in Christ.

Lauri Thurén

Lauri Thurén's call for 'source criticism' of Paul's letters[19] is an appeal to recognize that their primary aim was not to disclose his thinking but to persuade his audience. In his monograph *Derhetorizing Paul*, Thurén distinguishes between a 'static' and a 'dynamic' reading of the epistles.[20] The former approach is taken by those who read the letters as though their purpose was to make statements of timeless, universal theology. Such readings mistake the nature of Paul's writings, regardless of whether the reader then concludes that Paul was or was not coherent in his theological claims. A dynamic reading, on the other hand, recognizes that Paul wrote not textbooks, but letters intended to influence the thinking and behaviour of his addressees. Indeed, in the service of these aims, he frequently invoked such common rhetorical ploys as exaggeration, vituperation, and the creation of straw men, or 'soft opponents'. An awareness of the rhetorical nature of his discourse will prevent us from taking all that he wrote at face value.

Is it a mistake, then, to consider Paul a theologian? Thurén thinks not. Certainly the arguments with which Paul attempted to convince his audiences were theological; in that sense we can say that he saw *himself* as a theologian. Nor should we conclude from the fact that Paul addressed particular situations in his correspondence that he was merely a situational thinker. The task of the Pauline interpreter is to identify his persuasive devices, 'filter out' their effect on what he wrote, and see whether or not, underlying it all, there is a coherent theological system.

With that in mind, Thurén turns to the subject of the law. Conscious of Paul's persuasive purposes, we ought not to be surprised by the negative

19 See the opening remarks of his contribution to this volume.
20 Lauri Thurén, *Derhetorizing Paul: A Dynamic Perspective on Pauline Theology and the Law* (WUNT, 124; Tübingen: Mohr [Siebeck], 2000), pp. 23–35.

content and tone of his comments about the law in Galatians, nor ought we to conclude that Paul's own attitude towards the law was negative: anxious that his readers not submit to certain ritual aspects of the law, Paul would have undermined his own message if he had spoken in more positive ways. On the other hand, when Paul attempted to deal with the delicate relationship between Gentile and Jewish Christians in Rome, a more balanced treatment was required. In 1 Corinthians, Paul was concerned to modify his readers' interpretation of his own former teaching without (of course!) suggesting that the latter should be rejected. Hence the pattern of initial agreement with his addressees on a point at issue, followed by the introduction of other considerations that alter the picture.

When rhetorical considerations are taken into account, Thurén believes that a 'fairly clear and solid' view of the law emerges from Paul's writings.[21] Here we must be content to note three areas in which he argues this to be the case.

1. Paul has been held to use the term 'law' in different senses in Galatians without signalling any shift. But since Paul's opponents discussed cultic rules, such rules inevitably dominate his purpose-driven response. On the other hand, when Paul finds the core of the law in the love commandment (Gal. 5.14), he is not reducing the law to its moral component, but insisting (in a way that has a number of Jewish parallels) that a single basic intention or demand lies behind both the moral *and* the cultic prescriptions of the law. Nor should Paul's claim in this verse that love fulfils the law be thought to contradict his talk elsewhere of Christian freedom: freedom from the law, in Paul's mind, does not entail an exemption from the basic principle underlying its many regulations.

2. In speaking of the law both as intended to convey life (Rom. 7.10) and as incapable of doing so (Gal. 3.21), Paul has simply chosen, for persuasive purposes, to highlight different aspects of what he believed about the law in different contexts. All becomes clear once a further premise is spelled out: the law has the ability to give life, but since nobody complies with its demands, that ability is never realized. Not even in Galatians does Paul challenge the notion that the law gives life to any who obey it (cf. Gal. 3.12); nor does he ever suggest in Romans that the law *in fact* produces life (cf. Rom. 7.7-9; 8.3).

3. Paul contrasts justification by faith with justification by the works of the law. Both those scholars who base their reconstruction of a 'legalistic' Jewish soteriology on these texts and those who think Paul here distorts Jewish soteriology have failed to heed the rhetorical nature of the argument. Paul is not attempting a neutral description of what others believe, nor does he explicitly charge others with 'legalism'. The contrast

21 Thurén, *Derhetorizing Paul*, 185.

he draws is meant to highlight the gracious aspect of his own position; in the process he presses what he construes as the implication of others' views to an absurd, and therefore discredited, conclusion.

On the other hand, if Paul were not exaggerating a recognizable aspect of others' soteriology, his argument would carry no conviction. His rhetoric presupposes that, regardless of how much Jews or Jewish Christians emphasized the grace of God, they also acknowledged the importance of good works for salvation. And, indeed, further studies have shown a one-sidedness in Sanders' depiction of Jewish soteriology. There was more to the difference between Paul and Judaism than the conviction that Jesus is the Christ; rarely do we find in Jewish texts parallels to Paul's radical depiction of all humanity's guilt, or to his explicit discounting of any human contribution to salvation.

Why, according to Thurén, does Paul reject the law? Perhaps Paul believed that the Jewish law must be done away if the universal monotheism spoken of by the prophets is to be achieved. Or perhaps he thought it important to exclude the boasting before God that is liable to accompany pretensions of keeping the law.

Sundry Observations

1. Half a century ago, Krister Stendahl warned us against attributing the introspective conscience characteristic of a later age to a first-century apostle whose own conscience was remarkably robust.[22] I cannot resist the impression that Räisänen (following Sanders) has attributed the crisis of faith experienced by many in the modern age to a first-century apostle[23] whose own faith, or self-assurance, or assurance of faith, or whatever one wants to call it, has always struck readers (friends and foes alike) as (gloriously or maddeningly) robust. Professor Räisänen must pardon some of us for whom the picture of a Paul (a *Paul?*) plagued by doubts about the tenability of his own basic convictions will take a little getting used to.

2. Whatever the explanation, it is clear that Räisänen and Kuula repeatedly see inconsistencies and contradictions in Paul's writings where others see complementary lines of thought. When, for example, Paul explains Jewish rejection of the gospel both as the outworking of a divine plan and as an expression of culpable human *dis*obedience (Romans 9 and 10), the two explanations are deemed mutually complementary by some, mutually contradictory by others. A further example: in principle there

22   Krister Stendahl, 'The apostle Paul and the introspective conscience of the West', in *Paul Among Jews and Gentiles* (Philadelphia: Fortress, 1976), pp. 78–96.
23   Note, e.g., the references to Paul's 'anguish' and his 'desperate' wrestlings with doubts and dilemmas in Räisänen's contribution to this volume.

can be no disobedience where there is no requirement to be obeyed; in that sense law (broadly defined) must precede (and even, in a sense, be the instrumental *cause* of) the sinful act. On the other hand, were there in human beings no inclination to disobey, presumably the imposition of a requirement would not lead to disobedience; in that sense, (a kind of dormant) sin precedes the law. It is perhaps not surprising that some find Paul's attempts to illuminate different aspects of this chicken-and-egg relationship contradictory, while others find them revealing.

3. Sanders' work was an important corrective of earlier caricatures of Judaism. Ironically, however, I believe that it imposes on Judaism distinctions between grace and works that are derived from Paul but foreign to the thinking of his non-Christian compatriots. Of *course* Jews believed in, and were grateful for, the grace of God. Of *course* their observance of the law was, at its best, an expression of love for God and gratitude for his goodness. These are important reminders. But Jews did *not* programmatically assign God's election of his people, or their own place in the age to come, to divine grace as opposed to human deeds or merit. Paul did, for reasons linked to the nature of his (Christian) soteriology. It is thus misleading, I believe, to say that the relation between grace and works is the same in Judaism as in Paul's writings. In this respect I agree with observations made by Thurén (noted above).

4. On the other hand, I do not think (as Thurén does) that Paul exaggerates the 'legalism' of Judaism for rhetorical purposes. As I read Paul, he saw Judaism simply as life under the Sinaitic covenant which, though gloriously (2 Cor. 3.7-11) and graciously (Rom. 9.4) given by God to Israel, did require deeds in conformity with its prescriptions as its path to life (Rom. 2.13; 10.5; Gal. 3.12). Moreover, for Paul, the position of Jews under the Mosaic law is, essentially, no different from that of every human being: all are expected to do good and avoid evil if they are to be granted eternal life (Rom. 2.6-13). That Jews have been given the law in written form puts them in a position to instruct Gentiles – who nonetheless possess within themselves an awareness – of the goodness required of Jews and Gentiles alike (Rom. 2.6-27).[24] It is because the positions of Jews and Gentiles in this regard are both distinct *and* analogous that Paul can sometimes speak of Gentiles as not under the law, at other times as (like Jews) its subjects.

5. Thurén seems to me to grasp the point of Paul's superficially contradictory statements that the law was given 'for life' (Rom. 7.10) and that it cannot justify: i.e., the law promises life to those who obey its commands, but human sin blocks this path to salvation. I would add that the latter turn of events does not, for Paul, represent a failure in the plan

---

24 Here Paul approximates those Jewish thinkers who identified Torah with Wisdom, or with 'the law of nature'.

or purpose of the God who gave the law, nor does it make the giving of
the law pointless: good is good, evil is evil, and a righteous God cannot
but require moral beings to respect the difference. It is the great merit of
Laato's monograph to have introduced consideration of Paul's 'pessimistic' anthropology into the post-Sanders debate.

6. Eskola is one of a number of scholars[25] who have reminded us that,
in many Second Temple texts, the covenant is no longer thought to be
salvific for the majority of Jews – because of the sins of God's people.
Paul, to be sure, goes further: *all* are under (the power of) sin, *no one* is
righteous, *no one* is justified by the works of the law. Still, the parallels are
striking, and call in question the frequent claim[26] that, in the context of
Jewish covenantal nomism, with its provisions for atonement and
forgiveness, Paul could not have rejected the Sinaitic law and covenant
in the belief that sin had nullified their efficacy.

7. Kuula (following Sanders) maintains that Paul could not have
opposed the law because it is based on works rather than on grace since he
was not in principle against human 'activism': after all, Paul no less than
the Mosaic law demands righteous behaviour of his converts.[27] In fact
there *are* times when Paul insists, in a programmatic way rarely found in
contemporary Jewish texts, that God operates on the basis of his grace to
the exclusion of human works (e.g., Rom. 4.4-6; 9.16; 11.6). But 'activism'
as such is not the issue. The point for Paul (as suggested above) appears to
be rather that the law demands righteous works of people 'under sin', in a
'flesh' that is hostile to God. If the 'ungodly' (a category that included
Jews like Paul as well as Gentiles; cf. Rom. 4.5; 5.6, 8) are to be justified, if
those 'under sin' are to be transferred to the realm of grace, if the dead are
to be made alive, then the change will have to take place without any
contribution from the dead, the slaves of sin, the ungodly. Thus for Paul
salvific grace must exclude human contributions in a way that is not
typically articulated or necessary in Jewish texts. That Paul expects those
made alive in Christ to live righteously should neither be overlooked nor
allowed to obscure Paul's conviction that a divine creative act must first
put them in a position to do so.

8. Much that is important to Paul is lost to view when he is said to have
rejected the Jewish law and covenant simply because no alternative to
christocentric soteriology could be entertained. On that argument,
Judaism becomes (together with all other alternatives to Paul's scheme)
simply one of the false religions of Paul's day. But there is no reason to
doubt Paul when he says (what he would not have said of non-Jewish

25   See in particular Mark Adam Elliott, *The Survivors of Israel: A Reconsideration of the
Theology of Pre-Christian Judaism* (Grand Rapids: Eerdmans, 2000).
26   E.g., Kuula, *Law*, vol. 2, pp. 90–91, 167.
27   Kuula, *Law*, vol. 2, pp. 109, 134, 150, etc.

religions) that the Mosaic law embodies the good that God requires of human beings (compare Rom. 2.10 and 13; note also 2.17-20) and that, as part of the covenant, it is given to the most favoured of peoples (Rom. 9.4). Their failure to live up to its terms thus becomes for Paul the ultimate demonstration of the depth of human sinfulness (so Rom. 3.19: if even the favoured people of God are shown to be sinners, then all the world is culpable) and of the necessity of a fresh and extraordinary revelation of the righteousness of God (Rom. 3.21-22, following vv. 19-20). That same failure is the reason why, of the blessing that the covenant promises to those who obey its laws and the curse it pronounces on transgressors, Paul believes that only the latter is operative (2 Cor. 3.7, 9; Gal. 3.10; cf. Rom. 7.10). Only when these basic Pauline convictions are overlooked or rejected can one claim that Paul's gospel represents bad news for the Jews rather than good news for all nations.

9. To sum up: Paul saw *no* tension between the law's condition of obedience as its path to life and his conviction that salvation is to be found in the Christian gospel: the same requirement of righteousness underlies both. It is precisely *because* human beings are not righteous in the ordinary way (i.e., by doing the righteous deeds spelled out in the law) that God has provided, in the gospel, an extraordinary means by which sinners can be found righteous (Rom. 3.23-24; 4.5, etc.). Romans 5.1-11 suggests that Paul found, at the most existential level, profound joy rather than tormenting *angst* at this resolution of the 'problem' of the law.

10. So I read Paul. What is in any case clear is that different positions in the current debate have strong advocates among contemporary Finnish scholars.

PART II

Chapter 2

TORN BETWEEN TWO LOYALTIES: ROMANS 9–11 AND PAUL'S CONFLICTING CONVICTIONS

Heikki Räisänen

The Problem and the Task

The question of Paul's (in)consistency has been an exegetical storm centre for a quarter of century now. Although the problem is age-old, it seems to have gained new urgency in 1983, when E.P. Sanders pointed to a lack of 'inner unity' in Paul's thought,[1] and I claimed that inconsistencies should be accepted as constant features of Paul's treatment of the law.[2] Sanders and I are time and again singled out as a pair of villains – some contending that I am the worse one, others simply lumping us together.[3] James Dunn, for instance, labels us as interpreters 'content to find and to leave Paul's teaching inconsistent and irreconcilable in its contradictions'.[4]

---

1   E.P. Sanders, *Paul, the Law, and the Jewish People* (Philadelphia: Fortress, 1983), p. 147.

2   Heikki Räisänen, *Paul and the Law* (WUNT, 29; Tübingen: Mohr Siebeck, 2nd edn, 1987), p. 11 and *passim*. For a fair summary see Stephen Westerholm, *Israel's Law and Church's Faith: Paul and His Recent Interpreters* (Grand Rapids: Eerdmans, 1988), pp. 93–101, repeated and provided with a couple of helpful additional notes in his *Perspectives Old and New on Paul: The 'Lutheran' Paul and His Critics* (Grand Rapids: Eerdmans, 2004), pp. 170–77. I do not suggest, however, that 'Paul himself misunderstood Judaism' (contra Westerholm, *Perspectives*, p. 178). My point is rather that in a polemical situation he gave a one-sided picture of it, which does *not* mean that his 'twisted *purpose* is to give a distorted picture of Judaism', a view falsely ascribed to me by Timo Eskola, *Theodicy and Predestination in Pauline Soteriology* (WUNT, 2/100; Tübingen: Mohr Siebeck, 1998), p. 281. As I wrote: 'The question is *not* one of Paul's knowledge. The question is whether Paul, writing in a conflict setting, does *justice* to the form of piety he has given up. He would probably be a unique reformer in religious history if he did full justice to the surrendered form of life.' Heikki Räisänen, *Jesus, Paul and Torah* (JSNTSup, 43; Sheffield: Sheffield Academic Press, 1992), p. 33.

3   I think that Sanders correctly explained that we disagree(d) only about terminology: Sanders, *Law*, p. 148.

4   James D.G. Dunn, *The Theology of Paul the Apostle* (Grand Rapids: Eerdmans, 1998), p. 131 with note 16.

It was not just a question of a 'psychological explanation' of Paul's problems.[5] Sanders did speak of Paul's emotions, such as anguish, but he also made it clear that Paul was faced with a theological, or salvation-historical, *dilemma*: God gave the law, and yet its role was largely negative.[6] Paul wrestled with the resulting problem of discontinuity, trying to hold together '*conflicting convictions*': salvation is only by faith (in Jesus); yet God's promise to Israel is irrevocable.[7] I emphasized psychological factors more, but subsequently underlined the theological dilemma as well,[8] also pointing out that the problem is one which Paul *shares* with early Christianity at large, though it is he who brings it to a head.

Rather than returning to the issue of Paul and the law, I shall in this article summarize my interpretation of Romans 9–11, a section in which Paul's conflicting convictions, as I see them, come to light very clearly.[9] First, however, some comments on the ongoing discussion are in order.[10]

The inconsistency thesis does not enjoy vast popularity. It is said to attribute nonsense to Paul (Elizabeth Johnson)[11] and to be based on an 'atomistic' analysis (James Dunn).[12] It is found to be

5   Contra Troels Engberg-Pedersen, *Paul and the Stoics* (Edinburgh: T&T Clark, 2000), p. 15; cf. *ibid.* p. 341, note 11.

6   Sanders, *Law*, p. 68 etc.

7   *Ibid.*, p. 198.

8   Räisänen, *Paul and the Law*, pp. xxv–xxvi; *idem*, 'Paul, God, and Israel: Romans 9–11 in recent research', in Jacob Neusner et al. (eds), *The Social World of Formative Christianity and Judaism* (Festschrift H.C. Kee; Philadelphia: Fortress, 1988), pp. 178–206 (196).

9   For more comprehensive treatments see Heikki Räisänen, 'Römer 9–11: Analyse eines geistigen Ringens', *ANRW* II.25.4 (1987), pp. 2891–939; *idem*, 'Paul, God and Israel'.

10   I have not been in a position to follow the debate in detail. My observations are therefore of a rather casual nature.

11   E. Elizabeth Johnson, 'Romans 9–11: The faithfulness and impartiality of God', in David M. Hay and E. Elizabeth Johnson (eds), *Pauline Theology: Romans*, vol. 3 (Minneapolis: Fortress, 1995), pp. 211–39 (214). Cf. Engberg-Pedersen, *Paul and the Stoics*, p. 347 n. 30: Sanders and I have created a wreck from which subsequent interpreters have tried to salvage what they could.

12   This is an allegation repeatedly put forward by Dunn, e.g., in *Theology*, p. 159 note 160 – and still in 2007: *idem*, 'Not so much "New Testament Theology" as "New Testament Theologizing"', in Cilliers Breytenbach and Jörg Frey (eds), *Aufgabe und Durchführung einer Theologie des Neuen Testaments* (WUNT, 205; Tübingen: Mohr Siebeck, 2007), pp. 225–46 (236 note 27). Contrast, e.g., Westerholm, *Israel's Law*, p. 219: 'Räisänen's case is serious ... his argumentation rigorous and sensitive to nuances.' Whatever justification Dunn's accusation may have had twenty-five years ago, repeating it after I have published several comprehensive and detailed contextual analyses of Romans 9–11 borders on the ridiculous. Dunn would do well to engage with the books of Kari Kuula, who after thorough (certainly not atomistic!) analyses reaches conclusions very close to mine: Kari Kuula, *The Law, the Covenant and God's Plan: Paul's Polemical Treatment of the Law in Galatians*, vol. 1 (PFES, 72; Helsinki: The Finnish Exegetical Society and Göttingen: Vandenhoeck and Ruprecht, 1999); *idem*, *The Law, the Covenant and God's Plan: Paul's Treatment of the Law in Romans*,

'extreme';[13] claims of inconsistency, it is asserted, should be an interpreter's 'last resort'.[14] The polemical tone in much of this criticism seems, however, disproportionate in view of the general agreement that Paul's thoughts on the law *are* very difficult to grasp. Sven Hillert is justified in pointing out that the discussion on 'the radical positions taken by Räisänen and Sanders' (on contradictions) 'may give the impression that scholars disagree more than they actually do. A closer look reveals that there is an almost general agreement that "Paul was *not* a systematic theologian".'[15] This is not just a modern sentiment; the observation of inconsistency is an age-old insight[16] which some recent interpreters yet once more have tried to suppress. Attempts to deny inconsistency largely boil down to giving it a different name.[17] Alternatively, critics – notably

---

vol. 2 (PFES, 85; Helsinki: The Finnish Exegetical Society and Göttingen: Vandenhoeck and Ruprecht, 2003). Kuula's work should not be set aside with the mere comment that it comes from Helsinki (thus Westerholm, *Perspectives*, p. 227: Kuula's 1999 monograph 'leaves no doubt about its academic paternity'). In fact, Kuula's first 'academic father' was Lars Aejmelaeus; Kuula had already finished his master's thesis on Paul and the law when I came to know him. For a perceptive review of Kuula's 2003 book see Mark Reasoner, *CBQ* 68 (2006), pp. 151–52.

13   Daniel Boyarin, *A Radical Jew: Paul and the Politics of Identity* (Berkeley: University of California Press, 1994), p. 294 note 23.

14   James D.G. Dunn, *Jesus, Paul and the Law* (London: SPCK, 1990), p. 215.

15   Sven Hillert, *Limited and Universal Salvation: A Text-Oriented and Hermeneutical Study of Two Perspectives in Paul* (ConBNT, 31; Stockholm: Almqvist & Wiksell, 1999), pp. 238–39 (quoting Jouette Bassler). Cf. David Brown, *Tradition and Imagination: Revelation and Change* (Oxford: Oxford University Press, 1999), pp. 307–8 with reference to Dunn: '[E]ven those most well disposed to Paul find themselves remarking on the oddity of his arguments.'

16   Cf. my comments on Porphyry in *Paul and the Law*, pp. 2–3 and Margaret Mitchell's perceptive discussion of John Chrysostom's view of Paul: '"A variable and many-sorted man": John Chrysostom's treatment of Pauline inconsistency', *Journal of Early Christian Studies* 6 (1998), pp. 93–111. Malina and Neyrey agree with my 'assessment of Paul from the viewpoint of a twentieth-century northern European', but claim that I do not 'offer any suggestion as to whether Paul is typical or atypical in this regard': Bruce J. Malina and Jerome H. Neyrey, *Portraits of Paul: An Archaeology of Ancient Personality* (Louisville: Westminster John Knox Press, 1996), p. 11. Strangely, they only refer to a short early article of mine (of 1980); had they looked at *Paul and the Law*, they would have found that I do compare Paul with a number of his contemporaries and also pay attention to criticisms raised against him by some ancient authors.

17   Such attempts include development theories which assume contradictions between different letters (e.g., H. Hübner, U. Schnelle); a distinction between the coherent theme of Paul's gospel and its contingent application (J.C. Beker); a differentiation between a convictional and a theological level (D. Patte); a separation between intentions and objectifications (G. Klein); a distinction between practical aims and argumentative strategies (F. Watson). The effect is the same, sometimes against the intention of the interpreter in question: Paul is found consistent only if the interpreter knows how to tell the coherent kernel from the unimportant husk. See Hans Hübner, *The Law in Paul's Thought* (trans. J.C. G. Greig; Edinburgh: T&T Clark, 1984); Udo Schnelle, *Wandlungen im paulinischen Denken*

many practitioners of rhetorical criticism – produce consistency by putting forward quite idiosyncratic readings of individual passages.[18] Advocates of what is now sometimes called the 'new Paul' (Paul the loyal Jew)[19] stand out by reinterpreting whole sections, passage after passage, in most peculiar ways.[20]

   To be sure, serious attempts to see Paul as a coherent systematic theologian after all have been recently undertaken by Boyarin and Engberg-Pedersen, who, however, play down Paul's most negative statements. According to Boyarin, what Paul affirms is the 'spiritual sense' of the Torah; what he denies is its literal sense.[21] Engberg-Pedersen claims that Paul's thought 'makes coherent sense once it is seen in the light of ... the ancient ethical tradition' (of the Stoics in particular).[22] But

---

(SBS, 137; Stuttgart: Katholisches Bibelwerk, 1989); *idem, Paulus: Leben und Denken* (Berlin: Walter de Gruyter, 2003), e.g., pp. 585–91; J.C. Beker, *Paul the Apostle: The Triumph of God in Life and Thought* (Philadelphia: Fortress, 1984); Daniel Patte, *Paul's Faith and the Power of the Gospel: A Structural Introduction to the Pauline Letters* (Philadelphia: Fortress, 1983); Günther Klein, 'Gesetz III. Neues Testament', *TRE* 13 (1984), pp. 58–75; Francis Watson, *Paul, Judaism, and the Gentiles: A Sociological Approach* (SNTSMS, 56; Cambridge: Cambridge University Press, 1986).

   18   In this vein, Theo van Spanje devoted a whole monograph to the refutation of my claim that Paul is inconsistent: *Inconsistency in Paul? A Critique of the Work of Heikki Räisänen* (WUNT, 2/110; Tübingen: Mohr Siebeck, 1999). While the description of my position in the first part of the book is fair enough, the refutation itself is full of problems. At times van Spanje is content with discussing minor points (pp. 173–80); he even refutes at length a position which he attributes to me but which I explicitly reject (pp. 180–88). Moreover, he often puts forward idiosyncratic interpretations of his own; were they correct, they would 'refute' not only my interpretations but also those of almost everybody else: cf., e.g., pp. 208–10 on Gal. 3.10-13; p. 222 on Rom. 7.1-6; p. 227 on a strange distinction between the law per se and the law in God's overall plan of salvation, etc. See also Barry Matlock's review of van Spanje in *RBL*: http://www.bookreviews.org (2000).

   19   This position is not to be confused with the 'new perspective on Paul' introduced by Sanders and Dunn.

   20   Gager makes a virtue out of necessity by asserting that in Romans 9–11 Paul chose the strategy of '*unreliable* implied author'; generations of interpreters have fallen prey to this strategy. John G. Gager, *Reinventing Paul* (New York: Oxford University Press, 2000), pp. 131, 134: Paul '*misleads* in order to convince' (p. 131, my italics), dropping his guise only in 11.11b-32 (p. 138). Gager is following Stanley K. Stowers, *A Rereading of Romans: Justice, Jews, and Gentiles* (New Haven and London: Yale University Press, 1994). An even stranger set of readings is offered by Mark D. Nanos, *The Mystery of Romans: The Jewish Context of Paul's Letter* (Minneapolis: Fortress, 1996), pp. 239–88.

   21   Boyarin, *Radical Jew*, p. 132. The letter which kills is, according to Boyarin, the literal meaning (p. 56). Boyarin holds that Paul had a conscious 'hermeneutical' law theory, but his systematic reading of Paul fails to convince. For example, Paul's assertion that through the Torah he died to the Torah (Gal. 2.19) means, according to Boyarin, that Paul discovered the opposition of the true (allegorical) Torah to that which is understood as Torah by other Jews (p. 122).

   22   Engberg-Pedersen, *Paul and the Stoics*, pp. 171–72, 348–50, takes Gal. 3.19 as a reference to the law's 'curbing transgressions'; see against this Kuula, *Galatians*, pp. 145–47,

Engberg-Pedersen constructs Paul's Stoic-like philosophy on a very abstract level, and Boyarin actually accepts that Paul did have conflicting convictions with regard to the election of Israel[23] – which would seem to undermine his case.

Some prominent scholars have no problem at all in attributing inconsistency to Paul. Michael Goulder is outspoken: Paul believed contradictory things, he was 'in an impossible position' and was 'reduced to offering a series of arguments which were weak and contradictory'.[24] Gerd Theissen explicitly agrees with me: Paul's 'thought is full of contradictions. One does more justice to him, when one does not explain them away, but interprets them historically and psychologically.'[25] Most strikingly, David Brown, a systematic theologian and a former colleague of Dunn, looking at the biblical tradition from a larger theological perspective, comments that Paul 'resorts to a bewildering variety of arguments against the law'. The 'more natural interpretation' is, he claims, 'that Paul is desperately floundering in his attempt to find suitable arguments to undermine its central role, rather than that he has a coherent theology about its significance'.[26] What need have we of any further witnesses?

Why should finding inconsistency be a 'last resort' in the first place? Is it so self-evident that humans in general 'strive for consistency in their thinking'?[27] In general, theologians (or their critics) are not overly

---

153, 155–56, 174–75. Engberg-Pedersen (p. 173) practically ignores the very negative verse Gal. 3.20 and tries to improve the problematic argument of Rom.1.18–3.20 by claiming that, according to this passage, Jews and Gentiles merely *risk* sinning (pp. 207–8, 218).

23   Cf. Boyarin, *Radical Jew*, p. 323 note 1: Boyarin states that he finds the section on the Jewish people in Sanders' *Law* successful. Yet in this very section Sanders makes most forcefully the point concerning 'conflicting convictions'.

24   Michael D. Goulder, *St. Paul versus St. Peter: A Tale of Two Missions* (London: SCM, 1994), pp. 33–34.

25   Gerd Theissen, 'Röm 9–11 – eine Auseinandersetzung des Paulus mit Israel und mit sich selbst: Versuch einer psychologischen Auslegung', in Ismo Dunderberg et al. (eds), *Fair Play: Diversity and Conflicts in Early Christianity* (Festschrift Heikki Räisänen; NovTSup, 103; Leiden: Brill, 2002), 311–41 (311). Agreeing with me, Theissen states that 'Paul is in his theology concerned with legitimising new experience with old traditions. One who pours new wine in old wineskins must run the risk that the wineskins burst or that the new wine within them remains hidden...'. See also Dieter Mitternacht, *Forum für Sprachlose: Eine kommunikationspsychologische und epistolär-rhetorische Untersuchung des Galaterbriefs* (ConBNT, 30; Stockholm: Almquist & Wiksell, 1999); he regards my work as a convincing refutation of the notion that Paul was a great thinker or even a philosopher (pp. 55–56), also mentioning that he had to totally change his own view in the course of his research.

26   Brown, *Tradition*, p. 307 with note 103. Mark Reasoner recalls in his review of Kuula a remark by Robert M. Grant in the mid-1980s: 'The longer I read Paul, the more I wonder – did this man know what he was talking about?' *CBQ* 68 (2006), p. 151.

27   Timo Laato, *Paulus und das Judentum: Anthropologische Erwägungen* (Åbo: Åbo Akademi Press, 1991), p. 105. N.T. Wright is very reluctant to find inconsistency in Paul, but

reluctant to find inconsistency or self-contradictions even in 'good' thinkers. Consider Boyarin's section 'Bultmann against Bultmann'. On a central point, Bultmann 'contradicts his own view', 'Bultmann the exegete contradicting Bultmann the systematic theologian'.[28] What Boyarin allows in Bultmann, he would not allow in Paul.

I now proceed to analyse what I take to be Paul's inconsistent reasoning, his 'conflicting convictions', in Romans 9–11. It will be seen that I do not take the situation in the congregations of Rome (which Paul had neither founded nor yet visited) as the key to interpreting the letter, although Paul undoubtedly had gained some information about it. The really burning issue was hardly the situation in Rome (although Paul has something to say about that, too, at least in chs 14–15);[29] the main issue in the letter seems to be a problem of his own making.[30] Paul's moving wrestling in chs 9–11 suggests to me that he is in the process of making sense of his own experience in Galatia (and in Corinth), which had been filled with controversy. This exercise prepares him for his visit to Jerusalem in the near future, a visit which worried him and for which he asked the Roman fellow-believers to pray. It also serves (or so he must have hoped) to expel the suspicion that the Jewish Christians in Rome may have had concerning his mission, and to move them to come to his aid in realizing his planned mission to Spain. It seems reasonable to view at least chs 9–11, if not Romans as a whole, 'as being Paul's reflection on the problem of Jew and gentile in the light of his past difficulty in Galatia and the coming encounter in Jerusalem'.[31] Rhetorical approaches to the section can be helpful, but their significance may today be overrated. Now as before it seems to me that Paul is not just concerned about persuading others with this or that rhetorical feat. He is hard put to convince *himself* that God's word has not failed.

---

in speaking of Jewish 'monotheism and its modifications' he notes that 'most humans are quite good at holding together things which can be shown to be mutually contradictory': *The New Testament and the People of God* (Minneapolis: Fortress, 1992), p. 258. When he continues by stating that therefore 'the different positions are not necessarily incompatible', I confess that I don't understand his logic.

28 Boyarin, *Radical Jew*, pp. 82–85.

29 It is less certain that the Roman situation is in view in Rom. 11.13-24 where Paul warns Gentile Christians of boasting over 'the original branches' of the metaphorical olive tree. Interpreters generally take this as a reference to the attitude of (some?) Gentile Christians in Rome to their Jewish Christian brothers and sisters. But Paul does not here refer to a Gentile Christian attitude to Jewish *Christians* (who have, of course, *remained* in the 'tree'), but to 'unbelieving' Jews who have been 'cut off'. It is therefore not at all clear that the problem of chs 14–15 is already referred to in 11.13-24. Cf. Dieter Zeller, *Der Brief an die Römer* (RNT; Regensburg: Friedrich Pustet, 1985), pp. 15–16.

30 Cf. Otto Kuss, *Der Römerbrief*, vol. 3 (Regensburg: Friedrich Pustet, 1978), p. 700.

31 Sanders, *Law*, p. 31.

Romans 9.1-5

In his letter to the Galatians (Gal. 3–4), Paul had gone a long way towards virtually denying any significant continuity between Israel as a people and his faith communities.[32] In Galatians he does not seem to think of Abraham as an ancestor of the covenant people at all, but only 'as an exemplary individual who received promises that aimed far into the future' (Gal. 3.15-18).[33] The history of Israel as God's chosen people is ignored.[34] In Gal. 4.21-31 Paul does draw a 'historical' line, but it is a line of slavery: the covenant of Sinai gives birth to slaves (4.24-25). Non-Christian Jews are descendants of the slave woman Hagar; the Jesus-believers alone are 'children of the promise, like Isaac'. '[T]raditional Jewish terms, motives and approaches ... are reinterpreted in such a manner that the continuity remains only nominal.'[35] In such a context the expression 'God's Israel' (Gal. 6.16) can only refer to the Christian communities.[36] The church, which is in the process of formation, is the true Israel.

Paul's troubled relation to Israel did not leave him untouched, however. In Romans 9 he gives expression to 'great sorrow and unceasing anguish' because of his people (Rom. 9.2-3; cf. 10.1).[37] He even expresses the unreal wish that he could be 'accursed' (*anathema*) and 'cut off from Christ' for their sake. This implies that they must be in the very plight he is willing to enter for their sake: they are anathema.[38] This outburst opens an exposition which covers three long chapters. Recent interpreters agree that Paul is here concerned with the problem of Israel, which is also the

---

32   It is often claimed that Paul merely extends Israel's covenant to embrace even Gentiles. Yet in Galatians, there *is* no salvific covenant previously established into which Gentiles could be included in the first place. Paul may once have started his mission simply by demanding that Gentiles be included within the covenant, but by the time of dictating Galatians he has left this position behind. The notion of an expanded covenant fits the position of Paul's Galatian opponents better. This has been convincingly argued by J. Louis Martyn, 'Events in Galatia: modified covenantal nomism versus God's invasion of the cosmos in the singular Gospel. A Response to J.D.G. Dunn and B.R. Gaventa', in Jouette M. Bassler (ed.), *Pauline Theology: Thessalonians, Philippians, Galatians, Philemon*, vol. 1 (Minneapolis: Fortress, 1991), pp. 160–79 and, following him, Kuula, *Galatians*, p. 199.

33   Kuula, *ibid.*, p. 82.

34   See also Ulrich Luz, *Das Geschichtsverständnis des Paulus* (BEvT, 49; Munich: Chr. Kaiser, 1968), pp. 279–86. In Galatians, the Jews have been 'allegorized out of real historical existence': Boyarin, *Radical Jew*, p. 156.

35   Kuula, *Galatians*, p. 94.

36   Gerd Lüdemann, *Paul: The Founder of Christianity* (Amherst, New York: Prometheus Books, 2002), p. 155.

37   On the connection of the section with other parts of the letter, chs 3 and 8 in particular, see Räisänen, 'Römer 9–11', pp. 2894–95.

38   Hans Hübner, *Gottes Ich und Israel: Zum Schriftgebrauch des Paulus in Römer 9–11* (Göttingen: Vandenhoeck & Ruprecht, 1984), p. 16.

problem of the trustworthiness of God's promises. There is also a growing awareness that earlier research focused excessively on Paul's theological ideas. Chapter 9 once provided the classic support for the doctrine of predestination; ch. 11 predicted the conversion of the Jews. Bultmann could still hold that Romans 'develops in purely theoretical fashion [!] the principle of Christian faith in antithesis to the principle of the Jewish Torah-religion'.[39] Yet the social context and function of Paul's writing has to be taken seriously. My interpretation starts from the assumption that Paul's social experience as the 'apostle to the Gentiles' is reflected throughout the section.

Scholars agree that the chapters are 'as full of problems as a hedgehog is of prickles'.[40] Their solutions go in quite different directions. To me, the internal tensions provide a key to the interpretation of the section.

Paul raises the worrisome question of how the gospel can be taken to represent a triumph for God, even though most Jews have rejected it. He gives a long list of their advantages (which must come as a complete surprise to someone who has read Galatians): 'They are Israelites, and to them belong the sonship, the glory, the covenants, the giving of the law, the worship and the promises; to them belong the patriarchs, and of their race, according to the flesh, is the Christ . . .' (Rom. 9.2-4). Yet what gain will Israelites have for all these privileges, if they remain outside the salvation in Christ?

Romans 9.6-23

God's integrity is at stake: has his word failed, if Israel stays outside?[41] Paul answers by redefining 'Israel' – or, in Hübner's words, by 'juggling' with the concept of Israel:[42] all those who are 'of Israel' (the empirical

---

39   Rudolf Bultmann, *Theology of the New Testament, Volume 1* (trans. Kendrick Grobel; New York: Charles Scribner's Sons, 1951), p. 209. Notoriously, Bultmann did away with Paul's vision of Israel's salvation in Rom. 11 as 'speculative fantasy', which he did not discuss under 'The Theology of Paul' at all in his NT theology, deferring it to his section 'The Development Toward the Old Church': *Theology of the New Testament, Volume 2* (trans. Kendrick Grobel; New York: Charles Scribner's Sons, 1955), p. 132.

40   N. Thomas Wright, *The Climax of the Covenant: Christ and the Law in Pauline Theology* (Edinburgh: T&T Clark, 1991), p. 231.

41   Kuula describes the underlying problem well: 'As a native Jew, Paul had learned that God has made an eternal covenant with his people Israel. But the fundamental conviction of Paul the apostle that the Jews must turn to Christ in order to be saved, implies that the covenant is no longer the way of salvation. This appears to mean that God has cancelled the covenant, and in this he has been unfaithful to his promises ... But this is contrary to everything that holy scriptures teach about the covenant, which is eternal, and about God, who is trustworthy.' Kuula, *Romans*, p. 294.

42   Hübner, *Gottes Ich*, p. 17.

people) do not really belong to Israel. Who belongs and who does not is freely decreed by God. He has always freely called some, such as Jacob, and not others, such as Esau, without any regard to their character or ancestry (9.7-13). Paul does not think, say, of God's foreknowledge of wicked deeds. God is wholly sovereign in his decisions, so much so that he loved Jacob and hated Esau even before they were born. Therefore the gospel is not being rejected by the elect of God, for the majority of ethnic Israel never belonged to the elect![43] The gospel is being rejected by the non-elect and accepted by the true 'Israel'. Everything is as God meant it to be.

Paul goes to great lengths in undergirding the thesis of God's free election. That God can show unexpected mercy is in line with the surprising experience that he has lately called Gentiles to enter his people.[44] But to make this point, the 'positive' v. 15 would suffice: 'I will have mercy on whom I have mercy, and I will have compassion on whom I have compassion.' Such a concern alone does not, however, account for the negative side of God's action (vv. 17–18). Since Paul's problem is the rejection of his message by most Jews, he is led to develop this other side of God's sovereignty as well. Not only does God freely choose whom he wills to be saved; just as freely he also 'hardens whom he wills' (9.18).[45] This lesson is drawn from the biblical example of God's dealing with Pharaoh in Exodus; astonishingly, this classical enemy of Israel here stands for the Jews of Paul's time.[46]

Verse 19 shows that Paul senses that a moral problem is involved in his argument: how can humans be held responsible for their doings if

---

43   It is quite inadequate to summarize the point of Rom. 9.6-13 as Dunn, *Jesus*, p. 148 does: 'Those who are Israelites, but who *fail to recognize* the covenant character of their status as Israelites, have to that extent sold their own birthright' (my italics); cf. *idem*, *Romans 9–16* (WBC, 38B; Dallas: Word Books, 1988), p. 540: 'Paul's argument concerns the character and mode rather than the fact of election.' No, it concerns precisely the 'fact'! Eskola, *Theodicy*, p. 152 note 35 speculates that my above conclusion (stated already in 1988: 'Paul, God and Israel', p. 182) 'must be based on the conviction that Paul accepted the concept of double predestination and was here attempting to solve the dilemma of divine election'; this is very odd, since I actually draw the opposite conclusion (cf. 'Paul, God and Israel', p. 186).

44   It is often thought that this is the problem which Paul sets out to tackle in the section; thus, e.g., Lloyd Gaston, *Paul and the Torah* (Vancouver: University of the British Columbia Press, 1987), p. 97; Gager, *Reinventing*, p. 132; Nanos, *Mystery*, p. 263.

45   For instance, E. Elizabeth Johnson, *The Function of Apocalyptic and Wisdom Traditions in Romans 9–11* (SBLDS, 109; Atlanta: SBL, 1989), pp. 148ff. and Wright, *Climax*, pp. 238–39 do not take this negative side seriously enough. Eskola, *Theodicy*, pp. 153, resorts to the explanation that Paul employs the hardening theme 'as a kind of metaphor for Israel's fall and sin'. Kuula, *Romans*, p. 299 note 9 rightly asks why Paul should have wasted so much ink in speaking metaphorically about *God's* decisions if he only meant *humans*' response to the gospel.

46   Hübner, *Gottes Ich*, p. 45.

everything is effected by God?[47] All Paul can do is to assert that the Great Potter has the right to create what he wants, even 'vessels of wrath' prepared for destruction (9.22).[48] This would logically imply double predestination.[49] The unbelieving Jews of Paul's time are to be seen as such vessels of wrath. Gerd Lüdemann rightly points out: 'The fact that we know from Rom. 11 that this is not Paul's last word on the problem of Israel and salvation history must not be a reason for toning down the sharpness of Paul's argumentation in an interpretation of verses 22–23, or doing away with it on dialectical grounds.'[50]

Romans 9.24-29

Paul then shows from Scripture that God always intended to also call Gentiles to be his sons.[51] He further argues from Scripture that not all Israel will be saved, but only such seed as God has left in it (9.24-29). The idea of a remnant does not entirely agree with the one just presented that all Israel was never elected; it presupposes that in the beginning there was an elected 'whole'. Even so, Romans 9.6-29 gives a clear answer to the question: has God's word failed (v. 6)? No, it has not, for God never promised anything for *ethnic* Israel, for the whole empirical people.[52] Paul started the section with an impressive catalogue of Israel's privileges, but by now he has in effect denied them to the Israel 'according to the flesh'.[53] It seems clear that the majority of the Jews will remain outside of salvation. At this point a reader hardly feels that the treatise should go on.

47   John C. O'Neill, *Paul's Letter to the Romans* (Penguin Books: London; 1975), pp. 157f. frankly states that v. 18 contains a 'thoroughly immoral doctrine'; the objection in v. 19 'is entirely warranted, and the reply does nothing to answer it'. Cf. Kuss, *Römerbrief*, vol. 3, p. 730: the picture of God given in these verses contains 'despotic, tyrannical, Sultanic' traits.

48   Robert Jewett, *Romans: A Commentary* (Hermeneia; Minneapolis: Fortress, 2006), p. 596 is content to emphasize the 'positive' side of the verse, its mention of God's patience.

49   It is probably no coincidence, however, that the sentence ends as an anacoluthon. Paul appears to be uncomfortable with the notion of double predestination; cf. Kuss, *Römerbrief*, vol. 3, p. 732.

50   Lüdemann, *Paul*, p. 158.

51   It now seems as if the inclusion of the Gentiles is the point of the whole chapter, the thing in need of justification; such a view is indeed taken by some interpreters. But this was not the starting-point of ch. 9. It is not the inclusion of Gentiles that could have aroused the suspicion that God does not keep his promises. Paul's thought has taken on a new turn in v. 24.

52   Kuula, *Romans*, p. 304 correctly notes (contra Dunn, *Theology*, pp. 510, 514) that 'the redefinition of Israel on the basis of God's specific call in Christ amounts to a denial of the election of the historical Israel'.

53   It is therefore inappropriate to use the catalogue 9.4-5 as evidence that Paul had not broken with the religion of his fathers.

Nothing seems to be lacking; there is no need for a continuation.[54] Yet Paul does not leave the issue at that.

Romans 9.30–10.21

The next section introduces a quite different point of view. Paul explains why Israel, now seen as an ethnic entity after all, has failed to attain righteousness, whereas Gentiles have found it (9.30-33). We now hear nothing about sovereign divine hardening or about God's freedom to reject whom he will. On the contrary, God has held out his hands towards Israel 'all day long', patiently inviting her to salvation; Israel, however, remains 'a disobedient and contrary people' (10.21).[55] Clinging to works, she has refused to obey God and to accept his action in Christ with faith. Thus she has stumbled over the stumbling stone, Christ (9.32-33). Salvation is meant for all: there will be righteousness for everyone who believes (in Christ, 10.4); 'everyone who calls on the name of the Lord (Christ) will be saved' (10.13).

Romans 11.1-36

Then, however, Paul suddenly asserts that God cannot have rejected his people, *ethnic* Israel (11.1-2). This is rather surprising after ch. 9, but it continues the argument about the remnant which started in 9.27. Paul states that God cannot possibly reject his people, but in light of what follows this only seems to mean that God cannot totally reject *all of* his people. For Paul himself, one of the few believing Israelites, is a living testimony to the existence of a chosen remnant (v. 1) – hardly a very convincing argument if the unbelief and destiny of the great majority of the people is the problem.[56] Ethnic Israel has split into the elect remnant and the hardened rest (11.7). The election of the remnant is based on God's grace alone (v. 6). The others have been hardened: '*God gave* them a sluggish spirit, eyes that would not see and ears that would not hear' (v. 8). The psalm citation in v. 9 could suggest, however, that the hardening is a punishment for the way of life of the hardened (their 'table' is to become 'a stumbling block and a retribution for them'), which would connect this

---

54 Hübner, *Gottes Ich*, p. 59.

55 It is unjustified simply to identify 'disobedient' with 'hardened by God'; thus Johnson, *Function*, p. 140; Dieter Sänger, *Die Verkündigung des Gekreuzigten und Israel: Studien zum Verhältnis von Kirche und Israel bei Paulus und im frühen Christentum* (WUNT, 75; Tübingen: Mohr Siebeck, 1994), pp. 159, 162.

56 Kuula, *Romans*, p. 328 notes that 'it would be more logical to infer that since only a small minority of the Jews have accepted the gospel, God has surely rejected the majority of the people'.

section with 9.30–10.21. In any case it is clear that no happy end is envisaged for the great majority of the people.

Now the argument takes a new turn, and there is a remarkable change of tone. Paul goes on to suggest that the hardening of Israel has a positive purpose in God's plans: somehow[57] it serves to bring salvation to the Gentiles (11.11-12).[58] In vv. 12 and 15 Paul hints at the possibility that God will after all accept the people of Israel, which comes as a surprise after what the apostle has said so far. To be sure, still in v. 14 he speaks in a cautious manner: in helping Gentiles to gain salvation he, the 'apostle of the nations', may perhaps rouse in his kinsmen (positive) 'jealousy' towards the happy Gentiles; thus he may be able to attract '*some*' fellow Jews to the path of salvation. Yet the next verse (15) hints at something much greater which has to do with eschatological fulfilment, the resurrection of the dead; it seems that Paul already has in his mind the 'mystery' which he is to disclose a little later (vv. 25-26). In v. 16 he brings two images that appear somewhat loose in the context (but anticipate v. 28) to the effect that a whole is holy, if its core is holy. The whole must mean Israel; the core, which is compared to the 'dough offered as first fruits' (to the priest) on one hand and to the root of a tree on the other, probably (in light of v. 28) signifies its patriarchs. Because of them, or rather because of the promise given to them, the people still have a special relationship with God.

The image of a holy root which causes even the branches to be holy leads to the parable of the olive tree. Israel is like a cultivated tree from which some branches have been broken off and onto which branches of a wild tree have been grafted (11.17-24).[59] In effect Paul is saying that Israel remains God's people; some apostates have been excluded, and some believing Gentiles have been included as proselytes. The parable stands in a curiously ambiguous relation to the notion of the remnant, for the image of a tree and branches suggests (contrary to the social reality) that only a small minority of Israel ('some' branches) has 'fallen away'. Paul is here speaking to Gentile Christians who are not to 'boast over the original branches' (v. 18), even though some of these have, at present, been 'cut

---

57   Because otherwise the parousia would have occurred immediately?

58   In v. 14 'the apostle to the Gentiles' (v. 13) gives a strange account of his motives: the real purpose of his mission is to aid the salvation of *Israelites* by making them 'jealous' of Gentile Christians. Yet such an idea cannot have been the driving force behind Paul's missionary effort; the notion of jealousy, discovered by Paul in Deut. 32.21 by way of an idiosyncratic reading, serves an apologetic purpose with regard to Jewish Christians (who may have thought that Paul's liberal practice is an obstacle to the Christian mission among Jews) and is to be deemed a secondary rationalization of Paul's efforts; thus also Schnelle, *Paulus*, p. 387. When Paul speaks of his call in Gal. 1.15f., he explicitly mentions the task to win Gentiles, referring to Isa. 49.1 (a passage that has Gentiles, not Israelites, in view).

59   On the possibility of such a horticultural operation see Jewett, *Romans*, pp. 683–85.

off' (vv. 17, 20) – due to human failure, not by a divine decree. Gentiles are admonished to remain in faith so that they will not be 'broken off' as well (v. 22). Here the idea of divine hardening would be out of place. But God has the power to graft back again those Israelites who have fallen, 'if they do not persist in their unbelief' (v. 23).

God deals equally with everybody, Jews as well as Gentiles, depending on whether they continue in his kindness or fall into unbelief. The tone is similar to that found in section 9.30–10.21: the plight of Israel is due to its own false attitude. But now there is hope in the air as well: the situation can be changed.

And indeed a miracle will happen. Paul discloses a 'mystery': the hardening will not be final. When the 'full number of the Gentiles' has 'come in', then[60] *all Israel* – not just a remnant[61] – will be saved (11.25). Paul appeals to a word of Isaiah which he seems to connect with Christ's parousia:[62] 'The Deliverer will come from Zion, he will banish ungodliness from Jacob...' (vv. 26-27). This will happen because the Israelites are 'beloved *for the sake of their forefathers*'; 'the gifts and the call of God are irrevocable' (v. 29). Paul implies that he has received this knowledge (a 'mystery') as a revelation, possibly through a spirit-guided exegesis of Scripture.

The bold idea of the salvation of 'all Israel' differs completely both from the stern judgement Paul had presented in 1 Thess. 2.14-16 (supposing that these verses are not an interpolation)[63] and from his attitude to Israel

---

60   The expression καὶ οὕτως can be taken in a temporal sense ('then') which does not exclude a modal nuance either ('in this manner'): Jewett, *ibid.*, p. 701.

61   No mitigation of this expression should be accepted. For such attempts see, e.g., Wright, *Climax*, pp. 250f.: the salvation of all Israel means that *Gentiles* will join Abraham's family; Schnelle, *Paulus*, p. 389: Paul is only thinking of that part of Israel which will come to believe in Jesus. Correctly Jewett, *Romans*, p. 702: 'It seems most likely that Paul's "mystery" was believed to include all members of the house of Israel, who, without exception, would be saved.'

62   Thus, e.g., Jewett, *ibid.*, p. 704 (contra, e.g., Wright, *Climax*, p. 250). Some scholars decline the connection with parousia, thinking that Paul has a spectacular future success of the mission among Jews in mind: Sanders, *Paul*, p. 196; Jürgen Becker, *Paulus: Der Apostel der Völker* (Tübingen: Mohr Siebeck, 1989), pp. 500f. Since the returning Christ should come from heaven, not from Zion, Paul may simply be referring to Jesus' 'first' coming (in which case the future tense only indicates that this was a future event for Isaiah). In addition, the other passages in which Paul deals with the parousia (1 Thess. 4; 1 Cor. 15) are difficult to harmonize with this one. Kuula (who accepts the parousia interpretation) notes that 'Paul has not consistently integrated the idea of the conversion of the whole Israel into his overall scheme of the parousia' (*Romans*, p. 338). A very peculiar interpretation is given by Nanos, *Mystery*, pp. 278f.: the one who will come 'from Zion' is Paul himself, returning from his journey to Jerusalem!

63   They are considered an interpolation by Birger A. Pearson, '1 Thessalonians 2.13-16: a Deutero-Pauline interpolation', *HTR* 64 (1971), pp. 79–94, and many others.

in Galatians.[64] Therefore some scholars assume that Paul's theology developed in this regard essentially between Galatians and Romans.[65] But the thesis of this section is also completely different from Paul's thesis a couple of pages before in ch. 9. This fact militates against the development theory (unless one assumes that Paul's theology took a decisive new turn during a possible dictation break between Romans 9–10 and Romans 11 – or between 11.10 and 11.11!).[66]

Recently a novel interpretation of Romans 11.25-27 has gained some ground: Paul is taken to presuppose that Israel will be saved *independently of Christ's work*, simply on the basis of God's covenant with Abraham. On this interpretation, faith in Christ is the intended road to salvation for Gentiles, but not for born Jews. Paul is thought to maintain a theology of 'two covenants': Jews will be saved because of the covenant with the fathers, and Gentile Christians because of the new covenant established in Christ.[67] This theory is often connected with the idea that Paul remained a practising 'good Jew', fully loyal to his old tradition.[68] The theory is

---

64   Sänger, *Verkündigung*, p. 196 note 737, tries to harmonize 1 Thess. 2.14-16 with Romans 11 in a singularly unconvincing manner: Paul is aggressive in writing 1 Thess., as he knows that the Jews are sawing their own branch since the salvation of Gentiles is a necessary condition for their own salvation. On this reading, the salvation of Israel is a special concern of Paul in 1 Thess. 2.14-16. No wonder Sänger omits to comment on the divine wrath εἰς τέλος of v.16b.

65   Ulrich Wilckens, *Der Brief an die Römer* 2 (EKKNT, VI/2; Neukirchen: Neukirchener Verlag, 1980), p. 185; Hübner, *Gottes Ich*, p. 134.

66   Some interpreters do assume that in 11.11-32 Paul puts forward something which he did not yet have in mind when he expressed his sorrow in 9.1-3; e.g., Nikolaus Walter, 'Zur Interpretation von Römer 9–11', *ZTK* 81 (1984), pp. 172–95 (176). This is, of course, not impossible, provided that one does not build a full theory of theological development on this foundation (in which case it seems odd that Paul did not delete Romans 9 altogether). On the other hand, Georg Strecker, *Theologie des Neuen Testaments* (ed. Friedrich Wilhelm Horn; Berlin/New York: Walter de Gruyter, 1996), p. 220, regards Rom. 11.25-27 as a mere tactical concession due to the 'church-political' situation, to be assessed critically in light of Paul's own theology of justification by faith.

67   E.g., Gaston, *Paul*; Gager, *Reinventing*.

68   Thus Nanos, *Mystery*. Gager, building on the work of Gaston and Stowers, passionately argues that Paul presented no criticism at all of the Torah. All critical points about curse, condemnation and death concern the Torah only in the case that it is imposed on Gentiles: ('W)hen Paul appears to say something (e.g., about the law and Jews) that is unthinkable from a Jewish perspective, it is probably true that he is not talking about Jews at all. Instead we may assume that the apostle to the Gentiles is talking about the law and Gentiles' (*Reinventing*, p. 58, in the original italicised). This 'new Paul' is a highly unlikely creation. Paul himself states quite clearly that he, 'being all things to all men', lives among Jews '*as if* he were a Jew' (1 Cor. 9.20); he has become as one of the Galatian Gentiles (Gal. 4.12). The view of Paul as a 'good Jew' leaves unexplained why he was repeatedly whipped in the synagogue (2 Cor. 11), why he got the reputation of seducing others away from the law (Acts 21) or why conservative Jewish Christians still in the second century regarded him as their worst enemy. It is another thing that Paul always regarded himself as a Jew, and as one

admirable in its ecumenical scope, but there is very little exegetical evidence for it.[69] The 'mystery' of Romans 11 is a tenuous basis for an assertion which would nullify everything that Paul writes elsewhere (including Romans 10!) about the crucial significance of Jesus for all humanity, for the Jew first(!) and also for the Greek. The idea of the salvation of 'all Israel' – in whatever way this is conceived to happen – is at odds with Paul's other statements and has rightly been called a 'desperate theory'.[70] When Paul ends up by emphasizing that God's promises to his people will after all remain valid, he is in fact defending his own mission: what happens in the near future will justify his liberal practice which has upset born Jews.

Much is made of the parable of the olive tree in Romans 11 by those who emphasize Paul's continuity with Judaism. But this parable does *not* reflect Paul's usual 'ecclesiology' (which is that of the body of Christ). Paul's all-important 'in Christ' language is missing in Romans 9–11 altogether. Paul's normal position is, in Sanders' words, that both Jews and Gentiles had to 'join what was, in effect, a third entity'.[71] On that basis, Paul could have devised a parable of a *third* olive tree into which faithful Jews and converted Gentiles were 'grafted': in the church of Christ Jewish and Gentile Christians lived together without scrupulously observing the revealed Torah, the central symbol of Jewish identity – a practice which brought Paul the reputation of being a renegade (Acts 21.21, 28).

From the viewpoint of a non-Christian Jew, Paul's vision of the salvation of all Israel is not nearly so generous as many Christians, often in connection with Jewish–Christian dialogue, tend to think. In effect, Paul is saying that Jews will be saved since they will eventually become Christians, so that the eschatological 'mystery' assures 'the ultimate vindication of the church'.[72] This salvation is for non-Christian Jews 'a

---

of the few true Jews at that. Cf. already Donald W. Riddle, 'The Jewishness of Paul', *JR* 23 (1943), pp. 240–44 (244): 'Always regarding himself as a faithful and loyal Jew, his definitions of values were so different from those of his contemporaries that, notwithstanding his own position within Judaism, he was, from any point of view other than his own, at best a poor Jew and at worst a renegade.'

69 Paul states in 1 Cor. 9.20 that even Jews must be 'won', i.e., converted. If Jews were not expected to believe in Jesus, why should Paul complain about their unbelief (Rom. 11.20, 23) or disobedience (11.31)? What is supposed to arouse the 'jealousy' of Israel, if the Gentiles have not gained anything that Israel would not possess already? For a fuller critique see Räisänen, 'Paul, God, and Israel', pp. 189–92.

70 Kuss, *Römerbrief*, vol. 3, p. 792; similarly Sanders, *Law*, p. 198; Kuula, *Romans*, p. 344.

71 Sanders, *Law*, p. 172.

72 Rosemary Ruether, *Faith and Fratricide: The Theological Roots of Anti-Semitism* (London: Seabury, 1974) pp. 105f. Sänger, *Verkündigung*, tries to refute Ruether's thesis, but unintentionally ends up by confirming her point: see my review in *JBL* 116 (1997), pp. 374f.

bitter gospel not a sweet one' because it is conditional precisely on abandoning their separate cultural and religious identity.[73] 'If the only value and promise afforded the Jews, even in Rom. 11, is that in the end they will see the error of their ways, one cannot claim that there is a role for Jewish existence in Paul.'[74] From a traditional Jewish perspective Paul's theology, even in Rom. 11, is 'supersessionist',[75] and it may even have done a lot of *harm* to Jews, as it has kindled Christian hopes for their grand-scale conversion. Since this has not happened, the disappointment has been ever so great (playing a part in the hardening of old Luther's attitude, for instance).

God may not have rejected his people (11.1-2), but by the end of ch. 11 Paul has in effect rejected the arguments he had set forth in ch. 9. To be sure, everything still depends in 11.25-32 on God's sovereign action, but all emphasis now rests on his compassionate mercy. One gets the impression that even the sin and disobedience of all, Jews as well as Gentiles, is willed and effected by God (a thesis which stands in sharp contradiction to Romans 1–2) so that he can show his irresistible grace towards all and sundry: 'God has consigned all men to disobedience, that he may have mercy upon all' (v. 32). The section fittingly ends with a doxology that praises the endless richness of God's wisdom.[76]

Paul's Dilemma

Paul's arguments fluctuate back and forth, as if he is desperately searching for a solution to the problem of continuity and discontinuity which is, however, too difficult to be solved.[77] He tries different solutions:

(1) Israel as a people was never chosen by God. God has in advance elected only a small 'remnant' to be saved. The others he has from the start prepared for destruction; they have been hardened by him. Salvation depends on God's arbitrary choice. Many interpreters (notably Dunn) fail to take this side of Paul's argument seriously. Explaining away Paul's clear statements on God's arbitrary manner of acting in this passage makes it easier for them to assert that the argument of Romans 9–11 is coherent.

---

73   Boyarin, *Radical Jew*, p. 152.

74   *Ibid.*, p. 151.

75   Boyarin, *ibid.*, p. 202. To be sure, the doctrine is nevertheless not 'anti-Judaic' (correctly Boyarin, *ibid.*, p. 205).

76   Some scholars think that by resorting to a doxology, Paul tacitly admits that he has landed in a *cul-de-sac*; cf. Kuss, *Römerbrief*, vol. 3, p. 826; Walter, 'Zur Interpretation', p. 177.

77   In a similar vein, e.g., Ruether, *Faith*, pp. 105f.; Kuss, *Römerbrief*, vol. 3, p. 825; Sanders, *Law*, pp. 197–99; Theissen, 'Röm 9–11'; Walter, 'Zur Interpretation', pp. 173, 176: Paul is attempting to 'square the circle'; Schnelle, *Paulus*, p. 390; Lüdemann, *Paul*, p. 162.

(2) God has not hardened anyone. Israel herself has been stubborn; those (Jews or Gentiles) who accept Christ in faith will be saved.

(3) God has provisionally hardened the great majority of the people of Israel. In the end, however, the whole people will be saved, since God has in his grace elected it long ago. Salvation is based on the promises given by God to (the patriarchs of) Israel.

Undoubtedly Paul has Jewish *Christians* in mind when he speaks of God's merciful election in 9.6-23 (the first solution). The shape of his argument prevents him, however, from spelling this out; otherwise the train of thought which rests on God's total sovereignty would lose its force. One of the many peculiarities of this section is the fact that 'faith' is not mentioned in it at all.[78] The opposite of 'works' is here not 'faith' (as usually in Paul) but 'his call' (v. 12). Nor would a mention of 'faith' fit into this passage; it would damage it. Where *any* human activity is excluded, even faith inevitably disappears from the picture. In Romans 9.6-23 Paul speaks as if humans are saved simply by God's arbitrary action: their destinies are decreed by God before they are born. Verse 14 shows that Paul is not insensitive to the problematic nature of this thesis. He even tries to refute some predictable objections, but all he can do is to assert that the Almighty cannot be unjust since he has the power to do whatever he wants. In all this, however, Paul is not developing a 'doctrine'; he is wrestling with a burning practical mission problem: why does Israel not accept the message?

Elsewhere (2 Cor. 4.3-4) Paul occasionally attributes the blindness of the unbelievers, not to the God of Israel, but to the 'god of this aeon'. This fact shows for its part how far he is from possessing a consistent 'doctrine' of divine hardening. The introduction of Satan into Rom. 9 as the cause of Israel's stubbornness would have totally destroyed the argument based on God's sovereignty.

Compared with the general tenor of his letters, Paul here goes 'too far' as the argument leaves no room for faith. The idea of double predestination emerges as a side effect: it is an argument which Paul tries but which he soon drops. In Romans 11.25-36, by contrast, he seems to go 'too far' in the opposite direction. In fact the logic of the argument would here seem to lead to the notion of *apokatastasis*, the 'restoration' of all: 'God has consigned all men to disobedience, that he may have mercy upon all' (v. 32).[79] Here, too, faith seems dispensable; God's overwhelming grace is enough. The difference of this assertion from the roughly parallel

78 Cf. Kuss, *Römerbrief*, vol. 3, p. 709; Hübner, *Gottes Ich*, pp. 24f.

79 Some scholars think, however, that the 'universalist' idea of the salvation of all and sundry was indeed Paul's ultimate aim in this section; see Jewett, *Romans*, p. 712: 'The expectation of universal salvation in this verse is indisputable, regardless of the logical problems it poses for systematic theologians.'

statement in Gal. 3.22 is instructive. The latter belongs to a context where
the realization of God's plan is connected with 'justification by faith' (as
usual in Galatians): 'The Scripture consigned all things to sin, that what
was promised to *faith in Jesus* might be given to *those who believe*.' It is
difficult to emphasize human faith and divine omnipotence simultaneously.
In fact, the most 'normal' passage in the self-contradictory section Romans
9–11 is, in light of the total picture that emerges from Paul's letters, the
middle part (9.30–10.21) which stresses the crucial nature of a faith decision
(10.9-13) and the importance of the task of proclaiming the gospel.[80]

With all its tensions, Rom. 9–11 vividly illustrates how central and how
difficult the questions of identity and continuity were for Paul. The section
shows him in a struggle to legitimate his mission and to assert his and his
little group's identity in terms of traditional values. If God has made Jesus
Christ the only road to salvation, his covenant with Israel and his election
of the people seem to lose their significance. Yet Scripture affirms that the
covenant will be valid forever and that the Torah is given as an eternal
order. In Romans 9–11 Paul defends both the new and the old order of
salvation, but the attempt to do justice to both inevitably ends up in
contradictions. In the olive tree parable, Paul talks as if his church were a
mainstream synagogue with some new proselytes from which a few
apostates have been expelled. The social reality was quite different: to
speak in the language of the parable, almost all the old branches had been
'cut off' and a very small number of new branches of a 'wild olive tree' had
been 'grafted' onto the old tree. In Rom. 11 Paul attempts to argue for
salvation-historical continuity, but without much success. In the end, he
resorts to the desperate idea that the continuity will be realized at the
parousia at the latest. 'Paul's fundamental will is to establish a continuity
since God's trustworthiness demands it, but the inevitable logic of his
soteriology speaks against it.'[81] For Paul, 'two loyalties were absolute and
both were constitutive of his identity: to Jewishness and to Christ. Neither
was negotiable, intellectually or emotionally…'.[82]

It is the tension between a novel liberal practice and the pressure
towards a more conservative ideology that gets Paul into difficulty. His
practice, the abandonment of circumcision and food laws, amounted to a
break with sacred tradition; but his legitimating theory in Romans stresses
continuity, so that he can even assert that it is he who truly 'upholds the
law' (Rom. 3.31).

80 Cf. Kuula, *Romans*, p. 331.

81 Kuula, *ibid.*, p. 344. Kuula astutely observes that 'Paul finds himself in a similar
situation to the wretched "I" in Rom. 7: his will points to one direction but the hard facts of
reality in another.'

82 J.L. Houlden, *The Public Face of the Gospel: New Testament Ideas of the Church*
(London: SCM Press, 1997) p. 35; cf. Sanders, *Law*, p. 199.

Yet Once More: Consistency and Inconsistency

I return to the issue of consistency that has become a watershed in Pauline scholarship. It may be mentioned as a footnote to the history of Finnish studies on Paul, with which this volume is concerned, that I first became aware of the tensions in the thought of the apostle when preparing *The Idea of Divine Hardening*, a book that appeared in 1972.[83] In this early work I was comparing qur'anic and biblical texts that dealt with God's 'negative' activity (such as hardening people or leading them astray). At this point I was not yet aware of the many problems involved in Paul's treatment of the law; I was introduced to them a few years later through Hans-Joachim Schoeps's work.[84] But already at that early stage, after a rather sketchy discussion of the idea of hardening in Romans 9–11, I could not but conclude that contradictory trains of thought are present in these chapters. I found guidance and support in liberal German scholarship;[85] *Hardening* largely follows scholars of older generations such as Otto Pfleiderer, Heinrich Julius Holtzmann and Heinrich Weinel.[86]

It may be more interesting, though, to take note of the stimuli provided by the commentary on Romans by C.H. Dodd.[87] Dodd greatly appreciates Paul, but he does not shrink from singling out points where the apostle, in his opinion, presents a bad argument or is simply wrong. For example, the prediction of the conversion of the Jews appears artificial from a modern standpoint, but in addition it is 'doubtful whether it is really justified on Paul's own premises'. There are two divergent and 'perhaps inconsistent' lines in his argument, as Dodd cautiously formulates. *Either* the nation of Israel is the heir of the promise, *or* its place has been taken by 'the New Israel, the body of Christ in which there is neither Jew nor Greek'. In the latter case there is no ground for allowing special treatment for the nation of Israel. Dodd notes that 'Paul tries to have it both ways. We can well understand that his emotional interest in his own people, rather than strict logic, has determined his forecast.'[88] In the hardening passage Rom. 9.17-23 Paul takes 'a false step' and 'pushes what

---

83   Heikki Räisänen, *The Idea of Divine Hardening: A Comparative Study of the Notion of Divine Hardening, Leading Astray and Inciting to Evil in the Bible and the Qur'an* (PFES, 25; Helsinki: The Finnish Exegetical Society, 2nd edn, 1976).

84   Cf. Räisänen, *Paul and the Law*, p. v.

85   I guess that more modern German commentaries were mostly too theological in a 'roundabout' way (more or less covering up the internal discrepancies) to be really helpful.

86   Räisänen, *Hardening*, pp. 79, 85f.

87   *Ibid.*, pp. 79–83.

88   C.H. Dodd, *The Epistle of Paul to the Romans* (MNTC; London: Hodder and Stoughton, repr., 1947), pp. 182f.

we must describe as an unethical determinism to its logical extreme'.[89] The comparison with the potter which represents God 'as a non-moral despot' is 'the weakest point in the whole epistle', but then again it does not remain Paul's last word.[90] In not being afraid of 'calling a spade a spade' Dodd represents British common-sense thinking at its best. In this tradition I have later found a fair number of like-minded estimations of such points in Paul's thought that I must consider self-contradictory.[91]

As stated in the beginning, biblical scholars are often quite reluctant to admit contradictions in Paul's thought. Such an assumption is often regarded as a last resort. Yet I had to note in connection with *Hardening* that Christian scholars have not had inhibitions when it comes to pointing out self-contradictions, or ethically problematic features, in a foreign tradition – in the Qur'an or, say, in Qumran.[92] In connection with the New Testament, however, one prefers to speak of paradoxical tensions and the like.

Behind many (not all!)[93] criticisms of the thesis that Paul is inconsistent lurks religious anxiety. As one critic states, it is important to find 'coherence in Paul's argument if his theology is ultimately to inform our own perspectives and behaviour'. He asks, 'Why should I take seriously the opinions of someone who is himself so confused that he contradicts himself in the space of fifteen hundred words [Romans 9–11] on a matter central to these chapters... ?'[94]

It is difficult not to see here a residue of the old doctrine of inspiration, if not of inerrancy. Is there not even a 'docetic' tendency in the attempts to find coherence at all costs in Paul's thought? Real humans (including great theologians of the stature of Bultmann)[95] *are* inconsistent and may well contradict themselves! Sanders' work, which emphasizes Paul's conflicting convictions, has the great merit of making the apostle a being of flesh and blood: Paul wrestled 'desperately' with his dilemmas; Sanders speaks of his

89   Dodd, *ibid.*, pp. 157f. Jewett, *Romans*, pp. 585f. counters Dodd by stressing that Paul's rhetoric worked among his audience, since the idea of hardening 'was widely accepted throughout biblical literature. That Yahweh would harden Pharaoh's heart was repeatedly stated in the exodus narrative ... There was no scandal in reiterating this theme for Paul's audience ... Paul applies the widely shared teaching about Pharaoh's hardening in order to make the much more controversial case that God's mercy is sovereign.' But to bring out this positive intention, no emphasis on the hardening would have been necessary.

90   Dodd, *Romans*, p. 159.

91   Cf. Räisänen, *Paul and the Law*, pp. 11f.

92   Cf. Räisänen, *Hardening*, pp. 97f.

93   The point made here cannot be applied, e.g., to the contributions of Engberg-Pedersen or Gager (see above, pp. 22–3) nor, of course, to those of the Jewish expositors of Paul, such as Boyarin.

94   Douglas J. Moo, 'The theology of Romans 9–11', in David M. Hay and E. Elizabeth Johnson (eds), *Pauline Theology*, vol. 3, pp. 240–58 (240).

95   See above, p. 22.

'passion of expression', 'torment and passion', anguish, fear and even doubt.[96]

It is also complained that if the 'positive' attitude in Rom. 11 is an anomaly in Paul, then it becomes difficult to use that chapter as a Christian foundation for dialogue with Jews.[97] I am afraid that this is indeed the case and that we should face it.

There are different ways of taking a person seriously. The religious problem is somewhat mitigated, if we can take Paul as a *discussion partner* rather than as an authority. Why couldn't even a Christian join Boyarin when he states: 'I am wrestling alongside [Paul] with the cultural issues with which he was wrestling, and I am also wrestling *against* him in protest against *some* of the answers he came up with'?[98] Rather than taking any of Paul's statements as direct answers to our questions, it might be helpful to see his struggle as a potential example in our situation as well, when embracing cultural pluralism is imperative. Paul is wrestling with his sacred tradition in light of his new experience (positively, the living together of different ethnic groups in his churches; negatively, the rejection of his message by most Jews). We, too, try to make sense of our traditions in light of *our* experience, which includes the necessity of a critical approach to all traditions and an awareness of the terrible things that have happened and are happening in the world, partly because of some of our own traditions.

It is a fair demand that an interpreter of Paul try to 'understand' him as far as possible – and yet one should not try *excessively* hard, for Paul's is *one* stance in a conflict situation. If one presses equally hard to make sense of positions other than, or opposing, Paul's, one may be forced to admit that there are problems in Paul's position. I find 'fair play' all-important in biblical study, i.e., the taking seriously of the fact that we are listening to *one* party in a conflict in which the other side generally remains mute. Responsible scholarship must try to do justice both to Paul and to those Jews and Christians who disagreed with him. Probably every side had a point and some understandable concerns, and we should try to do justice to this diversity. Nascent Christianity was a religion with conflicting convictions. Not only were persons and groups engaged in conflict in the visible world; the struggle between tradition and innovation also took place in the microcosm of the mind and heart of Paul, a controversial Jew with conflicting convictions.

---

96   Sanders, *Law*, pp. 76, 79, 197f.
97   Moo, 'Romans 9–11', p. 240.
98   Boyarin, *Radical Jew*, p. 3. Cf. Engberg-Pedersen, *Paul and the Stoics*, p. 304.

Chapter 3

'God's Righteousness' – Once Again

Timo Laato

1. *Preface*

Pauline research continues to triumph. The debate broadens and deepens, yet it also becomes more difficult and complicated. Writing a research history seems next to impossible. In a brief article it is necessary to limit not only one's subject but also the number of scholars to include in one's notes. Who could demand more? No need to settle for less.

The present debate was launched in 1977 with the publication of E.P. Sanders' extensive work *Paul and Palestinian Judaism: A Comparison of Patterns of Religions*. Later there was talk of a whole new perspective: the New Perspective on Paul.[1] This concept comprises a large number of scholars who do not always agree on interpretations. Yet they do have something in common, otherwise it would not make any sense to speak of a new wave of research. The christological argument can at least be mentioned as one common denominator: Paul did not discard the Jewish religion based on its assumed legalistic soteriology – that it was built on merit and led to vainglory. His main reason was simply (and slightly simplified) that it was not *Christ*ianity, in other words it denied Christ as Saviour, Messiah.[2] This argument is also accompanied by a strong emphasis on salvation that is meant for everyone, heathen as well as Jew. As an apostle to the Gentiles, Paul had to regard God's plan of salvation more broadly than before. He could no longer stay inside the narrow

---

1 To read more closely about the research history, see Stephen Westerholm, 'The "New Perspective" at Twenty-Five', in Carson, O'Brien and Seifrid (eds), *Justification and Variegated Nomism: The Paradoxes of Paul*, vol. 2 (WUNT, 2/181; Tübingen: Mohr Siebeck, 2004), pp. 1–38.

2 E.P. Sanders, *Paul and Palestinian Judaism: A Comparison of Patterns of Religions* (London: Fortress Press, 1977), p. 501. His short and provocative thesis was: 'In short, *this is what Paul finds wrong in Judaism: it is not Christianity.*'

boundaries of Mosaic Law. Particularism had to give way to universalism. The old covenant had been replaced by the new.[3]

The debate has since advanced. The christological argument has been accompanied and in a way explained by anthropological analysis: Paul's view on man's ability to obey the law became much more pessimistic after he experienced conversion on the road to Damascus. He no longer believed in the ability of free will to break the power of sin. No man can help himself. The synergism of Judaism (co-operation of God and man within the prerequisites of the Sinaic covenant) must be rejected as worthless. It leads man to trust in the 'flesh' and to boast of self-righteousness (Gal., Rom. 3.27, 4.2-5, 9.30–10.3, Phil. 3.3-9). Man is totally corrupt and therefore fully unable to save himself or even contribute to his salvation. His only hope lies in the boundless mercy of God, which is received on account of Christ through faith alone.[4] In this we hear a reformation heartbeat – naturally! – although at some point it was thought or claimed to be silenced and the most enthusiastic hastened to toll the death knell in order to precipitate the burial.[5]

Although at this point it is too early to draw any final conclusions, I dare claim that anthropological analysis has entered the present debate on the relationship between Paul and Judaism to stay. It cannot be ignored anymore – except in tendentious research.

There is still disagreement on many details, but the importance and centrality of the main subject is the most significant and essential point. To support my claim I present here some brief scientific surveys of the present state of the debate. D.A. Hagner concludes:

> The result is that Paul abandoned the synergism of Jewish soteriology for the monergism of total dependence upon the grace of God in Christ. Laato concludes, rightly in my opinion, that Paul thus repudiates the

---

3 Especially E.P. Sanders: *Paul, the Law and the Jewish People* (Philadelphia: Fortress, 1983), and after him many others.

4 See, e.g., Timo Laato: *Paulus und das Judentum: Anthropologische Erwägungen* (Åbo: Åbo Academy Press, 1991) or *Paul and Judaism: An Anthropological Approach* (trans. T. McElwain; South Florida Studies in the History of Judaism, 115; Atlanta: Scholars Press, 1995). Cf. below.

5 Cf. Westerholm's summary ('The "New Perspective" ', pp. 37–38): 'That Luther, to this extent at least, gets Paul "right" is part of what I intended when I once suggested, somewhat epigrammatically, that Pauline scholars can learn from the Reformer. ... Still, one has only to read a few passages of his writings (most any will do) to realize that, in crucial respects, he inhabits the same world, and breathes the same air, as the apostle. ... Such kindredness of spirit gives Luther an inestimable advantage over many readers of Paul in "capturing" the essence of the apostle's writings. On numerous points of detail, Luther may be the last to illumine. For those, however, who would see forest as well as trees, I am still inclined to propose a trip to the dustbins of recent Pauline scholarship – to retrieve and try out, on a reading of the epistles, the discarded spectacles of the Reformer.'

Jewish understanding of righteousness and the Jewish soteriology. We may compare these conclusions to those of Stephen Westerholm.... [6]

Furthermore, S. Westerholm performs a broad survey of Jewish literature and concludes finally:

> The anthropologies of Paul and Judaism cannot, then, be considered in isolation from their respective 'soteriologies': different plights demand different solutions, and (as Sanders has reminded us) different solutions demand different plights. Broadly speaking, our survey of the literature supports the notion that Paul's anthropology, in corresponding to his 'soteriology', is a good deal more 'negative' than the anthropology typical among his contemporary Jews. [7]

M. Seifrid agrees fully:

> The very issue that Sanders's paradigm isolates within Paul's post-Damascus thought and thus removes from consideration, namely, the nature of the human plight, turns out to be the pivotal juncture at which Paul engages his contemporaries. [8]

P.T. O'Brien states:

> ...there are significant anthropological differences between Judaism and Paul. ... Sanders' contention, however, has been challenged: the

6 Donald A. Hagner, 'Paul and Judaism: the Jewish matrix of early Christianity: issues in the current debate', *BBR* 3 (1993), pp. 111–30 (p. 122).

7 See Stephen Westerholm, 'Paul's anthropological "pessimism" in its Jewish context', in J.M.G. Barclay and S.J. Gathercole (eds), *Divine and Human Agency in Paul and His Cultural Environment* (LNTS, 335; London: T&T Clark, 2006), pp. 71–98. In this chapter, I have used only the 'web-version' of his article which is found at http://www.abdn.ac.uk/divinity/Gathercole/paper-westerholm.htm. In another text ('The "New Perspective"', p. 37) Westerholm writes: 'But (the post-Damascus) Paul believes that human beings, at enmity with God and in slavery to sin, have neither the ability nor the inclination to submit to God's law. (Laato, among others, has reminded us that the pessimism of Paul's "anthropology" is not typically Jewish, and that it inevitably leads to a distinctive soteriological emphasis.) It follows (as those who stress the "apocalyptic" aspects of Paul's thought are wont to remind us) that, for Paul, a new divine act of creation is needed before people can be "put right" with God.' In addition see, e.g., Charles A. Gieschen, 'Paul and the law: was Luther right?', in C. A. Gieschen (ed.), *The Law in Holy Scripture: Essays from the Concordia Theological Seminary Symposium on Exegetical Theology* (St Louis: Concordia Publishing House, 2004), pp. 113–47 (132–38). He has the following subheading for II D: 'The Contrasting Anthropologies of First-Century Judaism and Paul'.

8 Mark Seifrid, 'Unrighteous by faith: apostolic proclamation in Romans 1.18–3.20', in Carson, O'Brien and Seifrid (eds), *Justification and Variegated Nomism*, vol. 2, pp. 105–45 (144). Earlier he wrote accordingly: 'In anticipation of our following discussion, we may say that Paul's surprising statements concerning the law make sense given his view of the fallen state and moral inability of the human beings (Laato 1995).' See Mark Seifrid, *Christ, our Righteousness: Paul's Theology of Justification* (NSBT, 9; Leicester: Inter-Varsity Press, 2000), p. 95.

anthropological presuppositions of Judaism clearly differ from those of the apostle.[9]

Similarly, T. George writes:

> In one of the most incisive criticisms of the new perspective published thus far, Timo Laato, building on the work of H. Odeberg, has compared the anthropological presuppositions of covenantal nomism, as sketched by Sanders, and Paul's own soteriology.[10]

H. Blocher concludes:

> Exegetical studies in the present volume have shown that Paul did elaborate the doctrine of human guilt, helplessness and condemnation as the foundation of his gospel.[11]

On the other hand, T.R. Schreiner generally states:

> E. Sanders (1977) rightly criticizes the caricature of Jewish legalism that has infiltrated biblical scholarship. But he goes too far to the other extreme. Laato (1991) contends rightly that Paul repudiates a synergism that was present in Jewish theology....[12]

J.R. Harrison summarizes the present state of research as follows:

> T. Laato (*Paul and Palestinian Judaism: An Anthropological Approach* [Atlanta 1995]) is a sound example of the approach required. He charts from the intertestamental and rabbinic literature how Judaism embraced an optimistic anthropology in its concentration on human free will (*ibid.*, 65–75). The synergistic approach of Judaism, Laato argues, stands in contrast to Paul who, because of his pessimistic anthropology of human depravity (*ibid.*, 75–146), emphasised salvation by grace alone (*ibid.*, 147–168).[13]

9   Peter T. O'Brien, 'Was Paul a Covenantal Nomist?', in Carson, O'Brien and Seifrid (eds), *Justification and Variegated Nomism*, vol. 2, pp. 249–96 (270).

10   Timothy George, 'Modernizing Luther, domesticating Paul: another perspective', in Carson, O'Brien and Seifrid (eds), *Justification and Variegated Nomism*, vol. 2, pp. 437–63 (453).

11   Henri Blocher, 'Justification of the Ungodly (*Sola Fide*): theological reflections', in Carson, O'Brien and Seifrid (eds), *Justification and Variegated Nomism*, vol. 2, pp. 465–500 (484).

12   Thomas R. Schreiner, *Romans* (BECNT, 6; Grand Rapids: Eerdmans, 1998), p. 174. Furthermore, in another context he concludes: 'Laato (1991) argues that the central difference between Paul and Palestinian Judaism lay in their estimate of anthropological ability. I believe he is largely correct here' (*ibid.*, p. 154 n. 14 *et passim*).

13   Henry J.R. Harrison, *Paul's Language of Grace in its Graeco-Roman Context* (WUNT, 2/172; Tübingen: Mohr Siebeck, 2003), p. 101 n. 18. Probably the first person to give a statement like those above was Lars Aejmelaeus in his 'Review (Timo Laato, *Paulus und das Judentum: Anthropologische Erwägungen*)', *SJS* 13 (1992), pp. 168–70 (170): 'Laatos Dissertation ist eine klargeschriebene und scharfe Apologie für den Heidenapostel, der in den letzten Jahrzehnten wegen seiner Polemik der jüdischen "Werkgerechtigkeit" gegenüber

These surveys show the present state of the research quite adequately. In this article I will not further examine anthropology because it has been discussed elsewhere.[14] However, it is still useful to keep in mind what has been said above, as it provides background to what follows.

Thus, it is necessary to take the anthropological analysis into account when contemplating or drawing the outlines of a new perspective on Pauline theology. A mere christological argument is not enough. On the other hand, one can rightly ask – with reference to the present scientific debate – whether the christological argument is understood in depth or even correctly without anthropological analysis. In Pauline theology both are interconnected: Jesus died for the sins of the whole world. This raises the question: what does such an atoning death mean? Naturally this is too vast a subject to be treated in one paper or short article. Might not eternity be too short a time to fully explore it? As a human with limitations and also a time limit one must limit one's task strictly. There are many options and freedom of choice may be applied. Romans especially emphasizes that the Gospel of Jesus Christ (1.3-4) declares to a mankind living without righteousness 'God's righteousness' which is received through faith (1.16ff).[15] This is where the anthropological analysis and the christological argument meet. What is their connection? Why do they presuppose each other? Below we will focus on the meaning of the term 'God's righteousness', with an emphasis on Romans. The central verses are 1.17; 3.5, 21, 22, 25, 26; 10.3 (2x) and 2 Cor. 5.21 (cf. 1 Cor. 1.30 and Phil. 3.9).[16] Subsequently, the outcome of the study will be compared with the earlier research, including the question of the centre of Pauline theology. Last, but not least, a homiletic application will be sketched out in the hope of making use of exegetics in the Christian Church.

einen schlechten Ruf bekommen hat. In diesem Buch wird ein Modell konstruiert, womit man die paulinische Logik und Argumentation in seiner Auseinandersetzung mit dem Judentum verständlich machen kann, ohne daneben gleichzeitig selbst antijudaistisch werden ....'

14 See, e.g., my articles 'Römer 7 und das lutherische simul iustus et peccator', *LuthBei* 8 (2003), pp. 212–34 and 'Paul's anthropological considerations: two problems', in Carson, O'Brien and Seifrid (eds), *Justification and Variegated Nomism*, vol. 2, pp. 343–59.

15 Cf. e.g., Ernst Käsemann, 'Gottesgerechtigkeit bei Paulus', *ZTK* 58 (1961), pp. 367–78 (367). He begins his famous article with the following statement: 'Der Römerbrief stellt die gesamte Verkündigung und Theologie des Paulus unter das eine Thema der sich offenbarenden Gottesgerechtigkeit.'

16 See, e.g., Leon Morris: *The Epistle to the Romans* (Leicester: Eerdmans, 1988), p. 101.

2. The Concept of 'God's Righteousness' in Romans

2.1. A Judicial Concept

In secular Greek the word 'righteousness' (*et alia*) was mainly an ethical term. It expressed what was morally acceptable and advisable. In the Old Testament the emphasis lies elsewhere. There, justification is also and foremost a part of judicial language. He is righteous who is acquitted in a court of law. Without righteousness is he who is found guilty.[17] Paul uses the same language. This is especially explicit in his letter to the Romans 1–3 where he underlines the sinfulness and guilt of man before God. His choice of words reads like a court transcript.

Rom. 1–3 depicts in fact vast court proceedings where the whole world stands accused. Paul acts as the prosecutor (3.9, προῃτιασάμεθα ἁη). Before his accusations both Gentiles (1.20) and Jews (2.1) are without excuse or defence (ἀναπολόγητος). Not even the attempt to show solidarity towards the judge by starting to condemn others in his stead will help anyone escape judgement. On the contrary, such action testifies to outrageous vileness and deserves an even harsher judgement (2.1-4). At the final judgement each will be judged according to his works (2.6). God judges no one with bias; he does not show favouritism (2.11). His coming judgements will meet each sinner without distinction (2.12-13). No excuses or defences of conscience will suffice then (2.15). Paul continues his harsh interrogation with some inconvenient questions that reveal the apparent untruth and hypocrisy of the defendant (2.21-24). After repealing the speech of the defence (3.1-8), he concludes triumphantly that all are guilty of persistent offence and work under the tyranny of sin (3.9). God will judge them according to his book of law (3.10-18) and their mouths will be silenced by his harsh judgements (3.19). In accord with the indictment, the death penalty will eventually follow (1.32). But even before that the criminals will be disciplined severely and handed over to the court wardens (παραδίδωμι) and left to contend with their various passions (1.24, 26, 28).[18]

Along with the judicial connotations it is also notable that in the original language words based on the root *dik*- emerge and unify the text. To mention a few examples:

---

17 *Ibid.*, p. 101. In addition, see Charles E.B. Cranfield, *A Critical and Exegetical Commentary on the Epistle to the Romans: Introduction and Commentary on Romans I–VIII*, vol. 1 (ICC; Edinburgh: T&T Clark, 1982), pp. 93–95. The meaning of the justification in the Old Testament will be returned to later in section 4.4.

18 See commentaries *ad loc*. Cf. my article 'Paavali ekumeenisena erotuomarina: Mistä löytäisin perustelut yhteiselle julistukselle?', in S. Kiviranta and T. Laato (eds), *Turhentuuko uskonpuhdistus? Rooman kirkon ja Luterilaisen Maailmanliiton uusi selitys vanhurskautta-misopista* (Kauniainen: Perussanoma, 2nd edn, 1998), pp. 79–102 (91). On the interpretation of Rom. 1–2, see Laato, *Paulus und das Judentum*, pp. 98–119.

1.18   ἀδικίαν, ἀδικίᾳ
1.29   ἀδικίᾳ
1.32   δικαίωμα
2.5   δικαιοκρισίας
2.8   ἀδικίᾳ
2.13   δίκαιοι, δικαιωθήσονται
2.26   δικαιώματα
3.4   δικαιωθῇς
3.5   ἀδικία, δικαιοσύνην
3.8   ἔνδικον
3.10   δίκαιος
3.19   ὑπόδικος
3.20   δικαιωθήσεται[19]

It may further be pointed out that exactly at this crucial point after the verdict has been read the court proceedings take a surprising new turn. On behalf of the accused and convicted, one man steps up who has atoned for all their transgressions and also served their sentence in full. Because of him justice is tempered with mercy (3.21-26). This is the gospel, good news, that declares 'God's righteousness'. Our subject is to further unravel this and to better understand it.[20]

Based on what has been presented above it seems quite untenable to claim that justification is not (or at least not primarily) a judicial proceeding. Perhaps not merely judicial but certainly and primarily that![21] At the same time it has also become evident that anthropology and justification by Christ are – as stated above – closely interconnected.

2.2. *Old Testament Background*

When writing (or rather dictating) the letter to the Romans, Paul especially wanted to emphasize that the gospel he declared was consistent with Old Testament scripture. His intention is evident initially (1.2-4) and it actually permeates everything that is said. Especially in chs 9–11 Paul quotes scriptures more frequently than ever. About half of all his Old

19   Seifrid, 'Unrighteous by faith', p. 108 n. 7.

20   Rom. 1–3 has a lot in common with the structure of the book of the prophet Amos. He starts by passing sentence on the Gentile nations (1.1–2.3). Then he suddenly turns against Judah and Israel (2.4-16). It is not until the very end that he prophesies of a coming time of salvation and of re-erecting the collapsed tabernacle of David (9.11-15). For more on the structure of Amos see, e.g., Rolf Rendtorff, *Das Alte Testament: Eine Einführung* (Neukirchen-Vluyn: Neukirchener, 6th edn, 2001), pp. 232–35.

21   The judicial aspect of Paul's doctrine of justification, and the continuing discussion on it, will be returned to later in section 4.

Testament quotations appear in Romans, one third in exactly the three chapters mentioned![22]

The same emphasis is also to be seen in the theme verses of Romans (1.16-17), where our central concept of 'God's righteousness' is first mentioned. Paul quotes Hab. 2.4 for support, as is known. He also seems to join the Old Testament teachings and choice of words in a much broader sense. As an illustration of this here are presented in parallel Ps. 98.1-3 and Rom. 1.16-17a. The similarities are striking:

Ps. 98.1-3	Rom. 1.16-17a
'Sing to the Lord a new song, for he has done marvelous things; his right hand and his holy arm have worked salvation for him. The Lord has made his salvation known and revealed his righteousness to the nations. He has remembered his love and his faithfulness to the house of Israel; all the ends of the earth have seen the salvation of our God.'	'I am not ashamed of the Gospel, because it is the power of God for the salvation of everyone who believes: first for the Jew, then for the Gentile. For in the Gospel a righteousness from God is revealed from faith to faith.'

Usually research has found the following similarities between these two passages:

1) God *is revealed*, he makes himself known;
2) God shows his great *power*, his glory makes itself seen;
3) God's *salvation*, and
4) God's *righteousness* are revealed.

The concepts 'salvation' and 'righteousness' overlap here. They are synonymous.[23]

Moreover the list of similarities can be complemented with the following:

1) The salvation acquired by God belongs to *all*, not only Jews, but also Gentiles.
2) God's salvation is something to rejoice in and boast of; it is not to be hushed up, not something to be ashamed of. (The opposite of being ashamed is in Romans' mostly bold boasting and public testifying, cf. 5.2-5 and 10.10-11; see further, Ps. 98.4-5).[24]

---

22 On the relationship between Paul and the Old Testament, see Timo Laato, *Romarbrevets hermeneutik: En lärobok för teologer om vetenskaplig metod* (Församlingsfakultetens skriftserie, 7; Göteborg: Församlingsförlaget, 2006).

23 See in the first place, John Murray: *The Epistle to the Romans* (NICNT, 5; 2 vols.; Michigan: Eerdmans, 1982), pp. 28–29.

24 Murray – along with many others! – does not mention the last two similarities.

There are parallels in the Old Testament to Ps. 98.1-3. Especially in the latter part of Isaiah the concepts 'salvation' and 'righteousness' are frequently mentioned in parallel (see e.g., Isa. 46.13; 51.5-8; 56.1; 62.1, cf. 54.17; 61.10-11). Yet we will not focus on these passages as a mention here should suffice.[25]

Since the observation has been made that, in Romans, particularly, Paul is building an Old Testament scriptural basis for the gospel he is proclaiming, and does so also and primarily in the theme verses of the epistle, there is a good ground to explore further his concept of 'God's righteousness'.

2.3. *God's Own Righteousness*

Against the Old Testament background it is obvious that 'God's righteousness' means primarily precisely God's own righteousness. Lutheranism has traditionally shuddered at such a thought. Luther's 'tower experience' has received a one-sided – if not false – interpretation. It has been claimed or insinuated that 'God's righteousness' means to the reformer God's gift of righteousness. As true as it is that such an emphasis is clear in his writings, he never claims that God would grant righteousness arbitrarily, without any just cause. I am sure we systematics and exegetes all agree today that 'God's righteousness' (Rom. 1.17) does not mean God's *punishing* righteousness that will befall mankind. Yet by this we must not conclude that God's righteousness does not mean God's righteousness![26]

25   See e.g., Murray, *ibid.*, pp. 28–29.

26   Afterwards Luther writes on his own reformatory breakthrough in the following way: 'I had indeed been captivated with an extraordinary ardor for understanding Paul in the Epistle to the Romans. But up till then it was not the cold blood about the heart, but a single word in Chapter 1 [.17], "In it the righteousness of God is revealed", that had stood in my way. For I hated that word "righteousness of God", which, according to the use and custom of all teachers, I had been taught to understand philosophically regarding the formal or active righteousness, as they called it, with which God is righteous and punishes the unrighteous sinner. ...I did not love, yes, I hated the righteous God who punishes sinners, and secretly, if not blasphemously, certainly murmuring greatly, I was angry with God... Nevertheless, I beat importunately upon Paul at that place, most ardently desiring to know what St Paul wanted. At last, by the mercy of God, meditating day and night, I gave heed to the context of the words, namely, "In it the righteousness of God is revealed, as it is written, 'He who through faith is righteous shall live.'" There I began to understand that the righteousness of God is revealed by the gospel, namely, the passive righteousness with which merciful God justifies by faith, as it is written, "He who through faith is righteous shall live". Here I felt that I was altogether born again and had entered paradise itself through open gates. There a totally other face of the entire Scripture showed itself to me. Thereupon I ran through the Scriptures from memory. I also found in other terms an analogy, as, the work of God, that is, what God does in us, the power of God, with which he makes us strong, the wisdom of God, with which he makes us wise, the strength of God, the salvation of God, the

If the Old Testament background helps to better understand the apostle's vocabulary, he is himself also capable of choosing his words and writing clearly. Based on the near context it seems fully clear that v. 17 speaks of God's own righteousness. In vv. 16–18 the following expressions appear: v. 16: 'God's power', v. 17: 'God's righteousness', and v. 18: 'God's wrath'. In vv. 16 and 18 the genitive structure expresses a quality that belongs to God and is his own. It is hardly likely that the same structure in v. 17 would merely express something that he grants to the believer or attributes to faith, e.g., a righteous 'position' or 'state' (*status*). Thus based on the near context, it would be wrong to limit the concept of 'God's righteousness' to mean merely a 'gift of righteousness'.[27] This point is worth returning to later.

The next time Paul addresses the subject of God's righteousness is in Romans 3. He speaks of the godlessness of Jews or people in general, which will be judged:

> Let God be true, and every man a liar. As it is written: 'So that you may be proved right [= justified] when you speak and prevail when you judge.' But if our unrighteousness brings out God's righteousness more clearly, what shall we say? That God is unjust in bringing his wrath on us? (I am using a human argument.) (vv. 4–5)

Here clarifying God's righteousness has above all to do with God being just. As a righteous judge he judges iniquity and will therefore judge the

---

glory of God.' The quotation is taken from *Luther's Works: Career of the Reformer IV*, vol. 34 (ed. L.W. Spitz; Philadelphia: Concordia Publishing House, 2nd edn, 1976), pp. 336–37. Luther's difficulty in understanding the concept of 'God's righteousness' was not with the idea that God is righteous, but with the kind of teaching that God is righteous and he therefore *punishes* the sinner. The solution Luther found was not that God would not be righteous, but that he is righteous and he therefore *justifies* the sinner, through his gospel. The concepts 'God's power' and 'God's wisdom' in the quotation above must also be understood accordingly. The intent is naturally not that God gives us his power and wisdom, without himself being almighty and omniscient. Thus Luther did not want to deny God's own righteousness in understanding the concept of 'God's righteousness'. In this respect he has – once again! – been quoted against his own intention. In addition, see below sections 4.2.–4.4.

27 Cranfield, *Romans*, p. 96. He thinks this is a strong argument, but rejects it nevertheless! Correctly for instance Joseph A. Fitzmyer, *Romans: A New Translation with Introduction and Commentary* (AB, 33; New York: Doubleday, 1993), p. 262. Heinrich Schlier, *Der Römerbrief* (HTKNT, 6; Freiburg: Herder, 1977), p. 44 concludes in a singular way and lacking any grounds whatsoever: 'jedenfalls ist nicht eine Eigenschaft Gottes gemeint [!], auch nicht eine in seinen Werken wirksame Eigenschaft, wie das in den Qumrantexten häufig der Fall ist ...'. Cf. surprisingly Jas 1.20. There the 'wrath of man' and 'God's righteousness' are contrasted. The former refers to an anger felt and expressed by man. Therefore, the latter must refer to God's own righteousness and a life, action and attitude that are in accord with it. In Paul's vocabulary the concepts 'God's wrath' and 'God's righteousness' must be understood accordingly – yet in harmony with the special features of his theology.

whole world. At least on this point the meaning of the text is clear. This will do and there is no need to review other details (yet cf. below).[28]

The notion of God's own righteousness arises later. His patience in letting sins go unpunished – especially in the old covenant times – threatened to turn against him and make his righteousness questionable. It was only the atoning death of Christ that proved that God was not an unjust judge who would let the iniquities of the world go unjudged. Instead he waited patiently until justice was tempered with mercy and the wrongs of the world were washed away with one single and total sacrifice:

> ...and are justified freely by his grace through the redemption that came by Christ Jesus. God presented him as a sacrifice of atonement, through faith in his blood. He did this to demonstrate his justice, because in his forbearance he had left the sins committed beforehand unpunished – he did it to demonstrate his justice at the present time, so as to be just and the one who justifies those who have faith in Jesus. (vv. 24–26)[29]

These verses will be returned to later.

To summarize so far, it can be stated that the concept of 'God's righteousness' comprises centrally the notion of God's own righteousness. He is just. There is no iniquity in him.

2.4. *God's Saving Action for Restoring Righteousness*

Already the central Old Testament passages (see above) show that God in his righteousness takes action to restore righteousness in Israel, and even the whole world. It is not merely that he is righteous. He also creates righteousness. This is his saving action. We already noted that righteousness and salvation are synonymous concepts. They express one and the same way of thinking.[30]

As the righteous judge, God should not justify an unrighteous man (cf. e.g., Exod. 23.7, Prov. 17.15 and Isa. 5.23). His own righteousness by itself would clearly not save anyone. It would rather lead to perfect doom and destruction. A sinner cannot prevail before Holiness. A righteous judge gives a righteous verdict for all unrighteousness of all kinds. That is what the final judgement means. That is the terrifying day of the Lord in the Old Testament.[31]

This is why it seems so surprising that God's righteousness and his saving action are seen as parallel. You would hardly believe it if you did not read it with your own eyes! The impossible suddenly becomes

---

28 Most commentaries agree. However, cf. below sections 2.4. and 2.5.

29 See especially John Piper, *The Justification of God: An Exegetical and Theological Study of Romans 9.1-23* (Grand Rapids: Eerdmans, 2nd edn, 1993), pp. 140–47.

30 See above.

31 Cf. Murray, *Romans*, pp. 30–31.

possible. The same kind of parallel is drawn by the apostle in Romans. He speaks of the gospel which is 'the power of God for the salvation of everyone', *because* in it 'God's righteousness' is revealed (1.16-17). Therefore the gospel saves precisely because it reveals God's righteousness. This is something previously unheard of, that indeed was prophesied in the Old Testament, but has not been declared for all until now.[32]

In the third chapter Paul clarifies and specifies his teaching. He uses the same vocabulary as in the epistle's theme verses. After he has proved the sinfulness and guilt of the world before God he finally gets to his point. Now 'God's righteousness' has appeared in the world without law (v. 21), the righteousness that is owned by faith and through faith (v. 22), and that Christ has earned by his bloody death (vv. 24–25a). Mercy and forgiveness are in him. He has acquired atonement. This is how God has finally fulfilled the demands of his righteousness, and at the same time made salvation possible for a fallen humanity. In the Old Testament times his vast patience with sin had called his righteousness into question. Does he really ignore the fact that his holy will is broken? Also in new covenant times his great mercy towards sinners shows his righteousness in an unfavourable light. Should he not rather condemn and punish? Now the awkward questions have been answered. When letting Christ die on the cross for mankind, God has indisputably proven his righteousness. He is righteous in justifying through faith (vv. 25b-26) even the godless (4.5).[33]

The same kind of reasoning continues later in ch. 10. Israel is accused of not having submitted to God's righteousness (v. 3). To them it obviously has gone (and goes) without saying that God himself is righteous (cf. above). It was (and is), however, not clear to them that God's righteousness has been revealed in Christ. This is what the context is about. There is also an emphasis on the salvation history perspective. Christ is 'the end of the law' so that there may be righteousness for everyone who believes (v. 4). Such righteousness speaks (!) and warns the listener against 'bringing Christ down' or 'bringing Christ up' (vv. 6–7), referring to his incarnation and resurrection, the beginning and end of his saving work. In all this God's righteousness is revealed and yet it is curiously rejected by God's own people. The graveness and strangeness of the situation makes Paul – apostle to the Gentiles – thoughtful. He prays and even weeps for his fellow Jews (9.1-3; 10.1).[34]

The unity of the argumentation in Romans is further highlighted by the parallel sections 3.20-22 and 10.3-4. The following similarities emerge:

---

32   Cf. Laato, *Romarbrevets hermeneutik*, pp. 55–58.
33   See especially Piper, *Justification*, pp. 135–50.
34   Laato, *Paulus und das Judentum*, pp. 249–54 and *Romarbrevets hermeneutik*, pp. 94–106.

- no one is justified by the law (3.20) – Israelites are unable to establish their own righteousness (10.3);
- therefore God's righteousness is revealed apart from the law (3.21), namely in Christ (see 3.22ff.) – Christ is the end of the law (10.4a), and besides
- God's righteousness belongs to all who believe (3.22 and 10.4b).

Even the expression 'to which the law and the prophets testify' (3.21) is parallel with the arguments in ch. 10: first the testimony of the law (vv. 6–8) and then that of the prophets (vv. 11ff.) are mentioned.[35]

So an essential part of God's righteousness is his action to save man. This perspective is not to be forgotten even at 3.5 – which is often the case in commentaries! A parallel is clearly to be found in 6.1. In both passages we hear the voice of the 'opponent' – according to the style of an ancient Greek diatribe. It is presented as a mocking question that is averted with a pompous exclamation: 'Certainly not! By no means!' (3.6; 6.2). Then an effective counter question is added, one that starts with the word 'How?' (3.6; 6.2). In the meantime the writer has had time to contemplate aloud how one should react or reply to such gross blasphemy (3.5; 6.1). Both passages also contain the same idea. The aim is to justify sin with God's goodness. Chapter 6 appeals to God's mercy, ch. 3 to his righteousness. Again God's righteousness cannot refer only to God being just. Simultaneously it comprises the idea of his saving action. Trust is being put in it and the hope is expressed that in the end – despite all godlessness! – one would be exonerated, freed from harsh judgement. There is no need to narrow the content of the concept of 'God's righteousness' here or to limit its meaning. Paul has already in the theme verses of his epistle presented God's righteousness as a saving righteousness and thereby followed the Old Testament example (see above). What else could his readers have concluded by what has been said? At this point research has a need for slight correction and self-criticism.[36]

---

35 Especially Douglas J. Moo, *The Epistle to the Romans* (NICNT; Grand Rapids: Eerdmans, 1996), p. 640 n. 2. See further Laato, *Romarbrevets hermeneutik*, pp. 97–98. Cf. Anders Nygren, *Pauli brev till romarna* (TNT, 6; Stockholm: SKD:s bokförlag, 1979), p. 381.

36 Research often notes *only* the connection between verses 3.5 and 9.14. See e.g., Heikki Räisänen, 'Zum Verständnis von Röm 3, 1–8', in *The Torah and Christ: Essays in German and English on the Problem of the Law in Early Christianity* (PFES, 45; Helsinki: Finnish Exegetical Society, 1986), pp. 185–205 (197). Piper especially (*Justification*, pp. 126–34) has criticized modern research for an all too one-sided view. In the same context he also refers briefly to Rom. 6.1 (p. 129). Moo stresses that Piper's 'interpretation of Paul's concept of God's righteousness as it unfolds in the passage as a whole is very close to ours' (*Romans*, p. 190 n. 67). Schreiner continues the conversation in his commentary on *Romans* (pp. 154–57). Yet he neglects the fact that Piper writes not only of God's *saving* righteousness.

2.5. *The Righteousness Granted by God*

In the previous section, it has many times become clear that God's saving action to restore righteousness requires faith on man's part. God's righteousness is revealed, 'from faith to faith' (1.17). At the same time God's righteousness is revealed without law and is granted 'through faith' to all who believe (3.20-21). In Jesus' work on the cross God has revealed his holy righteousness and is therefore capable of justifying those who believe (3.25-26). Israel should give up the attempt to establish its own righteousness and finally submit to God's righteousness by heeding what the righteousness that comes by faith recommends (10.3ff.).

So there is still one important side to the concept of 'God's righteousness' – the state of righteousness that is in force before God through faith only. Without faith God's saving action will benefit no one. Faith receives and owns his saving work. Therefore 'God's righteousness' is precisely 'righteousness by faith'. Paul says that the aim of proclaiming the gospel is 'obedience to faith' (1.5 and 16.26, cf. 15.18). By this he means above all obedience to the gospel, accepting 'God's righteousness' in faith.[37]

For reasons that are understandable this perspective recedes in 3.5. Here the opponent speaks, an opponent that does not care much for faith (or anything else in particular). There is not much point in discussing righteousness by faith in such a context. Therefore Paul does not engage in a prolonged quarrel. He refutes the objections promptly and curtly. It is nevertheless remarkable that even and also in this passage the concept of 'God's righteousness' itself at least refers to an acceptable state before God. The opponent attempts to speak himself free of the last judgement, and supports his argument with the idea that his godlessness actually confirms God's righteousness. If God's righteousness merely meant his integrity and justice, there would not be the least hope of avoiding punishment. Appealing to that would be pure madness: the argument should lead to an even harsher judgement! If God's righteousness, on the other hand, means also and simultaneously his saving action and his merciful will to place the sinner righteous before him (cf. above), then the reasoning suddenly becomes quite logical. In that case the opponent is appealing to the theme of the whole epistle and simply turning it upside down. The gospel becomes a travesty of mercy. The arguments are – as stated above – parallel with the objections later in ch. 6.[38]

---

37 Thus, in general, many scholars who are connected to the reformation tradition. Yet it has already been noted above that Luther had a broader understanding of the concept of 'God's righteousness'!

38 Cf. Piper, *Justification*, pp. 126–34. Rom. 3.4 quotes Ps. 51.6, which undoubtedly speaks primarily of God's punishing righteousness. In this Penitential Psalm, David, however, submits to his verdict only to appeal to mercy and to plead for forgiveness for his

2.6. *Summary*

'God's righteousness' is a very broad concept. The following meanings are connected with it in Romans:

1) God's own righteousness (his justice);
2) God's saving action to establish righteousness; and
3) the righteousness granted by God.[39]

Already in the Old Testament the concept of 'God's righteousness' not only expressed God's own righteousness, but it essentially comprised the idea of salvation that he has acquired and granted to the whole world. So Romans continues to use the same language.

Usually researchers have a one-sided interpretation of the concept of 'God's righteousness'. They only focus on one meaning and disregard the others. Or they note the different meanings but in separate passages: they find one meaning in one verse, another in another verse. As a result the main message and theme of Romans becomes narrow and fragmented. Yet there is no reason for such interpretation of the texts. Paul's language is rich with nuances. It reveals at the same time many sides of one idea. This is exactly the nature of the concept of 'God's righteousness'.

3. *The Concept of 'God's Righteousness' Outside Romans*

The concept of 'God's righteousness' appears only once outside Romans, in 2 Cor. 5.21,[40] although 1 Cor. 1.30 and Phil. 3.9 are both conceptually and semantically directly connected with our topic. Therefore they will also be examined.

3.1. *2 Corinthians 5.21*

The context of the verse is about God's reconciliation with the whole world (see vv. 18–20). Fully of his own accord, he has acted in his great mercy to restore his fallen creation. Because of Christ's vicarious death (the preposition ὑπέρ, vv. 14–15 and 21), transgressions will no longer be counted as fault and the proclamation of the gospel transmits this good news to be received in faith (v. 19). The irreconcilable conflict between a

---

malice. He will not remain doomed! This reasoning also suits the goal of the opponent. He tries to talk himself out of punishment by re-interpreting Scripture – according to his own fancy.

39   Cf. Murray, *Romans*, pp. 30–31 and further James D.G. Dunn, *Romans 1–8* (WBC, 38A; Dallas: Paternoster Press, 1988), pp. 40–42. In Finland similar thoughts have been presented by Jukka Thurén, *Roomalaiskirje* (Helsinki: SLEY-Kirjat, 1994).

40   Elsewhere (= outside the Pauline Epistles) the concept of 'God's righteousness' occurs thrice: Mt. 6.33, Jas 1.20 and 2 Pet. 1.1 (Morris, *Romans*, p. 101).

holy God and a sinful world is now gone. Therefore nothing stands in the way of reconciliation at least on his part.

Verse 21 is actually a summary of what has been said before. It concerns God who made 'him who had no sin' (Christ) 'to be sin for us', so that 'in him' we might become 'the righteousness of God'. The concept of 'God's righteousness' expresses first and foremost that once Christ has suffered for the sins of the whole world he has completely fulfilled God's righteous demands (cf. above). Hence he has effected exactly that saving righteousness of God that is declared in the gospel and proclaimed through the apostolic ministry. The one who now believes the proclamation of reconciliation becomes righteous, is freed from guilt and enters a state where she or he prevails before God – even at the last Day of Judgement.[41]

Thus, in 2 Cor. the concept of 'God's righteousness' has the same meaning as above in Rom. It contains three main aspects:

1)   God's own righteousness;
2)   God's saving righteousness; and
3)   the righteousness that prevails before God.

The concept of 'God's righteousness' is therefore not to be limited, for example, to mean only 'not counting men's sins against them' (v. 19b). Then the whole idea would remain rudimentary and mainly comprise only number two from the list above: after all 'not counting men's sins against them' is followed by the apostolic 'message of reconciliation' (v. 19c) which – received in faith – only sets man in the right state before God. Man would never reach this state before God if God had not first himself reconciled the wickedness of the whole world and the integrity of his holiness (v. 19a). So for the sake of logic, points one and three above are also fully inevitable.

Further, the exceptional language in v. 21 is worthy of note. Paul does not write that 'we would become righteous before God in Christ'. He expresses himself more obscurely and utters a rather strange phrase: 'so that in him we might become the righteousness of God'. Why? The answer may in part remain a guess. It is well known that Paul sometimes expresses himself obscurely (cf. 2 Pet. 3.15-16)! Perhaps he is quoting an earlier church tradition that has to do with Isaiah's words on 'God's suffering servant' (see Isa. 53.10-11).[42] In any case he seems to deliberately avoid the phrase that Jesus was made a *sinner* (cf. Rom. 8.3). Instead he

41   Hans Johansson, *Andra Korinthierbrevet 1–7* (KTNT, 8a; Uppsala: Verbum, 1990), pp. 144–45, 152–56.

42   See e.g., Ralph P. Martin, *2 Corinthians* (WBC 40; Waco: Paternoster Press, 1986), pp. 138–41, 156–57 with references to other scholars, especially Käsemann (the problematic character of his interpretation is discussed further in section. 4.2).

says that God made him to be *sin*. Accordingly he is speaking of 'us', not as being righteous before God, but as being 'God's righteousness'. By this he emphasizes the polarity between 'us' and Christ. Christ takes away from us what separates us from God. We receive from Christ or rather in Christ that which unites us with God. This reciprocity explains (at least to a great extent!) the unusual language.[43] Further there may be in the background an allusion to 'the Lord, our righteousness', one of the pseudonyms of the Messiah (Jer. 23.6 and 33.16).[44]

Both linguistically and in thought 2 Cor. 5.21 resembles 1 Cor. 1.30, which will be studied next.

3.2. *1 Corinthians 1.30*

The concept of 'God's righteousness' does not appear as such in 1 Cor. yet a parallel expression is to be found in 1.30. There is mention of Christians who are said to be 'of God' and 'in Christ', and 'God made' their 'righteousness'. One could hardly express more strongly that the righteousness of a Christian is alien righteousness (in systematic theology the expression *iustitia aliena*), which is not acquired or produced by himself. He only exists because God has called him into being; now he exists only in another, namely in Christ, and Christ is to him his righteousness that has come from without and from above, from God. These characterizations define more closely the meaning of 'God's righteousness'. At least there is no trace of self-righteousness in it![45]

A comparison of 1 Cor. 1.30 and 2 Cor. 5.21 shows that the reasoning is very similar. In light of the context both passages emphasize that:

1) the salvation of a Christian is of God (cf. expressions ἐξ αὐτοῦ, 1 Cor. 1.30; ἐκ τοῦ θεοῦ, 2 Cor. 5.18);
2) existence for a Christian is being 'in Christ';
3) the righteousness of a Christian is Christ himself, and
4) this kind of righteousness is granted by God or it is God's righteousness.[46]

---

43   See Philip E. Hughes, *Paul's Second Epistle to the Corinthians: The English Text with Introduction, Exposition and Notes* (NICNT; Grand Rapids: Eerdmans, 1962), pp. 213–14.

44   More closely on the prophecy of Jeremiah, see Walter J. Kaiser, Jr., *The Messiah in the Old Testament* (Studies in Old Testament Biblical Theology; Grand Rapids: Eerdmans, 1995), pp. 187–89, 191.

45   Cf. Hans Conzelmann, *Der erste Brief an die Korinther* (MeyerK, 5; Göttingen: Vandenhoeck & Ruprecht, 2nd edn, 1981), pp. 72–73, Wolfgang Schrage, *Der erste Brief an die Korinther: 1 Kor 1,1–6,11*, vol. 1 (EKKNT, 7/1; Neukirchen–Vluyn: Neukirchener 1991), pp. 213–17.

46   Cf. Johansson, *Andra Korinthierbrevet*, p. 142: 'Tankegången [in 2 Cor. 5.21] liknar den i 1. Kor. 1.30 där Kristus är "vår rättfärdighet" för oss från Gud.'

Thus, both 1 Cor. 1.30 and 2 Cor. 5.21 say the same thing, but in slightly different words.

Furthermore, the context of 1 Cor. 1.30 shows that it is closely connected with the theme verses of Romans (1.16-17).[47] This is evident by the following points:

1) Paul is not ashamed of the gospel, although the wise of this world often reject it (1 Cor. 1.18-29). He has decided not to proclaim anything other than Christ crucified (1 Cor. 2.1-5);

2) The gospel is the power of God (1 Cor. 1.18 and 24; 2.5);

3) As God's power the gospel brings salvation (1 Cor. 1.18);

4) Salvation belongs to those who believe (especially 1 Cor. 2.5);

5) The gospel is meant foremost for Jews, then also for all Gentiles (1 Cor. 1.22 and 23);

6) Because the word of the cross as God's power (1 Cor. 1.18) is actually Christ himself (v. 24), and God has made Christ our righteousness (v. 30), God's righteousness is revealed precisely in the gospel, and

7) The Old Testament scriptures prove what the gospel proclaims (1 Cor. 1.19 and 31).

In the light of these similarities the two expressions 'Christ, whom God has made our righteousness' (1 Cor. 1.30), and 'God's righteousness as it is revealed in the gospel' (Rom. 1.17) have exactly the same meaning.[48] In both letters to Corinthians it is more explicit than in any other of Paul's epistles, that God's righteousness is after all a person, Jesus Christ himself. He has fulfilled the righteous demands of God by dying for the sins of the world, in him God's saving righteousness is present and in him the believer is righteous or he is even the righteousness of God.[49]

---

47   Peter Stuhlmacher, 'The Theme of Romans', in K.P. Donfried (ed.), *The Romans Debate* (Peabody: T&T Clark, 3rd edn, 2005), p. 338: 'The way in which the gospel from Rom. 1.11ff. [= Rom. 1.1ff.] fits together with 1.16f., i.e., the gospel of Christ with the revelation of the righteousness of God, can be seen in a formulation used by the apostle in 1 Corinthians... First Corinthians 1.30 allows the sending of Christ (in accordance with Rom. 1.3f.) and the revelation of the divine righteousness (in accordance with Rom. 1.16f.) to be brought together conceptually in the sense Paul intended...'

48   Cf. Fitzmyer, *Romans*, p. 256.

49   Not even in Romans is the thought of Christ as God's righteousness missing: Laato, *Romarbrevets hermeneutik*, pp. 50–52, 97 and 101. Cf. further Robert Badenas, *Christ the end of the law: Romans 10.4 in Pauline perspective* (JSNTSup, 10; Sheffield: JSOT Press, 1985), p. 110 and in addition Karl Kertelge, *'Rechtfertigung' bei Paulus: Studien zur Struktur und zum Bedeutungsgehalt des paulinischen Rechtfertigungsbegriffs* (NTAbh, 3; Münster: Aschendorff 1967), p. 98.

3.3. *Philippians 3.9*

Philippians does not use the concept of 'God's righteousness' either (cf. 1 Cor. above). The closest parallel is Phil. 3.9. There Paul expresses as his goal 'to be found in Christ', having a righteousness that comes from God and by faith, and which therefore is the exact opposite of his own acquired righteousness. Just a bit earlier (see vv. 4-6) he has listed what belongs to his own righteousness and what he has left behind.[50]

Both in language and in thought Phil. 3.9 and 1 Cor. 1.30 (cf. 2 Cor. 5.21) are parallels. The similarities are evident by the following points:

1) Paul's existence (as a Christian) is being in Christ;
2) In Christ Paul (the Christian) owns righteousness;
3) This righteousness comes from God;
4) It is owned by faith (1 Cor. 1.30 presupposes faith, although does not mention it);
5) A righteousness that is acquired through the law and which one can boast of 'in flesh' (Phil. 3.3-6 and 9), as well as the best and wisest achievements of both Jews and Greeks leading to boasting in 'flesh' (1 Cor. 1.18-29), are in stark contradiction with righteousness by faith, and
6) Paul wants to discount all false righteousness (Phil. 3.7-8, cf. also 1 Cor. 1.18-28) and to know only Jesus Christ and him crucified (1 Cor. 2.2, cf. also Phil. 3.7-10).[51]

These similarities show that Phil. 3.9 is in full harmony with the passages studied above. It especially emphasizes the position, in which granted righteousness that comes by faith puts one before God. God accepts nothing but the righteousness that Christ himself has acquired and that is found in Christ himself. Nothing else will do, because in all other cases salvation would have to be earned and that would leave room for false bragging.

3.4. *Summary*

Paul treats the subject 'God's righteousness' most extensively in Romans (see above, section 2.6.), but elsewhere less frequently. He has proved quite logical in his teaching. The same emphases emerge everywhere. In Corinthians the focus lies on Christ himself as God's righteousness. In a deeper sense it is not about an ideology or doctrine, but a living person; therefore the gospel requires not only knowledge, but also real faith.

---

50 On Paul's boasting in 'flesh' see Laato, *Paulus und das Judentum*, pp. 256–61.

51 Commentaries (and other research) often refer quite superficially to the parallelism of verses Phil. 3.9 and 1 Cor. 1.30, but the similarities are not examined.

4. *The Concept of 'God's Righteousness' and the Present State of Research*

Since it is always useful to weigh new research against the old, the definition of the concept of 'God's righteousness' that has been reached above will next be compared with contemporary theological currents.

4.1. *Research History: Mission Impossible*

Writing a research history of the innumerable interpretations of Paul's doctrine of justification, the differences and similarities of those interpretations or their relations, is not a matter of one paper, nor even a longer series of lectures. How much time would such a task require? It would not be done in a minute. On the contrary it seems like a 'mission impossible'. C.E.B. Cranfield writes in his commentary on Romans of the situation in research history:

> But the bulk of it [i.e. the discussion concerning the meaning of 'God's righteousness'] is so immense and the positions maintained by different scholars depend to such an extent on detailed arguments, that it is impossible to give, within reasonable limits, an account of the debate which is fair to those who have contributed to it.[52]

On the other hand Cranfield states that the work of E. Käsemann is a sort of milestone in research history. He has in many ways guided the present debate. He is either agreed with, or to an increasing extent taken distance from, and the so-called Lutheran(!) tradition that he represents is being severely criticized.[53] Therefore, it is worthwhile to assess what he could contribute today.

4.2. *Ernst Käsemann's Case*

E. Käsemann presented his own widely noticed and interest-provoking theory of Paul's doctrine of justification, especially in relation to the existential analysis of his teacher R. Bultmann.[54] It is not possible to fully

---

52 Cranfield, *Romans*, p. 92. In footnote 2 he states further as if being quite resigned: 'Even those who have devoted whole monographs [sic] to the subject of the righteousness of God in Paul's thought have been conscious of the difficulty to which we refer...' Nevertheless, cf. e.g., Ulrich Wilckens, *Der Brief an die Römer: Röm. 1–5*, vol. 1 (EKKNT, 6/1; Köln: Neukirchener, 1978), pp. 202–33 (Exkurs: 'Gerechtigkeit Gottes').

53 Cranfield, *Romans*, pp. 96–99. In addition, see e.g., Manfred T. Brauch: 'Perspectives on "God's righteousness" in recent German discussion', in E.P. Sanders, *Paul and Palestinian Judaism: A Comparision of Patterns of Religions* (London: Fortress Press, 1977), pp. 523–42 (524): 'Such a turning-point in the history of interpretation must be seen in the publication of E. Käsemann's essay "Gottesgerechtigkeit bei Paulus"... Käsemann's essay provided the impetus and the direction for a renewed discussion of the problems ...'

54 Ernst Käsemann, 'Gottesgerechtigkeit', pp. 367–78.

examine this controversy here, especially because it is well known and it is hardly necessary to repeat previous discussions.[55] Only some central points of view that concern the subject will be brought up next.

On closer observation, Käsemann's interpretation is not without flaws. After all he presents a difficult equation: he separates the ideas of justification and atonement from each other. The passages about the latter are always pre-Pauline early church tradition that the apostle indeed quotes, but that he does not specifically teach himself. It is rather that he has a tendency to discard Jewish cultic theology and broaden his soteriological teaching to comprise the whole world. So he in fact corrects and completes the traditional model. Instead of atonement as the basis of justification there is Christ's active and radical obedience towards the first commandment that he showed even unto the cross. There he fulfilled the law for all. Now they gain salvation as his gift, and this inspires them to follow and obey him according to his example.[56]

Justification – without atonement for sins! The claim in itself is very contradictory and hardly convincing. Besides research has clearly shown that atonement is an essential part of Pauline theology. He does not merely quote early church tradition for its own sake and then change the subject. It seems quite arbitrary to start dissecting someone else's ideas that do not match one's own mental construct.[57] It has also become clear above that atonement is closely connected with justification. The concept of 'God's righteousness' means salvation that Christ has acquired and earned when he gave his blood for the world (see especially Rom. 3.21-26 and 2 Cor. 5.18-21). He fulfilled the demands of God's own righteousness and in him faith receives a complete gift of righteousness.

However, when explaining the concept of 'God's righteousness', Käsemann ends up with a different result. According to him it is not only about a gift (*Gabe*), but also and primarily about power (*Macht*). They both belong together: in God's gift his power and authority are revealed. That is why justification and sanctification also always belong

---

55   See e.g., Brauch, 'Perspectives', pp. 526–29.

56   Cf. Käsemann, 'Gottesgerechtigkeit', p. 374. Later he dedicated one rather brief paper to Paul's atonement theology: 'Erwägungen zum Stichwort "Versöhnungslehre im Neuen Testament"', in E. Dinkler (ed.), *Zeit und Geschichte* (Festschrift R. Bultmann; Tübingen: Mohr Siebeck, 1964), pp. 47–59. On the critique of Käsemann's atonement theology, see especially David Way, *The Lordship of Christ: Ernst Käsemann's Interpretation of Paul's Theology* (Oxford Theological Monographs; Oxford: Clarendon Press, 1991), pp. 220–21 and Paul F.M. Zahl, *Die Rechtfertigungslehre Ernst Käsemanns* (Calwer Theologische Monographien; Stuttgart: Calwer Verlag, 1996), pp. 66–74, 199–201.

57   See first of all Peter Stuhlmacher, *Versöhnung, Gesetz und Gerechtigkeit: Aufsätze zur biblischen Theologie* (Göttingen: Vandenhoeck & Ruprecht, 1981). Cf. e.g., Piper, *Justification*, pp. 136–40. Way (*Lordship*, p. 221 n. 125) lists a group of scholars who have drawn away from Käsemann's one-sided view.

together. Being counted righteous and being made righteous are in the end synonymous. Christ's dominion is the true content of the gift of righteousness. They too are inseparable and their separation should not be attempted.[58]

Käsemann's interpretation of the concept of 'God's righteousness' follows in part directly from the fact that justification according to him has nothing to do with atonement, and that he sees justification as primarily a result of Christ's obedience (cf. above). What else could come out of such postulates or presuppositions than an emphasis on making man righteous – sanctification? At the same time legalism is rapidly approaching – if this is not indeed already pelagianism.[59]

Surely it is worth pointing out that the concept of 'God's righteousness' is not mere theory. It also emphasizes God's awesome dominion. It reveals his eternal authority. In it his vast power is at work. It is said of the gospel that it *is* 'the power of God' for in it (and only in it!) is righteousness from God revealed (Rom. 1.16-17). In this aspect Käsemann is right,[60] but he goes too far in denying Christ's absolute work of atonement and focusing on the change in man. The emphasis moves away from christological salvation history. It is known that Käsemann attempted to correct Bultmann's anthropological and individualistic interpretation of the doctrine of justification. With hindsight one might ask how well he actually succeeded in the attempt. He does indeed speak of justification from a perspective of power and authority. Further he speaks of Christ's cosmological dominion. And yet the thought evolves constantly around what happens (or should happen) in man, how he changes and how he then fulfils his vocation to follow Christ. It seems downright incredible that Käsemann's veiled and subtle criticism of Bultmann after all does not lead to any decisively new interpretation. Do both, under the influence of existential philosophy, remain prisoners of its postulates and prerequisites? Could it be a coincidence that their 'Vorverständnis' seems to be troubled by an anthropocentrism of the kind described above? It does after all guide their interpretations in the wrong direction. The concept of 'God's righteousness' loses its meaning without the atonement Christ has acquired and its content withers in a most fatal way.[61] The gospel as God's power (Rom. 1.16) is Christ (1 Cor.

58   Käsemann, 'Gottesgerechtigkeit', pp. 368–74. In his article he draws a parallel between making righteous and sanctification. To make righteous in itself can also be understood judicially, forensically. The root word is simply the Latin *iustificare* (*iustus* + *facio* = to make righteous).

59   Cf. Zahl, *Rechtfertigungslehre*, pp. 73–74.

60   See Dunn, *Romans*, p. 42. Cf. Cranfield, *Romans*, pp. 96–99.

61   T. Eskola, 'Vanhurskaaksi julistamisen ja vanhurskaaksi tekeminen uusi tulkinta yhteisen julistuksen raamattuargumentaatiossa: Näkökulmia saksalaisen eksegetiikan ohjaamaan teologiaan', in S. Kiviranta ja T. Laato (eds), *Turhentuuko uskonpuhdistus?*

1.24), and him crucified (1 Cor. 2.2). In him a new existence opens; in him the different aspects of salvation are connected, e.g., righteousness and holiness (1 Cor. 1.30, cf. above).[62] To put it in terms of existential philosophy, man finds his true self only outside himself. This is achieved in real (not symbolic or imagined) unity with Christ crucified, who took away the sins of the world. In the gospel as God's power, the foremost thing is what he has already done in his saving righteousness, not what he does through the gospel in man.

Käsemann's approach also causes the judicial nature of justification to fade. Although he does not deny it, it is clearly left aside. It seems that he brings it up occasionally for formal reasons, in accord with the usual and traditional way of speaking.[63] After all a judicial point of view cannot have much to contribute to an interpretation that denies the atonement Christ has achieved, and which focuses on the 'cosmologic' dimensions of Christ's dominion. Yet it has become clear above that judicial language and predisposition are crucially important in Romans. That is why we can here refer to earlier presentation and then move on.

It may still be noted that Käsemann – in my view with reason! – stresses 'in a Lutheran way' the crucial importance of the doctrine of justification in Romans. However his overall interpretation is in many ways non-Lutheran (although I leave this statement to be more closely substantiated by systematics). Thus, it seems unfair that the increasingly frequent criticism against Käsemann is automatically understood to be criticism against Lutheranism. Does the heartbeat of the reformation really sound in his theology?[64] Scholars who have criticized him most harshly often represent the 'new perspective'.[65] Therefore we will next examine their theories.

Rooman kirkon ja Luterilaisen Maailmanliiton uusi selitys vanhurskauttamisopista (Kauniainen: Perussanoma, 2nd edn, 1998), pp. 115–28 (123–24, 127–28) has creditably noted the anthropocentrism of Käsemann's interpretation.

62   1 Cor. 1.30 is not concerned so much with sanctification in the sense of 'new life', but rather with being set apart for God and his use, which is something that Christ, preached in the gospel, has mediated in Corinth.

63   Morris, *Romans*, p. 102.

64   Thus, among others, Zahl, *Rechtfertigungslehre*, pp. 197–98, in defence of Käsemann! Cf. Mark Seifrid, 'Paul's use of righteousness language against its Hellenistic background', in Carson, O'Brien, and Seifrid (eds), *Justification and Variegated Nomism*, vol. 2, p. 67: 'It is important to recognize that current discussion of righteousness and justification inescapably stands in the *Wirkungsgeschichte* of the Reformation, no matter what form that discussion might take. This history of effects, moreover, often becomes confused with the historical Reformers themselves, with the result that they come to be charged with the weaknesses of later generations.'

65   See e.g., Zahl, *Rechtfertigungslehre*, pp. 188–98.

4.3. *'The New Perspective on Paul'*

Supporters of 'the new perspective' do not form a very uniform school. There are differences of opinion and emphases which we cannot go into here. Yet they (nearly?) always stress that the doctrine of justification is not to be seen as the centre of the theology of Romans, or of Pauline theology in general. According to them, the most central points in his thinking are so-called participatory categories, passages that talk about the existence of the Christian in Christ (in the Spirit) or his participation in Christ (the Spirit). The real content and meaning of salvation is expressed in these most clearly. The doctrine of justification is (usually) seen as only one attempt to argue why Gentiles are admitted into the people of God, without following Jewish law.[66]

A sharp polarization of participatory and judicial terminology is at least in part artificial. Both ways to express the reality of salvation rather support and explain each other. Often they even appear side by side in the same verse. To illustrate this, I have presented participatory expressions in CAPITALS and judicial ones in *italic* below:[67]

> Of him you are IN CHRIST JESUS, who has become for us wisdom, *righteousness*, holiness and redemption from God. (1 Cor. 1.30)

> God made him who had no sin to be sin for us, so that IN HIM we might become the *righteousness* of God. (2 Cor. 5.21)

> If, while we seek to be *justified* IN CHRIST, it becomes evident that we ourselves are sinners, does that mean that Christ promotes sin? Absolutely not! (Gal. 2.17)

> ...and be found IN HIM, not having a *righteousness* of my own that comes from the law, but that which is through faith in Christ – the *righteousness* that comes from God and is by faith. (Phil. 3.9)

Compare further these similar passages:

> ... and are *justified* by his grace as a gift, through the redemption that is IN CHRIST JESUS, whom God put forward as a propitiation by his blood [IN HIS BLOOD], to be received by faith. This was to show God's *righteousness*... (Rom. 3.24-25)

> Therefore, there is now no *condemnation* for those who are IN CHRIST JESUS. (Rom. 8.1)

> But you were washed, you were sanctified, you were *justified* IN THE NAME OF THE LORD JESUS CHRIST AND BY THE SPIRIT OF OUR GOD. (1 Cor. 6.11)

---

66   Laato, 'Paul's Anthropological Considerations', pp. 343–53.
67   Cf. *ibid.*, pp. 348–49.

> So the law was put in charge (παιδαγωγός) to lead us to Christ that we
> might be *justified* by faith. ... You are all sons of God through faith IN
> CHRIST JESUS. (Gal. 3.24 and 26)

Based on these examples, Paul emphasizes the existence of Christians in
Christ, to be exact, not so much the presence of Christ in Christians![68]
That means he does not change the objective nature of justification into a
merely subjective experience. Justification always occurs outside the
believer. He is counted righteous in Christ. In addition there is always a
kind of 'instrumentalism' or 'sacramentalism' to justification. The
participation in Christ and in his righteousness is fulfilled in the
proclaimed and written gospel (*passim*), in baptism (Rom. 6.1ff; 1 Cor.
6.11 and Gal. 3.24-27) and in Holy Communion (1 Cor. 10.16-17 and
11.23-29). It does not build on internal experience – although it surely has
a connection to it.[69]

Considering what has been said above about participatory and judicial
terminology, it is no longer very useful to ponder which expresses the

---

68 Cf. an astonishingly similar interpretation that Luther presents in his commentary on
Jn 14.20: 'Das sie diese zwey stücke fassen (als die höchsten und nötigsten zu unserm trost),
wie wir inn Christo und Christus inn uns ist. Eins gehet uber sich, das ander unter sich. Denn
wir müssen zuvor inn im sein mit alle unserm wesen, sunde, tod, schwacheit und wissen, das
wir fur Gott davon gefreiet und erlöset und selig gesprochen werden durch diesen Christum.
Also müssen wir uber uns und ausser uns inn in schwingen, ja gar und ganz inn im verleibt
und sein eigen sein, als die auff in getauft und sein heilig Sacrament darauff empfahen. ...
Das ist (sage ich) das erste heubtstück, dadurch der mensch ausser und uber sich inn
Christum feret. Darnach gehets wider von oben herab also: Wie ich inn Christo bin, also ist
widerumb Christus inn mir. Ich hab mich sein angenomen und bin inn in gekrochen aus der
sund, tod und Teuffels gewalt getretten. So erzeigt er sich wider inn mir und spricht: Gehe
hin, predige, tröste, Teuffe, diene dem nehesten, sey gehorsam, gedültig. Ich wil inn dir sein
und alles thun. Was du thust, das wil ich gethan haben. Allein sey getrost, keck und
unverzagt auff mich und sihe, das du inn mir bleibest, so wil ich gewislich widerumb inn dir
sein. ... Darumb mus diese kunst gelernet sein, wer da wil bestehen und dem Teuffel obligen,
das wir genzlich schliessen, das wir inn Christo sind, das ist, das er unser lieber Herr und
Heiland ist, so fur uns gestorben, und wir durch seine gerechtigkeit und leben von sund und
tod erlöset sind. Darnach auch, das er inn uns sey und aus uns rede und wircke, was wir
schaffen und thun inn der Christenheit, das er solchs heisst sein thun und schaffen. Und unser
zungen, augen, ohren, hende, herz und alles sein sey.' See *D. Martin Luthers Werke: Kritische
Gesamtausgabe: Weimarer Ausgabe*, vol. 45 (Graz: Akademische Druck u. Verlagsanstalt,
1964 = Weimar: Hermann Böhlaus Nachfolger, 1911), pp. 591–92. On the central role of
Christ in Luther's doctrine of justification see my article 'Yksimielisyyden Ohjeen oppi
vanhurskauttamisesta: Luther-tutkimuksemme kompastuskivi', in S. Kiviranta ja T. Laato
(eds), *Turhentuuko uskonpuhdistus? Rooman kirkon ja Luterilaisen Maailmanliiton uusi selitys
vanhurskauttamisopista* (Kauniainen: Perussanoma, 2nd edn, 1998), pp. 181–94.

69 Paul naturally applies participatory and judicial categories also to the area of ethics.
They are then not to be confused with his teaching of justification (cf. e.g., Rom. 1–4 and 6).
This is where James D.G. Dunn makes a cardinal error! Cf. 'The New Perspective: whence,
what and whither?', *The New Perspective on Paul: Collected Essays* (WUNT, 185; Tübingen:
Mohr Siebeck, 2005), pp. 1–88 (80–86).

centre of Paul's theology better or more authentically. Understood rightly they both mean exactly the same thing in his thinking. They are as two sides of one medallion. One does not exist without the other.[70]

4.4. 'The Old Testament Perspective on Paul'

In recent years Old Testament research has brought new light into the discussion on the doctrine of justification. Naturally all cannot be presented here. Especially worth mentioning is M. Seifrid's important contribution 'Righteousness language in the Hebrew scriptures and early Judaism'.[71] In it he draws, among others, the following remarkable conclusions:

1) Being declared righteous is a judicial proceeding, in which God not only gives (orally) an acquitting verdict, but also acts to carry righteousness into effect.

2) Declaring one part righteous means necessarily condemning the other (for instance destroying God's adversaries). Therefore the word 'righteousness' does not simply translate into 'salvation'.

3) The concept of 'righteousness' is not only a *Verhältnissbegriff*, describing the relationship between two parties (in a way they themselves define and decide). Central parts of it are also the norms and sanctions that are valid in all cases regardless of possible particular agreements.[72]

---

70   In a different way Kari Kuula: *The Law, the Covenant and God's Plan: Paul's Polemical Treatment of the Law in Galatians*, vol. 1 (PFES, 72; Helsinki: Finnish Exegetical Society, 1999), pp. 37–41. Correctly Dunn, 'The New Perspective', pp. 83–84 n. 354: 'It is important at this point to avoid the polarisation of "justification" and "participation" encouraged by the well known assertion of A. Schweitzer.... ' Yet in the same context he does not recognise the need to distinguish between soteriological and ethical aspects. According to him, justification and sanctification blend together and thus salvation is reduced to '*a process of transformation* of the believer' (see. p. 84). Cf. above and Peter Stuhlmacher, *Biblische Theologie und Evangelium: Gesammelte Aufsätze* (WUNT, 146; Tübingen: Mohr Siebeck, 2002), p. 54: 'Führende Vertreter der New Perspective propagieren aufs neue die uralte Zweiteilung der paulinischen Soteriologie in einen juridischen und einen partizipatorischen Teil.... Diese Aufteilung wird überflüssig, wenn man den von Paulus selbst klar herausgestellten Zusammenhang von Rechtfertigung, Sühne und Versöhnung beachtet und bedenkt, dass der Christus Jesus für den Judenchristen Paulus immer auch eine korporative Repräsentationsfigur ist.... '

71   Mark Seifrid, 'Righteousness language in the Hebrew scriptures and early Judaism', in Carson, O'Brien and Seifrid (eds), *Justification and Variegated Nomism*, vol. 2, pp. 415–42. See further Seifrid, 'Paul's use', pp. 40–44.

72   Seifrid, 'Righteousness language', pp. 415–30 and 'Paul's use', pp. 40–44.

Seifrid further emphasizes that justification is to be understood precisely from the point of view of creation and not so much that of covenant. The concept of 'righteousness' means God's sovereign action as Creator ('ruling and judging') to reinforce and carry into effect the order of creation in all fallen creation; his righteous wielding of power should not – as is usually done – be narrowed into mere covenantal loyalty. On the contrary, covenantal loyalty should be referred to as righteousness, as one (important) part of it.[73]

In many aspects Seifrid has furthered the discussion with his profound or even pioneering research. It is not often that one gets to read as thorough a concept analysis as his article proves to be. Nevertheless I dare propose two minor adjustments that actually spring from what he has written himself.

The concept of 'righteousness', as God's sovereign action to restore the order of creation in all of creation, could also be expressed in other words, perhaps from a slightly different angle: it is in the end and in the most profound sense a matter of the Creator's own being, his own righteousness, which appears in his acts and works. The broad body of Old Testament passages that Seifrid has collected speaks, to my understanding, fully for this conclusion.[74] He also states later, in another context, that Greek philosophy defined the ethically 'right' abstractly out of the idea of good, whereas the Old Testament ties it to God himself, who reveals to Israel his holy will and the commandments that are in accord with his will.[75] Research history seems to show that, in the interpretation of Pauline theology, the emphasis on a connection between righteousness and creation comes especially from E. Käsemann, who emphasized broader cosmologic aspects in opposition to the anthropological individualism of R. Bultmann.[76] His student P. Stuhlmacher largely followed the same track.[77] Thence Seifrid worked on his important publications in Tübingen and dedicated one of his articles to Stuhlmacher. Without presenting any real criticism, I would like to move the focus slightly and speak of the Creator himself instead of creation. He is righteous and all righteousness is therefore in accord with his own being. God's righteousness is therefore also his own righteousness (cf. above section 2.3.).[78]

Another point that, as I understand, lacks clarity and specificity is the

---

73   Seifrid, 'Righteousness language', pp. 423–28 and 'Paul's use', pp. 41–42.

74   Seifrid, 'Righteousness language', pp. 418–30.

75   Seifrid, 'Paul's use', pp. 43–44.

76   See above section 4.2.

77   Peter Stuhlmacher, *Gerechtigkeit Gottes bei Paulus* (FRLANT, 87; Göttingen: Vandenhoeck & Ruprecht, 2nd edn, 1966).

78   Brauch, 'Perspectives', p. 542: 'The overwhelming emphasis on God's creative action in the interpretation of Paul, which Stuhlmacher shares with Käsemann, must be seen as an over-emphasis. Where the expression *dikaiosynē theou* appears in Paul, the concept of his

relation between righteousness and salvation. At least in Psalms, and especially the latter part of Isaiah, both concepts very often merge.[79] That is why their contents are frequently put in parallel in research. Seifrid is right in warning about the danger of one-sidedness: in the Old Testament the prospect of judgement remains as a kind of flip-side to saving righteousness (see above point 2).[80] He warns of a similar danger with Paul's soteriology, which in its central parts follows the terminology of Psalms and the latter part of Isaiah.[81] Even here there is no need to present any real criticism against Seifrid. Yet one feels the urge to propose – actually based on his own presentation! – the death (and resurrection) of Jesus as a solution to the problem. On the cross God's righteous judgement is fulfilled in a way that brings salvation to all mankind. There his holy wrath and burning love are fulfilled *simultaneously*.[82] Thus the danger of one-sidedness is avoided and the true meaning of the gospel is grasped. This is why God's righteousness means both his saving action to restore righteousness and the righteousness he grants through faith (cf. above sections 2.4. and 2.5.).

The apostle Paul's thinking, that springs from his Jewish background, helps (at least to some extent) to shed light on why the concepts 'righteousness' and 'covenant' hardly ever appear in the same context in the Old Testament.[83] According to Rom. 3.25-26, God has not shown his righteousness until now in the new covenant, when he has atoned for the sins that he previously left unpunished 'in his forbearance' during old covenant times.[84] The old covenant was not based upon the righteousness of Israel (see Deut. 9.4-6), and logically not even upon God's righteousness (the fulfilment of which would rather have demanded punishment and destruction of the rebellious people), but upon his promises, that in the deepest sense referred to the coming of the Messiah and the atonement he would perform. In this sense God's righteousness is 'covenantal loyalty' (a concept Seifrid is not comfortable with):[85] that which in the old covenant was only realized through 'divine forbearance', is now revealed in the new covenant without any reserve, on account of Christ's death on the cross. In a broad sense God's righteousness springs from his own

---

action as Creator is always in the background, but nowhere at the centre. It seems that Paul is primarily concerned with the *medium* (the Christ-event) and the *result* (the redemption of man) of that creative action of God, rather than with that action itself.'

79   See above section 2.2.
80   Seifrid, 'Righteousness language', pp. 415–18 and 'Paul's use', pp. 42–43.
81   Seifrid, 'Paul's use', pp. 58–59.
82   Cf. *ibid.*, pp. 58–59, 63.
83   See Seifrid, 'Righteousness language', pp. 423–25.
84   See above sections 2.3. and 2.4.
85   Seifrid, 'Righteousness language', pp. 423–28 and 'Paul's use', pp. 41–42.

nature and comprises his faithfulness in the order of creation as well as the covenant he has made and all his other promises.

4.5. *Summary*

Paul's doctrine of justification and the language he uses both originate in the Old Testament. In addition, he expresses the same point in different concepts (e.g. participatory categories), that spring from the religious experience – typical for him. Neither the German school that Käsemann represents nor representatives of the so-called new perspective have done full justice to the apostle's arguments. Neither have they sufficiently considered the Old Testament roots of his thinking.

5. *The Concept of 'God's Righteousness' and the Centre of Pauline Theology*

What at least still remains unanswered is the traditional question: what status does the doctrine of justification have in Paul's theology as a whole? Is it to him only one – yet important! – doctrine among many others? Classical Lutheranism considers it the centre, around which all other doctrines are grouped and to which they must be related. This is not the case in all of Christendom. Within the field of scientific exegetics, similar thoughts were earlier presented by W. Wrede. In his opinion the doctrine of justification is only a sub-plot (*Nebenkrater*) in the body of Pauline theology. As is known, A. Schweitzer argued similarly. Today supporters of the so-called new perspective often adopt his basic theory, although in many details they differ from his interpretations.[86]

To define the status of the doctrine of justification in Paul's theology, at least the following points must be considered:

1) The teaching of God's righteousness is a theme that covers all of Romans (see 1.16-17). In addition the concept of 'God's righteousness' arises in central verses (the ultimate purpose of Christ's atonement, 3.25-26; the deepest reason for Israel's disbelief, 10.3).

2) As a concept 'God's righteousness' also refers to God's own being, to himself. That means it is a *theocentric* expression and precisely therefore central.

3) Especially in Corinthians the concept of 'God's righteousness' refers to Christ as the Saviour of the whole world (see 1 Cor. 1.30, 2 Cor. 5.21). This means it is a *christocentric* expression and that is exactly what makes it central.

---

86 To read more closely about the research history, see e.g. Stephen Westerholm, *Perspectives Old and New on Paul: The 'Lutheran' Paul and His Critics* (Grand Rapids: Eerdmans, 2004). On the contributions of Wrede and Schweitzer, see especially pp. 101–16.

4) The true content of the gospel is 'God's righteousness'. That is what Paul, apostle to the Gentiles, is called to proclaim everywhere (Rom. 1.16-17). Therefore his entire life's work is defined by this concept.

5) Proclaiming the gospel is an apocalyptic event (cf. the verb ἀποκαλύπτεται, Rom 1.17), the ultimate revelation of the final times. Although it is proclaimed by man, God is revealed in it and expresses his saving will in it. Another revelation or a revelation of a different kind is not to be expected.[87]

6) The concept of 'God's righteousness' can by its content be expressed in different words without altering it (cf. above e.g., participatory categories). A mere statistical analysis fails to tell the whole story.[88]

7) Gathering an offering to benefit the congregation in Jerusalem is in Romans mentioned as an important undertaking (15.25-27). It had been agreed on in the apostles' meeting previously (Gal. 2.10). In Judaism, the offering made by Gentiles that had converted from idolatry and various vices for the benefit of the poor (of Israel!) was understood as proof of their righteousness. They had taken their faith and religion really seriously.[89] This explains Paul's zeal in the matter. He wants to prove that Gentile Christians have reached righteousness in faith and are therefore making an offering for the Jewish Christians. Accepting the offering in Jerusalem and Judea means that all of Christendom is unanimous about the basis of justification: it is by grace through faith in Jesus Christ. Yet, because Paul cannot be certain that the Jewish Christians will accept the 'earmarked' funds, he requests an intercession on behalf of the undertaking, all the way from the Christians in Rome (15.30-32). Success would mean final triumph for the gospel he is

---

87 As is known, Käsemann has extensively discussed the 'apocalyptic nature' of Paul's theology (see e.g., 'Gottesgerechtigkeit', pp. 375–78). Yet he does not sufficiently (if indeed at all) notice what Günter Bornkamm already wrote in his volume *Paulus* (Stuttgart: Kohlhammer, 6th edn, 1987), p. 126: 'Das Evangelium selbst *ist* "Gottes Kraft zur Rettung für jeden, der glaubt" (Röm 1, 16). Das passt in kein apokalyptisches Konzept mehr hinein. Was jüdische und urchristliche Apokalyptik in ferner oder naher Zukunft erwarten, ist Gegenwart im Evangelium!'

88 It is therefore false to claim that justification is an isolated 'island' in Paul's letters, and that no practical conclusions follow from it. Against Sanders, *Paul and Palestinian Judaism*, pp. 453–72, 502–8, see Rom. 6, where participatory and judicial categories unite and together argue for the duty of a Christian to live according to his faith. Cf. above, section 4.3.

89 See especially Klaus Berger, 'Almosen für Israel: Zum historischen Kontext der paulinischen Kollekte', *NTS* 23 (1977), pp. 180–204. He writes for instance: 'Vielmehr ist in späterer Zeit das Almosen an die Armen Ausweis der Gerechtigkeit ganz allgemein und Ausdruck der Ernsthaftigkeit, mit der die Bekehrung aufgefasst wurde' (p. 190), and: 'Weggabe der Habe an Arme ist zugleich Kriterium für den Willen zur Zugehörigkeit. Theologische Aspekte und konkretes Gruppenverhalten greifen ineinander' (p. 192).

proclaiming 'from Jerusalem all the way around to Illyricum' (15.19). Then the proclamation of 'God's righteousness' would be the 'way of salvation' for all the church of Christ everywhere (in systematic theology the expression *articulus cadentis et stantis ecclesiae*).[90]

According to this list, the doctrine of justification is without doubt the centre of Paul's theology. His main epistle, the entire letter to Romans, his teaching of God, Christ and salvation, his own calling to become apostle to the Gentiles, his understanding of the end times, his many practical applications and exhortations, are all connected to the concept of 'God's righteousness'. Paul's theology is in fact intertwined with his doctrine of justification. This is obviously the key to his thinking.

6. *The Concept of 'God's Righteousness' and the Proclamation of the Church: A Homiletic Application*

Exegetics should benefit the church – that is, if it is truly desired that the church should take the latest results of exegetic research into account. Exegetes or theologians in general stay employed as long as the message of the church finds its audience in the people. It is hard to imagine a theological faculty without any close relationship with the Christian faith. A historic view shows that the whole Western university system has its roots in the triumph of the gospel in Europe. In this sense exegetics is and remains a maid of the church (*ancilla theologiae*). It needs to grasp and internalize its own role in God's dispensation of mercy![91] Therefore a brief homiletic application of the results reached in this article will be presented below. If and when the concept of 'God's righteousness' is the essence of the gospel, and the absolutely most important mission of the church is to proclaim the gospel always and everywhere, then how should we preach of God's righteousness and preach God's righteousness 'for the salvation of souls'?

One contemporary trend in preaching is to encourage the listeners to 'accept God'. They are encouraged to 'accept that they are already accepted'. This kind of preaching is commonly heard in folk churches, but it is also to be found in evangelistic movements, where new members or

90   Strangely Berger gives almost no thought to how the offering, taken up by Paul, and the gospel of God's righteousness, preached by him, relate to one another, although this is the aspect that in my opinion explains his theological intentions about the whole undertaking! It was not only an ecclesiastical pursuit to preserve the unity of the church ('Almosen', pp. 195–204), but also a soteriological struggle about the sufficiency of grace as the only means of salvation.

91   See e.g., Päiviö Latvus, *Ymmärryksen siivet: Miksi tiede on länsimaista?* (Vaasa: Omega, 2nd edn, 2002).

believers are sought through enthusiastic missionary work. Yet the crucial question is rarely brought up: does God want to, or is he even able to, accept a sinner into his fellowship? Often the presumption is made that of course he wants to and of course he can. Then God's own righteousness is discarded; his righteous and holy requirements are demeaned or at least trivialized. The question is left unanswered – on what grounds can he, the righteous Judge, justify the godless? What is proclaimed is not the gospel, which reveals 'God's *own* righteousness'.[92]

Another feature of contemporary religiosity is that fulfilment of 'our different (human) needs' dominates, and is mainly sought after in religion. Often these needs are also understood in a 'psychologized' fashion. There is talk of loneliness, alienation, frustration, fears, anxiety, indisposition, etc. Then the Christian message is accommodated to such needs. The church becomes more and more of a 'psycho-church', as the recent development has been aptly described.[93] Of course a spiritual community is concerned with psychology, human relationships and their twists and turns, but surely that is not the whole picture. When will preachers find the courage to say that sometimes loneliness and alienation can have their roots in egoism, bitterness or hatred? Or that frustration and fear might result from neglect of prayer or downright disbelief? Or that anxiety may spring from some unconfessed evil or fall? Such preaching would no longer be mere psychologizing, but preaching about the spiritual pitfalls. Heaping false guilt on the listeners must absolutely be avoided, but guilt should hardly be avoided altogether. After all, the fault is most often ours! No silencing or ignoring it will do. Only the gospel can help. It grants full forgiveness, acquired by Christ with his innocent blood on Calvary. So this is where 'God's *saving* righteousness', acquired by God in Christ, is revealed.[94]

The same line of thought can be continued further. Many Christian 'virtues' are also often psychologized today. Joy, for example, is turned into being content with oneself and one's life. Peace becomes inner peacefulness of the soul. Love means enjoying good company in the congregation and so on. Surely these definitions are at least half-true and

---

92   Justification is not only about the stronger one showing his right, a mere manifestation of force (according to the principle 'might is right'). The crucial thing is the fulfilment of God's own rightfulness: Does he do the right thing in proclaiming the sinner righteous? On what grounds is it the right thing? Cf. Donald A. Carson, *The Sermon on the Mount: An Evangelical Exposition of Matthew 5–7* (Carlisle: Paternoster Press, 4th edn, 1998), p. 128. John Stott, among others, makes an account of the conversation carried out in the matter throughout church history. See his book *The Cross of Christ* (Leicester: Inter-Varsity Press, 2003), pp. 111–32.

93   See Janne Kivivuori, *Psykokirkko: Psykokulttuuri, uskonto ja moderni yhteiskunta* (Tampere: Gaudeamus, 1999).

94   Cf. Carson, *Sermon*, p. 128.

that is why they may be worth adopting. Yet many biblical (and especially Pauline) themes are put aside, such as rejoicing in the Lord, peace with God and love for God and even for enemies. And where and when does anybody ever preach of such Christian virtues as honesty, truthfulness, humility, purity and holiness? Preaching of these urges the listeners to examine their position especially before God and in relation to him, and not only to occupy themselves with studying their own emotions. Very often such self-examination leads even deeper into contrition. The gospel of Christ's atonement is needed to clarify God's grace, because in it – as already stated above – is revealed 'God's *saving* righteousness', acquired by God in Christ.[95]

The proclamation of the folk church has culminated today in its most extreme form in the statement 'everyone gets to heaven'.[96] The one-sidedness of the pointed statement is hardly worth examining here. It will be enough to state that at least for those who, according to their own testimony, do not even desire to go to heaven, getting there would mean being thrown in – and then heaven would not be heaven any more. Seen in the light of the doctrine of justification, this kind of proclamation does not contain even the slightest light of truth. It is not a proclamation of the gospel, where 'God's righteousness', *granted* through faith and by faith, is revealed.

Therefore preaching of 'God's righteousness' is not an easy task. All the nuances and connotations of the concept (see sections 2.3.–2.5. above) should be clearly drawn. No aspect should be omitted and none should be altered or downright distorted. Luther said that preaching of justification is the hardest and most demanding task ever. This is, in his opinion, where the true doctors of theology stand out.[97]

7. Conclusion

My mission in this research was to examine what the concept of 'God's righteousness' means in Paul's theology. In summary it can be stated that

95 Cf. *ibid.* See also Carl Fr Wisløff, *Ordet fra Guds munn: Aktuelle tanker om forkynnelsen* (Oslo: Lunde Forlag, 5th edn, 1988). He repeatedly exhorts preachers to proclaim especially the 'first tablet' of the commandments, so that not only will the listeners hear moral principles and psychological constructions of ideas, but they can face the living God, who demands that they respect himself as well as love their neighbour. See pp. 101–2, 112–13, 125–26, 160–61.

96 Antti Kylliäinen, *Kaikki pääsevät taivaaseen: Välttämättömiä tarkistuksia kristillisiin opinkohtiin* (Helsinki: Nemo, 2nd edn, 1997).

97 See especially Luther's commentary on Galatians: M. Luther, *Pyhän Paavalin Galatalaiskirjeen selitys* (trans. A.E. Koskenniemi; Helsinki: SLEY-Kirjat, 1957), pp. 17–26, 74–75, 97–98, 134–36, 147–50, 189–91, 363–65, 380, 397–98, 404–8, 435–37, 521–24, 556–57, 562–64.

it forms in his epistles a kind of spectrum, through which different nuances of the same concept are reflected. H. Hübner has used the illustrative expression 'Bedeutungsspektrum' in various contexts.[98] It fits the concept of 'God's righteousness' as well, because that has at least the following three meanings:

1) God's own righteousness;
2) God's saving action for establishing righteousness; and
3) righteousness granted by God.

These connotations appear side by side and are intertwined. It would not be meaningful – not to mention right – to stress only one side at the expense of another, one aspect instead of the whole. We should rather 'see the wood for the trees and the trees for the wood'. Then a broad enough understanding will be reached of what is to be seen and read in the texts and from the texts. In short: 'God's righteousness' is the righteous act of a righteous God to justify the sinner in a righteous way. It is in other words righteousness of faith in Christ and by Christ's atonement.

Righteousness was (and is) a central topic in Judaism. When Paul talked about it or taught it, his thought did not slide into some especially Christian perspective. He remained a pupil of the Old Testament scriptures even after his conversion, but now he believed in their fulfilment, Jesus Christ, and salvation that is granted in him. That is why he also stressed that justification is a gift. As an apostle to the Gentiles he preached as a Jew, to Jews, of the Jewish religion – although with poor results. Yet, as such, his preaching issues a challenge even to present-day Judaism.

Challenges remain also for the Lutheran church and Lutheranism. In the fourth Assembly of the Lutheran World Federation in Helsinki in 1963, no consensus was reached on how to express the doctrine of justification in ways that were relevant for 'people of today'.[99] Regrettably the matter has never really been brought up again, although ecumenical negotiations over the doctrine of justification have many times been undertaken both on national and international levels. So far it seems that the meaning of Paul's (or Luther's) doctrine of justification is not clear in the Lutheran community.[100] That is why this attempt has been made above to explicate his teachings as well as those of the great reformer.

98   Thus in his lectures in the theological faculty of Göttingen in 1989–1991, and in several of his books.
99   *Vanhurskauttaminen ja uusi elämä: Asiakirja n:o 3: LML:n neljäs yleiskokous 30.7.– 11.8.1963, Helsinki–Suomi* (Pieksämäki: Sisälähetysseuran Raamattutalo, 1963), p. 3. On this problem see more closely e.g., C.E. Braaten, *Justification: The Article by Which the Church Stands or Falls* (Minneapolis: Fortress Press, 1990), pp. 12–15.
100   Cf. Laato, 'Paavali ekumeenisena erotuomarina', pp. 101–2.

Chapter 4

GRECO-ROMAN PHILOSOPHY AND PAUL'S TEACHING ON LAW

Niko Huttunen

Scholars have traditionally interpreted Paul's teaching on law from the ancient Jewish point of view, since 'law' (νόμος) and expressions like 'commandment' (ἐντολή) often refer to the Torah in Paul.[1] This viewpoint was substantially deepened by E.P. Sanders with his insightful book *Paul and Palestinian Judaism: A Comparison of Patterns of Religion*.[2] Sanders provided the impetus for the discussion on the so-called covenantal nomism and 'new perspective' on Paul, in turn giving rise to an immense number of works which are inspired by Sanders. Besides Paul and the law, many works include surveys of Jewish writings.[3]

Paul's Jewishness is evident, but this is no reason to limit the discussion on Paul's Jewish heritage. In the following, I will show that Paul was a *Hellenistic* Jew whose teaching on law had Greco-Roman philosophical components. I will demonstrate this aspect of his teaching by a comparison between Paul and Epictetus, a Gentile Stoic philosopher. Epictetus was one of the most prominent Stoics, and his philosophy illustrates the intellectual milieu of the first and second centuries CE.[4]

1 See Räisänen, H., *Paul and the Law* (WUNT, 29; Tübingen: J.C.B. Mohr [Paul Siebeck], 2nd edn, 1987), pp. 16–18.

2 London: SCM Press, 1977.

3 E.g. A.A. Das, *Paul, the Law, and the Covenant* (Peabody: Hendricksons, 2001) and the compiled works edited by F. Avemarie and H. Lichtenberger, *Bund und Tora. Zur theologischen Begriffsgeschichte in alttestamentlicher, frühjüdischer und urchristlicher Tradition* (WUNT 92; Tübingen: J.C.B. Mohr [Paul Siebeck], 1996) and by D.A. Carson, P.T. O'Brien, and M.A. Seifrid, *Justification and Variegated Nomism* (WUNT, 2/140 and 2/181; 2 vols.; Tübingen: Mohr Siebeck, 2001 and 2004). A comprehensive overview on the exegetical industry in this field is done by Stephen Westerholm in his book *Perspectives Old and New: The 'Lutheran' Paul and His Critics* (Grand Rapids: Eerdmans, 2004).

4 For Epictetus' life and philosophy, see e.g. W.A. Oldfather, 'Introduction', in Epictetus, *The Discourses as Reported by Arrian, the Manual and Fragments* (trans. W.A. Oldfather; LCL; 2 vols; repr., London: William Heinemann, 1985 and 1995), pp. vii–xii and A.A. Long, *Epictetus: A Stoic and Socratic Guide to Life* (Oxford: Clarendon Press, 2002), pp. 10–11. For the intellectual milieu, see J.A. Francis, *Subversive Virtue: Asceticism and Authority in the Second-Century Pagan World* (University Park, Pennsylvania: Pennsylvania

It is no wonder that Paul's teaching on law contains philosophical components, since Judaism had been under Greco-Roman influence for centuries. There are Stoic strains, for instance, in Sirach, in Wisdom of Solomon, in the 4 Maccabees, and in Philo.[5] However, I do not compare Paul with Hellenistic Jewish writings for methodological reasons. It is difficult to assess if the similarities between Paul and a Hellenistic Jewish writing are due to Jewishness or to the philosophical components. Similarities with Epictetus cannot be traced back to inner-Jewish discussions. Epictetus' philosophy is independent of Judaism and Christianity despite his incidental notes on Jews and Christians.[6]

Next, I will compare certain passages of Paul's epistles with Epictetan passages and, thus, show the similarities between Paul's and Epictetus' teaching on law. These analyses suggest further comparisons between Paul and ancient philosophers in order to get a clearer grasp of the philosophical components in Paul's teaching of law.[7]

God's Commands and Stoic Theology of Social Positions

Paul states in 1 Cor. 7.19: 'Circumcision is nothing, and uncircumcision is nothing; but obeying the commandments of God (τήρησις ἐντολῶν θεοῦ) is everything', whereby 'obeying the commandments of God' sounds like a Jewish principle to obey the Torah (Sir. 32.23; Wis. 6.18).[8] Paul, however, regards circumcision – the focal commandment in the Torah – as indifferent! There were tendencies to find 'spiritual' content of the Mosaic commandments in diaspora Judaism, and some extremists even rejected the literal meaning of the commandments in favour of an allegorical

---

State University Press, 1995), p. 1; R. MacMullen, *Enemies of the Roman Order: Treason, Unrest, and Alienation in the Empire* (Cambridge, Massachusetts: Harvard University Press, 1975), pp. 47–48. The following translations of Epictetus are by Oldfather (bibliographical references above in this footnote) if not otherwise indicated.

5 For Sirach, see e.g. U. Wicke–Reuter, *Göttliche Providenz und menschliche Verantwortung bei Ben Sira und in der Frühen Stoa* (BZAW, 298; Berlin: Walter de Gruyter, 2000). For Wisdom of Solomon, see e.g. J.M. Reese, *Hellenistic Influence on the Book of Wisdom and Its Consequences* (AnBib, 41; Rome: Biblical Institute Press, 1970), p. 4. For the 4 Maccabees, see e.g. S. Sandmel, *Judaism and Christian Beginnings* (New York: Oxford University Press, 1978), pp. 277–79. For Philo, see e.g. M. Pohlenz, *Die Stoa: Geschichte einer geistigen Bewegung*, vol. 1 (Göttingen: Vandenhoeck & Ruprecht, 1948), pp. 369–78.

6 Long, *Epictetus*, p. 35. Few scholars have held a different view. They are listed by M. Spanneut, 'Epiktet', in T. Klauser *et al.* (eds), *RAC* V (Stuttgart: Anton Hiersemann, 1962), pp. 599–681 (630).

7 This article is based on my manuscript of a monograph on law in Paul and Epictetus.

8 E.g. F. Lang, *Die Briefe an die Korinther* (NTD, 7; Göttingen: Vandenhoeck & Ruprecht, 1986), p. 96; Räisänen, *Law*, p. 68.

reinterpretation (Philo, *Migr. Abr.* 89–93).[9] Paul, however, presents no allegory. Circumcision is not reinterpreted but ignored: circumcision is *nothing*. Can 'the commandments', thus, still refer to the Torah?

Some scholars see 'the commandments' as a reference to the commandment to love one's neighbour (Lev. 19.18).[10] For Paul, this commandment is a crystallization of the whole Torah (Rom. 13.9; Gal. 5.14). Yet, it is difficult to understand the plural ('commandments') as a reference to *one* commandment, especially in a context where there is no mention of love.[11] If there is any link between the Torah and 'the commandments', it is a superficial association. The basic meaning of 'the commandments' should be understood in its close context, which does not mention the Torah at all.

The core in 1 Cor. 7.17-24 is God's call. God calls each one to become Christian within one's own social position: 'Let each of you remain in the condition (ἐν τῇ κλήσει) in which you were called' (v. 20). The call has a double meaning: the call to become Christian, and at the same time, to remain in the same social position.[12] No matter, if one is circumcized or not, slave or free, they should equally 'lead the life that the Lord has assigned (ἐμέρισεν)' to them (v. 17). In this context, the commandments of God seem to mean the requirements of one's social position. It is God's command to 'lead the life that God has assigned'. The plural 'commandments' here refers to the different requirements of different positions.

There is a clear analogy with Epictetus' thoughts. He understood social positions as God-given and admonished others to fill one's position in obeying God's commandments.[13] For example, in *Diatr.* 3.24.95–98, Epictetus suggests that a good and excellent man fills his place (ἡ χώρα) obeying God until it is time to depart. Then, he answers the question on how one should depart from this life:

> (98) Again, as Thou didst wish it, as a free man, as Thy servant (ὑπηρέτης), as one who has perceived Thy commands and Thy

    9 Räisänen, *Law*, p. 34–41.
    10 Lang, *Korinther*, p. 96 and C. Wolff, *Der erste Brief des Paulus an die Korinther* (THKNT, 7; Leipzig: Evangelische Verlagsanstalt, 1996), p. 149.
    11 Cf. A. Lindemann, *Der erste Korintherbrief* (HNT, 9,1; Tübingen: J.C.B. Mohr [Paul Siebeck], 2000), p. 171.
    12 K.A. Plank, *Paul and the Irony of Affliction* (SemeiaSt; Atlanta: Scholars Press, 1987), p. 26 and W. Schrage, *Der Erste Brief an die Korinther* (EKKNT, 7/2; Solothurn: Benziger Verlag, 1995), p. 137. Pace Wolff (*Korinther*, p. 149), who takes the social position as being irrelevant for a call.
    13 J.C. Gretenkord, *Der Freiheitsbegriff Epiktets* (Bochum: Studienverlag Brockmeyer, 1981), p. 302. Pace A. Bonhöffer, *Epiktet und das Neue Testament* (Religionsgeschichtliche Versuche und Vorarbeiten, 10; Gießen: Verlag von Alfred Töpelmann [vormals J. Ricker], 1911), pp. 171–72 and F.G. Downing, *Cynics, Paul and the Pauline Churches* (Cynics and Christian Origins, 2; London: Routledge, 1998), p. 112.

prohibitions (ὡς ᾐσθημένος σου τῶν προσταγμάτων καὶ ἀπαγορευμάτων). (99) But so long as I continue to live in Thy service, what manner of man wouldst Thou have me be? An official or a private citizen, a senator or one of the common people, a soldier or a general, a teacher or a head of a household? Whatsoever station and post (χώραν καὶ τάξιν) Thou assign me, I will die ten thousand times, as Socrates says, or ever I abandon it.[14] (100) And where wouldst Thou have me be? In Rome, or in Athens, or in Thebes, or in Gyara? Only remember me there. (*Diatr.* 3.24.98–100.)

'Thy commands and Thy prohibitions' regulate the departure in death, but they are also associated with the right lifestyle. A just person lives in accordance with God's will, obeying his commands and prohibitions – in a word, obeying the law of God. 'Commands and prohibitions' is a Stoic definition of law.[15] A just person does not leave the God-given social position, but fulfils it voluntarily like a free servant (ὁ ὑπηρέτης), not like a compelled slave (ὁ δοῦλος).[16] Epictetus emphasizes the voluntary obedience many times, for instance in *Diatr.* 4.3.9-10, where social position ('office') is also referred to: 'I am a free man and a friend of God, so as to obey Him of my own free will (ἑκὼν πείθωμαι). No other thing ought I to claim, not body, or property, or office, or reputation – nothing in short.' Epictetus adds: 'I cannot transgress any of His commands (τῶν ἐντολῶν)' (v. 10).

In *Diatr.* 3.24, Epictetus illustrates the absolute demand to accept outer circumstances with reference to Gyara, the barren island and a place of exile.[17] The obedient fulfilling of the duties is important anywhere and in any social position:

(113) Now He brings me here, and again He sends me there; to mankind exhibits me in poverty, without office, in sickness; sends me away to Gyara, brings me into prison. Not because He hates me – perish the thought! And who hates the best of his servants? Nor because He neglects me, for He does not neglect any of even the least of His creatures; but because He is training me, and making use of me as a witness to the rest of men. (114) When I have been appointed to such a service, am I any longer to take thought as to where I am, or with whom, or what men say about me? Am I not wholly intent upon God, and His commands and ordinances (πρὸς τὸν θεὸν τέταμαι καὶ τὰς ἐκείνου ἐντολὰς καὶ τἀπροστάγματα)? (*Diatr.* 3.24.113-114.)

14 Possibly a free paraphrase of Plato, *Apol.* 28e-29a (cf. *Diatr.* 1.9.23-24; 3.1.19-20).

15 Bonhöffer, *Epiktet*, p. 231.

16 For the difference of ὁ ὑπηρέτης and ὁ δοῦλος, see K.H. Rengstorf, 'ὑπηρέτης κτλ', in R. Kittel *et al.* (eds), *TDNT* 8 (Grand Rapids, Michigan: Eerdmans, 1974), pp. 530–44 (532–33).

17 R.F. Dobbin (ed.), *Epictetus, Discourses Book I* (transl. R.F. Dobbin. Oxford: Clarendon Press, 1998), p. 208.

One should fulfil a God-given social position in obedience to God's commands and ordinances. Obeying makes the expelled person a worthy witness of the power of philosophy. God calls persons to be a witness, especially at the moment of a social descent (*Diatr.* 1.29.44-49):[18] an exemplary man lives 'as a witness summoned by God' (ὡς μάρτυς ὑπὸ τοῦ θεοῦ κεκλημένος) (*Diatr.* 1.29.46; cf. 2.1.39) even after having lost his office. One should not disgrace 'the summons which He gave you' (τὴν κλῆσιν ἣν κέκληκεν) by blaming God for the descent (*Diatr.* 1.29.49).

Epictetus connects the issues regarding God's commands, social positions and God's call, which are all contiguous with Paul's ideas in 1 Cor. 7.17-24.[19] What, however, makes these affinities striking, is their emergence in the context of a similar paradox: the social positions are indifferent, but they should be occupied. This paradox is based on the Stoic theory of value which is the heart of Epictetus' philosophy. According to Epictetus, all human beings have a so-called moral purpose (ἡ προαίρεσις) which denotes the faculty of a moral decision.[20] Other things are external (τὰ ἐκτός), they are 'not up to us' (τὰ οὐκ ἐφ' ἡμῖν) or 'not our own' (τὰ ἀλλότρια). Those external things lie outside the moral purpose (*Diatr.* 1.29.47). For example, body, property, reputation, office are external (*Ench.* 1.1). The external things are materials (ὕλαι) for the

---

18   Pace Bonhöffer (*Epiktet*, 37) and W. Deming (*Paul on Marriage and Celibacy: The Hellenistic Background of 1 Corinthians 7* [SNTSMS, 83; Cambridge: Cambridge University Press, 1995], p. 167) who claim that there is no change of social position when God calls one to be his witness. When Epictetus reports losing the governorship, an interlocutor (possibly Epictetus himself) asks: 'In what rôle, do you mount the stage *now* (νῦν)?' The answer is: 'as a witness...'. The text clearly suggests that one is witness as a consequence of the change of social position.

19   This is true despite a minor difference in call: according to Epictetus, only few persons are called to be a witness because of their hard circumstances. Paul ascribes God's call to all Christians in any circumstances. Much greater is the difference between God's call in 1 Cor. 7.17-24 and in Epictetus' parable of the voyage (*Ench.* 7) which Deming (*Paul*, 167–68) sees as analogical. In the parable, Epictetus compares this life to a time in which a ship is anchored in a harbour. A passenger should immediately go to the ship, when the captain calls, or he/she will be thrown on board all tied up. As the time in the harbour is life, the call indicates the time to die: one can meet death freely or 'all tied up'. Epictetus, however, remarks that an older person can miss the call without being thrown on board. This is a reference to suicide which is recommended by the Stoics in particular situations, especially in older age (A. Bonhöffer, *Die Ethik des Stoikers Epictet: Anhang: Exkurse über einige wichtige Punkte der stoischen Ethik* [Stuttgart: Verlag von Ferdinand Enke, 1894], pp. 29–39, 188–93 and J.M. Rist, *Stoic Philosophy* [Cambridge: Cambridge University Press, 1969], pp. 233–55). Thus, the older person in Epictetus' parable is a person who has not commited suicide in the proper time. As the call in *Ench.* 7 is a call to die, the analogy with 1 Cor. 7.17-24 is very loose.

20   R.F. Dobbin, 'Προαίρεσις in Epictetus', *Ancient Philosophy* 11 (1991), pp. 111–35. Long (*Epictetus*, pp. 210–20) has a lengthy discussion on the character of ἡ προαίρεσις, and he prefers to translate it 'volition'. Because I quote Oldfather's version of Epictetus' texts, I congruently use his translation 'moral purpose'.

moral purpose (v. 2), and the 'materials are indifferent' (ἀδιάφοροι) (*Diatr.* 2.5.1), not good or evil. Real good and evil are value judgements (τὰ δόγματα) that arise out of the moral purpose, not out of external things. If any external thing appears to us to be good or evil, it is so because of our value judgements.[21] All external things are indifferent as such.

Despite the fact that Epictetus regards external things as indifferent, he does not encourage us to ignore them: 'Materials are indifferent, but the use (ἡ χρῆσις) which we make of them is not a matter of indifference' (*Diatr.* 2.5.1). Epictetus deals with the right use of indifferent things in *Diatr.* 2.16 entitled 'That we do not practise the application of our judgements about things good and evil'. He claims that we can dismiss our troubles with the help of right judgements. Then he asks what those right judgements are:

> (27) And what are these? The things which a human being ought to practise all day long, without being devoted to what is not his own, either comrade, or place, or gymnasia, nay, not even to his own body; but he should remember the law (μεμνῆσθαι δὲ τοῦ νόμου) and keep that before his eyes. (28) And what is the law of God (τίς δ' ὁ νόμος ὁ θεῖος)? To guard (τηρεῖν) what is his own, not to lay claim to what is not his own, but to make use (χρῆσθαι) of what is given to him, and not to yearn for what has not been given; when something is taken away, to give up readily and without delay, being grateful for the time in which he had the use of it (ἐχρήσατο) (*Diatr.* 2.16.27-28; transl. revised.)

Epictetus reminds us that we should not be devoted to what is 'not our own' (τὰ ἀλλότρια) – this means the external things: body, property, reputation, office, etc. Instead (δέ) we should take heed of the law of God. The law requires us to guard (τηρέω) what is our own, namely our judgements (cf. *Diatr.* 2.16.24,26), without laying claim to any external thing. This, however, does not suggest passivity with regard to external things. They are on loan and we should make use (χράομαι, χρῆσις) of them.[22] Because external things are only on loan, we should give them back without constraint. The only morally justified attitude is gratefulness.

Besides some similar words in Paul and Epictetus (τηρέω, τήρησις,

---

21 'For in general remember this – that we crowd ourselves, we make close quarters for ourselves, that is to say, the decisions of our will (τὰ δόγματα) crowd us and make us close quarters' (*Diatr.* 1.25.28). Epictetus means that an impression of an oppressive crowd is in fact (1) an impression of a crowd and (2) our value judgement ('the decision of our will') that the crowd is oppressive. Thus, oppressiveness is not in a crowd but in our value judgement.

22 Bonhöffer, *Ethik*, p. 43; A. Bonhöffer, 'Epiktet und das Neue Testament', *ZNW* 13 (1912), pp. 281–92 (284–285). Cf. *SVF* 3.117, 119, 122, 123.

χράομαι besides ἡ κλῆσις and expressions for law),[23] we also find a similar theory of value. Paul suggests the idea of the indifference of social positions. Circumcision and uncircumcision are nothing (v. 19) and a slave should not be concerned about his or her social position (v. 21). Despite the indifference of the social positions, Paul does not suggest ignorance. He admonishes one to stay in one's position and to fulfil its duties, because the position represents God's commandment. Epictetus' theory of value makes this paradox understandable: the externals are indifferent as such, but their use is not.[24]

How did the theory of value influence social ethics? Both Paul and Epictetus share the same logic in this matter: if the social positions are indifferent, they also make indifferent the divergences between people. For Paul, it is indifferent if one is circumcized or not, free or a slave (cf. 1 Cor. 12.13; Gal. 3.28).[25] In 1 Cor. 7.22-23 the changing metaphors point to equality. First, Paul turns slavery and freedom upside down: the slave is a freedman of the Lord and a free person is slave of the Lord (v. 22) as though there was a status reversal. Then the metaphor changes: all Christians are slaves bought (ἀγοράζω) by the Lord (v. 23).[26] Now, there is no status reversal, but all are equal slaves. The changing metaphors prove the indifference of social divergences among Christians. This sounds much like Epictetus who spoke of the principal equality between slaves and those who are free. The slave is 'your own brother, who has Zeus as his progenitor and is, as it were, a son born of the same seed as yourself and of the same sowing from above'. To bear this in mind is to look at 'the laws of the gods' (*Diatr.* 1.13.3-5). These words of Epictetus also make clear a difference: he grounded the equality on human nature, not on being 'in the Lord' (1 Cor. 7.22). This difference, however, does not erase the fact that Paul's and Epictetus' teachings are in other respects fundamentally alike.

---

23   S. Vollenweider, *Freiheit als neue Schöpfung: Eine Untersuchung zur Eleutheria bei Paulus und in seiner Umwelt* (FRLANT, 147; Göttingen: Vandenhoeck & Ruprecht, 1989), p. 241.

24   In 1 Cor. 7.29-31 Paul returns to the Stoic theory of value with apocalyptical overtones. See Gretenkord, *Freiheitsbegriff*, pp. 293–97; Vollenweider, *Freiheit*, pp. 242–43; Deming, *Paul*, pp. 177–97; J.L. Jaquette, *Discerning What Counts: The Function of the Adiaphora Topos in Paul's Letters* (SBLDS, 146; Atlanta: Scholars Press, 1995), pp. 173–79. Pace, W. Schrage, 'Die Stellung zur Welt bei Paulus, Epiktet und in der Apokalyptik: Ein Beitrag zu 1Kor 7, 29–31', *ZTK* 61 (1964), pp. 125–54.

25   Jaquette, *Discerning*, pp. 170–72.

26   Verb ἀγοράζω denotes a buying of a slave for service, not a payment of freedom. See F.S. Jones, *'Freiheit' in den Briefen des Apostels Paulus: Eine historische, exegetische und religionsgeschichtliche Studie* (GTA, 34; Göttingen: Vandenhoeck & Ruprecht, 1987), p. 31 and D.B. Martin, *Slavery as Salvation: The Metaphor of Slavery in Pauline Christianity* (New Haven: Yale University Press, 1990), p. 63. Cf. 1 Cor. 6.19-20.

Some of the similarities are already recounted in earlier scholarship.[27] My analysis, however, has shown that the similarities are not superficial, but that they extend to the heart of Stoic moral philosophy: Paul presupposes the theory of value. In this context, it is natural to interpret 'the commandments of God' along the Stoic lines – they are requirements of God-given social positions.

The Torah as Stoic Law of Nature

In Rom. 2.9-16, Paul affirms that the Jews and the Gentiles will be judged impartially, because even the Gentiles know the law, i.e. the Torah. He says that Gentiles fulfil the things of the law by nature (φύσει τὰ τοῦ νόμου ποιῶσιν), they are a law to themselves and the work of the law (τὸ ἔργον τοῦ νόμου) is written in their hearts. It is possible that the dative φύσει in Rom. 2.14 is closely tied with the previous words. Thus, it would denote Gentile extraction as ἐκ φύσεως does (Rom. 2.27; cf. Rom. 11.21, 24; Gal. 2.15). However, it is more probable that φύσει defines the following words and denotes the way in which Gentiles know the Torah.[28]

In Paul, nature refers to the essential character of a person or a thing,[29] and as such, it may also be a guide for proper life (Rom. 1.26-27; 1 Cor. 11.14-15).[30] This fits with Rom. 2.14 where the Gentiles 'are a law to themselves'. The nature of the Gentiles contains the law, and thus, nature

27   E.g. Bonhöffer, *Epiktet*, p. 171; Jones *'Freiheit'*, pp. 37, 53; Vollenweider, *Freiheit*, pp. 211, 241, Deming, *Paul*, p. 159; Downing, *Cynics*, p. 113.

28   Rom. 2.14 is one of the three occurrences of the dative φύσει in Paul. In the two other cases it precedes the word it defines (Gal. 2.15; 4.8). Similarly in Rom. 2.27, ἐκ φύσεως denoting Gentile extraction precedes the word it defines. See G. Bornkamm, *Studien zu Antike und Urchristentum: Gesammelte Aufsätze*, vol. 2 (München: Chr. Kaiser, 1959), p. 103; J.D.G. Dunn, *Romans* (WBC, 38A; Dallas: Word Books, 1988), p. 98. Pace C.E.B. Cranfield, *A Critical Exegetical Commentary on the Epistle to the Romans*, vol. 1 (ICC, Edinburgh: T&T Clark, 1975), p. 156; S.J. Gathercole, 'A law unto themselves: the Gentiles in Romans 2.14-15 revisited', *JSNT* 85 (2002), pp. 27–49 (36–37). Beside the place of φύσει, Gathercole claims that there is no parallel for the thought of doing law by nature. There is, however, a rough parallel in Gal. 4.1-11: Gentiles have been slaves to the elements of the world which is identified with slavery to the law. Thus, Gentiles have obeyed the elements-law (cf. E.P. Sanders, *Paul, the Law, and the Jewish People* [London: SCM Press, 1985], p. 69; Räisänen, *Law*, 20–21.)

29   E.D.W. Burton, *A Critical and Exegetical Commentary on the Epistle to the Galatians* (ICC; Edinburgh: T&T Clark, 1948), p. 228; cf. H. Koester, 'φύσις κτλ', in R. Kittel *et al.* (eds), *TDNT* 9 (trans. G.W. Bromiley; Grand Rapids: Eerdmans, 1974), pp. 251–77 (271–72).

30   In 1 Corinthians Paul surprisingly personifies nature, but he seems to think in terms of the order of creation. See M. Pohlenz, 'Paulus und die Stoa', *ZNW* 42 (1949), pp. 69–104 (77); Koester, 'φύσις κτλ', pp. 272–73. It is not clear why men have short hair *by nature*. Epictetus seems to think just the contrary (*Diatr.* 4.8.5; Bonhöffer, *Epiktet*, 147).

is the basis for doing the law.[31] The idea of moral law based on nature was typical for Stoics, but it is known also for instance from Plato (*Leg.* 890d).[32] I, however, argue that Paul refers to the *Stoic* version of natural law, since Paul's description of 'nature' rules out the Platonic version.

In Romans, 'nature' does not occur for the first time in 2.14, but in 1.26-27 where Paul condemns the homosexual practice as contrary to nature. It seems clear that in the condemnation Paul affiliates himself with the Greek tradition of natural law. Not only Stoics understood homosexual practice as being opposed to nature. Plato already held the same view (*Leg.* 636c, 836c-841d), and there were also other critical voices in the Greco-Roman world.[33] However, the philosophical background of Paul's statements is not Platonic but Stoic, for he describes the homosexual desires in a way that unmistakably recalls the Stoic philosophy of emotions.

According to Paul, homosexual practice is the result of a decline which began in futile thinking and continued in idolatry. As a result 'God gave them up in the lusts of their hearts to impurity, to the degrading of their bodies among themselves' (Rom. 1.24). This is explained in Rom. 1.26-27: Gentiles have fallen to female and male homosexual practice which is contrary to nature (παρὰ φύσιν).[34]

Possibly Paul saw homosexual practice as being opposed to the proper gender roles.[35] Yet, it does not mean that nature is the same as the gender roles. In Rom. 2.14 the criteria of naturalness are anchored in human nature: Gentiles are a law unto themselves. In Rom. 1.26-27 this law is the physical construction of male and female. The words denoting the sexes (ἡ θήλεια, ὁ ἄρσην) emphasize the particular characteristics of the sexes, including the physical ones.[36] Paul probably understood homosexual

31 Pohlenz, 'Paulus', p. 77; O. Kuss, *Der Römerbrief*, vol. 1 (Regensburg: Verlag Friedrich Pustet, 1963), p. 69; O. Michel, *Der Brief an die Römer* (MeyerK, 4; Göttingen: Vandenhoeck & Ruprecht, 1978), p. 117.

32 Bonhöffer, *Epiktet*, p. 149. See also the comment on Plato, *Leg.* 890d in H. Thesleff, 'Divine and human law in early Platonism', in T. Veijola (ed.), *The Law in the Bible and in its Environment* (PFES, 51; Helsinki: The Finnish Exegetical Society, 1990), pp. 91–108 (103): 'As such, this passage has almost a Stoic ring.' Aristotle claimed that a person can be a law unto himself or herself (*Eth. nic.* 1128a; *Pol.* 1284a). More parallels: see Bornkamm, *Studien*, pp. 104, n. 22 and 105, n. 24.

33 M. Nissinen, *Homoeroticism in the Biblical World: A Historical Perspective* (trans. K. Stjerna; Minneapolis: Fortress, 1998), pp. 79–88.

34 The general reference to unnatural intercourse in v. 26 may refer to any sexual vice committed by women. The thought of homosexual practice is quite close due to the analogy made with v. 27. See, B.J. Brooten, *Love Between Women: Early Christian Responses to Female Homoeroticism* (Chicago: University of Chicago Press, 1996), pp. 246–50, 253–54.

35 Nissinen, *Homoeroticism*, pp. 107–8.

36 Kuss, *Römerbrief*, p. 50; Cranfield, *Romans*, p. 125; Dunn, *Romans*, p. 64.

practice as something which is contrary to the *bodily* construction since he says that the Gentiles degrade their *bodies* (v. 24).[37]

Similarities with Epictetus are striking. He says that homosexual practice is contrary to the proper gender roles as the passive man in a homosexual relationship loses his manhood. The proper sexual practice is, however, not based on gender roles since the active partner also loses his manhood (*Diatr.* 2.10.17). In Roman times, only the passive role was seen as shameful.[38] Epictetus does not explain his divergent view though he generally recommends to act as those who understand the constitution of nature (παρακολούθουν τῇ φυσικῇ κατασκευῇ) (*Diatr.* 2.10.4). What this constitution means in sexual matters becomes clear when he approves the heterosexual relationship in *Diatr.* 1.6. Epictetus tries to prove that everything is so marvellously constructed that providence must exist. One of those marvellous things is the heterosexual relationship.

> τὸ δ᾽ ἄρρεν καὶ τὸ θῆλυ καὶ ἡ προθυμία ἡ πρὸς τὴν συνουσίαν ἑκατέρου καὶ δύναμις ἡ χρηστικὴ τοῖς μορίοις τοῖς κατεσκευασμένοις οὐδὲ ταῦτα ἐμφαίνει τὸν τεχνίτην;

> And the male and the female, and the appetite of each for intercourse with the other, and the faculty which makes use of the organs which have been constructed for this purpose; do these things not reveal their artificer either? (*Diatr.* 1.6.9, transl. slightly revised.)

When this short passage is read in the context of Epictetus' philosophy we grasp his grounds for natural sex. The two sexes are called 'male' and 'female' (τὸ ἄρρεν, τὸ θῆλυ) instead of the common terms 'man' and 'woman'. The expressions bring attention to the physical characteristics, in this case to the genitals ('the organs') and their use (δύναμις ἡ χρηστικὴ τοῖς μορίοις τοῖς κατεσκευασμένοις). This is close to Paul's thought concerning natural sex (ἡ φυσικὴ χρῆσις) which is based on physical characteristics (Rom. 1.26-27).

What is more striking is the philosophy of emotions Paul suggests. There is no distinct category for homosexual desires in Paul. His words for desire (ἡ ἐπιθυμία, πάθος ἀτιμίας, ἡ ὄρεξις) are general ones and only the context specifies the sexual connotation. These words recall the Stoic

---

37 This is also the interpretation of copyist D*: the females 'exchanged natural creation (κτίσιν) for unnatural intercourse (χρῆσιν)' (Rom. 1.26).

38 Nissinen, *Homoeroticism*, pp. 70–73; D.M. Halperin, 'Forgetting Foucault: acts, identities, and the history of sexuality', in M.C. Nussbaum and J. Sihvola (eds), *The Sleep of Reason: Erotic Experience and Sexual Ethics in Ancient Greece and Rome* (Chicago: University of Chicago Press, 2002), pp. 21–54 (29–34).

vocabulary,[39] and Stoic theory of emotions. This becomes clear when we look at Epictetus' theory of emotions in respect of sex.

In *Diatr.* 1.6.9 Epictetus refers to sexual appetite with the word ἡ προθυμία which denotes natural and involuntary desire. It is a subcategory of ἡ ὄρεξις, which denotes all desires in general, including natural and unnatural, voluntary and involuntary desires.[40] Involuntary desires are always natural (*ergo* morally acceptable) as distinct from voluntary desires which are either natural or unnatural. Thus, heterosexual desire as ἡ προθυμία is natural and morally acceptable for Epictetus.

An involuntary desire ἡ προθυμία is like a drive or an instinct in contrast to voluntary desire which presupposes a value judgement. In Epictetus, voluntary and unnatural desire is ἡ ἐπιθυμία and a subcategory of the passion (τὸ πάθος), the voluntary and unnatural emotion.[41] What is wrong with ἡ ἐπιθυμία is the wrong object of desire: one has made a value judgement that something external, like sex, is a good thing in itself and worthy of desire. External things, however, are indifferent but their right use is not: sex is a matter of indifference, but not our conduct in sexual matters. Epictetus clearly condemns same-sex relationships, since they involve a mistaken value judgement: the object is wrong. Thus, Epictetus considers homosexual desire to be voluntary and unnatural ἐπιθυμία which violates the involuntary and natural προθυμία.

When reading Paul we must pay attention to two points in Epictetus' theory of homosexual desire: (1) its unnaturalness, which is due to (2) a wrong object of desire. In Romans 1 Paul argues that Gentiles have ceased to give honour and thanks to God. This theological lapse was followed by

---

39 Brooten, *Love*, pp. 254–55; Nissinen, *Homoeroticism*, p. 104. From a formal Stoic perspective the expression πάθος ἀτιμίας is pleonastic, for πάθος as such already denotes a morally questionable emotion. This fact, however, does not make the Stoic reading impossible (Pace Bonhöffer, *Epiktet*, p. 124). The abundance of expression is common in diatribe, as in Epictetus and Paul (see e.g. T. Schmeller, *Paulus und die 'Diatribe': Eine vergleichende Stilinterpretation* [NTAbh, Neue Folge, 19; Münster: Aschendorf, 1987]), and the expression 'dishonourable passion' does not include the possibility of honourable passion. See D.B. Martin, 'Heterosexism and the interpretation of Romans 1.18-32' *BibInt* 3 (1995), pp. 332–55 (347).

40 I present common Stoic terminology although Epictetus is sometimes imprecise in terminological matters. See A. Bonhöffer, *Epictet und die Stoa: Untersuchungen zur stoischen Philosophie* (Stuttgart: Verlag von Ferdinand Enke, 1890), pp. 233–49, 278–84. In the analysed text, ἡ προθυμία has its common Stoic meaning. See Bonhöffer, *Epictet und die Stoa*, p. 248 and R. Sorabji, *Emotion and Peace of Mind: From Stoic Agitation to Christian Temptation: The Gifford Lectures* (Oxford: Oxford University Press, 2000), pp. 52–53.

41 In Stoicism, the main categories of the passion are wrong desire (ἡ ἐπιθυμία), pleasure (ἡ ἡδονή), fear (ὁ φόβος) and grief (ἡ λύπη). For Stoic theories of the passions, see *SVF* 3.386–388, 391–394 and e.g. T. Brennan, 'The old Stoic theory of emotions', in T. Engberg-Pedersen and J. Sihvola, *The Emotions in Hellenistic Philosophy* (The New Synthese Historical Library, 46; Dordrecht: Kluwer Academic Publishers, 1998), pp. 21–70 (30–31) and Sorabji, *Emotion*, pp. 29–30.

intellectual lapse (futile thinking, senseless and darkened mind, a debased mind) and, for example, by homosexual desires. Thus, homosexual desires are not created by God, and in this sense they are unnatural. These unnatural desires are followed by practices which are parallel to the theological lapse. In both cases Gentiles have *changed* the right object to a wrong one: instead of God they have honoured idols, instead of heterosexual practice they have adopted the homosexual one. This is what Epictetus thought: homosexual desire as ἡ ἐπιθυμία is due to a wrong object.

Paul's and Epictetus' similarities become clear when we consider Plato's views. For Plato, there is a passionate part in the human soul, and, thus, all desires have a natural origin though one has to restrain their excess (*Resp.* 434d-441c; *Phaedr.* 253c-256d). For Plato, the origin of homosexual practice is not in a wrong value judgement, but rather in the incapacity to restrain desire for pleasure (δι' ἀκράτειαν ἡδονῆς) (*Leg.* 636c). Paul's text does not blame Gentiles for excessive sex but for the change of sexual object. Gentiles are not skimming off more and more sexual pleasures, but they have *left aside* (ἀφέντες) natural sex while searching for unnatural sex. Hence, Paul's view is Stoic, not Platonic.[42]

Paul's sayings concerning homosexual practice illustrate the significance to him of the *Stoic* natural law. Moreover, they illustrate the way he thought Gentiles to be a law unto themselves (Rom. 2.14). The Gentiles have their human nature as law, and in this sense they had a law unto themselves. Paul's condemnation of homosexual practice also shows what he means by paralleling the natural law to the Torah (Rom. 2.14-15). The Torah condemns male homosexual practice (Lev. 18.22; 20.13) and Hellenistic Jews supported this condemnation with Stoic arguments.[43] Paul is heir to this Jewish tradition, but the Torah is conspicuously absent in his condemnation. This is Paul's deliberate decision, since Gentiles cannot be blamed for the rejection of the Torah. They have never had the Torah, but rather the natural law (Rom. 2.12-14).

State law, the Torah and Political Philosophy

The close reading of Paul's condemnation of homosexual practice has shown that Paul had the *Stoic* version of natural law in mind, rather than that of the Platonic. This is also the case in Romans 7 as I have shown

---

42   Pace Martin ('Heterosexism') who rejects the idea of disoriented desire as a creation of modern heterosexism without a reference to the Stoic position. Rightly, T. Engberg-Pedersen, *Paul and the Stoics* (Edinburgh: T&T Clark, 2000), p. 210.

43   Nissinen, *Homoeroticism*, pp. 89–97.

elsewhere.[44] Of course, Paul has blended Stoic ideas with other elements, for example with an apocalyptic idea of the last judgement (Rom. 2.16). Paul was not a Stoic philosopher and he adjusted Stoic doctrines to his teaching when he deemed it suitable and purposeful.

I argue that in Romans 13 Paul's teaching on law is *not* Stoic. A comparison with Epictetus will prove this. Nevertheless, the comparison not only attests to Paul's disagreement with Stoicism, but also reveals his clear connections to another kind of Greco-Roman political philosophy. Thus, my comparison encourages further comparisons between Paul and ancient philosophy.

Paul does not mention state *law* in Rom. 13.1-7, but his teaching on obedience to authorities also goes for state laws. This obedience is linked with God's ordinance (ἡ διαταγή) (Rom. 13.2) and love command (Rom. 13.8-10). At the same time, the love command prepares for the discussion on the weak and the strong (Romans 14–15) as verbal similarities between the passages show.[45] Moreover, the issue of the strong and the weak is present not only in Romans 14–15, but also in Paul's teaching on authorities (Rom. 13.1-7) as I will show. Thus, Romans 13–15 is linked together by love and the issue of the weak and the strong.

What is Epictetus' teaching on authorities? In *Diatr.* 1.12.7, Epictetus suggests that 'a good and excellent person subordinates (ὑποτέταχεν) his or her will to God like good citizens do as regards the state law'. Thus, he suggests obedience to state law, but not without qualifications. This becomes clear when he discusses weakness and strongness in respect to a tyrant's claim over the judgements.

> (12) You fail to realize that the judgement overcame itself, it was not overcome by something else; and nothing else can overcome moral purpose, but it overcomes itself. (13) For this reason too the law of God is most powerful and most just: 'Let the stronger always prevail over the weaker.'[46] (14) 'Ten are stronger than one,' you say. For what? For putting in chains, for killing, for dragging away a man's property. Ten overcome one, therefore, in the point in which they are stronger. (15) In what, then, are they weaker? If one has correct judgements, and the ten have not. (*Diatr.* 1.29.11-15; transl. slightly revised.)

Epictetus accepts that the stronger always prevail over the weaker, but makes a division between moral and physical strength. Physical super-

44 N. Huttunen, 'The human contradiction: Epictetus and Romans 7', in Antti Mustakallio (ed.), *Lux Humana, Lux Aeterna: Essays on Biblical and Related Themes* (Festschrift L. Aejmelaeus; PFES, 89; Helsinki: The Finnish Exegetical Society, 2005), pp. 324-33.

45 Räisänen, *Law*, p. 64; Dunn, *Romans*, p. 797.

46 I prefer the translations 'stronger' and 'weaker' (Oldfather: 'better' and 'worse') as there is a question of physical strength. See also ἰσχυροτέρων in *Diatr.* 1.29.16.

iority does not mean moral superiority. This makes it possible to criticise authorities and their laws from a moral point of view: 'Law is not simply anything that is in the power of a fool' (νόμος δ' οὐκ ἔστι τὰ ἐπὶ μωρῷ) (*Diatr.* 4.7.34). Philosophy provides the criteria for good laws. In *Diatr.* 4.3 Epictetus calls the Stoic theory of value 'God's commands', viz. laws which should be obeyed: 'These are the laws that have been sent you from God, these are His ordinances (οὗτοί εἰσιν οἱ ἐκεῖθεν ἀπεσταλμένοι νόμοι, ταῦτα τὰ διατάγματα); it is of these you ought to become an interpreter, to these you ought to subject yourself (τούτοις ὑποτεταγμένον), not the laws of Masurius and Cassius.' (*Diatr.* 4.3.12.) Masurius and Cassius interpreted old Republican laws in the imperial context,[47] and, thus, 'the laws of Masurius and Cassius' are state laws. Thus, Epictetus denies obedience to state laws.

Epictetus' reserved attitude towards state laws is clearly different from Paul's teaching on authorities. Paul suggests a power structure in society: there are rulers and subjects. He refers to the rulers generally as those who happen to be (αἱ δὲ οὖσαι). Paul clearly means that people in power change and one should be subject to anyone in power, since God appoints authorities. What remains unaltered is the power structure: there are always rulers and subjects in the society. As God has appointed authorities, their power is the hallmark of God's ordinance (ἡ διαταγή). This is not a hallmark in the Hebrew Bible.[48] For example, Saul was the factual king long after Samuel had anointed David. Paul, in contrast, assumes straightforwardly that God has appointed those who now hold the power. This is an echo of philosophical theories that the stronger will always prevail over the weaker.

Paul, unlike Epictetus, does not make any division between political and moral authority. Because authority is appointed by God, Paul concludes that it also represents God's moral requirements. 'For rulers are not a terror to good conduct, but to *bad*... But if you *do what is wrong*, you should be afraid, for the authority does not bear the sword in vain! It is the servant of God to execute wrath on *the wrongdoer*' (Rom. 13.3-4; italics mine). The morality of rulers is confirmed in the following passage (Rom. 13.8-10) where Paul says that the core of the Torah is the command to love one's neighbour (Lev. 19.18). He clarifies: 'Love *does no wrong* to a neighbor' (Rom. 13.10; italics mine). Good, bad and love also occur as cornerstones of Christian ethics in Rom. 12.9, 17, 21, and it is natural to

47   J. Kodrebski, 'Der Rechtsunterricht am Ausgang der Republik und zu Beginn des Prinzipats', in *ANRW* II.15 (Berlin: Walter de Gruyter, 1976), pp. 177–96 (190–96).

48   For the Jewish background of Paul's teaching on authorities, see e.g. J. Friedrich, W. Pöhlmann, and P. Stuhlmacher, 'Zur historischen Situation und Intention von Röm 13,1–7', *ZTK* 73 (1976), pp. 131–66 (145–46); V. Riekkinen, *Römer 13: Aufzeichung und Weiterführung der exegetischen Diskussion* (AASF, Dissertationes Humanarum Litterarum, 23; Helsinki: Suomalainen tiedeakatemia, 1980), pp. 54–57.

understand good and bad similarly throughout Romans 12–13.[49] One cannot avoid the impression that authorities enforce people to do the good the Torah and Christian ethics require.[50] In a word: the sword compels to love.

Paul's approval of the imperial sword opposes Epictetus' views. Epictetus argued that one can be *fearless* in the middle of the punishments that are executed by state authorities (*Diatr.* 4.7). He says that one must please God rather than any of the authorities (τίνα τῶν ὑπερεχόντων). The power (ἡ ἐξουσία) and the armed guards (οἱ ἐπὶ τῆς μαχαίρας) amount to nothing (*Diatr.* 1.30.1, 6–7). This is due to his theory of value which does not ascribe any value to violent punishments or to approval since they are indifferent externals. Epictetus' view is squarely opposite to Paul's, who even says that one *must* (ἀνάγκη) obey authorities because of wrath (Rom. 13.5)![51] Both accept the law of the stronger, but only Paul assumes that the physically weaker must morally obey the stronger. In accepting the avoidance of fear as a basis for obeying, Paul is closer to Epicurus (Diogenes Laertios 10.151) than to the Stoics. Paul's community-centred thinking in Romans 14–15 also points to Epicureans rather than to Stoics.[52] Yet, we should remember that the division between the weak and the strong has a long history beginning with Hesiod,[53] and continuing through Plato (*Apol.* 30c-d; *Gorg.* 483c-e) until the times of Paul (Seneca, *Ep.* 90.4).[54]

Rom. 13.1-7 can be read as a part of the Greco-Roman discussion on the state,[55] and we can say the same about Epictetus. Similarities between Epictetus and Paul are due to the fact that they participate in the more

---

49　U. Wilckens, *Der Brief an die Römer* (EKKNT, 6/3; Zürich: Benziger Verlag, 1982), p. 31; cf. Riekkinen, *Römer 13*, p. 209.

50　Pace E. Käsemann, *An die Römer* (HNT, 8; Tübingen: Mohr, 1973), p. 338 and Michel, *Römer*, p. 401.

51　Compulsion (ἀνάγκη) can be understood in several ways (Aristotle, *Met.* 1015a-b), and Paul speaks of it in double meaning: (1) a compulsion independent of human action and (2) an unavoidable ethical requirement. The former meaning is connected with wrath while the latter is connected with the conscience. Cf. K. Haacker, *Der Brief des Paulus an die Römer* (THKNT, 6; Leipzig: Evangelische Verlagsanstalt, 1999), p. 267.

52　C.E. Glad, *Paul and Philodemus: Adaptability in Epicurean and Early Christian Psychagogy* (NovTSup, 81; Leiden: Brill, 1995).

53　A.A.T. Ehrhardt, *Politische Metaphysik von Solon bis Augustin*, vol. 1 (Tübingen: J.C. B. Mohr, 1959), p. 27.

54　H. Räisänen, *Jesus, Paul and Torah: Collected Essays* (trans. D.E. Orton; JSNTSup, 43; Sheffield: JSOT Press, 1992), pp. 81–82.

55　H. Cancik, ' "Alle Gewalt ist von Gott." Paulus, Röm. 13 im Rahmen antiker und neuzeitlicher Staatslehren', in B. Gladigow (ed.), *Staat und Religion* (Düsseldorf: Patmos Verlag, 1981), pp. 53–74 (60).

general Greco-Roman discussion on the state.[56] The comparison has shown that Paul did not accept Epictetus' Stoic stance, but that Paul's teaching on state laws, God's ordinance and the Torah has strong links to Greco-Roman philosophy.

Paul, Law and the Philosophers

The philosophical components of Paul's teaching on law have been dwarfed by the traditional approaches. My comparison between Paul and Epictetus has showed that there is a Stoic matrix of Paul's teaching on law in 1 Corinthians 7 and in Romans 1 and 2. In Romans 13 Paul differs from Epictetus' Stoic views. Even this result was fruitful as the comparison exposed Paul's consciousness of philosophical theories on the state and law.

Paul was a Christian preacher with deep roots in Judaism which, in turn, was a part of the Greco-Roman world. Surprisingly, this well-known fact has been overlooked in the scholarly work on Paul's teaching on law, and the scope of Paul's philosophical background has been neglected. I encourage a fresh approach from the ancient philosophical point of view in order to exhibit the philosophical components of Paul's teaching.

---

56 See e.g. Xenophon, *Mem.* 1.2.41-46; Aristotle, *Pol.* 1324a-b; *Eth. nic.* 1180a; Cicero, *Off.* 2.22-29; Seneca, *Clem.* as a whole; Marcus Aurelius, *Med.* 9.29. See also A. Strobel, 'Furcht, wem Furcht Gebührt: Zum profangriechischen Hintergrund von Rm 13.7', *ZNW* 55 (1964), pp. 58–62; van W.M. Unnik, 'Lob und Strafe durch die Obrigkeit: Hellenistisches zu Röm 13, 3–4', in E.E. Ellis and E. Gräßer (eds), *Jesus und Paul* (Festschrift W.G. Kümmel; Göttingen: Vandenhoeck & Ruprecht, 1975), 334–43; Riekkinen, *Römer 13*, pp. 60–65; Downing, *Cynics*, pp. 58–70.

Chapter 5

THE PAULINE LUTHER AND THE LAW: LUTHERAN THEOLOGY RE-ENGAGES THE STUDY OF PAUL

Risto Saarinen

1. *The Lutheran Paul vs. the New Perspective*

In his recent study *Perspectives Old and New on Paul: The 'Lutheran' Paul and His Critics*, Stephen Westerholm surveys a topic that is, as he puts it, 'warmly debated in the saunas of Finland'.[1] Since the topic in question concerns the apostle Paul's teaching of law, grace and justification, it is debated elsewhere as well. Continuing and rewriting his earlier work, *Israel's Law and the Church's Faith*,[2] Westerholm outlines an extensive research history which in the last decades has oscillated between two basic views. There is (1) the 'Lutheran' Paul who teaches that human beings are sinners, but justified by faith in Jesus Christ, not by the works they do. According to this classical view of justification, the law does not contribute to salvation but crushes human self-righteousness and drives human beings to seek mercy from God. Even as justified the Christians remain sinners who fail to do good with their own will. Thus we all continue to ponder the existential problems of Paul expressed in Rom. 7.14-25.[3]

In conscious opposition to this received view, many twentieth-century biblical scholars have outlined (2) a 'new perspective', according to which Paul teaches that Christians can in fact live according to the Spirit. This new interpretation of Paul further holds that the struggle with law and sin essentially belongs to the pre-Christian existence of humans. According to the new perspective, Paul's conscience was not burdened by his own sins,

---

1 Grand Rapids: Eerdmans, 2004, here: p. 226. Westerholm refers to Finnish debates after Heikki Räisänen, *Paul and the Law* (WUNT, 29; Tübingen: Mohr Siebeck, 2nd edn, 1987). With minor modifications, this article appeared in *Pro ecclesia* 15 (2006), pp. 64–86. Reprinted by permission. I have meanwhile continued the discussion in Saarinen, 'How Luther got Paul right', *Dialog* 46 (2007), pp. 170–73.

2 Grand Rapids: Eerdmans, 1988.

3 Westerholm, *Perspectives*, pp. 88–97, 134.

but the Christian Paul is only critical of the shortcomings and wrong judgements of non-Christians, in particular the Jews.[4]

The new perspective emerged when the biblical scholars realized, or were assumed to have realized, that they had read Paul through the lenses of Augustine and Martin Luther. In these two later Western theologians, however, we are confronted with a notion of introspective conscience that is not found in Paul. Whereas Augustine and Luther display an introspective awareness of sin and individual guilt, Paul in fact possesses a robust conscience and does not practise self-analysis. Already as a Jew Paul thought that he could lead a rather blameless life, and as a Christian he expected to be able to live his life according to the Spirit.[5]

When Paul, from his particularly Christian perspective, criticizes the Jewish and Gentile ways of life, he is therefore not reporting his own personal and existential problems, but rather making a theological point. A Christian can see that salvation does not come from the works of the law. However, it is only the viewpoint reached 'in Christ' that reveals the basic problem of our former striving after perfection. And since the Christian can achieve and has achieved spiritual fulfilment, he or she does not need to be worried about the existential problem of failing to do good. In sum, both Jew and Christian may have a robust conscience and both in fact believe that they can do good works. The Christian knows that Jews and pagans are wrong in believing this, but the Christian also thinks that in the Spirit he is no longer under sin's power and can thus fulfil the law.[6]

A prominent argument in favour of the new perspective concerns the interpretation of the word 'I' in Romans 7. The 'Lutheran' view of Paul has interpreted this word to refer to Paul's own inner struggles with the law. Given this, one is almost compelled to understand justification as a theocentric event in which humans remain 'justified and sinners at the same time'. Humans cannot do the works of the law; they can only believe in God's promise in Jesus Christ. Paul's self-description in Romans 7 thus becomes a paradigmatic description of that individual introspection which is presupposed in the Lutheran doctrine of justification.[7]

Exegetes of the twentieth century, in particular W.G. Kümmel and Krister Stendahl, have argued, however, that the 'I' to which Paul refers does not represent his own personal experience. It is rather a rhetorical or an exemplary 'I' which is employed in order to demonstrate a general state of affairs. Paul uses an exemplary 'I' in several places, e.g. in Rom. 3.7, 1

---

4 For the extensive discussion, see, in addition to Westerholm, *Perspectives*, D.A. Carson *et al.* (eds), *Justification and Variegated Nomism* (WUNT, 2/140 and 2/181; 2 vols; Tübingen: Mohr Siebeck, 2001 and 2004). A brief summary is offered in vol. 2, pp. 1–38, by Stephen Westerholm, 'The "New Perspective" at twenty-five'.

5 Westerholm, *Perspectives*, p. 144.

6 *Ibid.*, pp. 144–49.

7 *Ibid.*, pp. 140–44.

Cor. 6.12, 15, 13.1, and Gal. 2.18, but in Romans 7 this is not self-evident. Without going into the exegetical discussion in detail, it may be said that the presupposition of an exemplary 'I' helps us to understand why the law is criticized but not abrogated by Paul in Romans 6–8.[8]

According to the 'new perspective' it is neither the general Christian experience nor Paul's personal experience that is portrayed in Rom. 7.14-25. Instead, Paul here describes the general condition of humanity under the law. The exemplary 'I' refers to a human condition which is not particulary Christian nor particularly Jewish, but shows the general relationship between sin and the law. In doing this the passage 'demonstrates the utter moral impotence of humanity under the law, a gloomy contrast to the glorious picture of redemption in Romans 6 and 8'.[9]

Why is this new perspective on Romans 7 antagonistic to the 'Lutheran' Paul? Not because of this demonstration, but because Paul's own situation as a Christian is no longer represented under the universal human condition of sinfulness. For those who are in Christ Jesus, this condition is no longer valid (Rom. 8.1). Christians, including Paul himself, are rescued from 'this body of death' by Jesus Christ (Rom. 7.24-25). Thus the exemplary 'I' of Rom. 7.14-25 describes the pre-Christian situation of human sinner. The justified Christian is no longer subject to this condition. And this is contrary to Lutheranism which teaches that our struggle with sin, lack of good will and life under the cross continue throughout Christian existence.

We may also note that the exemplary 'I' does not depict a Jewish dilemma, but a universal human dilemma which, however, only appears as such a dilemma when it is looked at from the specific viewpoint provided by Christianity. In a somewhat paradoxical manner, the new perspective thus presents the situation described in Rom. 7.14-25 as a universal human dilemma which nevertheless only appears as such once the human being has been set free of this dilemma by Jesus Christ and the Spirit of life (Rom. 8.2).[10]

This argument was outlined by Kümmel and Stendahl many decades ago, but it gained new support in E.P. Sanders's work *Paul and Palestinian Judaism*.[11] Sanders showed that the Jews of Paul's time did not boast of human achievement but believed in the grace of God which was in keeping with the observance of the law. Luther's contrast between righteousness of

8   *Ibid.*, pp. 135–45, summarizing W.G. Kümmel, *Römer 7 und die Bekehrung des Paulus* (UNT, 17; Leipzig: Hinrichs, 1929) and Krister Stendahl, *Paul among Jews and Gentiles* (Philadelphia: Fortress, 1976).
9   Westerholm, *Perspectives*, p. 144.
10   Cf. *Ibid.*, pp. 144–49.
11   Philadelphia: Fortress, 1977.

works and justification by faith and grace alone does not meet the historical situation of Paul since, for first-century Judaism, 'salvation is always by the grace of God'.[12] On the other hand, Paul according to Sanders observed a 'work-ethic' himself: already as a Jew he believed himself to be leading a rather blameless life, and as a Christian he was set free in the effort to do good because, as mentioned above, the Spirit enables Christians to do what the law requires.[13]

So, although the human condition, expressed in Romans 7, in a way remains a universal dilemma, it is relativized in three different ways: 1. the dilemma is not relevant with regard to Judaism in particular; 2. Christians have actually surpassed this dilemma because the Spirit enables them to fulfil the law; and 3. the whole dilemma only appears to be a universal dilemma from the specifically Christian viewpoint.

All three points seem to go radically against Luther and Lutheranism, since in Lutheran theology (i) the insufficiency of the law in overcoming sin has been seen as the problem of a Jewish righteousness of works; (ii) Christians are justified but they nevertheless remain sinners at the same time and thus remain faced with the dilemmas of Romans 7; and (iii) the experience of the Pauline 'I' in Romans 7 is seen as a universal problem: all humans wonder why 'I do not do what I want, but I do the very thing I hate' (Rom. 7.15).

Continuing Westerholm's argument, we may note that the allegedly Lutheran reading of Rom. 7.15-20 contains yet another problem. The exegetes have questioned the subject of this doing, but also the doing itself remains far from clear. What does the speaker not do? According to the 'Lutheran' interpretation, the justified Christian, or Paul himself, continues to sin. But does the speaker (A) do always and everything wrong, and contrary to his will? It would be very odd to think that the paradigmatic Christian Paul, apostle and saint, would always do everything wrong and contrary to his will. There must be some qualifications in this non-willed doing. But how are we to read these qualifications into the text?

The 'new perspective' seems to offer an elegant solution, since the Christian speaker only refers to the doings of the exemplary I (B) in some earlier period, during which the extent of wrongdoing may have varied and need not bother the present speaker. A third logical possibility would be that the speaker is, as Rom. 7.14 explicitly says, the old and carnal

---

12 Westerholm, *Perspectives*, p. 342 quoting Sanders, *Palestinian Judaism*, p. 297.

13 Westerholm, *Perspectives*, p. xiv, 163. For the sake of brevity, I leave out here many different versions of non-Lutheran Paul in recent discussion, for instance N.T. Wright's discussion of 'I' as referring to Israel. See Westerholm, *Perspectives*, pp. 179–83 and Wright, *The Climax of the Covenant: Christ and the Law in Pauline Theology* (Minneapolis: Fortress, 1991).

person who is describing (C) his current powerlessness. But this possibility must face the contradiction that, on the one hand, the speaker claims to understand his carnal situation while, on the other, he claims not to understand (Rom. 7.15) his own action. Assuming that there is a temporal difference between the present speaker and the exemplary 'I' of the past, such contradictions can be solved.

Is the traditional Lutheran position thus declared to be exegetically invalid? No, since the exegetical case is not yet closed. In his extensive survey Westerholm actually believes that the new perspective of Sanders, Stendahl and others has not solved all the problems. He consoles Lutherans by saying that they have nevertheless 'rightly captured Paul's rationale and basic point',[14] namely that salvation is by faith and through grace in Jesus Christ.

In fact, Westerholm himself moderately argues in favour of the 'Lutheran' Paul. According to Westerholm, many slogans of the 'new perspective' are exaggerations which need to be tested and qualified. He is critical of Sanders' results, because the Jewish harmony of obedience to the law, on the one hand, and trust in the gratuity of God's covenantal election, on the other, finally differs from the understanding of grace in Lutheran and Protestant Christianity. In its interplay of grace and works, first-century Judaism, as portrayed by Sanders, in fact resembles Pelagianism as refuted by Augustine and Martin Luther.[15] In spite of these qualifications, it is nevertheless clear that the new perspective has presented powerful and plausible alternatives to the traditional Lutheran reading of Pauline theology of justification and the law. Therefore Westerholm attempts to take seriously both the 'old' and the 'new' perspectives.

In the following, my interest will not be exegetical. I will highlight some points which are relevant for our understanding of Luther and Lutheranism. For exegetes like Westerholm, Stendahl, Sanders and many others, the problem has been that the earlier New Testament scholars have read the texts through the lenses of Martin Luther and Lutheranism. Given this point of departure, they aim at liberating exegesis from the myopia caused by maladjusted lenses. They have not considered, however, what kind of Lutheranism has caused this myopia.

Is Martin Luther really saying all that the exegetical paradigm of the 'Lutheran Paul' has said? Or can it be that both Luther and Paul have been distorted or at least rigidly systematized by some later interpreters? Could it be that also in Luther studies we have, since the times of W.G. Kümmel, developed new perspectives? Could one even discover a more

---

14 Westerholm, *Perspectives*, p. 445.
15 *Ibid.*, pp. 346–51.

'Pauline' Luther with the help of contemporary historical, theological and also exegetical insights? Such questions will be the focus of my attention.[16]

2. Participation in Christ: Biblical Scholarship, Ecumenism and Luther Studies

Before turning to Luther, some general comments on the recent history of New Testament scholarship, ecumenical theology and Luther studies ought to be made.

Participation in Christ in Pauline theology. Stephen Westerholm's presentation of the 'Lutheran Paul' vs. the 'new perspective' is related to another and broader exegetical issue dealing with the relative importance of the doctrine of justification in Paul's theology. It is clear that justification is important for Paul, but many biblical scholars have claimed that it need not be seen as the most important and central doctrine or as a concept which would be operative as the overall criterion of all other theological themes in Paul.

Already Albert Schweitzer has paid attention to the theme of 'being in Christ' as an extremely important issue of Pauline theology. In the twentieth-century exegetics, this view of the 'new life in Christ' or 'participation in Christ' has not seldom been regarded as a topic which is more important for the apostle than the doctrine of justification. One way to make this argument is to say that Paul's language of justification is prominent in Romans and Galatians because of the particular disputes and circumstances relevant for those letters. But in many other letters justification is not treated, whereas the language of participation in Christ and being in Christ is prominent everywhere in the Pauline letters irrespective of the particular disputes at hand.[17]

Moreover, many exegetes claim that even in Romans and Galatians the problems of justification are in fact solved with the theology of 'being in Christ' and participation. Without entering into this exegetical argument in detail, it can be said that the 'being in Christ' can be regarded as the actual centre and argumentative foundation of Paul's soteriology, whereas

16   Although my interest is similar to that of Timothy George, 'Modernizing Luther, domesticating Paul: another perspective', in Carson *et al.* (eds), *Justification and Variegated*, vol. 2, pp. 437–63, my claims will be different. I share, however, his opinion (442) that 'the strength of the new perspective does not rest on the accuracy of its depiction of Luther'.

17   See e.g. Martien Brinkman, *Justification in Ecumenical Dialogue* (Utrecht: IIMO, 1996), pp. 57–78; Mark A. Seifrid, *Justification by Faith: The Origin and Development of a Central Pauline Theme* (NovTSup, 68; Leiden: Brill, 1992). Carson *et al.* (eds), *Justification and Variegated*, vols 1–2 highlight the latest updates of this enormous discussion.

justification remains a more circumstantial topic, mostly relevant for Paul's disputes with Judaism.[18]

Generally speaking, many advocates of the above-mentioned 'new perspective' with regard to the law often also adopt the priority of participatory language in their interpretations of Pauline soteriology. This preference often strengthens their criticism of the 'Lutheran' Paul who was, in their opinion, forced to teach forensic justification by faith. Given this, the best exegetical option left to the 'Lutheran' Paulinists, for instance Ernst Käsemann and his students, was to broaden the idea of justification to include various aspects of sanctification, liberation and life in Christ. While this option is helpful for systematic theologians and has received some support in the exegetical study of Paul, it can be criticized by both strict Lutherans and the advocates of the 'new perspective' for making the language of justification unclear.[19]

One may nevertheless mention in passing that some exegetes have meanwhile learned to see Luther's view of justification not only as imputation but also and perhaps primarily in terms of 'Christ present in faith'. Mark A. Seifrid notes that Luther highlights this Pauline idea in his *Commentary on Galatians*, but does not speak of the imputation of Christ's righteousness. Seifrid remarks that the more narrowly forensic language stems from Melanchthon and comes 'into widespread usage only after the Osiandrian controversy (1551)'.[20]

Ecumenism. In their ecumenical agreements, contemporary Lutherans normally defend a view of justification that is both forensic and effective. In so doing they follow the above-mentioned exegetical option of broadening the language of justification in order to embrace the Pauline view of 'being in Christ'. Another strategic reason for doing this is that the ecumenical partners may not regard the forensic justification by faith as the highest criterion of true Christianity. But all churches speak of 'being in Christ' in the Pauline sense and connect this language with other aspects of Pauline soteriology, thus offering points of ecumenical convergence.[21]

According to the ecumenical strategy of many recent Lutheran agreements, justification is not merely a matter of God's favour or

---

18 So Brinkman, *Justification*, pp. 59–63, explaining e.g. the 'participationist eschatology' of Sanders, *Palestinian Judaism*.

19 Cf. Brinkman, *Justification*, pp. 63–69.

20 Seifrid, 'Paul's use of righteousness language against its Hellenistic background', in Carson *et al.* (eds), *Justification and Variegated*, vol. 2, pp. 39–74 (71).

21 See e.g. Brinkman, *Justification*; Risto Saarinen, 'Justification by faith in the ecumenical dialogues of the Lutheran World Federation', in Bert Beach (ed.), *Lutherans and Adventists in Conversation* (Silver Springs: SDA, 2000), pp. 89–105, and the Lutheran–Roman Catholic text *Joint Declaration of the Doctrine of Justification* (e.g. Grand Rapids: Eerdmans, 2000).

'counting', but the divine favour is accompanied by a sacramental grace which effects and transforms the life or even the very person of the justified Christian. While the Christian, to a certain extent, remains a sinner, he or she is nevertheless 'in Christ' and thus participates in the new creation. This effective grace may be called sanctification or life in the Spirit, but is often understood as an aspect of justification. Justification thus not only comprise juridical relationships, but it also endows the believer with the gift of sacramental and christocentric reality.

A typical example of this strategy is the British-Nordic *Porvoo* agreement between Lutherans and Anglicans. Although the Anglicans participated in the European Reformation, they did not adopt the forensic justification or the distinction between law and gospel in a strictly Lutheran manner. In order to meet broader Anglican soteriology in a manner compatible with Lutheranism, the *Porvoo* agreement formulates this as follows: 'Both our traditions affirm that justification leads and must lead to "good works"; authentic faith issues in love. We receive the Holy Spirit who renews our hearts and equips us for and calls us to good works. As justification and sanctification are aspects of the same divine act, so also living faith and love are inseparable in the believer.'[22] This description comes rather close to those adherents of the 'new perspective' who teach that Christians have the Spirit and are able to do some good.

'Being in Christ' in Luther Studies. If one were to judge the state of Luther studies on the basis of Westerholm's exegetical research history, one could but wonder how one-sided it has remained. But it is very clear that modern interpreters of Luther have paid a lot of attention to the non-forensic and Christ-centered language in the reformers' writings. In part this may have been a reaction to the challenge set by the exegetes since the days of Albert Schweitzer, but a more obvious reason has been that the language of participation and 'being in Christ' is as prominent in Luther as it is in Paul.

As I have shown in detail elsewhere,[23] the prominence of this language was observed already by Albrecht Ritschl and Wilhelm Herrmann, but it became a major issue for many scholars of the German Luther

---

22 'Porvoo Common Statement' 32 c, in C.J. Podmore (ed.), *Together in Mission and Ministry* (London: Church House, 1993).

23 Risto Saarinen, *Gottes Wirken auf uns: Die transzendentale Deutung des Gegenwart-Christi-Motivs in der Lutherforschung* (VIEG, 137; Wiesbaden: Frans Steiner, 1989). With regard to the present article, this book can be read so that the 'transcendental' interpretation of German Protestants was an attempt to cope with the 'being in Christ' language while preserving the almost non-sacramental, forensic view of justification. I disagree with this interpretation as such, but already its elaborated appearance shows that the importance of 'being in Christ' language for Luther was already, for a long time, observed by Luther scholars.

Renaissance, for instance Karl Holl, Erich Vogelsang, Reinhold Seeberg and Erich Seeberg. Also dialectic theologians like Karl Barth and Ernst Wolf wrestled with the fact that Luther so often speaks of the presence of Christ in faith. A variety of different interpretations emerged in order to show that this seemingly mystical and ontological language in Luther was in fact meant to be eschatological, moral/forensic or existential. Later scholars like Gerhard Ebeling, Marc Lienhardt, Albrecht Peters and Otto Hermann Pesch have built on this research trend.[24] Contemporary Lutheran dogmatics of Wolfhart Pannenberg and Robert Jenson interpret Luther's view of justification in more ontological terms as the 'presence of Christ in faith'.[25]

In the present paper I am not, however, concerned with these interpretations as such. What needs to be pointed out is only that the 'Pauline Luther' of the twentieth-century Luther scholars has been found to speak in the manner of Paul. Moreover, this observation has challenged a one-sided forensic interpretation of justification by faith. As a result of this history, the effective-sacramental description of justification as gift and as participation in Christ has been widely discussed in academic Luther research. Throughout the twentieth century, Luther research has emphasized that Luther characterizes salvation in terms of '*fides Christi*' or as 'presence of Christ in faith'.

This effective or 'union with Christ' view of justification has been outlined, defended and further developed by contemporary Finnish Luther research, begun by Tuomo Mannermaa's book *Der im Glauben gegenwärtige Christus* (1989).[26] This Finnish school has not followed exegetical developments, but it has proceeded from the Scandinavian variety of Lutheranism, emphasizing the sacramental dimension of Christian faith and lacking the various antagonisms with Catholicism, characteristic of German Protestant theology. Although the new Finnish school is critical of the theological underpinnings of older German research, it also continues that research tradition of the German Luther Renaissance which has given more weight to the Pauline idea of communion with Christ.

24 See e.g. the research history in Simo Peura, *Mehr als ein Mensch? Die Vergöttlichung als Thema der Theologie Martin Luthers von 1513 bis 1519* (VIEG, 152; Mainz: Philipp von Zabern, 1994).

25 Wolfhart Pannenberg, *Systematische Theologie*, vol. 3 (Göttingen: Vandenhoeck & Ruprecht, 1993), pp. 242–54; Robert Jenson, *Systematic Theology*, vol. 2 (Oxford: Oxford University Press, 1999), pp. 293–300. See also Jenson, 'Luther's contemporary theological significance', in Donald K. McKin (ed.), *The Cambridge Companion to Martin Luther* (Cambridge: Cambridge University Press, 2003), pp. 272–88.

26 AGTL, 8; Hannover: Lutherisches Verlagshaus, 1989. See also Carl Braaten and Robert Jenson (eds), *Union with Christ, The New Finnish Interpretation of Luther* (Grand Rapids: Eerdmans, 1998).

Thus, the last one hundred years of Luther scholarship display a clear parallel between the exegetical discovery of the 'participation in Christ' language in Paul and the historical rediscovery of '*fides Christi*' or 'presence of Christ in faith' paradigm in Luther. Because of this parallel it may further be said that Lutheran ecumenical theology has with good conscience adopted this broader understanding of justification and/or soteriology. I do not think that this needs to be debated much further since, in order to criticize successfully Lutheran ecumenism, one should also criticize the results of Luther studies and exegetical scholarship as well. In this sense the 'broader' understanding of justification, although perhaps not a very elegant construct within a strictly historical Pauline exegesis, serves well in ecumenism and systematic theology.

What remains a challenge for Lutheranism, however, are the issues which Stephen Westerholm has investigated in such great detail. These issues concern our permanent sinfulness and they can be expressed in terms of the three contradictions defined above: (1/i) whether Paul's proclamation of the insufficiency of the law is particularly meant to be a radical alternative to Jewish self-righteousness; (2/ii) whether Christians remain permanently unable to fulfil the law; and (3/iii) whether the 'I' of Romans 7 expresses both Paul's own permanent struggle and a universal problem of non-Christians and Christians alike. A positive answer to all these questions would imply that Luther does not embrace the new perspective with respect to the theology of law and sinfulness. But a negative answer to any of these questions would at least mean that Luther is more complicated on these issues than the exegetes have assumed him to be. It may also mean that subsequent Lutherans have misread Luther to an extent.

3. *The Pauline Luther: Counter-evidence to Westerholm's Luther*

Stephen Westerholm provides a concise summary of his understanding of Luther. This summary represents the exegetes' theological assumptions in an exemplary manner. The summary consists of six theses:

1. In our relationship with God, faith in God's goodness rather than the good works we do is decisive.
2. The law, like a mighty hammer, is meant to crush human self-righteousness and to drive human beings, made aware of their sinfulness, to seek mercy from the Saviour.
3. We are justified by faith in Jesus Christ, not by the works we do.
4. Though believers are righteous in God's eyes, they remain sinners throughout their earthly lives.
5. The law must be banished from the thinking of believers when their relationship with God is the issue. Yet it must continue its role of identifying and judging their sin.

6.   God predestined believers to salvation.[27]

We will keep this summary in mind when we proceed to the three alleged contradictions between Luther and contemporary exegetes. I am not attempting to make a new study of Luther, but will only briefly present results of some new studies and complement them with a few quotes from the German reformer. My argument will be that, in many respects, Luther is closer to the 'new perspective' than has been assumed.

3.1. *How Radically Different is the Christian Alternative to the Mosaic Law?*

Our first contradiction (1/i) is closely related to the fifth thesis of Westerholm. Since the role of the law is a vast topic both in Luther's own writings and in the secondary literature,[28] I will restrict my discussion on some general features which I consider to be representative, though not sufficient to outline Luther's whole theology of the law. Since I will focus on the law, I will not speak much of the Christian's 'being in Christ'. It should be kept in mind, however, that I presuppose the importance of this language for Luther's theology of justification and the law.

Although Luther emphasizes the freedom of the Christian, he remains critical of the so-called antinomism. While the Antinomians downplay the significance of the Decalogue for Christians, Luther stresses in contradiction to this that 'the law will not be abolished in all eternity; rather, it will remain – with the condemned as one to be fulfilled, with the blessed as fulfilled one'.[29] Luther also keeps the Ten Commandments as the starting-point of his Catechisms. In his *Von den Konziliis und Kirchen* Luther says that moral quality is an 'external', that is, uncertain, mark of the church, and a total lack of moral quality and good works clearly signals that

27   Westerholm, *Perspectives*, pp. 22–23. This view becomes somewhat more moderated and qualified in Westerholm's subsequent discussion. It should not be understood as a professional scholarly position, but rather as a report of the view common among exegetes.

28   For older studies, see Bernhard Lohse, *Luthers Theologie in ihrer historischen Entwicklung und ihrem systematischen Zusammenhang* (Göttingen: Vandenhoeck & Ruprecht, 1996), pp. 283–93. New important books are: Andreas Wöhle, *Luthers Freude an Gottes Gesetz: Eine historische Quellenstudie zur Oszillation des Gesetzesbegriffes Martin Luthers im Licht seiner alttestamentlichen Predigten* (Frankfurt: Haag & Herchen, 1998); Antti Raunio, *Summe des christlichen Lebens: Die 'Goldene Regel' als Gesetz der Liebe in der Theologie Martin Luthers von 1510 bis 1527* (VIEG, 160; Mainz: Philipp von Zabern, 2001); John Witte, *Law and Protestantism: The Legal Teachings of the Lutheran Reformation* (Cambridge: Cambridge University Press, 2002). My interpretation to a great extent follows Wöhle and Raunio.

29   *WA* 39/1, 350, 3–4. For this quote and the Antinomian controversy, see most recently Reinhard Hütter, *Bound to Be Free: Evangelical Catholic Engagements in Ecclesiology, Ethics and Ecumenism* (Grand Rapids: Eerdmans, 2004), pp. 136–40. We may note that Westerholm (*Perspectives*, pp. 92–93) clearly sees the presence of this feature in 'Lutheran' Paulinists also.

something is lacking.[30] Even though the church cannot be defined in terms of morals, Luther thus does not consider moral quality to be indifferent in the church.

In Luther's extensive collection of sermons on Matthew 5–7 (1530–32), the Sermon on the Mount is normally treated as an ethic of Christian individuals.[31] Luther thinks that Jesus here clarifies and purifies the original will of God. However, the same will is basically expressed in the Decalogue.[32] The ethics of Jesus are thus neither an abrogation of the Jewish law nor a higher and different ethic. It is rather a cleansing of the Decalogue, a law to be followed in the Christian community.[33] Recent studies have emphasized the unity of the law in Luther's theology,[34] and I think that this unity is also maintained in Luther's interpretation of Matthew 5–7 as an ethic for Christians. Although the law does not justify, it thus remains relevant for the believers in their relationship with God.

Luther's exposition of Matthew 5–7 has often been viewed critically since the reformer writes against enthusiasts who want to rule the world with the Sermon on the Mount. The doctrine of two kingdoms means for Luther that the world must be ruled according to the civil use of the law, whereas the Sermon on the Mount is meant for individual Christians in order to describe the fruits of their faith.[35] Thus, although Matthew 5–7 is not a higher ethic of perfection, neither is it a civil law. Interestingly, the Sermon on the Mount remains a Christian ethic.

Although one may criticize Luther for making Matthew 5–7 a merely interior and individualistic law, one is, for the same reason, also compelled to say that the Sermon on the Mount remains a description of the Christian individual's moral practice. As a Christian practice it cannot be 'banished from the thoughts'[36] when the believer's relationship to God is at stake. On the contrary, the point of Christian ethics is found in the interior sense attached to moral action rather than in the external action. And this inner sense is related to the believer's relationship to God.[37]

---

30 *WA* 50, 649.

31 See e.g. H.G. Geyer, 'Luthers Auslegung der Bergpredigt', in Geyer (ed.), *Wenn nicht jetzt, wann dann?* (Festschrift H.J. Kraus; Neukirchen-Vluyn: Neukirchner Verlag, 1984), pp. 283–93.

32 See e.g. *WA* 32, 299, 15–19.

33 Luther says often that Jesus in Matthew 5–7 cleanses the Decalogue, or the original will of God, from later confusing interpretations, e.g. *WA* 32, 362, 30–363, 25.

34 See in particular Antti Raunio, 'Natural law and faith: the forgotten foundations of ethics in Luther's theology', in Braaten and Jenson (eds), *Union with Christ*, pp. 96–124.

35 E.g. *WA* 32, 318, 30–35; 370, 28–371, 25.

36 Cf. Westerholm's (*Perspectives*, pp. 22–23) thesis 5 above.

37 See e.g. Luther's explanation of 'clean heart' (Mt. 5.8), *WA* 32, 325, 33–366, 8, and also *WA* 50, 643, 27–31. Of course, this evokes many additional questions pertaining to the ethical theory at hand. Cf. e.g. Oswald Bayer, *Martin Luther's Theologie: Eine Vergegenwärtigung* (Tübingen: Mohr Siebeck, 2003), e.g. pp. 110–39, 256–96 and Risto

Given this, one may ask whether Luther's view in fact comes closer to the 'new perspective' of Pauline exegesis, according to which the apostle observes a work ethic while believing that salvation is by grace.

Although these observations show that Luther was not indifferent to Christian behaviour, Lutheran theology has often left a gap between faith and works, or between law and grace. Many new studies proceed, however, from a more integrative vision. Antti Raunio outlines Luther's view of Christian neighbourly love, expressed by the so-called Golden Rule (Mt. 7.12) as an antagonistic alternative to the medieval view of 'order of love' *(ordo caritatis)*. While the medieval view presupposes a human being who evaluates the objects of the universe and then loves them according to this evaluation, the Golden Rule actually tells us to give to others what they need. It is thus not a law of desire or evaluation, but a law of gift-love, a law of giving to others what they lack.[38]

For Luther, this Christian love emerges from the imitation of the love of God which 'does not find, but creates that which is pleasing to it'.[39] God is able to love even emptiness and the sinner – this is the capacity of *agape* to fulfil the imperfections and needs of the universe. When Christians try to live according to the Golden Rule, they should imitate this rule of divine love. Humans should meet their neighbour's needs, aiming to be Good Samaritans to them as Christ has been our Samaritan. This, however, would require an attitude which runs contrary to natural, egoistic and desire-based human reasoning.[40]

Raunio points out that Luther outlines a true Christian practice of a Christian community.[41] The rule of divine love is not a new law which would be at variance with the Mosaic law. But it is nevertheless something that is not instinctively found in the natural intuitions of all humans. A truly Christian neighbourly love, though in consonance with the Decalogue and perhaps even with the natural moral law, requires a

---

Saarinen, 'Ethics in Luther's theology', in Jill Kraye and Risto Saarinen (eds), *Moral Philosophy on the Threshold of Modernity* (The New Synthese Historical Library, Text and Studies in the History of Philosophy, 57; Dordrecht: Kluwer Academic, 2005), pp. 195–215. As Geyer, 'Bergpredigt', p. 293, points out, the new ethics does not remain only interior.

38 See Raunio, *Summe*, and, for a brief summary in English, Veli-Matti Kärkkäinen, 'The Christian as Christ to the neighbour: on Luther's theology of love', *International Journal of Systematic Theology* 6 (2004), pp. 101–17. Even though Raunio and Kärkkäinen outline a heuristically fruitful interpretation, the dynamics of gift-love and need-love is extremely complicated both historically and systematically. For some other new interpretations, see e.g. Risto Saarinen, *God and the Gift: An Ecumenical Theology of Giving* (Collegeville: The Liturgical Press, 2005) and Jean-Luc Marion, *Le phénomène érotique* (Paris: Grasset, 2003).

39 So Luther's famous thesis 28 of the *Heidelberg Disputation* (1518), *WA* 1, 365, 2–3.
40 Cf. Raunio, *Summe* and Kärkkäinen, 'Love'.
41 For the communal and diaconal dimension of the church as communion, see e.g. Braaten and Jenson (eds), *Union with Christ*, pp. 116–20.

theological model, a rule of divine love to be imitated. In this sense the Christian following of the Golden Rule is a fruit of faith and presupposes grace. It would probably be misleading to call this behaviour a 'work ethic', but we see that the relationship with God also qualifies the observance of the law in a new way.

Following Raunio, Reinhard Hütter remarks that the law's content can be 'restored to its original intent as the genuine expression of God's will: the law of love'. This law, received in Christ, is welcomed with delight, and, as Luther tells us, 'whenever there is this delight, it does what God commands. Then the law does not cause a guilty conscience, but causes joy, because one has become another person already.'[42] Hütter's quote from Luther comes astonishingly close to the emphasis of the 'new perspective', claiming that the Pauline Christian can fulfil the law in Spirit, the person being already almost another person than the one described in Romans 7. The Christian alternative outlined here does not appear, however, as a radical alternative to Jewish law, but rather as its fulfilment or as its restoration to express the original will of God.

Many good Lutherans probably think that my presentation has twisted Luther's theology of the law. I have selected a number of features from the reformer that run contrary to the traditional picture, as summarized by Westerholm. The positive meanings ascribed to the Christian observance of the law do not mean that sinners could be justified by works of law; this is not meant by the advocates of the 'new perspective' either. Although I have not told the whole story of both law and gospel in Lutheranism, I think that the evidence presented here has some weight. As in Paul, we find evidence in Luther for both the 'old' and 'new' perspectives, with regard to the issue of law.

3.2. *Do Christians Remain Permanently Unable to Fulfil the Law?*

In all their ecumenical dialogues, Lutherans have stressed that a Christian is and remains a sinner even when he or she is justified. There can be little doubt that both Martin Luther and the later Lutherans have always emphasized the being of a Christian as 'righteous and sinner at the same time' (*simul iustus et peccator*) and that Lutherans have been the most ardent Christian combatants against self-righteousness.

But there must be a theological limit to this emphasis. If we go beyond this limit, we would simply claim that Christianity would do no good for you, since you will always remain the same sinner. Most likely Lutherans do not claim this, but sometimes other churches think that Lutherans are

---

42   Hütter, *Bound*, p. 11, quoting Luther, *WA* 16, 285, 9.

in danger of emptying the grace of God in their claim of the permanent sinfulness of all Christians.[43]

At least in systematic theology, one is therefore bound to admit that the Christian faith has some bearing upon Christians, even though all people remain sinners and cannot fulfil the law by their own powers. In Luther research, scholars traditionally discuss whether Luther allows for any progress (*profectio*) in Christian life and whether Luther teaches the so-called 'partial' meaning of *simul iustus et peccator*, according to which one would be 'to an extent' (*partim*) sinful and, to an extent, righteous.[44]

The new Finnish interpretation of Luther has argued that justification, as it becomes expressed in terms of participation with Christ, has an effective bearing upon the justified sinner. This interpretation, outlined in particular by Tuomo Mannermaa and Simo Peura, has met with criticism especially in Germany. But even positions critical of this view have often affirmed that there must be an ontological side in the theological understanding of justification.[45] Moreover, the Finnish interpretation, although critical of many earlier paradigms, in fact continues the long trend which considers the 'being in Christ' language to be of special importance for Luther.[46]

Tuomo Mannermaa pays attention to Luther's *Commentary on Galatians* in which Christ is said to become the subject of the good works of the Christian. Through Christ present in the faith of the believer, the believer can become 'a new person' that brings forth good fruit. Faith thus first 'makes' the person, and this Christian person can do good works.[47] Although this event remains hidden and occurs under the cross, and although it is nevertheless Christ who remains the only meritorious subject in this process, one can understand how faith indeed has an effective bearing upon the person in question. Interestingly, Luther's view of bringing forth a new person, an allusion to Mt. 7.17, also here displays a parallel with the soteriology of the 'new perspective' in which the new person fulfills the law.

In spite of this parallel, there certainly remain differences between Luther and the new perspective. Whereas Paul as a Christian is assumed

43   One example would be the discussion on remaining concupiscence in the context of the Lutheran–Roman Catholic text *Joint Declaration on the Doctrine of Justification*. For a responsible theological assessment of this problem, see Theodor Schneider and Gunther Wenz (eds), *Gerecht und Sünder zugleich? Ökumenische Klärungen* (Freiburg: Herder, 2001).

44   For literature and different views, see Lohse, *Theologie*, pp. 274–82; Bayer, *Theologie*, pp. 193–230 and Braaten and Jenson (eds), *Union with Christ*.

45   See e.g. Reinhard Flogaus, *Theosis bei Palamas und Luther: Ein Beiträg zum Ökumenischen Gespräch* (FSÖT, 78; Göttingen: Vandenhoeck & Ruprecht 1997), p. 433, and Wilfried Härle, *Dogmatik* (de Gruyter Lehrbuch; Berlin: de Gruyter, 1995), p. 363, 397.

46   Saarinen, *Gottes Wirken* documents this trend in Germany.

47   Mannermaa, *Der im Glauben*, pp. 56–62.

by the exegetes to be able to fulfil the law in a quasi-Pelagian manner, Luther's reading of Galatians only affirms that a new tree can bring forth good fruits. The tree or the believer, however, is no autonomous subject but is empowered to do this because of the union with Christ. The good work remains an '*opus theologicum*', a theological action or deed, whose meritorious subject is Christ, not the Christian.[48] Luther wants to preserve the anti-Pelagian view of human powers, whereas the historical Paul, as interpreted by the new perspective, is probably not restricted by such considerations.

For our theological re-evaluation of Luther, however, it is important to see that Luther has a positive view of the fulfilment of the law by Christians in their union with Christ. The so-called 'third use of the law' as well as the sanctifying role of God's moral commands were much discussed by the older research.[49] I do not want to identify the bringing forth of good fruits with the third use of the law. Nor do I find the old distinction between law and 'command' (*Gebot*) very helpful. Recent studies, in particular Andreas Wöhle, have attempted to describe this feature in Luther in new and fresh ways. Reinhard Hütter speaks boldly of 'original unity of gospel and law'[50] which, for Luther, existed in paradise.

For many Lutherans, such a unity would be a confusion between law and gospel. I think that Antti Raunio's above-mentioned insistence on the unity of the law already establishes a permanent place for the law. I can side, however, with David Yeago's observation, according to which Luther in his interpretation of Genesis 2 recognizes a divine law that presupposes the presence of grace and not sin. This reveals, so Yeago and Hütter suggest, the original and fundamental significance of the law which is 'to give concrete, historical form to the "divine life" of the human creature deified by God'.[51]

In this sense there seems to be a 'fulfilment of the law' in committed Christian life as well. It is not a traditional 'third use',[52] since the uses of the law presuppose a human subject. In this theological deed or action,

48 Cf. Reijo Työrinoja, 'Opus theologicum: Luther and medieval theories of action', *NZST* 44 (2002), pp. 119–53. *WA* 40/1, 417, 23–26. As Työrinoja points out, the Christian might nevertheless keep his or her 'subjecthood' in some other sense.

49 See Lohse, *Theologie*, pp. 293–94.

50 Hütter, *Bound*, p. 140; Wöhle, *Freude*.

51 Hütter, *Bound*, p. 140, quoting David Yeago, 'Martin Luther on grace, law, and moral life', *The Thomist* 62 (1998), pp. 163–91 (177).

52 Lutheran theology traditionally distinguishes among three 'uses': 1. through the law external discipline may be maintained; 2. the law leads people to a recognition of their sins; and 3. the law conducts the entire life of the reborn Christians (R. Kolb and T. Wengert [eds], *The Book of Concord, The Confessions of the Evangelical Lutheran Church* [Minneapolis: Fortress, 2000], p. 502). Through the history of Lutheranism, the adequacy of the 'third use' has been controversial, since Christians are in some Pauline sense no more 'under the law'.

Christ present in the faith, or the grace of God present in Adam, makes the believer a new person who 'brings forth' good works. In this 'bringing forth' the fundamental subject remains hidden, since we are dealing with a theological action that takes place in union with Christ. But we may, I think, nevertheless say that the goodness of the good work is related to the same moral standard, the law or the original will of God, which accuses humans of their sin and which is preached in the Sermon on the Mount. In this sense there is a unity of the law and a fulfilment of the one law, the moral standard of both Old and New Covenant.

Given this, we may say that the point of Lutheran axioms like 'theology of the cross' and 'righteous and sinner at the same time' is not to say that Christianity and faith would have no bearing upon human existence. Rather, these axioms emphasize that all renewal and all emerging righteousness remain hidden 'under the opposite': under weakness, suffering and imperfection. As far as the fulfilment of the law is concerned, the axioms are not meant to deny morality, but they are critical of the human ability for judging the progress of others and even of oneself. Therefore, even though points 2 and 4 of Westerholm's summary are as such true, they do not sketch out the full picture of Luther's theology of law and good works. This observation may also have some bearing on theses 1 and 6.

Luther can employ the term 'law' in this positive sense, as 'love of law' (*dilectio legis*) in his exposition of many Old Testament texts.[53] Also Luther's exposition of the Sermon on the Mount contains an interesting excursus dealing with the issue of 'doing good' as criterion for entering into the Kingdom and receiving the wages in heaven.[54] Luther emphasizes that as Christians we are all equal. There are, however, external differences relating to the various gifts and callings of different Christians. Since the Sermon on the Mount speaks of the good works of those who are already forgiven and possess grace, one cannot say that the different fruits produced by different Christians would somehow merit this grace. All fruits, that is, good works, result from grace.[55]

The remuneration by the Father and other such promises, so often repeated in Mt. 5–7, are meant to console Christians in their daily struggle for the good. With the help of such promises you may carry on in spite of all adversities and injustices.[56] But although we speak of wages, finally God gives everything and in Christ we are all equally participants of grace. It is the case, however, that some work more and some suffer more than others. They may need more consolation and remuneration.

---

53 See Wöhle, *Freude* and Hütter, *Bound*, p. 269.
54 *WA* 32, 535, 29–544, 7.
55 *WA* 32, 541, 14–25.
56 *WA* 32, 542, 22; 543, 3.

Interestingly, Luther admits that among Christians there are differences in their talents and in their industriousness. He says that this may result in differences in their future 'luminosity' or 'brightness' (*Klarheit, Herrlichkeit*). This does not pertain to the fundamental equality or to the merits of obtaining grace. And in heaven everyone rejoices at the brightness and glory of others.[57]

Without stretching too much the interpretation of this passage we may say that Luther here struggles with the relative activity of different Christians in bringing forth the fruits of faith. He is very clear in his insistence on the fundamental equality of all humans and in the axiom that we cannot earn grace. At the same time he does not want to downplay the moral commitment of doing good, expressed so emphatically in the Sermon on the Mount. We must bear in mind that Matthew 5–7 is, for Luther, concerned with the life of the justified Christian who is already 'another person' in his or her unity with Christ. Therefore, doing good in this context does not mean earning grace, but it relates to the bringing forth of good fruit. These fruits are concerned with the observance of the law, but their motivational background is not the so-called 'third use of the law'. They are fruits which arise from different callings and talents, whereby referring to them serves the purpose of consolation, and the resulting differences in 'brightness' do not alter the fundamental equality of all in Christ. Thus we find in this text a similar view of 'divine life' and 'delight of law' as in the above-mentioned expositions of the Old Testament.

3.3. *Who Is Speaking in Romans 7? And What Does the Speaker Not Do?*
Even in Luther's exposition of Romans 7 we may observe a curious pattern which offers counter-evidence to Westerholm's portrayal. First we must admit that the New Testament scholars are right in their basic point. It is evident that Luther, following Augustine, understands the 'I' to mean the apostle Paul as a spiritual person. This is emphatically stated in *Lecture on Romans* (1515/16) when Rom. 7.7 is exposed.[58] We may note in passing that Luther repeatedly mentions the other alternative, the 'I' as a carnal person. But, when the 'I' in Rom. 7.14 claims to be carnal, Luther remarks that this claim only proves his point. For a spiritually wise man knows his own flesh and despises it, whereas a foolish carnal person would boast of his spirituality.[59] We may note that these two alternatives correspond to models A and C in our section 1 above.

---

57   *WA* 32, 543, 30–544, 7.
58   *WA* 56, 339, 4–8: 'Quod Apostolus ab hoc textu usque ad finem loquatur in persona sua et spiritualis hominis et nequaquam in persona tantum Carnalis, primum b. Augustinus locupletissime et constanter asserit in libro contra Pelagianos.'
59   *WA* 56, 340, 24–29.

In Rom. 7.17 the 'I' claims that it is not himself, but the 'sin in me' that is operative in the person. Luther says that many, offended by this verse, interpret it to mean that the 'I' must be the carnal person, since if the speaker were spiritual, he would have no sin. But this opinion of some real or imagined contemporaries of Luther[60] is false and harmful. In reality, the verse proves that even the spiritual person remains sinful.[61] In terms of our earlier discussion, alternatives B and C are thus ruled out.

This does not mean for Luther, however, that the speaker in question would perform a morally bad action. How come? Given that Romans 7 has been understood as a prooftext of permanent sinfulness, this is a surprising turn, a turn which has been neglected in the allegedly 'Lutheran' reception history of this text. Luther admits that a human reader of Romans 7 is inclined to draw the conclusion that Paul simply commits a 'morally and metaphysically' bad action. But this is not the case. As a holy and spiritual person the apostle Paul would like to perform a good action in a totally pure and free fashion, but because of the flesh he cannot perform it in this perfect way, but rather he does good only with some repugnance and aversion.[62] After saying this, Luther starts to build a massive qualification around what we called, above, alternative A.

The sin of the apostle consists of the inner aversion. Expressions like 'to will something other than what one does' in Romans 7 mean that the apostle as a spiritual person wills to perform his action with such perfection that no aversion remains in the subject. Because of the flesh, this does not happen. But the good action is performed with some remaining carnal repugnance. Therefore the apostle does not do what he wants to do, but he does what he does not want.[63] In other words, doing

---

60   For useful background information, see Leif Grane, *Modus loquendi theologicus: Luthers Kampf um die Erneuerung der Theologie 1515–1518* (Acta Theologica Danica, 12; Leiden: Brill, 1975), pp. 94–100. Although I agree with Grane in most of what he says (e.g. that Luther in fact deviates here from Augustine), the patristic and scholastic interpretation history remains more complex than Grane assumes. There may have been various 'new perspectives' around.

61   *WA* 56, 349, 22–350, 8.

62   *WA* 56, 341, 27–33: 'Non est putandum, Quod Apostolus velit intelligi se malum, quod odit, facere et bonum, quod vult, non facere, ut moraliter et methaphysice, quasi nullum bonum, Sed omne malum faciat; sic enim humano sensui verba eius sonant. Sed vult, quod non tot et tantum bonum nec tanta facillitate faciat, quantum et quanta vult. Vult enim purissime, liberrissime et laetissime, sine molestiis repugnantis carnis agere, quod non potest . . .'. For the interpretation of 'moraliter et metaphysice', see Grane, *Modus*, p. 95.

63   *WA* 56, 342, 13–19: 'Quia "vult aliud quam facit", hoc est, habet beneplacitum et voluntatem per spiritum diffusa charitate promptam ad bonum et odium ad malum, et tamen resistente carne et adversa concupiscentia non potest hanc voluntatem implere et perficere. Si enim perficeret et impleret, sine resistentia bonum operaretur et delectabiliter; hoc enim vult voluntas eius. Nunc autem non ita operatur; ideo quod vult, non facit, Sed quod non vult, facit.'

the external good with an intensity of, say, 80 per cent, would still be an instance of '*non enim quod volo hoc ago*' (not doing what I want to do, Rom. 7.15), because the speaker wants to do good with an intensity of 100 per cent, willing totally and without repugnance. And the remaining 20 per cent, although a merely latent inner counter-movement, is counted as sin and is enough to qualify the externally good action as '*quod nolo illud facio*' (doing what I do not want to do, Rom. 7.16), and in this sense as sin.

This sounds like sophistry and it is evident that through this interpretation Luther wants to rescue Paul from saying that the apostle sins morally in his external action. But it is remarkable for our study that Luther in fact thinks, actually in keeping with his famous *simul iustus et peccator*, that the Apostle Paul in Romans 7 does pursue the good, although externally and with some inner aversion. The sin does not consist in a bad action, but in the fact that while he wills perfectly, he can actualize this will in his deed only imperfectly and in this qualified sense fails to do what he wants to do. Using scholastic terminology, Paul in Luther's interpretation does not display moral weakness (*akrasia, incontinentia*), but continence (*enkrateia, continentia*). In fact, Luther here continues the extensive medieval discussion on the so-called '*appetitus contrarii*'.[64]

The same argument appears in a condensed fashion in two later writings, namely in Luther's *Resolutiones* written after the Leipzig disputation of 1519, and in the preparatory part of the *Heidelberg Disputation* of 1518. In Leipzig, Luther defended the view that nobody does good without sinning. In *Resolutiones*, this view is explained with the help of Romans 7. A hasty reader of this condensed text may wonder how on earth Paul's argument could be employed for such a purpose. But, if the text is read together with Luther's *Lecture on Romans*, the point becomes clear: even the most holy apostle must admit that all his actions are contaminated by the repugnant flesh and therefore he fails to achieve the perfect and 'full' implementation of the law which he wants to achieve. Therefore, nobody does good without sinning.[65]

---

64 For this terminology, see more extensively Risto Saarinen, *Weakness of the Will in Medieval Thought: From Augustine to Buridan* (STGMA, 44; Leiden: Brill, 1994) and especially Theodor Dieter, *Der junge Luther und Aristotele: Eine historisch-systematische Untersuchung zum Verhältnis von Theologie und Philosophie* (Theologische Bibliothek Töpelmann, 105; Berlin: de Gruyter, 2001), pp. 130–36.

65 The decisive text is *WA* 2, 412, 13–20: 'Primum hic idem unus homo Paulus, sanctus Apostolus, plenus gratia, simul delectatur in lege dei, simul repugnat legi dei, simul vult bonum secundum spiritum, non tamen agit propter carnem, sed contrarium: ergo peccat, dum bene facit. Nam repugnare legi dei, quis aliud quam peccare audeat intelligere? Non agere bonum, nonne contra legem dei est? At dum ergo nunquam sit sine repugnantis, nunquam sine vitio bene facit, nunquam ergo plene implet legem dei.'

In preparing the *Heidelberg Disputation*, Luther claims that the righteous person sins even 'between' his good works. This is proved with the help of Rom. 7.19 and 7.22. During all our life, Luther says, the good will and the resisting bad will struggle with one another. There is never a 'total' or whole will, but all will remains 'mixed' in this way.[66] For this reason there is always some sin present even in and between our good works. When Luther here claims that a person 'wills the good according to the Spirit, but does not do it, but does the contrary', he does not mean that the person would externally follow the worse option. The 'contrary' mentioned here is 'some nill' (*quaedam noluntas*), which contaminates the good action so that it is not totally without sin.[67]

One should be careful not to read Luther so that the subject of Romans 7 would choose the wrong external option. The whole point of the two disputation texts is to claim that all, even the best, human actions remain sinful because the human being remains carnal. They are not claiming that the apostle Paul does not externally do what he wants to do. When the two texts are read together with the *Lecture on Romans*, the meaning becomes clear and supports Luther's point: even while doing good a Christian always sins. In fact, this is the well-known core of Luther's radicalization of *simul iustus et peccator*: the sin need not be manifest or external in order to be called sin. Already the repugnancy and the bad internal desire in itself is sinful.

This horizon is further presupposed in Luther's most exhaustive and most influential reading of Rom. 7.14–8.1 in his *Against Latomus* (1521). I will not go into the details of this very long interpretation[68] but mention only that Luther here defends the view that the imperfections of the justified Christian must be called 'sin'. In Romans 7, the Christian apostle Paul wills the good and consents to the good, but because of his twofold, that is, carnal and spiritual, existence neither the good nor the bad will is whole. In this sense, the external deed remains 'contrary' to the perfect good, willed by the good will.[69] This does not mean, however, that the

---

66 *WA* 1, 367, 2, 15–27 (see also next note). For 'voluntas tota' and 'mixta' in medieval tradition, cf. Saarinen, *Weakness*, pp. 20–86 and Andrea Robiglio, *L'impossibile volere: Tommaso d'Aquino, i tomisti e la volontà* (Milano: Vita e pensiero, 2002).

67 *WA* 1, 367, 18–21, 24–27: 'Simul vult bonum secundum spiritum, et tamen hoc non agit, sed contrarium. Hoc itaque contrarium quaedam est noluntas, quae semper est, quando est voluntas. Per hanc bene facit et per illam male facit. Nolle est ex carne et velle ex spiritu. ... Mixta enim sunt haec duo in omni vita et opere nostro. ... Ideo semper peccamus, dum benefacimus, licet quandoque minus, quandoque magis.'

68 See *WA* 8, 99–126. Luther's own detailed reading is given in 120, 31–125, 31, but it is useful to pay attention to the whole context of this reading.

69 *WA* 8, 120, 33–36: 'Mira compositio [Rom. 7.16]: consentit legi bonae, sed non totus, quia facit non totus, quod vult non totus, neque consentiens, neque faciens, neque nolens hic totus est, sed idem qui consentit bonae legi, facit quod non vult, id est, contrarium legi bonae, quam vult.'

flesh would overcome in action. The spirit dominates the action, but so that the flesh remains averted and repugnant and thus there is sin.[70] Therefore, both the pious and the impious remain sinful in their thought in a similar way; Luther even says that the sinful attack is greater for the pious. But since the pious have the 'antidote' given by their being in grace and in Christ, they do not commit sin in the same manner as the impious.[71]

Leaving aside many other aspects pertaining to this interpretation of Romans 7, we can say that Luther, on the one hand, expresses the view of the 'Lutheran' Paul: Romans 7 speaks of Paul as an exemplary Christian. He exemplifies the continuing struggle with sin, thus being a paradigm of Christian as *simul iustus et peccator*. On the other hand, however, this does not entail the view that a Christian is characterized by weak will and permanent failure to do good. On the contrary, Paul as subject of Romans 7 is characterized by a strong will and by an external ability to do good. He misses the mark only in the sense that he wants to be perfect and, being carnal, cannot reach absolute perfection. Thus our alternative A becomes so strongly qualified that it begins to resemble the 'new perspective' offered by B. Both in Luther and in B the Christian is said to fulfil the law. In both, this takes place in the Spirit.

Although Luther's exposition of Romans 7 remains at variance with the 'new perspective' insofar as it presupposes that the speaker is Paul the apostle, we may thus identify interesting and even surprising parallels with the new perspective. Both positions presuppose a work ethic in which the Christian can fulfil the law to a significant extent. Of course grace and forgiveness remain necessary, since there always remains some sin. The fact that the holy apostle Paul remains carnal and sinful does not entail that he would not lead a moral life. He is in Christ and thus he can to a great extent bring forth the fruits of Christian existence. Luther's point is only that the apostle nevertheless continues to participate in the carnal existence which is characterized by aversion and some non-will which qualify as sin. Thus the two different exegetical strategies lead to surprisingly similar conclusions, namely that the apostle in his union with Christ, in his life in the Spirit, as a spiritual person, can cope with the same law, the will of God, in a new and successful manner.

70   *WA* 8, 122, 11–12, 17–18: 'Alterum enim hic dicit per alterum impediri, sic tamen, ut spiritus praevaleat et illi tribuatur, quod non operetur, non velit malum. ... Nunc cum spiritus queruletur et accuset carnem, patet, quod non caro dominetur, sed dominanti spiritui molesta et rebellis sit.'

71   *WA* 8, 123, 9–12.

4. *Conclusion*

Our study has yielded the following picture: New Testament scholars claim that, because of the Lutheran axiom 'righteous and sinner at the same time', they have been misguided in their reading of Paul for centuries. Only recently have they liberated their understanding from this axiom. Therefore they can now see that, after his conversion, Paul thinks that he can fulfil the law in the Spirit and in Christ. The exemplary 'I' of Romans 7 refers to the pre-Christian existence, as it is described from a specific Christian viewpoint. This new result is an essential element of the so-called 'new perspective', achieved in the study of Paul during the last twenty-five years.

In our reading of Luther we have observed, however, that Luther also sometimes adopts a positive view of the law in the life of Christians. He thinks that the justified person in his or her union with Christ can perform 'theological actions' in which good results are brought forth spontaneously, as a good tree produces good fruit. In this theological action the person has been renewed. Through Christ present in the faith, the Christian is in the process of becoming 'another person'. The new person fulfils the moral law, although he is not 'using' the law as an instrument of his own sanctification. Christ remains the only meritorious subject of the theological actions of the new person. Nevertheless the Christian individual now displays moral practices which are consonant with the idea of fulfilling the law.

Luther adheres to the basic unity of the law. Although Jesus purifies and clarifies the law, he teaches the same morals as the Old Testament, namely the original will of God concerning good and bad. In bringing forth good fruits the Christian is fulfilling the one moral law, although in a theological manner, that is, in the Spirit and in union with Christ.

Luther's interpretation of Romans 7 between 1515 and 1521 does not entail the view that the apostle Paul, or the paradigmatic Christian, would remain unable to produce good actions. The axiom 'righteous and sinner at the same time' only means that good actions are brought forth in an imperfect manner and that the sin continues in this sense. Romans 7 is thus not a description of a weak-willed (akratic) Christian, but is a description of a continent or strong-willed (enkratic) Christian. Although the internal will of the Christian may be perfectly good, the resulting actions remain, at least theologically speaking, less than perfect. So, the Christian in Romans 7 does not simply fail to do good, but in 'doing what he does not want to do' he fails to be perfect and fails to become totally free of the sin brought about by carnal existence. In that sense he sins even while doing good. On the other hand, he in fact does do good.

All this brings Luther's theology significantly closer to the 'new perspective' than many exegetes and Luther interpreters have assumed. Of course this need not mean anything with regard to the historical study of Paul. Heuristic categories like 'Lutheran Paul' and 'new perspective' continue to possess their heuristic value irrespective of their historical accuracy. Given our results, however, we ought to ask at least who actually initiated the so-called 'Lutheran' reading of Romans 7. This question is left unanswered in the present study. My aim has been to show that, after the liberation of New Testament studies from Lutheranism, we may with some good reason initiate a counter-movement in which Lutheran theology aims at re-engaging the study of Paul. My proposal is that this re-engagement should not primarily consist of a criticism of the 'new perspective'. It may be more fruitful to show that Martin Luther's theology is closer to the insights of the new perspective than has been previously assumed.

PART III

Chapter 6

'CHRIST IS WEAK IN PAUL': THE OPPOSITION TO PAUL IN CORINTH

Lars Aejmelaeus

The Task

Nobody denies the importance of the Second Epistle to the Corinthians among Paul's letters. We would know much less about his life and have a much more one-sided picture of him if this document were lacking. Where do we find the most central thoughts in this letter? Many would have difficulties in choosing, but Erich Grässer in his commentary seems to be very sure of the answer to this question: '13,1-4 ist ein Abschnitt, den wegen der beiden Schlussverse (v. 3f.) kein anderer Text im 2 Kor an Wichtigkeit übertrifft'.[1] In his opinion verses 13.3-4 are 'the hermeneutic key' for the chapters 2 Cor. 10–13.[2] The two verses are not easy to translate. The translation of C.K. Barrett gives, however, a good starting-point: 'since you seek proof that it is Christ who speaks in me, Christ who is not weak towards you, but mighty in your midst. For indeed he was crucified because of his weakness, but he lives because of God's power. For indeed we are weak in him, but we shall live with him because of God's power and that in relation to you.'[3]

Although I do not fully agree with Erich Grässer in his interpretation of the verses and in his evaluation of precisely these verses as the most important verses in 2 Cor. compared with some others, I do think that they are most relevant and worthy of detailed examination. An essential part of the Pauline theology is concentrated in them, and not without a strange accent for us who still admire Paul after two thousand years. The verses grant us a good insight into Paul's way of argumentation. Through these two verses we also get a glimpse of Paul's dark ironic humour.

---

1 Erich Grässer, *Der zweite Brief an die Korinther: Kapitel 8,1–13,13* (ÖTK, 8/2; Gütersloh: Gütersloher Verlagshaus, 2005), p. 253.

2 *Ibid.*, p. 245. Concerning the verses that belong to 2 Cor., only the numbers of the verses without other abbreviations are used in this article.

3 C.K. Barrett, *The Second Epistle to the Corinthians* (BNTC; London: Black, 1973), p. 327. In other translations of the text of 2 Cor., I also use Barrett's translations.

The two verses are not isolated from their context. On the contrary, the reader is not able to understand them if she or he is not well informed about the purpose and content of the chapters 2 Cor. 10–13. Therefore we must begin with a short résumé of the background and purpose of these four chapters.

The Background and Context of the Verses 2 Cor. 13.3-4

Paul's purpose when he was writing the chapters 2 Cor. 10–13, or his 'Letter of Tears' (2.4), was clear: he wanted to bring the Corinthians back to a relationship of obedience. Paul's picture of the situation that he drew during his short visit from Ephesus to Corinth was that the congregation had been incited to rebellion against him by some new apostles from outside. They had come to the city after Paul's first visit and after the sending of his First Letter to the Corinthians. These new teachers criticized Paul as a weak apostle of Christ and they had been successful among the members of the congregation. After the unlucky short visit there Paul felt the situation to be very threatening. With the 'Letter of Tears' (2 Cor. 10–13), written in Ephesus and sent to Corinth with Titus, Paul tried to achieve what was yet possible. He could not be sure that the letter was enough and wanted to come himself to the city to face his opponents anew and settle the matter a short time after the letter.[4]

There is much material in the 'Letter of Tears' where Paul wants to correct the criticism of him in Corinth. In 10.10 he gives a direct quotation from the lips of his adversaries: 'For "his letters", he says, "are weighty and powerful, but his bodily presence is weak and his speech excites contempt".' When returning a little later to this criticism Paul writes: 'I may be unskilled in speech, but I am not unskilled in knowledge' (11.6). He has, in other words, other merits that compensate for the deficiencies in his rhetoric.

From these statements it would be easy to conclude that the quarrel in Corinth dealt with just the rhetorical skills of Paul and of the other apostles. It is well known that in antiquity being skilled in rhetoric was synonymous with being well educated and civilized. Yet it was a difference between rhetoric and rhetoric. Not everything that glitters is gold. In his letter, Paul makes a distinction between two things in a speech, between its content and its external form. Looking at the content, there is no deficiency

---

4 This reconstruction of the situation arises from the Pauline text itself. For the argumentation and discussion with other solutions, see my books *Streit und Versöhnung: Das Problem der Zusammensetzung des 2. Korintherbriefes* (PFES, 46; Helsinki: Finnish Exegetical Society, 1987) and *Schwachheit als Waffe: Die Argumentation des Paulus im 'Tränenbrief' (2. Kor. 10–13)* (PFES, 78; Helsinki, Güttingen: Finnish Exegetical Society, Vanderhoeck & Ruprecht, 2000), pp. 19–36.

of knowledge in Paul's speech, only a certain clumsiness of the form. Understanding his words so, Paul actually performs a skilled rhetorical counterattack against his opponents who have been questioning his rhetorical skills. People in antiquity were certainly able to see a difference between a sophistic playing with and twisting of words and a simple and direct speaking of truth. The most famous example in this area was Socrates, well known by everyone. In Plato's dialogues Socrates often plays the role of a silly and unlearned person and in this way puts the slick and loquacious sophists where they belong, in the shame corner. In his defence, Paul tries in other words to give the impression that he in his rhetorical weakness represents the Socratic rhetorical heritage while the new apostles in Corinth are comparable with the sophists. Paul does not write this directly, which adds weight to the rhetorical effect of his utterance.[5]

Ever since people have been arguing with each other, they have used the method of rhetorical misrepresentation. The attacker is not criticizing the thoughts of his opponent as they really are. He first makes a misconstruction of them and then attacks the caricature of the thoughts of the other. It is naturally much easier to overthrow a caricature and make it into a laughing stock than to argue with and discuss seriously the real thoughts of the opponent. This method must also be taken into consideration when we look at the Pauline attacks against his opponents in Corinth. His intimation that they are nothing but smooth sophists does not mean that they really were religious impostors. On the other hand a caricature of this kind would have no effect at all if it did not have any point of contact with reality. In the direct quotation from the opposition in Corinth (10.10) the weakness of Paul was pointed out. Such a criticism is possible only in a context where there are some persons who are better speakers than Paul. If the new apostles were not sophistic impostors, they were in any case good speakers – better than Paul. Is it possible to give a more accurate picture of the situation? What did the opponents really mean in their criticism of Paul and on what grounds did they think their own way of speaking was better than that of Paul?

The context of the whole 'Letter of Tears' makes it clear that the question cannot have been only about the technical skill of rhetoric, and also not only about the knowledge which one had about important matters. It was a struggle within a religious community and about the authority in it. This means that the question was first of all about the spiritual authority. Who is nearer to God, who can better manifest God's reality in his person among the congregation and convey his message to the people? A religious authority can never be achieved only through rational and earthly means. In a battle within a non-rational religious community a charismatic person always wins over a person who is less

---

5   More about this theme in Aejmelaeus, *Schwachheit*, pp. 115–28.

charismatic according to the standards of the community – regardless of how learned and skilled in rhetoric the latter is. On the other side, the religious and the rhetorical authority often go together and are inseparable.

Paul calls the new apostles who have come to Corinth after his first visit there 'super-apostles' in an ironical way (11.5, 12.11). Their battle with Paul was primarily about spiritual authority, about the question of who was the best envoy of Christ, who best represented Christ and his reality. The theme of speaking was only part, even if an important part, of the quarrel. The new apostles and the congregation inspired by them had also criticized the whole persona of Paul. The impression given of the entire personality of Paul is 'humble' (10.1). Although the adjective 'humble' (ταπεινός) in the later Christian language has a positive meaning, at the time when Paul was writing his letter it had a very negative connotation to his readers. It meant above all 'plain', 'common', 'slavish'.[6] Paul is criticized that when present he goes humbly among the members of the Corinthian congregation, but when absent, through his letters, he is bold towards them (10.1, 10). We can conclude that in this context of a religious quarrel the humbleness of Paul meant absence of spiritual authority and strength in his whole being, not only in his speech.

Prior to the appearance of the new apostles Paul had not had such problems in Corinth. He had had so much spiritual strength and authority that he had been able to lay the foundations of a flourishing and energetic congregation. The strength of Christ had been working through him even though his spiritual strength had from the very beginning been rather paradoxical. The Corinthians had their difficulties in understanding the essence of the Pauline *theologia crucis*. Paul preached salvation, which came to mankind through the death of God's Son on the cross (1 Cor. 2.1-5). This message had its consequences which were seen in the preacher himself and which ought to be seen also in the believers.[7] Already at the beginning of the conversion of the Corinthians their religious conviction depended mostly on their spiritual experiences which they received when they listened to Paul's message. They did not understand deeply the Pauline *theologia crucis* (1 Cor. 2.6–3.2). In any case they had accepted Paul and his way of being an apostle of Christ. Still, when writing 1 Cor. Paul gives orders and reproaches the Corinthians as a man who feels himself to be in full control of the situation and who does not doubt being the authoritative father of the congregation (e.g., 1 Cor. 4.21; 11.1, 34; 14.37; 16.1). That Paul is suddenly seen as a 'humble' man means that the

---

6 *Ibid.*, pp. 52–56.

7 About this theme see the thorough study of C.W. Strüder, *Paulus und die Gesinnung Christi: Identität und Entscheidungsfindung aus der Mitte von 1Kor 1–4* (BETL, 190; Leuven: Peeters, 2005).

Corinthians had got new criteria for the genuine way of being an apostle. The new apostles, who in their way of acting, being and speaking were different from Paul, had brought about this change in their evaluation.

The difference between Paul and his adversaries is, however, relative in its nature. As a matter of fact, there might have been a difference only in degree. Paul, too, was a charismatic apostle with spiritual gifts. He himself made his appearance as such when he came into contact with Christians who laid stress on following the rules of the law. The clearest illustration of this is the verses Gal. 3.1-5. They end with the question: 'Does he who supplies the Spirit to you and works miracles among you do so by works of the law, or by hearing with faith?' The new teachers in Corinth are, from this point of view, nothing but extreme and one-sided followers of the Pauline doctrine. They have exaggerated the same traits of liberal spiritual ecstasy which also constituted a central area of the Pauline view of Christian faith and life. In the exaggeration, the opponents had, however, thrown out other essential points of the Pauline theology. Their overall understanding of the christology and the eschatology had become strange to Paul. Between the genuine teaching of Paul and the teaching of the new apostles there is, however, no such clear contrariness as between Paul and the Jewish Christian teachers in Galatia, who demanded that the pagan Christians should let themselves be circumcized. This explains the difference between the Pauline manner of argumentation in the two letters, Galatians and the 'Letter of Tears'. The nature of the dispute in Corinth grants Paul no opportunity to use biblical-theological arguments such as he uses in writing to the Galatians. These opponents are too close to him from the point of view of their relationship to the Old Testament. In other religious-ideological disputes as well, the most dangerous opponent is he or she who differs only a little from one's own teaching. When it is difficult to disprove the teaching of the opponent with calm and logical argumentation one needs so much more vehemence and rhetorical effect.

Paul became angry because of the criticism of his humbleness. He promises he will change his style when he visits the congregation the next time. But the Corinthians will hardly take real pleasure in the change. Paul writes (10.2): 'I ask you not to compel me when present to show that confident boldness which I think I shall dare to use against certain people who think of us as if we conducted ourselves according to the flesh.'

Somebody in Corinth had formulated their criticism of Paul with the words that he 'conducts himself according to the flesh (κατὰ σάρκα)'. The word 'flesh' in biblical terminology has special meanings. It hints at perishableness, separation from God, and often also at antagonism towards God. The antithesis of 'flesh' is 'spirit'. In the terminology of Paul 'conducting oneself according to the flesh' means the opposite of 'conducting oneself according to the Spirit', which is synonymous with the genuine Christian life (cf. Rom. 8.9, 12-14). In Paul's own terminology 'flesh' in such an expression would have had clear ethical connotations. In this context, however, Paul is citing the criticism of his opponents and using their terminology, so that ethical connotations hardly play any role in the meaning of the expression. They have only claimed that Paul is not truly spiritual.

This interpretation is strengthened by the way that Paul immediately in the following corrects the evaluation made of him (10.3): 'For though we conduct our life in the flesh we do not make war according to the flesh.' Paul makes an important distinction between the two kinds of relationship to the 'flesh', i.e., to this perishable world which is far from God even if created by Him. His opponents have very likely not reflected such a distinction in the same way. During his life on the earth Paul, as a human being, belongs in the sphere of 'flesh', which means that he is part of the mortal creation, but at the same time, as a member of the new Christian movement, he is totally directed towards God and His coming kingdom. He still lives 'in flesh' – that is something that is his and everyone's destiny, his opponents' as well, although they may imagine otherwise – but not 'according to the flesh', i.e., according to the inward values of the perishable and godless world. One cannot choose and change the limits in which everyone has to live, but one is able to choose according to which values one lives within these limits of human life. Paul thinks that it is necessary to explain such elementary concepts because very likely there has been confusion of this kind in the criticism of him. Already now Paul hints at themes that he deals with later in the letter: his weakness, which is caused by his 'being in the flesh', does not amount to spiritual weakness. In the quarrel the disputants discuss the question of what the correct spiritual strength and authority are and how they appear in the apostles of Christ.[8]

One cannot give proof of spiritual ability and achievements in the same way as one can from events in normal life. Such a list of merits is written in 12.12 when Paul refers to 'the signs of an apostle', which were performed by him among the Corinthians. Paul only mentions these signs and does not build his apology on their foundation. Appealing to 'signs and portents and mighty works' (12.12) would have put Paul too much on the same level as the 'super-apostles' and Paul wants to avoid this kind of setting by all means. He is not like his adversaries. Paul is not 'fleshly' but highly 'spiritual' and defeats his opponents overwhelmingly in this respect when his 'spirituality' is seen genuinely in the correct light.

Paul's attempt to make the difference between him and his opponents as clear as possible and to exhibit his own spiritual ability clashes with the difficulty one has when one wants to boast of things which are not, as a

8 Aejmelaeus, *Schwachheit*, pp. 59–63.

matter of fact, one's own, but gifts granted by God. Paul's solution to the problem is ingenious: he is not boasting of his abilities but of his weaknesses and deficiencies. He does it with ironical comparisons and side hints in the direction of his opponents. By this means he is able to make it very clear to the readers, who understand that he has very high spiritual talents and attainments.

Paul's christology is the key that unlocks his argumentation in the 'Letter of Tears'. The reader must agree with Paul in his christology of the cross. Already at the very beginning of his mission work in Corinth Paul had preached only that Christ whose death on the cross, i.e., his uttermost weakness and defeat, effected the salvation of mankind (1 Cor. 2.1-5). Christ brought salvation to mankind through 'taking the shape of a slave' (Phil. 2.7), through 'becoming poor though he was rich' (8.9), through 'becoming a curse on behalf of us' (Gal. 3.13). If it was so with Christ, the shape and destiny of his apostle cannot differ greatly. No one should look for much external brilliance and strength in the real apostle of Christ.

Because Paul is building his argumentation precisely on this picture of Christ and his apostle (cf., e.g., 11.22-30) we can conclude that there was a clear difference between him and the 'super-apostles' exactly in this attitude towards the apostleship. The natural religious instinct of men towards the Christ event emphasizes the victory of Christ, his resurrection, the strong experiences with the Spirit and the eschatological hope that will soon be reality and that in its own way is already effective among the believers. All these aspects belong in their way to the Christian life and Paul also refers to them often and positively in his letters. It is however a question of balance. In the 'Letter of Tears' Paul is emphasizing the other side of the Christian life which should not be forgotten either. It also remains always as reality in the life of a Christian during his lifetime in this world. A believer lives here still 'in the flesh', in the midst of perishableness and of all the restrictions and sufferings of his or her age. Although a believer has the Spirit as the earnest (ἀρραβών, 5.5) of the coming age, the fulfilment and its glory are waiting for him or her only in the future (Rom. 8.9-11). If one forgets this, the style of living of a Christian becomes skewed and his or her faith is altered into overly spiritual indulgence in fancies. Paul was seeing something like this in the attitudes of the 'super-apostles' and of the members of the Corinthian congregation who had embraced them. Therefore his own attitude is crystallized in this context with the words 'when I am weak, then am I strong' (12.10).

The Content of the Verses 2 Cor. 13.3-4

At the end of his letter Paul writes about his plans for the future. He expresses to the Corinthians a clear threat (13.2): 'if I come for another visit I shall not spare you'. The two verses that Erich Grässer regards as the most important in the letter serve as a clarification of the threat. As text this clarification is very compact and includes linguistic structures that are difficult to transfer to another language. Every translation is an interpretation of Paul's thoughts and the exegetes have given varying interpretations of Paul's message and intentions here. The way that the translator has understood the central thoughts of the text before these verses, the Pauline rhetoric in the preceding chapters, the way that he or she has answered the question of the order and composition of 2 Cor. in its historical setting, the way that he or she understands the nature of the opposition to Paul in Corinth and some other factors, all have their effect upon the way that an exegete interprets the linguistic details of 13.3-4.[9] In the following pages I try to explain the verses in accordance with my overall view of the situation in which Paul wrote the 'Letter of Tears'.

It is not enough for Paul that he only warns of his severe visit to Corinth in the near future. The threat 'if (i.e., when) I come I shall not spare you' is so difficult for all participants that it demands more information – statements of reason and explanations. For this reason Paul writes first the statement of reason: (I shall not spare you) 'since you seek proof that it is Christ who speaks in me'. The statement is full of Paul's black humour: 'You will get what you yourselves have asked for.' The Corinthians have criticized Paul by daring to be strong only through his letters and when absent, whereas 'his bodily presence is weak and his speech excites contempt' (10.10). When he comes to the congregation Paul promises to give a demonstration that he is able to be strong when present as well. This demonstration will not be such as the Corinthians expected though, and it will also not be pleasant for them.[10] His strength will appear through punishing procedures and not only through mighty

9   An analysis and discussion of various ways to interpret the verses is in Aejmelaeus, *Schwachheit*, pp. 353–78 .

10   Murray J. Harris, *The Second Epistle to the Corinthians: A Commentary on the Greek Text* (NIGTC; Grand Rapids: Eerdmans, 2006), pp. 911–12, writes about the expectations of the Corinthians: 'Their expectation, perhaps, was for additional miraculous signs (cf. 12.12) or specialized ecstatic experiences (cf. 12.6) or aggressive authoritarianism (cf. 11.20) or polished rhetoric (cf. 10.10).' Harris is interpreting in a more detailed way what the expression 'Christ speaks in Paul' includes; he is interpreting it, however, in a too abstract and theological way: 'The question at issue was ... whether he was, as he claimed to be (5.20), an ambassador who reliably represented the intent of Christ in his words and deeds, whether the message he had delivered to the Corinthians by word and deed accurately reflected the mind of Christ.'

spiritual speeches like the speeches the Corinthians had heard with pleasure from the 'super-apostles', the lack of which from Paul's side had led them to doubt his spirituality. Paul will give the awaited proof, but he will give it in his own way. The speech which will not spare the Corinthians will be a speech of judgement given with the full authority of Christ and it will also have real consequences. The 'proof' will be delivered in Paul's act of 'not to spare'.[11]

The reason for the severe visit of judgement in the near future is thus the desire of the Corinthians to see if Christ speaks in Paul. After citing this desire Paul cannot ignore another quotation from Corinth. This citation treats the self-estimation of the Corinthians and has in its formulation a clear ironical twist with a taste of bitterness. They are not sure if Christ speaks in Paul – Christ 'who is not weak towards/in you, but mighty in your midst (or: in you)' (ὃς εἰς ὑμᾶς οὐκ ἀσθενεῖ ἀλλὰ δυνατεῖ ἐν ὑμῖν).[12] Verses 13.3-4 are, according to their essence, a dialogue between Paul and the members of the congregation. Paul is continually reverberating the statements of the Corinthians about him, themselves and Christ, changing them a little and answering them. The second quotation adjusts the content of the demanded proof: the Christ who possibly speaks also in Paul is the Christ who, according to the opinion of the Corinthians, is already mighty in their midst (or in them). They themselves need no proof. It is clear that this can be only their own opinion of their spiritual competence in this situation. Paul does not think so. Just before, in 12.19-21, he has written about his fear that God will humiliate him because of the poor state of his congregation, and that when he comes to Corinth he must mourn for many as one mourns for the dead because of their impenitent mind.[13] Therefore the words in the half-verse 13.3b must be a quotation, but hardly a word-by-word quotation.[14]

11   Grässer, *Der zweite*, pp. 250–51, 254, interprets the words of Paul so that his proof of his own legitimacy as an apostle will be given only through speech: 'In seiner Predigt ist Christus gegenwärtig. Damit und mit nichts sonst wird der geforderte Legitimitätsnachweis des Paulus erbracht. Die Antipauliner haben mit ihrer häretischen Christologie den Korinthern den Blick verstellt, das richtig zu erkennen.' Paul believes that he is able to carry out everything in Corinth through the same power of Christ which he already and always has in his weakness. According to Grässer Paul consequently stays in his theology of the cross and no changes happen in the means which he has at his disposal. Already the inner logic of verses 13.3-4 speaks against this interpretation. In addition there remains the difficult question: why did Paul not bring order to the congregation during his sad intermediary visit, if he had already then all the same means to handle the situation as during his third visit in the near future?

12   Harris, *The Second*, p. 912, emphasizes that the prepositions ἐν and εἰς have here the same meaning: the change from one to the other is 'simply a stylistic variant'.

13   Aejmelaeus, *Schwachheit*, pp. 342–53.

14   Margaret E. Thrall, *A Critical and Exegetical Commentary on the Second Epistle to the Corinthians: Commentary on II Corinthians VIII–XIII*, vol. 2 (ICC; London: T&T Clark,

After the Corinthians themselves have read the letter they will naturally have easily recognized the ironical quotations and the way that Paul is playing with them. We have here difficulties. The conclusion that 13.3b is a quotation is easy to draw, but the reconstruction of the original wording of it is more difficult and there can be no absolute certainty of it. The shape of the half-verse is in any case too tautological for a direct quotation. Why would the Corinthians have expressed the conviction about their own good relationship to Christ twice, first in a negative, then in a positive way?

From the whole content and situational background of the 'Letter of Tears' it is clear that it is Paul who has been criticized for his lack of spirituality, not the Corinthians. They had no reason to defend themselves on this subject that would explain the abundant emphasis on their good spiritual relationship to Christ. In the original statement that lies behind 3b the barb of the message was most probably also directed at Paul. They have talked about themselves only in comparison to Paul so that the quotation could have run in their mouth as follows: 'Christ is weak in Paul, but mighty in us' (Χριστὸς εἰς Παῦλον ἀσθενεῖ ἀλλὰ δυνατεῖ ἐν ἡμῖν). The letter otherwise reflects abundantly this kind of criticism of Paul and this kind of self-evaluation. It would have been easy for Paul to change such a critical quotation into the shape in which it appears in 3b, especially since the readers know well what lies behind the words 'not towards/in *you*'.

In Paul's line of thought, 3b marks only an excursion of a special kind. It reintroduces in the kernel, however, the theme and the terms that have been the main thread through the whole discussion of the letter in its earlier parts, namely the question of the true strength of Christ and of the weakness of Paul with its christological connections. Since 12.14 the main subject of Paul has been his third visit to Corinth in the near future with its severe purpose of putting all in the congregation in order. With the help of the quotation 13.3b, Paul is able to unite in the next verse the theme of his judgemental visit to the main theme of the whole letter. He is able to clarify the christological and theological premises of his coming third visit to Corinth, to show how the man who has been accused of being weak and who himself has also admitted it and even boasted of it (11.30) is able to threaten the Corinthians with a severe judgement. In 13.4 Paul thus gives a correction with adjusting explanation to the truth and the misunderstanding, both of which lie behind the quotation 13.3b. At

2000), p. 881, also holds 13.3b as an ironical citation. Harris, *The Second*, p. 912, thinks that the statement of the Corinthians that lies behind 13.3 might have run in the following way: 'We demand proof that Christ who works powerfully among us, is using you as his spokesman.'

the same time the basis of Paul's confidence in his being able to be strong in his visit is exposed.[15]

For the real understanding of Paul's argumentation one has to take into accurate consideration the structure and especially the conjunctions of 13.4:

καὶ γὰρ ἐσταυρώθη ἐξ ἀσθενείας, ἀλλὰ ζῇ ἐκ δυνάμεως θεοῦ. (13.4a)
καὶ γὰρ ἡμεῖς ἀσθενοῦμεν ἐν αὐτῷ, ἀλλὰ ζήσομεν σὺν αὐτῷ ἐκ δυνάμεως θεοῦ εἰς ὑμᾶς. (13.4b)

For indeed he was crucified because of his weakness, but he lives because of God's power.[16]
For indeed we are weak in him, but we shall live with him because of God's power – and that in relation to you.

The verse is divided into two strictly parallel sentences with the same conjunctions in the structure of each (καὶ γάρ ... ἀλλά, for indeed ... but). The terms and content in both sentences also strengthen in another way the impression of the parallelism: 'weakness', 'life' and 'God's power' play a central role in both sentences.

The rhetorical structure of the presentation requires that the 'for indeed' clauses refer to convictions held by both parties to the discussion. This is the only way that the two parallel Greek sentences can be connected with each other in an unforced way through the conjunction pair καὶ γάρ in verse 13.4.[17] The statement 'Christ was crucified because of his weakness, but he lives because of God's power' is a christological statement, with which the Corinthians also agreed. Some christological formulas and credo declarations in the Pauline letters in which the two phases of the Christ event are similarly emphasized resemble it. The lowering and the heightening of Christ are also described in 8.9, Gal. 4.4, Phil. 2.6-11, Rom. 1.3-4. Excluding Rom. 1.3-4 the emphasis in these verses lies in the lowering of Christ and in the benefits it brings to mankind. In the sentence 'Christ was crucified because of his weakness,

15   In a similar way, Thrall, *Critical*, p. 882.

16   The expression with the preposition ἐκ + gen. hints at the reason that caused the crucifixion and the living, but in this connection it also includes at the same time a broader shade of meaning. The verb in the present in the latter part of the sentence expresses this. God's power is not only the force that gave Christ his life back, but also the basis for his whole existence in this new situation. In an analogical way the weakness was not only the actual reason for the act of crucifixion, but the basic mode of existence which made it possible that the Son of God could be put to death by men. The meaning of the first part of the sentence could also be translated with the words 'he was crucified because he was weak'. Cf. Thrall, *Critical*, p. 882–84, Grässer, *Der zweite*, p. 252.

17   Scholars who do not interpret the beginning of the latter sentence ('Paul is weak in Christ') as a quotation also hold the latter conjunction pair καὶ γάρ as odd in their reconstructions of the Pauline way of thinking. See for example Thrall, *Critical*, p. 885.

but he lives because of God's power' the emphasis clearly lies in the last half, in the living in the power. The way that the christological sentence is connected with the self-estimation of the Corinthians in the former verse is best understood when we see it as the way that the Corinthians themselves wanted to justify their own attitude towards spirituality with christology: Christ lives in the resurrection power and his power is effective already in the life and spirituality of the congregation as well.[18] Paul agrees with the Corinthians in the christological formula. He himself has taught them how Christ, who suffered a shameful death on the cross, is now, through the resurrection, a heavenly ruler and lord (1 Cor. 15.25). The premise of the Corinthian thinking is right. Paul does not, however, accept the validity of the conclusion the Corinthians have drawn from the premise. Their conclusion was: because Christ is powerful and he lives in us, we are powerful, too. 'Christ is mighty in us' (13.3).

After having read the first part of 13.4 the Corinthians must have thought that Paul also professes the genuineness of their spirituality as a manifestation of the power of the heavenly Christ. Since Paul even continues writing 'for indeed we are weak in him' the Corinthians thought for a moment that Paul also professed the legitimacy of their criticism of him. It is best to interpret that the beginning of the second half-verse 13.4b is also a quotation from the Corinthians. Paul is referring here to the same criticism that seems to be behind the words in 13.3b, 'Christ is not weak towards/in you', which originally in the mouth of the Corinthians were probably 'Christ is weak towards/in Paul'. Paul himself presumably wanted to put the statement in the form 'I am weak in Christ', whereas the Corinthians preferred the form 'Christ is weak in Paul'. It was only a question of nuance to formulate the relationship this way or the opposite way (cf. Gal. 2.20, Phil. 3.9). The content of both formulations was so uniform that the Corinthians were not able to accuse Paul of misrepresenting their thoughts, but to put the statement this way was better suited to the rhetorical argumentation of Paul. The way that Paul expresses the subject in the beginning of the half-verse 13.4b (καὶ γάρ, 'for indeed') makes it clear that Paul is accepting the criticism about himself that he is quoting.

After this a surprise follows. After the quotation of the Corinthian

18   Thrall, *Critical*, p. 884, discusses the interpretation according to which the half-verse 13.4a would be a familiar christological formula and rejects it. There is too much linguistic divergence between this sentence and the proposed parallels in the New Testament. When, however, we take into account the scantiness of the sources, the lack of a close linguistic formula is not particularly significant. Most of the other formulas which are accepted as formulas make their appearence only once in the New Testament. Thrall writes further: 'it is unlikely that Paul would have made use of a formula designed to remove the offence of the crucified Christ'. If we assume that Paul cites the formula as a Corinthian justification of their attitude towards spirituality Thrall's argument loses its weight.

criticism of him, Paul continues to write with his own words and formulates the half-verse 13.4b into a sentence of two parts like the formula in the half-verse 13.4a. In this case the emphasis is again on the latter part of the sentence, on the strong but-clause. Just as there were two phases in the Christ event there are also two phases in the life of Paul. So far the Corinthians have been acquainted only with the weakness phase. Paul has thus far carried out his apostolic mission under signs of weakness. It has however been weakness 'in him', in Christ. The way that Paul has earlier in the 'Letter of Tears' expounded the positive nature of his apostolic weakness in Christ and in imitation of the voluntary weakness of Christ makes it clear to the reader that his weakness is in reality, if rightly understood, nothing but the greatest spiritual strength ('power comes to perfection in weakness … when I am weak, then I am strong', 10.9-10). Because it is so, he is able to accept with calmness the Corinthian evaluation of him.

The Corinthians themselves understood their criticism of Paul in a quite different way, as they also did concerning the christological formula in 13.4a when they drew from it very different conclusions from those of Paul. In any case both parties to the dispute could fully agree with the external expressions in the three first clauses in 13.4.

The superficial unanimity is broken, however, when Paul writes a surprising sequel to the clause in which he admits that he is weak. The weakness is reality now, but in the future Paul will, like Christ, live in God's power. When Paul adds that this life will be 'with Christ' the readers who knew Paul's typical expressions – including most probably the Corinthians – must have almost automatically thought that Paul is now speaking about the eschatological resolution and about the eternal life. The expression σὺν Χριστῷ, 'with Christ' is, in the Pauline language, a technical term hinting either at the baptism or at the situation in the eschatological resolution (see e.g. Rom. 6.8, 2 Cor. 4.14, 1 Thess. 4.17).[19] The future tense of the verb 'live' has heightened the impression of the first thought. Without the last two words εἰς ὑμᾶς in the verse there simply would not be any choice other than to understand the Pauline words as a hint at the eschatological end situation of Paul. The two words mean 'in relation to you' or 'towards you'. Without them Paul would have informed the Corinthians that although he is weak at this time, in the eschatological future, namely after the resurrection (or the eschatological 'changing', 1 Cor. 15.52) he will be as strong as Christ is already mighty after his resurrection. The two words εἰς ὑμᾶς confuse this clear pattern

---

19   Concerning the eschatological aspect of the verse 13.4, cf. Thrall, *Critical*, pp. 886–87. Her attempt to connect the expression 'with Christ' to the verse 1 Cor. 5.4 and to the theme of judging the sinner in that context is hardly right. The connections in the content and expressions are too slight.

which would have been supported by other verses in the letters of Paul (cf., e.g., Phil. 3.10-11). They do not seem to make sense in the context and therefore it is no wonder that they have been removed from some manuscripts of the letter.

Even though the words εἰς ὑμᾶς cause confusion in a context that seems to be purely eschatological, they, and just they, unite the last clause with its wider context and with the subject of the actual dialogue between Paul and the Corinthians.[20] Paul and the Corinthians are not discussing the principal differences between the situations now and in the future, but about the dispositions of the coming severe visit of Paul to Corinth and of his power to punish them. Paul wants to make clear how he, who had already been there and who had failed on that occasion to settle the matter and was evaluated as weak, now felt himself to be capable of a better performance. The verb 'live' in this connection is not the most natural verb, but Paul probably uses it here for the purpose of formulating his own situation and rhetorical stance as symmetrically as possible with the two-phase situation of Christ as described in 13.4a.[21]

According to verse 13.4, Paul seems to be absolutely sure that he has the eschatological power of God to perform the judgement when he comes to the congregation. What did he have in mind? He might have thought that the final eschatological judgement would be anticipated in a specific and odd way in Corinth simultaneously with his coming there. Alternatively he might have thought that Christ's *parousia* from heaven would coincide with his own return to Corinth. Although the last thought seems difficult to us it was not so to Paul, who eagerly awaited the return of Christ and who himself was sure of still being alive when this happened (cf. 1 Thess. 4.17, 1 Cor. 15.51-52). Paul had already earlier told the Corinthians that the saints would have a role as judges on the Last Day (1 Cor. 6.2). When Christ comes back and the new era begins, the weakness of Paul will be history.

Paul does not explain from where he got such certainty. It belongs to the secrecy of the private religious life of Paul. He had also had other direct messages from above and connections with his Lord (Gal. 1.15-16, 2.2, 2 Cor. 12.2-5, 8-9; cf. also 1 Cor. 2.10, Phil. 3.15). We could imagine Paul in deep prayer before the Lord in his discouragement after his failure

20 Grässer, *Der zweite*, p. 252: 'Als die eigentliche Pointe der Aussage sind die beiden Worte vom Kontext und vom Gedanken der ganzen Stelle her unbedingt gefordert.'
21 It is probably an overinterpretation when Harris, *The Second*, pp. 916–17, explains the meaning of the verb ζάω here as follows: 'it can also mean (in reference to things) "be in full vigor", and of people "be strong/efficient"... so that ζήσομεν may be paraphrased "we shall show ourselves alive and effective" or "I shall be full of life and vigour"'. Harris unites this meaning with his interpretation that Paul is here not speaking about some eschatological judgement but about his normal apostolic activities with the possibilities of using God's power when needed.

in the second visit to Corinth. As in the instance of 'the thorn in the flesh' (12.7-10) Paul did get an answer, which he interpreted in the way that it is written in 13.4. Maybe the divine answer was as simple and open in its nature as: 'Go to Corinth. You will win, because I am with you'. What would have happened if Paul had really gone to Corinth in the sureness of the eschatological power? We do not know that because the letter itself was already enough. The Corinthians had already begun to repent their behaviour towards Paul when Titus came to the city with the letter (7.15). Paul had probably exaggerated the seriousness of the quarrel in his isolation far away from Corinth. This can be read between the lines in the next letter (7.8-9).

The threatening by Paul and the way that he places it in the eschatological schedule in 13.3-4 is in harmony with his overall conviction of the Christian way of life. In this time the believer 'walks in the realm of faith, not of sight' (5.7). A believer has to follow Christ in the mode of existence Christ had before his resurrection, when he lived in abasement. During this time the power of God is broken in its nature, 'for power comes to perfection in weakness' (12.9). The indirect manifestation of God's power is possible only after the future break of eras when Christ comes back and begins to rule.

Chapter 7

REJOICING IN THE JUDAISERS' WORK? THE QUESTION OF PAUL'S
OPPONENTS IN PHIL. 1.15-18A

Nina Pehkonen

1. *Introduction*

The research on Paul's opponents in his letter to the Philippians has often
concentrated on the letter's chapter 3. And rightfully so, for ch. 3 includes
some of Paul's most vehement and slanderous language and as such is
clearly 'oppositional'. The majority of scholarship sees Judaisers behind
Paul's warning about the 'dogs' and 'evil workers', and this very
reasonable assumption will not be questioned in this paper.[1] There are,
however, also other texts in Philippians that deal with opposition of some
sort. These especially include passages such as 1.15-18a and 1.27-30. While
the latter of these two has been fairly securely resolved as dealing with
pagan opposition to the church in Philippi,[2] the former remains in many
respects a puzzle. Varying identities for the opponents in 1.15-18a have
been proposed, to the point where one can safely say that scholarship is at
the moment quite far from a consensus on the matter.

  This article will concentrate on solving the identity of the opponents in
1.15-18a and in particular on assessing their relationship to the Judaisers
in ch. 3. Assuming the same opponents behind these two passages has not

---

1 For arguments on Judaisers behind Philippians 3, see e.g. E.P. Sanders, 'Paul on the
law, his opponents, and the Jewish people in Philippians 3 and Corinthians 11', in P.
Richardson (ed.), *Anti-Judaism in Early Christianity: Paul and the Gospels*, vol. 1 (Studies in
Christianity and Judaism, 2; Waterloo: Wilfried Lauriel University Press, 1986), pp. 75–90
(80–84); M. Bockmuehl, *The Epistle to the Philippians* (BNTC; London: Black, 1997), p. 191;
G.D. Fee, *Paul's Letter to the Philippians* (NICNT; Grand Rapids: Eerdmans, 1995),
pp. 293–95.

2 Two things especially support this. First, Paul implies that the opponents in the text
have caused the Philippians (physical) suffering, which rules out the Judaisers. Non-Christian
Jews are not likely either, because they seem not to have been very numerous in Philippi.
Secondly, Paul says the Philippians are having the same struggle as he did, when he was with
them, which was clearly pagan/Roman-induced. See e.g. Bockmuehl, *Philippians*, pp. 100,
103; Fee, *Philippians*, p. 167.

been very common, at least in recent scholarship.[3] This has mostly been argued by the different tone Paul takes towards those he speaks about. It has been noted that whereas in ch. 3 Paul's resentment towards those he calls dogs is very tangible and explicit, in 1.15-18a he can even say he rejoices in the work of those referred to. The allegedly more lax disposition in 1.15ff. has thus been taken as a sign that Paul cannot mean the Judaisers there. In the following this very common view will be challenged, which of course accounts for the question in the heading: is Paul actually saying in 1.15ff that he rejoices in the work of the Judaisers?

We will proceed as follows: First a concise introduction to the text in 1.15-18a will be offered, including the three previous verses 1.12-14, which are intimately related to the section. After this a quick glance will be taken at some of the most notable and usual ways of solving the identity of the opponents in the text, with a summary of the main reasons for not seeing Judaisers in it. Thirdly a more thorough analysis of the text will be offered, with criticism of the previous views and testing of the Judaiser-hypothesis. Finally, some notes will be offered on how the Judaiser solution affects our understanding of the historical context of the letter.

2. The Text in 1.12-18a

1.12 Γινώσκειν δὲ ὑμᾶς βούλομαι, ἀδελφοί, ὅτι τὰ κατ'ἐμὲ μᾶλλον εἰς προκοπὴν τοῦ εὐαγγελίου ἐλήλυθεν,

1.13 ὥστε τοὺς δεσμούς μου φανεροὺς ἐν Χριστῷ γενέσθαι ἐν ὅλῳ τῷ πραιτωρίῳ καὶ τοῖς λοιποῖς πᾶσιν,

1.14 καὶ τοὺς πλείονας τῶν ἀδελφῶν ἐν κυρίῳ πεποιθότας τοῖς δεσμοῖς μου περισσοτέρως τολμᾶν ἀφόβως τὸν λόγον λαλεῖν.

1.15 τινὲς μὲν καὶ διὰ φθόνον καὶ ἔριν
τινὲς δὲ καὶ δι' εὐδοκίαν
τὸν Χριστὸν κηρύσσουσιν

1.16 οἱ μὲν ἐξ ἀγάπης,
εἰδότες ὅτι εἰς ἀπολογίαν τοῦ εὐαγγελίου κεῖμαι,

1.17 οἱ δὲ ἐξ ἐριθείας
τὸν Χριστὸν καταγγέλλουσιν,
οὐχ ἁγνῶς, οἰόμενοι θλῖψιν ἐγείρειν τοῖς δεσμοῖς μου.

---

3 For older commentators see e.g. J.B. Lightfoot, who reads Judaisers in both instances (*Saint Paul's Epistle to the Philippians* [New York: MacMillan, rev. edn, 1900], pp. 88–90).

1.18a Τὶ γάρ; πλὴν ὅτι παντὶ τρόπῳ,
       εἴτε προφάσει
       εἴτε ἀληθείᾳ
       <u>Χριστὸς καταγγέλλεται,</u>
       καὶ ἐν τούτῳ χαίρω.

Paul begins a new section after the thanksgiving (1.3-11) with a conventional epistolary disclosure-formula 'I want you to know…'.[4] He insists that 'what has happened' to him[5] has 'rather'[6] advanced the gospel. This has been so, because 'the whole *praetorium* and all the rest' have learned that Paul's chains are 'in Christ'. A second reason is that 'the majority of brothers' have gained courage 'in the Lord'[7] from Paul's chains to preach 'the Word' more fearlessly.

After these verses (1.12-14), which e.g. L. Gregory Bloomquist identifies as the rhetorical *narratio* of the letter,[8] Paul goes on to a chiastically structured description of 'some' (τινές), who preach Christ out of pure motives, and others (also introduced as τινές) whose intentions are impure – that is, the opponents. Bloomquist classifies this section as a rhetorical *partitio*.[9] As the underlined clauses above point out, both τινές are said to preach Christ. The 'good' τινές are told to do this out of goodwill (δι' εὐδοκίαν) and love (ἐξ ἀγάπης), and sincerely (ἀληθείᾳ). They also 'know' that Paul is put (in prison, by God) for the defence of the gospel (εἰδότες ὅτι εἰς ἀπολογίαν τοῦ εὐαγγελίου κεῖμαι).[10] The 'bad' τινές are said to preach out of envy, strife (διὰ φθόνον καὶ ἔριν) and partisanship (ἐξ ἐριθείας), and on a pretext (προφάσει). They are also said to 'think' they are rousing agony for Paul in his chains (οἰόμενοι θλῖψιν ἐγείρειν τοῖς δεσμοῖς μου). Paul concludes the section with a rhetorical question (Τὶ

---

4   γινώσκειν δὲ ὑμᾶς βούλομαι… See L.G. Bloomquist, *The Function of Suffering in Philippians* (JSNTSup, 78; Sheffield: JSOT Press, 1993), p. 77.

5   More literally τὰ κατ' ἐμέ means 'the things pertaining to me'.

6   The adverb μᾶλλον expresses an idea contrary to expectation (G.F. Hawthorne, *Philippians* [WBC, 43; Waco: Word Books, 1983], p. 34).

7   The qualifier ἐν κυρίῳ should be taken together with πεποιθότας, not with ἀδελφῶν, this being a typical Pauline usage (cf. Phil. 2.24 and also Gal. 5.10, Rom. 14.14). Fee (*Philippians*, p. 116) seems also correct in that 'the chains' is used in an instrumental way and 'the Lord' is meant to represent the true ground of the brothers' confidence.

8   Bloomquist, *Function*, pp. 123–24.

9   *Ibid.*, pp. 124–25.

10   Paul's expression is concise and one is forced to read the ideas given above in parentheses from between the lines. The verb κεῖμαι is a technical term for being appointed by God (cf. Lk. 2.34, 1 Thess. 3.3). That Paul means his appointment in prison – as opposed to his appointment as an apostle in a more general sense – is not evident from the text as such. It is, however, supported by Paul's use of a judicial word for the 'defence of the gospel' (ἀπολογία) and also by the fact that much of the surrounding material in the passage has to do with Paul's imprisonment.

γάρ;) that could be translated with the common modern-day interjection 'So what?'. After this he insists that he rejoices in Christ being preached regardless of how this is done (παντὶ τρόπῳ).

3. *Previous Solutions*

G.D. Fee's solution for the identity of the opponents in Phil. 1.15ff. leans heavily on two assumptions. First, that Paul is writing from Rome, and secondly, that the opponents he talks about are local Christians. Based on these Fee suggests that the situation depicted reflects an extension of the dispute between the 'weak' and the 'strong' in the Roman church, which Paul had already touched upon in his previous letter to the church. Fee assumes Paul found upon his arrival in Rome that his earlier attempt in this letter to mediate between the groups had not been successful. On the contrary, the Jewish–Christian 'weak' brothers had further sharpened their stance and now viewed Paul's imprisonment as an opportunity to preach their own mode of Christianity even more emphatically, and in Fee's words 'in part at least over against Paul's understanding of the gospel'. While Fee admits there is some theological difference between Paul and the opponents, he still denies that it could be something as serious as with the Judaisers warned against in ch. 3. The latter are, in Fee's interpretation, 'sheep stealers', who invade Pauline communities, while the former only evangelize and attach to their more Jewish mode of Christianity pagans who have not been previously converted. So Fee sees the opponents' theology as being somewhat different from Paul's, but still in essence 'milder' than the actual Judaisers' theology. This he then takes to account for Paul's lack of total condemnation of the opponents in 1.15ff.[11]

F.W. Beare and M.R. Vincent, both writing considerably earlier than Fee, also situate Philippians in Rome and believe Paul refers in 1.15ff. to local Christians. They argue for even less theological difference between Paul and the opponents than Fee. Both refer to the fact that the church in Rome had not had a well-established leadership before Paul arrived on the scene. This is then believed to have caused jealousy and rivalry in the local and smaller group leaders, which in turn resulted in their attempt to prove themselves Paul's equals by increased evangelism. This reaction is taken to account for Paul's accusation of the opponents' false motives. On the other hand, it is also taken to explain the lack of condemnation by Paul of the actual content of the opponents' message. Beare specifically explicates that Paul cannot mean Judaisers because he does not accuse the

---

11 Fee, *Philippians*, pp. 122–23. Bockmuehl (*Philippians*, pp. 76–81) essentially follows Fee.

opponents of teaching a perverted gospel. Vincent even calls the opponents 'Pauline Christians'.[12]

Robert Jewett for his part gives a very detailed depiction of the opponents.[13] He locates Philippians in Ephesus, but his overall theory is a little less dependent on the exact place of writing than the ones above.[14] He argues that the opponents in Phil. 1.15ff. are 'similar, if not identical' to the missionary evangelists Paul countered in 2 Corinthians.[15] In his opinion both groups criticized Paul for displaying weakness and humiliation unseemly for a true apostle of God. In the case of Philippians this was seen especially in Paul's imprisonment, which the opponents thought could jeopardize the cause of the gospel. Jewett uses as his main proof a rather elaborate reading of 1.13. He believes that Paul is with his sentence ... ὥστε τοὺς δεσμούς μου φανεροὺς ἐν Χριστῷ γενέσθαι ... implying more than just the fact that many people at Paul's place of imprisonment had heard that his charges were related to his Christ-message. Jewett finds, on grammatical grounds, a different dimension in the sentence. He states that 'the emphasis in Paul's expression, as shown by the word order, is that the "manifestation of my chains" is really "in Christ"'.[16] This, in his opinion, is written to counter a view held by the opponents that Paul's imprisonment as a sign of weakness could not be a manifestation of Christ's saving activity. Jewett finds this initial observation further supported by many features in the surrounding text. He reads opponents behind Paul's allegedly defensive μᾶλλον in 1.12 and interprets Paul's accusations of the opponents' envy, rivalry and partisanship as very literal descriptions of their highly competitive ethos. On the whole Jewett admits that the opponents were theologically in disagreement with Paul and that Paul does not treat them mildly at all. He believes the 'positive' side of Paul's depiction of the opponents is due to the fact that Paul, not having founded the church in Ephesus, was in no position to condemn local Christians there as outright heretics.

Morna D. Hooker's view on the opponents is somewhat related to both

12   F.W. Beare, *A Commentary on the Epistle to the Philippians* (BNTC; London: Black, 1959), pp. 59–60; M.R. Vincent, *A Critical and Exegetical Commentary on the Epistles to the Philippians and Philemon* (ICC; repr.; Edinburgh: T&T Clark, 1985 [1897]), pp. 18–19.

13   R. Jewett, 'Conflicting movements in the early church as reflected in Philippians', *NovT* 12 (1970), pp. 362–90 (363–71).

14   One needs to note here that Vincent's and Beare's overall view could just as easily be interpreted to fit with Ephesus, since Paul was not the founder of the Ephesian church either.

15   Jewett calls these 'divine-man' missionaries. Even if this designation, including many features assumed along with it, has nowadays been called into question, Jewett's description of the opponents in 2 Cor. is essentially correct and his overall theory need not be discarded simply on the grounds of a misguided category.

16   Jewett's grammatical notion is that the qualifier 'in Christ' actually applies to the whole remaining *accusativus cum infinitivo* construction.

the one given by Jewett and the one by Beare and Vincent. In line with the latter she believes the opponents are local Roman Christians, whose gospel is essentially correct in content. But similarly to Jewett she also thinks that the major problem with the opponents was their critical attitude towards Paul's imprisonment. They suspected it would damage the gospel's cause. Hooker believes the opponents might hold views on apostleship similar to the ones opposed by Paul in 1 Cor. 4.8-21, but denies the necessity to read 'divine-men' missionaries in the text like Jewett. Hooker further thinks that the opposition is more of a personal nature and that Paul can treat the opponents mildly because he sees them as still 'adolescent' in their Christian views, but nonetheless as Christians.[17]

This, admittedly quick and incomplete, glance at previous scholarship hopefully shows two things. First, that scholars have indeed attempted to solve the identity of the opponents in 1.15ff in very different ways. Secondly, it gives a general view of the main issues that have been taken up as proof that Paul cannot be speaking of Judaisers here. These are in essence the following: 1. Paul's estimate of the opponents in 1.15-18a is taken to be much milder than of those in ch. 3. Paul's rejoicing and the fact that he does not condemn outright the opponents' theology are taken as proof that the opponents cannot be theologically or otherwise as starkly opposed to Paul as the Judaisers. Some claim the opponents' theology must be correct from Paul's point of view. Others, like Fee and Jewett, allow for some theological difference. 2. Paul is taken to speak of local Christians at his place of confinement, not travelling missionaries such as the Judaisers were. Here Jewett is an exception. He believes Paul does in fact refer to missionary workers, but ones that are apparently affecting the Ephesian church – and thus from Paul's point of view in some sense locals there – and whose message is ultimately not a Judaising one. 3. The opponents are depicted as critical towards Paul's imprisonment. Vincent, Beare and Fee do not assume here that this was connected to their theological views, but only think that the opponents were happy to see Paul out of the way. Criticism of Paul's imprisonment is rarely stated as an explicit reason for not identifying the opponents as Judaisers, but apparently it makes the interpreters look for a different kind of solution here. Jewett notes in passing that 'there is no particular reason to believe that Judaisers would cast doubt on Paul's apostolicity simply because of an imprisonment'.[18]

17 M.D. Hooker, 'Philippians: phantom opponents and the real source of conflict', in I. Dunderberg *et al.* (eds), *Fair Play: Diversity and Conflicts in Early Christianity* (Festschrift H. Räisänen; NovTSup, 103; Leiden: Brill, 2002), pp. 377–95 (377–86).
18 Jewett, 'Conflicting movements', p. 366.

4. *Analysis*

4.1. *Negative Statements on the Opponents*
4.1.1. *False Motives*

Paul's negative statements on the opponents deal with the supposed foul motives that underlie their preaching activity. This is the crux of everything Paul says of them and can be substantiated both by the use of the preposition διά + acc.[19] and also by Paul's summary statement in 1.18a where the question of motivation is made explicit. Whatever else Paul says of the opponents in this passage should thus be read as 'the real reason' behind their 'pretext'.

Among the direct negative statements on the opponents' 'real' motives are the accusations of envy, rivalry and partisanship (φθόνος, ἔρις, ἐριθεία). These words are certainly very negative and something of their serious tone can be detected when we note the contexts where Paul uses them otherwise. All three appear in Paul's vice list in Gal. 5.20-21, where they designate those who will not inherit the kingdom of God. The first two are also included in the infamous vice list of Rom. 1.29 describing fallen humanity. 'Rivalry' is in Paul's language also one of the signs that the Corinthian Christians, having formed parties, are still 'fleshly' (1 Cor. 3.3). The remedy for this threat of disunity is expounded by Paul in terms of love (1 Cor. 13), which notably also appears as a positive statement on the 'good preachers' in Phil. 1.16.[20] 'Rivalry' and 'partisanship' are further repeated as undesirable qualities in 2 Cor. 12.20. The last two examples imply internal problems in a Pauline congregation and one might be tempted to read the same as being the case in Philippians, thus accounting for a 'milder' reference with the words. This is, however, not substantiated by the other appearances. It seems rather that these words are very conventional in Paul's polemical language and that their informational value should thus be deemed quite low.[21] Jewett surely hangs too much descriptive weight on these words, even if they do not act as the starting-point to his overall view. He also gives undue emphasis to the appearance of the same words in 2 Cor. 12.20, which he takes as a strong signal that the same or similar opponents are intended in Phil. 1.15ff. The conventional nature of the words and the fact that they appear elsewhere in Paul's letters reveal that the verbal similarities between these passages cannot denote a 'true' parallel in the sense of revealing an analogous situation also behind the text. However, the net sum of the words hardly

19 *Means* is expressed by διά + gen., *motive* by διά + acc. (see H.W. Smyth, *Greek Grammar* [rev. Gordon M. Messing; Harvard: Harvard University Press, 1956], 1679§).
20 See Hooker, 'Phantom opponents', p. 383.
21 G. Lüdemann, *Opposition to Paul in Jewish Christianity* (trans. Eugene M. Boring; Minneapolis: Fortress, 1989), p. 105.

amounts to nothing. It is noteworthy that all the words concentrate on the theme of disunity.[22]

Something of the serious tone of these accusations can be further detected by what Paul states as the reverse side of envy and rivalry, namely the notion of εὐδοκία. Commentators sometimes read this quite mildly as denoting only the human attitude of 'goodwill' on the part of the 'good preachers' towards Paul.[23] Even if this could be supported by the fact that a lot of what is said in these verses centres on Paul's person, it is still remarkable that Paul uses the word in the same letter as denoting *divine* will (2.13).[24] The indirect suggestion that the opponents do not preach in line with God's will and purpose certainly gives an alarmingly negative ring to Paul's words.

It is important to note from Paul's accusations on the opponents' motives that he is in fact making use of a known *topos* in ancient polemic. Accusations of teaching and preaching for ulterior motives such as love of money or glory are something of a commonplace in ancient polemical sources.[25] In the gospels the accusation is linked to the hypocrisy of the scribes (Mk. 12.40 par.). Even Paul himself is elsewhere found stressing that his own work is devoid of ulterior motives and fulfils the ideals of preaching the gospel for its own sake (2 Cor. 4.2 and 1 Thess. 2.5). Paul's choice of a *topos* that centres on the opponents' motives has often been taken as proof that this is the only area he had complaints about concerning the opponents. Reticence over theological issues in these accusations has been taken to mean that he has no, or at least very few, complaints on the content of the opponents' message.[26] It is true that Paul does not claim in these verses that the opponents preach 'another Jesus' (2 Cor. 11.4) or a 'different gospel' (Gal. 1.6; 2 Cor. 11.4). And to be sure, he *could* of course be offering here a non-selective image of some Christians who really are like this. But in reality, Paul's choice of 'motive-denigrating-*topos*' here should not be taken as a definite sign that he *could* not have condemned the content of the opponents' message too, had he chosen to, or did not in fact do it elsewhere – e.g. in ch. 3! It seems wise

22 Hooker ('Phantom opponents', pp. 382–83) has noted that the terms envy and strife (ἔρις, φθόνος) appear also in secular Greek as factors that endanger the common good and oppose concord in the community. She notes that Dio Chrysostom uses the words in this sense (*Invid.* 37–39) and may well reflect a common notion.

23 Fee, *Philippians*, p. 120 n. 15.

24 Hooker ('Phantom opponents', p. 383) and Bockmuehl (*Philippians*, pp. 78–79) read the same meaning in these two passages.

25 See Luke Timothy Johnson, 'The New Testament's anti-Jewish slander and the conventions of ancient polemic', *JBL* 108 (1989), pp. 419–41 (430–32).

26 Hooker ('Phantom opponents', p. 379) concludes from this that the opponents are 'doing the right thing for the wrong motive'. Hawthorne (*Philippians*, p. 37) states on this ground that the opponents' message in itself must be 'sound'.

to at least ask whether Paul could have had a tactical reason of some kind for choosing this way of describing the opponents rather than some other.

4.1.2. *Stance Towards Paul's Imprisonment*

Another major difficulty in establishing the nature and identity of the opponents in 1.15ff. comes from assessing what their relationship to and stance towards Paul's imprisonment was. Paul links the opponents to his imprisonment in two ways: First, in 1.14-15 he implies that the opponents have somehow, perversely, been encouraged by his imprisonment to preach Christ more boldly. The second linking appears in 1.17, and poses some challenge for interpretation.

The Greek in 1.17 reads as follows: οἱ δὲ ἐξ ἐριθείας τὸν Χριστὸν καταγγέλλουσιν, οὐχ ἁγνῶς, οἰόμενοι θλῖψιν ἐγείρειν τοῖς δεσμοῖς μου. The main difficulty lies with the last clause of the sentence, and especially with the dative τοῖς δεσμοῖς μου. The first possible option for understanding the dative is to rely on the identical expression in 1.14 and attribute the same instrumental meaning here too. In this reading it is possible that Paul is not the direct object of the affliction caused by the opponents. The clause could be understood roughly in the following manner: 'thinking to raise affliction (to some unidentified persons or generally) *by* making use of my imprisonment'. This reading may be behind certain reconstructions, where the opponents are depicted as aiming to increase eschatological suffering for Christians in the hope of hastening the day of the Lord. Of course, even in this case, Paul himself can also still somehow be implied as suffering from this, even if he does not appear as a grammatical object in the sentence.[27] It is in fact more common to see Paul in this sentence as somehow the object of the intended affliction. Along these lines the dative can also be read as dative of disadvantage ('thinking to raise affliction in order to complicate/aggravate my imprisonment') or something close to the dative proper ('thinking to aggravate my imprisonment').[28] The dative of location may also be suggested ('thinking to bring me affliction in my imprisonment').[29] For the last one, there is a closely parallel expression in Phlm. 10.

While we may reasonably suppose that Paul somehow intends himself

27   R.P. Martin (*Philippians* [NCBC; Grand Rapids: Eerdmans, 1980], p. 73) and Hawthorne (*Philippians*, 37) refer to the views of T. Hawthorn ('Philippians 1.12-19 with special reference to vv. 15, 16, 17', *ExpT* 62 [1950–51], pp. 316–17) who thought that the opponents' strife and rivalry were chiefly aimed at the Roman authorities in the hope of provoking persecution and even inviting martyrdom upon themselves as well as Paul, this being the necessary θλῖψις preceding the end-times.

28   Smyth, *Greek Grammar*, 1457§ (but note 1459§) and 1481§.

29   The locative aspect is reflected in many translations (GNB, CEV, NRSV). That Paul does not explicitly state himself as the object of the opponents' harmful intentions is not a problem, since it is clearly implied, in that the affliction is caused to/in *his* chains.

as the object of the affliction caused by the opponents, it is still to be decided whether he means that the opponents aim to cause him concrete physical affliction in prison or perhaps even influence the outcome of his trial, or whether something more subjective and abstract, such as his personal feelings, is meant. Some features in the text may be put forward in favour of the first option. First of all, for Paul θλῖψις is often connected to concrete physical suffering on behalf of/in imitation of Christ (cf. 1 Thess. 3.3, 2 Cor. 4.8, 10-12). This theme is strongly present elsewhere in Philippians, where Christ's obedience unto death runs like a *typos* throughout the letter (2.8; 2.30; 3.10). However, the word is given a somewhat less acute meaning in the same letter in 4.14, where it denotes Paul's economically deprived circumstances in prison (still physical though). Secondly, the way Paul chooses to emphasize 'the chains' and not his own person may be symptomatic of the fact that he has concrete bearings on his physical situation in mind. The idea may be further supported by Paul's possible reference to his forthcoming trial in the previous verse 1.16. If we are to understand that Paul with his reference to the 'defence of the gospel' means his trial and the fact that the 'good' brothers share in it somehow, it would only be natural to see the 'bad' brothers in 1.17 as rather wishing to have a negative impact on it.[30] However, there are also reasons for not interpreting the passage like this, the main one being the alleged *means* of the opponents for causing Paul affliction, that is, their preaching activity. It is hard to understand how preaching Christ more could make Paul's situation worse, but apparently not affect the opponents themselves. It is in fact more believable that Paul here speaks rather of his personal feelings. Thus, the pain Paul denies(!) feeling may result, for example, from witnessing the opponents' increased and successful preaching.[31]

But have the opponents also somehow used Paul's imprisonment as a tool for getting at him? This need not be decided solely on the basis of 1.17, which, as was seen above, does not necessarily bear an instrumental meaning. But even if the exact meaning of 1.17 could not be decided, verses 1.14-15 still give serious reason for suggesting that the opponents had indeed offered a negative interpretation of some sort on the meaning of Paul's imprisonment and ultimately used it against Paul. It has in fact been very common in scholarship to assume that the opponents promoted

---

30 Bockmuehl (*Philippians*, p. 77) notes that also the words 'envy' and 'contention' are 'attested in situations where in the context of court trials public adversaries engage in public manoeuvring to make life difficult for each other'. B.W. Winter (*Seek the Welfare of the City: Christians as Benefactors and Citizens* [Carlisle: Paternoster, 1994], pp. 93–95) suspects that the opponents intended to prejudice the outcome of Paul's trial by mobilizing ill-will towards him.

31 Hooker, 'Phantom opponents', p. 384.

some kind of a negative interpretation of Paul's ordeal. The question only remains *what* kind.

Before going into that question a further note should be made on 1.17, namely, that it seems clear from it that Paul's imprisonment as such is not the initial cause of disagreement between him and the opponents. If the opponents were otherwise faithful 'Paulines', but had only come to view Paul differently because of his imprisonment, we would not expect Paul to accuse them of wanting to *hurt* him. He would rather complain that the opponents lack faith concerning the divine purpose of his imprisonment or that they have abandoned him. The intent to hurt him goes a step further from this and conveys the image of kicking someone when he is down. This reveals that the opponents have most apparently been his enemies already before the most recent ordeal. It seems they used Paul's imprisonment as a further weapon against him, but is it possible to decipher from the text whether, and if so, what kind of, theology lay behind the opponents' alleged critique of Paul's imprisonment?

In Jewett's theory the opponents' critique of Paul's imprisonment is theologically motivated. Jewett believes the opponents viewed Paul's imprisonment as a sign of weakness unsuitable for a true apostle. He draws heavily on a polemical reading of 1.13 (cf. above) – but fails to convince at this point. First of all, while it must be admitted that the sentence structure in this verse is awkward, the sentence itself still hardly allows for a *polemical* reading. Paul's intent at this point is simply to report how the gospel has been furthered by his imprisonment. Jewett argues against this plain reading by doubting that simply learning Paul's charges had something to do with his Christ-message would be enough to convert anyone and thus result in truly furthering the gospel.[32] This may be true as such, but what Jewett forgets is that Paul's words are hardly an objective report. They are rather purpose-oriented rhetoric that allows for considerable exaggeration. Furthermore, in Jewett's reading it sounds somewhat strange that Paul would attribute the *correct theological interpretation* of his chains to 'the whole *praetorium* and all the rest'! Jewett's undue use of mirror-reading was already noted in connection to the words 'envy', 'rivalry' and 'partisanship' but he makes himself guilty of the same elsewhere too. He finds references to the opponents, for example, in 1.12, where Paul initially says that he wants the Philippians to be informed that his imprisonment has in fact furthered the gospel. In Jewett's interpretation this reflects a criticism by the opponents who claim that Paul's imprisonment has in fact been harmful to the gospel.[33] But it seems more reasonable on the grounds of the context that if someone is to be accused of having doubts about the situation it should be the ones Paul

32   Jewett, 'Conflicting movements', p. 367.
33   *Ibid.*, p. 366.

actually addresses, that is, the Philippians themselves. In the same vein Jewett also reads Paul's references to and justifications of suffering throughout the letter as arising out of the conflict with the opponents, who did not value these things.[34] Again, it seems more natural to understand these statements as either Paul's reflection on his own grim situation and/or as encouragement for the Philippians in theirs (cf. 1.27-30).

So Jewett's view remains, in many respects, suspect. He attempts to read information from passages that do not really contain it. Strangely enough he gives no attention to the pair of assertions in 1.16 and 1.17. Hooker interprets the situation in line with what we may assume Jewett might have done had he attempted to. She mirror-reads the opponents' stance from what Paul says of the 'good' brothers in 1.16, that is, that they 'know' Paul is put in prison for the defence of the gospel. She believes the opponents have misunderstood the significance of Paul's imprisonment, think it an embarrassment and fear that it might damage the gospel's cause. She thinks they might also hold a view on apostleship different from Paul's and more in line with what Paul opposes in 1 Cor. 4.8-21. This interpretation is, however, based on a too elaborate mirror-reading of a statement that cannot carry the suggested amount of weight. Even if the statement in 1.16 were an eligible source for mirror-reading, it is important to note that in no unequivocal sense can a 'theology of glory' be detected from behind it. That Paul was 'imprisoned for the defence of the gospel', that is, that Paul's imprisonment was part of God's plan, is something that anyone opposed to Paul – for whatever reason – would have been likely to refute. This is all the passage in reality allows for. Furthermore, it may even be the case that Paul's initial attempt with 1.16 may not be so much to describe the 'good' brothers – let alone reveal something about the 'bad' ones – but more to strengthen and to repeat the theological justification for his imprisonment for *the Philippians*. He touches upon the subject already in 1.7 with them in view. There he commends the Philippians for supporting him in his work in prison for the defence of the gospel, and seems at least partly interested in reassuring the Philippians that what he is going through and what they support is part of a divine plan. It may well be that Paul feels the need to stress and further explicate this in 1.16 and therefore makes this a quality of the 'good' brothers.[35] That the opponents did not engage in a 'theology of glory' is further substantiated by what Paul actually *does* say about them in 1.17,

---

34   *Ibid.*, pp. 367–68.

35   The 'good' brothers otherwise also reflect the ideal behaviour and stance Paul expects from the Philippians. 'Love' and 'divine will' are repeated in relation to the Philippians at 2.1 and 2.13. The qualities of the 'bad' brothers are also repeated as unacceptable in relation to the Philippians (e.g. 'partisanship' in 2.3).

which in no way reveals a 'theology of glory' stance. It would have been easy enough to form a sentence conveying such an idea had this really been the main problem. In fact, on closer examination there is not a single sign in the whole of 1.14-18a that reveals that the opponents hold some kind of 'theology of glory' or think that Paul's imprisonment is an unacceptable sign of weakness.

One further noteworthy feature in 1.17 deserves to be pointed out, namely Paul's emphatic denial of the opponents' negative impact on himself. When Paul insists the opponents only 'think' they are hurting him, he aims to deny that they in fact are able to. As will be suggested below, this attitude is perhaps something that explains Paul's depiction of the opponents at other points too. And of course, one needs to ask whether this kind of defensive reaction is more likely to appear in relation to a fairly harmless phenomenon, or rather in the face of something more serious.

As for the opponents' stance towards Paul's imprisonment we are thus left with Paul's insistence that some, who have already previously opposed him, have been somehow, in reverse manner, encouraged to preach Christ more because of his chains. It seems believable enough that the opponents had given Paul's imprisonment a negative theological interpretation, but we are left in the dark as to what kind. The text leaves room for various possibilities. If the opponents, for example, believed from the start that God did not approve of Paul's gospel, his imprisonment would easily have served as further evidence of this. It is to be noted that even if Paul in this text recognizes the opponents' gospel as a gospel, this does not prove that the same held the other way around. All in all, it can at least be stated that the way Paul relates the opponents to his imprisonment poses no obstacle for identifying Judaisers in the passage.

4.2. *Locals?*

That the opponents Paul takes up in 1.15-18a are local Christians at Paul's place of confinement is almost universally accepted. Elaborate theories on the opponents have been created almost on the basis of this notion alone, Fee perhaps being the clearest example. The letter has been located at Ephesus or Rome and the opponents interpreted accordingly. No substantial view has, however, been based on the third eligible option, Caesarea.[36] Clearly, the assumption that local Christians are meant in this passage has been a further reason for not identifying the opponents as Judaisers.

That the opponents are locals at Paul's place of confinement is not,

---

36   Of modern commentators Hawthorne situates Philippians in Caesarea (*Philippians*, pp. xli–xliv), but has very little to say about the opponents in 1.15ff. (*Ibid.*, pp. 36–39).

however, as is self-evident as often assumed. The fact that Paul clearly refers to local non-Christians in 1.13 does of course suggest that the same is meant of the 'majority of brothers' in the next verse. But this is not necessary. Locality may be further strengthened by Paul's insistence that the opponents have somehow reacted to his imprisonment. This seems more believable if they are present somewhere near enough to observe what is happening to him. But again, this does not make locality necessary, especially since Paul's words do not require that the opponents have attempted to cause any concrete trouble for him. Assuming that Paul was in his time probably quite a famous figure in the church, it is easy to imagine that news about him travelled fast. One did not necessarily have to be geographically close to learn about his fate and react to it. At least it should be noted that Paul nowhere explicitly states that the opponents – or the 'good' brothers for that matter – are locals. It seems he can just as well refer to a wider phenomenon.

Even if we were to assume that Paul speaks of local opponents here, which of course still remains a noteworthy possibility, perhaps even a probable one, we should nonetheless be careful not to exclude a connection with the Judaisers in ch. 3 on this basis alone. It has long been noted concerning ch. 3 that Paul is not describing a situation present at Philippi, but only giving a preliminary warning of some who might appear on the scene.[37] It is thus not completely impossible that he is warning about some whom he knows (also) from wherever he is imprisoned or some who are at least somehow connected to these local people. After all, Paul clearly assumes the opponents in 1.15ff. engage in evangelizing work (they preach Christ), even if actual long-distance missionary activity is not explicitly mentioned.

4.3. *Inclusive Statements and Implications on the Opponents*
4.3.1. *'Brothers Encouraged in the Lord to Preach Christ'?*

As we saw above, Paul's negative statements on the opponents can easily be fitted to describe Judaisers. Indeed, the main hindrance for identifying them here has resulted from the more positive statements and assumptions Paul makes about the opponents. Paul says, for example, in his summary statement (1.18a), that he is able to rejoice in the opponents work 'as long as Christ is being preached'. Also, he seems to include the opponents in the group of 'brothers' who have been encouraged 'in the Lord' to preach Christ more boldly (1.14). These statements convey a much more 'inclusive' stance towards the opponents than in ch. 3.

---

37   Jewett, 'Conflicting movements', p. 382; J. Becker, *Paul: Apostle to the Gentiles* (trans. O.C. Dean, Jr.; Louisville: Westminster/John Knox Press, 1993), p. 324. Hooker ('Phantom opponents', p. 377) and Bockmuehl (*Philippians*, p. 100) do not seem to regard Paul's warning here as being very acute.

As for Paul's inclusion of the opponents in the group of 'brothers' in 1.14 it needs to be noted that this reading has sometimes been problematized. On the surface one easily gets the impression that the two groups of 'τινές' in the following verse 1.15 are intended as subgroups to the 'majority of brothers' (πλείονες τῶν ἀδελφῶν). The fact that the 'bad' preachers clearly *do* preach and that Paul later depicts them as doing so somehow in relation to his imprisonment strengthens this connection. But Vincent, for example, has noted that it still rings a bit strange that the same people who are said to preach out of envy and rivalry would also be implied as having been divinely encouraged to do this ('in the Lord', cf. above, n. 7). Vincent suggests that Paul only means to identify the 'good' τινές with the πλείονες and set the 'bad' τινές against them. He finds grammatical support for this in a supposedly adversative καί following the τινές.[38] But this can hardly be correct since *both* the 'good' and the 'bad' τινές are introduced by the same term. Also the reduction of πλείονες to τινές in the case of the good preachers seems odd, although not too much weight should be placed on it; the latter τινές is probably due to repetition of the first one. Another possibility has been to see a break between the πλείονες in 1.14 and both τινές in 1.15. This could be supported by the completely adequate verbal structure of the sentence beginning with τινές, which means it need not be organically connected to the previous verse. Many have indeed seen the sentences beginning in v. 1.15 as excursus-like.[39]

Vincent's note on the inconsistency between what Paul says of the πλείονες in 1.14 and what he says of the opponents in the following verses is, in a sense, correct and should not be completely bypassed. There is an element here that does not fit. In 1.14 the ultimate motivation for the preachers' work is the Lord, but this is clearly something Paul denies of the opponents in the following verses! In fact, 1.14 sounds as if it were originally meant only as the second, completely positive, proof for the favourable repercussions of Paul's imprisonment. The line of thought could just as well have ended here. But still, even with a possible discontinuity in Paul's train of thought, it is grammatically correct to understand the two τινές-groups as subgroups to the πλείονες in 1.14.[40] Had this not been Paul's intention, he surely could have expressed the difference more clearly. The key as to why Paul in reality can include the 'bad' preachers in the group of 'brothers encouraged in the Lord' lies with the insistence that they too 'preach Christ'. As Fee has noted, this is the language of 'evangelism', that is, of preaching Christ to those who have

---

38   Vincent, *Philippians*, p. 18. It seems somewhat strange in this light, that Vincent still sticks to a very mild reading of the opponents.

39   Lüdemann, *Opposition*, p. 104; Bockmuehl, *Philippians*, p. 76.

40   Fee, *Philippians*, p. 118 n. 5.

not previously heard of him.[41] Fee, however, thinks it is necessary to assume that this is *all* the opponents ever did, that they were not 'sheep-stealers'. But I propose the question is more of what Paul here *chooses to say about the opponents*. In a technical sense the Judaisers hardly restricted their efforts to invading Paul's churches, but rather engaged in true evangelism also. Thus, when Paul concentrates on this side of the story, he is not being completely untruthful. He chooses not to take up the same issues as in ch. 3, but moves within a more neutral area, still, however, revealing a true resentment towards the opponents with his negative statements. The discontinuity between 1.14 and 1.15 may be a sign that Paul is somehow stretching his mind and rhetoric to include the opponents in the group of 'brothers encouraged by the Lord', and that in fact with the negative statements he reveals his true thoughts more accurately. The question remains of course, *why* he chooses to proceed like this.

4.3.2. *Paul's Joy over the Opponents*

Paul's insistence on joy over the opponents' work in 1.18a is often taken as further evidence that the opponents cannot represent something as being as 'bad' as the Judaisers. It is assumed that Paul simply *could not* say this if it were so.[42] But allowing the possibility that Paul is restricting the subject matter to 'evangelism', his joy does not sound quite as unbeliev-able.[43] Of course, that Paul would express something this positive over *anything* his archenemies do, smacks of an ulterior motive. It is in fact necessary to realize at this point that with his insistence on joy Paul is not so much saying something about the opponents as he is about himself. In fact, the opponents as such are still, even *in* this concluding statement referred to negatively as preaching on pretext (προφάσει). The whole point in Paul's insistence on rejoicing in fact gains its value from the contrast between the saintly Paul and the very negative opponents. In fact, I propose that the main reason why Paul does not here describe the opponents straight out as negatively as in ch. 3 is the way he wants to depict himself here in 1.18a. He wants to say that he is rejoicing over the opponents' work, and this would obviously not have sounded right had he claimed here that they preach another Christ.

So what does Paul say about himself here? Commentators often note, quite correctly, that the passage conveys an image of Paul as a large-

---

41   *Ibid.*, p. 123.

42   Lüdemann, *Opposition*, p. 104; Vincent, *Philippians*, p. 19.

43   This seems to be Lightfoot's rationalization, as he says: 'Here ... the choice is between an imperfect Christianity and an unconverted state; the former, however inadequate, must be a gain upon the latter, and therefore must give joy to a high-minded servant of Christ' (*Philippians*, 89).

hearted man, who is willing to look past personal disputes and forget personal misfortune for the sake of God's greater glory. Without a doubt, this is exactly what Paul wants the reader to see. But instead of just stopping here and praising Paul for his noble qualities – as the same commentators often do[44] – we should take a step further and see how all this works respectively for Paul and against the opponents. There are several aspects that Paul may be aiming at. First of all, by creating an image of himself as someone who, unlike the opponents, is genuinely only concerned for the gospel, Paul places his *ethos* well above that of his opponents. It is in fact common in ancient speeches that the speaker engages in confirming his *ethos* at the beginning of the letter.[45] The opponents bicker over personal and mundane issues, but Paul's motivation is 'divinely' oriented. So Paul is, compared to the opponents, the more reliable one. In fact, he is so much above the opponents, that he can *afford* to take an 'inclusive' stance towards them. Secondly, Paul's joy may be an attempt to deny that he himself is in any way responsible for the disagreements with the opponents. It may be his way of saying that, if it were up to him, he could even rejoice in the work of these 'brothers'. They, not Paul, are to blame for all the animosity.

Thirdly, and perhaps most importantly, Paul's joy works as a sign that the opponents have not succeeded in hurting him and as Paul's assurance that he feels in no way threatened by them. This is very much in line with his insistence in 1.17 that the opponents, despite their apparent intent, have not been able to add to his affliction in prison. A note may be made in this connection with Paul's overall use of the subject of joy in Philippians. It is repeated frequently and appears to be a theme word of some kind.[46] But considering Paul's difficult and worrisome situation in prison, with a possible death sentence looming large, there is really no reason to read the frequent references to joy as spontaneous and genuine expressions of his feelings, but rather as a rhetorical device or even a psychological sign of denial. One gets the impression that the worse the situation, the stronger the emphasis on joy. Assuming the same is at work with Paul's judgement on the opponents in 1.15ff., we are rather to see his insistence on joy at this point as a sign that he considers them a serious threat.

In addition to these polemic functions, there is also the possibility that Paul simply does not want to admit to the Philippians the whole extent of

---

44   Fee, *Philippians*, pp. 114, 118, 125; Hawthorne, *Philippians*, p. 38.

45   The place for this is most commonly the *exordium* (Cic. *Inv.* 1.15-18). According to Bloomquist (cf. n. 9 above) Phil. 1.15-18a already comprise the *partitio* of the letter. D.F. Watson ('A rhetorical analysis of Philippians and its implications for the unity question', *NovT* 30 [1980], pp. 57–88 [61–65]), however, identifies the whole section 1.3-26 as *exordium*.

46   Exhortations to joy appear in 2.18; 3.1; 4.4. The theme is also taken up at 1.25; 2.2; 2.28-29; 4.1.

his problems with the opponents. Inclusive language may be used here in order to embellish the picture of a situation that in reality was considerably more serious.

5. *Further Reasons for Seeing Judaisers in 1.15ff.*

It is a well-known fact that in the beginning of his letters Paul often gives a short introduction to the themes he will later develop at greater length. This is apparently a convention he picked up from the general ideals of ancient speech-writing. In this vein, it is very tempting to see 1.15ff. as an introduction to the issue of Judaisers in ch. 3. But this is not entirely unproblematic. First of all, Paul's introduction to the following themes is most often located in the thanksgiving part of the letter.[47] And as was shown above, verses 1.3-11 form the thanksgiving section in Philippians, thus not extending to 1.15ff. As is indicated by the conventional informational formula in 1.12, verses 1.15ff. are already clearly part of the epistolary body-middle.[48] However, in a rhetorical sense, 1.15ff. most likely form the *partitio* of the letter, which makes the problem with these verses as 'introductory material' less insuperable. For at least in forensic speeches this section seems to have an introductory function as the place where the speaker for the first time shows where he agrees with his antagonists and where disagreement remains (Cic. *Inv.* 1.22.).[49]

The second problem, however, is that the original unity of the letter is in itself a disputed matter. Some see ch. 3 as an inserted fragment of an originally separate letter, thus dissolving the need for an introduction to the matter in the first chapter.[50] In this case it can of course be asked why Paul would take up a group of opponents in the beginning of the letter and not return to the subject later on. The question of the need for an introduction is, however, overall quite a wavering one, since it can hardly be expected that Paul in every single one of his letters properly introduces every single theme taken up later. Also, the discussion relating to the unity of the letter easily ends up moving in circles.

Regardless of whether 1.15ff. could/should be read as an introduction to the matters in ch. 3, there is another issue that seems to make Judaisers

---

47   See R. Jewett, 'The epistolary thanksgiving and the integrity of Philippians', *NovT* 12 (1970), pp. 40–53.

48   Bloomquist, *Function*, pp. 107–109.

49   Bloomquist, *Function*, pp. 124–25 believes Paul moves in his *partitio* out of the sphere of deliberative rhetoric otherwise represented by the letter, into forensic rhetoric. According to Bloomquist, the main messages (*causa*) of the section under discussion are the different interpretations of Paul's imprisonment made by himself and his adversaries.

50   See J. Linko's essay 'Paul's two Letters to the Philippians? Some critical observations on the unity question of Philippians' in this publication for discussion on the unity of Philippians.

in 1.15ff. more likely. Namely, the function and purpose of the opponents depicted therein in relation to the recipients of the letter. Is it really believable that Paul would, right at the beginning of the letter, take up a situation that only has relevance for himself (and perhaps minimally even so, as in the views of Beare and Vincent)? What purpose would this serve for the Philippians? Of course, as we established above, Paul is very much interested in creating a certain kind of image of himself in this section, and this being the case, it is not completely unthinkable that he would use a more insignificant phenomenon to make his point. But redundancy seems not to be the best solution, especially at a crucial point like this in the letter. It seems, in fact, much more believable that Paul would here depict himself in a certain way in relation to some who have a real connection and a real significance to the readers. Thus, when he strengthens his *ethos*, he does it to convince the Philippians that they should listen to him rather than to the opponents. And this is, of course, something that fits the Judaisers better than just some random group, whatever Paul's attitude.

In fact, there are certain signs in Philippians that reveal Paul's worry over losing the Philippians. He heavily stresses the unity between himself and the Philippians right at the beginning of the letter (1.5) and expresses trust(!) that God will keep the Philippians on the path they have originally taken (1.6). That the worry has to do with the Judaisers is evident in ch. 3, where in the context of his warning about the Judaisers, Paul again expresses his wish that the Philippians continue in the same manner of 'walk' as hitherto (3.15-16). (Of course, this passage is significant only if the letter is originally of one piece). All of these passages convey a fairly positive and trusting attitude by Paul towards the Philippians, but this is not necessarily a sign that Paul's worry is not acute. That his worry appears in the guise of a more sugary approach, by way of affirmations of mutual love and commitment, may at least partly result from his vulnerable situation in prison. It would probably not have been very wise to appear extremely authoritarian in his situation.

6. *The Connection between 1.15ff. and Ch. 3*

A major, perhaps *the* major question concerning the possibility of Judaisers in 1.15ff., still remains unaddressed. Namely, is it possible to explain the different tone Paul takes towards allegedly the same opponents inside this one letter? The question of Paul's 'inclusiveness' towards the opponents in 1.15ff. was already explained above as the result of how Paul wanted to depict himself in relation to them and/or by his unwillingness to admit the seriousness of the situation. But how is it that Paul can express such victoriousness and self-assurance in 1.15ff. and then in ch. 3 resort to warning the Philippians in a not-so-stoic manner?

Perhaps a bit surprisingly, the most important key to solving the puzzle is found in the much debated verse 3.1, immediately preceding Paul's warning to the Judaisers in 3.2.[51] It reads as follows: τὸ λοιπόν, ἀδελφοί μου, χαίρετε ἐν κυρίῳ. τὰ αὐτὰ γράφειν ὑμῖν ἐμοὶ μὲν οὐκ ὀκνηρόν, ὑμῖν δὲ ἀσφαλές. This is the place where 1.15ff. connects to ch. 3 and also, where Paul reveals why he takes a more aggressive stance in the latter. First of all it is important to note that Paul begins with the same theme of joy (χαίρετε) used already in 1.15ff. Appearance of the word may well be a sign that he is thinking of the same phenomenon in connection with which he used it previously. But of more importance is the way he denies that what he is about to discuss is awkward *for him* (ἐμοὶ μὲν οὐκ ὀκνηρόν).[52] This is exactly what he wanted to prove in 1.15ff. as well. Apparently Paul feels the need to stress again at this point, before his aggressive warning, that he himself feels in no way intimidated by the Judaisers. But in the following – and this is in fact the explanation Paul himself gives for his different tone in ch. 3 – he needs to take a different tone and issue a stern warning against the Judaisers *for the safety of the Philippians* (ὑμῖν δὲ ἀσφαλές).

7. *Notes on the Historical Setting of the Letter*

The question of where and when Paul wrote his letter to the Philippians has been a source of much discussion and, so far, no consensus has been reached in the matter. Some believe Paul wrote the letter from Ephesus during his so-called third missionary journey.[53] Others opt for a later date after Paul's last trip to Jerusalem and locate the letter either in Caesarea, or more traditionally, in Rome.[54] Valid arguments can be put forward for each of these options, but within the confines of this article, there is no room to engage with all of them systematically. So, in the following, observations will be limited to how the overall solution offered above reflects on the matter.

First a few words on who the Judaisers were. In short: the Judaisers were Jewish-Christians who believed that those who converted to

---

51   See Linko, 'Two letters' on the different interpretations of 3.1.

52   'The same things' (τὰ αὐτά) Paul says he is writing about may or may not refer to 1.15ff. The necessity of this is dependent on whether Paul had already had time to write to the Philippians about the Judaisers before the letter at hand.

53   Jewett ('Conflicting movements', p. 364) suggests the years 54–55 A.D. Becker (*Paul*, p. 314) believes in the original disunity of the letter. He situates letter A (1.1–3.1; 4.1-7, 10-23) in Ephesus and letter B (3.2-21; 4.8-9) shortly after Paul's second visit to Philippi during the collection journey to Macedonia, but still before Paul's Caesarean-Roman imprisonment.

54   E.g. Hawthorne opts for Caesarea (cf. n. 36 above). Fee (*Philippians*, pp. 35–37), Bockmuehl (*Philippians*, pp. 30–32), and U. Schnelle (*Apostle Paul: His Life and Theology* [trans. M. Eugene Boring; Grand Rapids: Baker, 2005], pp. 366–69) opt for Rome.

Christianity from paganism should also become members of Israel in the conventional sense and accept circumcision and (at least certain of) the ritual commandments of the Torah. Paul, as is well known, had a different view on the matter. The Judaisers Paul refers to in Phil. 3 appear initially in Paul's letter to the Galatian churches. A strong case can be made for their Jerusalem/Judaean origin and that they were on a counter-mission of some sort to (at least some of) Paul's churches. A more debated question is whether the Judaising movement was in any way connected to the Jerusalem church and its leadership. Luke, of course, does not say this in Acts, but this has sometimes been taken as part of his placatory intent. In Luke's account a view similar to that of the Judaisers is the cause for assembling the Jerusalem meeting. In that meeting the view is refuted and a pact made by Paul and the Jerusalem apostles (Acts 15). This is something that Paul validates in Galatians (2.1-10). Historically the question is, however, what happened *after* the meeting. In Luke's story, the 'Judaising view' is still, during Paul's last visit to Jerusalem, something both Paul and the Jerusalem leadership reject (Acts 21.17-24). However, there is a real possibility that things started to change in the Jerusalem church after the meeting. James, who had replaced Peter as the number one apostle already before the meeting,[55] was more conservative in his outlook. It can be argued that, partly due to the escalating political tension in Judaea, he and the local Christians adopted a more tradition-ally Jewish stance and ultimately drifted further and further away from what was decided at the meeting.[56] That James either actively or passively supported the Judaisers in Galatia may be reflected in Paul's dismissive evaluation of him in Gal. 2.6 and by the fact that the Judaisers had evidently appealed to some authority figure who could be viewed as having a higher standing than Paul (Gal. 1.8-9). Even more remarkable is Luke's silence about the inclusion in his account of Paul's last visit to Jerusalem. It can be taken as a sign that the inclusion, which was originally intended as a token of unity (Gal. 2.10), was not accepted, and that Paul's last effort to strengthen or perhaps re-establish his connections with the Jerusalem apostles failed.[57] Another option is, of course, to take things more in line with how Luke depicts them. Even in this scenario the Judaisers still appear as a force to be reckoned with during Paul's last visit

---

55   This is clear among other things from Acts 12.17 as well as the order of names Paul uses when recounting the events of the Jerusalem meeting (Gal. 2.9). For further discussion see Lüdemann, *Opposition*, pp. 44–52.

56   *Ibid.*, p. 62.

57   Thus e.g. *Ibid.*, pp. 58–62 and Schnelle, *Paul*, pp. 360–62. In this alternative, one of course needs to explain what happened to the considerable sum of money Paul brought with him to Jerusalem. It seems at least clear that it was no longer at Paul's disposal, since he needs a gift from the Philippians.

to Jerusalem, in fact, one that had even grown in numbers and influence (Acts 21.20).

In the Ephesian solution for locating Philippians, the letter is assumed to be written well before Paul's last visit to Jerusalem. It is commonly assumed to be Paul's anticipatory warning to the Philippians written almost immediately upon the arrival of bad news from Galatia. Paul is thought to perhaps fear that the Judaisers might set out for Macedonia next. While ch. 3 as such works quite nicely within this reconstruction, the assumption of Judaisers behind 1.15ff. makes the matter more compli-cated. Especially the way Paul connects the opponents in 1.15ff. to his imprisonment would in this case have to be read as gross exaggeration. Paul's alleged Ephesian imprisonment could not have been a very extended one, which makes the likelihood of the opponents (in Galatia at the time) reacting to it quite slim.

More can be said in favour of a date after Paul's last visit to Jerusalem. First of all, Paul's imprisonment was at this point more severe and long-term. The opponents would have had plenty of opportunity to react to it. Moreover, Paul's imprisonment in Judaea was due to Jews who felt Paul was betraying their heritage (Acts 21.27-36). This would most probably have spoken to the Judaisers, who apparently felt the same way. It is in no way difficult to imagine that they would have interpreted Paul's imprisonment as God's way of silencing a heretic – and in turn would have been encouraged by this to preach their own message even more and perhaps even accelerate their counter-missionary actions. This in turn explains why Paul makes an extra effort to ensure that the Philippians stay on the right path. At this point it is important to make a note on the question of the locality of those Paul speaks about in 1.15ff. If Paul writes from Rome, Judaisers are most probably not locals. But perhaps a bit surprisingly, Caesarea allows for this perfectly. The Judaisers Paul in our view refers to might not have been all that active in Caesarea, but they were most certainly a *Judaean* phenomenon.

Paul's defensive stance towards the Judaisers in 1.15ff. is, of course, explainable regardless of whether they were connected to the Jerusalem leadership or not. In both cases they would have posed a threat and given Paul reason to stress that he is in fact fearless and unaffected. Both cases would also have given Paul reason to deny that the gospel (that is, *Paul's* interpretation of it) was not seriously endangered even if its main proponent was imprisoned (1.12). However, certain issues fit much better if we assume the background to be Paul's rejection by and rift with the Jerusalem church. First of all, that it would have been, after all, *the original Jerusalem church* with Jesus' biological brother as its leader that had rejected Paul, makes it understandable that Paul might have had

reason to attempt to conceal the real state of affairs.[58] In a situation like
this it might not have been all that clear where the Philippians' loyalties
would now lie. If Paul were now to fully admit the rift, it would only have
hastened the Philippians' need to start taking sides. Paul may have felt
more comfortable with the idea of making his case in person before
handing the guns to the listeners. It almost sounds as if Paul is at the same
time attempting to evade the truth and implicitly admitting it with his
attempt to clear himself from all guilt. And somehow, Paul is not even
completely distorted at this point: he had in fact travelled to Jerusalem
with unity in mind. This brings us to the second point that explains itself
better in this scenario, that is, the way Paul's accusations on the
opponents centre on their schismatic behaviour. It is hardly suprising that
Paul would, after his bitter experiences in Jerusalem, accuse the opponents
of factionalism. This is exactly what the situation was all about. In this
scenario a real change in tactic needs to be assumed from 1.15ff to ch. 3,
but one that can still be explained by what Paul expressedly says in 3.1: it
is for the protection of the Philippians.

8. *Conclusion*

We set out with a rather provocative question: does Paul in Phil. 1.18a say
that he is rejoicing in the work of the Judaisers? The answer proposed in
this article was, quite expectedly, somewhat more moderate – but yet
affirmative. It was suggested that Paul in this passage is able to say that he
rejoices in the work of the Judaisers, because he restricts his viewpoint to a
more neutral aspect of their work. He refers only to their genuine
evangelism, not their way of invading Paul's churches. He also remains
silent on the more conflicting theological issues with them and restricts his
critique to their allegedly impure motives. The reason for this choice of
viewpoint was explained by Paul's desire to show himself, by his joyous
and noble attitude, as having a higher *ethos* than the opponents and not
feeling threatened by them. It was also suggested that Paul might use his
joy as a tool for creating for the Philippians a softer picture of his relations

58   Evasiveness of how things really had gone may also appear in 1.12. Paul's obscure
words τὰ κατ᾿ ἐμέ ('what has happened to me') do not unequivocally limit the subject to
Paul's imprisonment (although it must be admitted that the next verses 1.13-14 do
concentrate on that specific question). It is, in fact, quite possible that with this non-specific
choice of words Paul refers more widely to his rejection by the Jerusalem church. It is also at
least slightly possible in this scenario that Paul's ambiguous words in 1.16, on 'knowing' that
he is 'appointed' by God, in fact carry a veiled reference to the rejection of his apostleship by
the Jerusalem leaders (cf. note 10). Of course, this need not be something that came up only
in connection to Paul's imprisonment (cf. Jewett's note, section 3 of this article). It was rather
something that Paul and the Judaisers (and the Jerusalem apostles) had disagreed on from
the start.

with the Judaisers than was the case in reality. This would have been especially valuable had the Judaisers in reality been connected to the official Jerusalem church, and had Paul only recently been rejected by them.

The crucial element for explaining the change in Paul's tone from 1.15ff. to ch. 3 was detected in verse 3.1, which was in fact taken as Paul's own explanation on the matter. In it, Paul is first seen to emphasize, completely in the spirit of 1.15ff., that he himself does not feel awkward when it comes to the opponents, but that the following, more aggressive (and more forthright) estimate of the opponents is intended *for the safety of the Philippians*.

Chapter 8

PAUL'S TWO LETTERS TO THE PHILIPPIANS? SOME CRITICAL
OBSERVATIONS ON THE UNITY QUESTION OF PHILIPPIANS

Jaakko Linko

1. *Introduction*

The sudden change in the tone of the text and the break in the line of thought at the beginning of chapter three of Philippians have given a reason to suspect Philippians of being originally a compilation of two or three separate letters. In the course of decades, numerous different division theories of two and three letters have been posed, especially in the 1960s when the mainstream of study seemed to deny the unity of the letter.

In the two-letter hypothesis, chapter three is considered to be an originally separate warning letter (letter B) that has later been added in the middle of Paul's first letter to the Philippians (letter A). In the three-letter hypothesis, the thanksgiving at the end of the letter (4.10-20) is also interpreted as an independent letter. When partitioning Philippians to three originally separate letters, verses 4.10-20 are called letter A, the warning letter is letter C and the rest of the text is letter B – written after A and before C. Against the division theories numerous unity theories have been suggested, especially during the last couple of decades.

The denial of the unity of Philippians is based on literary critical observations on the change of tone and contents of the text within the letter. Generally speaking, the changes in the contents of the text are the strongest arguments of the literary criticism for the fact that the text is non-uniform. The researchers, who divide Philippians into two or three original letters, perceive breaks in it, not only in the tone of the text, but also in the logical line of Paul's thought. If a part of the letter is supposed to be later than another, the same lexicon as in the older part should be found in it. Likewise the fresh supply or correction of subjects that have been dealt with earlier should be found. When the same matters are mentioned, the point of view would have to be different between the letters.[1] It is problematic that the connection of the lexicon and contents between the separate parts of the letter can also be used to justify those parts being parts of a uniform letter.

The newer theories which defend the unity of Philippians are usually based on some kind of rhetorical analysis or other so-called 'trendy literal observations'. The use of a merely different method complicates the discussion with division theories which usually lean on the literary critical method. For example, there is a fundamental problem in the use of rhetorical analysis to solve the unity question of Philippians. Rhetorical analysis supposes that a particular text to be examined is a unity which has a clear beginning and end.[2] Otherwise, the task of rhetorical analysis is not to clarify if one text is uniform, but the analysis presupposes that it is in principle uniform at least. In that case, the danger of a vicious circle is obvious.

The rhetorical analysis can seem convincing even if it does not really adhere to the actual problems of the unity of the text. In addition, as Carolyn Osiek states, there do not seem to be two similar views on the structure of Philippians which are based on a rhetorical analysis.[3] The unity question of Philippians cannot be considered permanently solved yet. Even if in recent decades a seeming consensus about the unity of the letter seems to have been created, the new unity theories are no more convincing than most old division theories. To find a convincing solution to the unity question it is necessary to be critical also of those newer unity theories and to take a good look at the observations of the division theories. In this article it is not necessary to go through the entire history of the study on the unity question. Instead, I present a weighing of a few of the strongest arguments both for and against the original unity of the letter and finally try to find a fair solution to the unity question of Philippians.

---

1   Lars Aejmelaeus deals with the methodology of the examinination of the composition of 2 Corinthians and summarizes the subject of James H. Kennedy's methodological observations (see James H. Kennedy, *The Second and Third Epistles of St. Paul to the Corinthians with Some Proofs of Their Independence and Mutual Relation* [London: Methuen & Co., 1900], pp. 79–80). The basic principles presented also agree as a starting-point for the clarifying of the unity question of Philippians (Lars Aejmelaeus, *Riidan ja sovun dokumentti: Kirjallisuuskriittinen ja tutkimushistoriallinen selvitys 2. korinttolaiskirjeen kokoonpanosta ja taustasta* [PFES, 39; Helsinki: Finnish Exegetical Society, 1983], pp. 4–5).

2   Lauri Thurén, 'Retoriikkaa, epistolografiaa ja argumentaatiotutkimusta', in R. Hakola and P. Merenlahti (eds), *Raamatuntutkimuksen uudet tuulet* (Helsinki: Yliopistopaino, 1997), pp. 76–86 (79).

3   See Carolyn Osiek, *Philippians, Philemon* (ANTC; Nashville: Abingdon Press, 2000), p. 18.

2. Are Verses 4.10-20 a Thanksgiving Letter?

How necessary is it to interpret verses 4.10-20 as a separate thanksgiving letter? According to William J. Dalton, this assumption should not be made because the communication between Paul and the Philippians was not necessarily restricted only to what Paul wrote. Paul may have already thanked the Philippians for the gift orally and therefore may have placed his thanks only at the end of the letter.[4] However, Dalton's argument entails too many guesses about the communication between Paul and the Philippians. It cannot yet prove the unity of the letter.

Duane F. Watson defends the original unity of Philippians and remarks that the rhetorically important parts – the *exordium, narratio* and *peroratio* – seem to be missing in the supposed separated letters.[5] However, it is a mistake to think that the short thanksgiving letter of one matter would necessarily have to have a perfect rhetorical structure. It is also uncertain how the rhetoric of antiquity was adapted in the letters.[6] Salutations and greetings may have been left out of this thanksgiving letter when the original letters were connected by a redactor. The arguments as presented above are not convincing.

Stronger arguments against interpreting the verses 4.10-20 as a separate letter are made by Jürgen Becker. If verses 4.10-20 are interpreted as a separate letter, the connection breaks between the references to Epaphroditus in chapter two (2.25-30) and four (4.18). Verses 4.14-15 are easily understood as part of the same letter as chapters one and two. Furthermore, Becker remarks that, as in Philippians, in 1 Cor. 16.1-4 the matter of collection is likewise not mentioned until the end of the letter.[7]

The arguments made by Becker are more convincing because at the same time he does not need to address the whole letter as uniform. According to Becker, without verses 3.2-21, Philippians would form a perfect whole.[8] Without the break in the contents and tone of the text in the beginning of chapter three, Philippians would not appear to be a composite-letter to anyone. Dalton and Watson get into trouble when connecting the solution of the question of the thanksgiving letter too closely together with the whole unity question of Philippians.

There does not seem to be such a break between verses 4.9 and 4.10 that one should suppose the verses 4.10-20 to be a separate letter. The only remaining argument for such an interpretation is the placement of the

4   William J. Dalton, 'The integrity of Philippians', *Bib* 60 (1979), pp. 97–102 (99).
5   Duane F. Watson, 'A rhetorical analysis of Philippians and its implications for the unity question', *NovT* 30 (1988), pp. 57–88 (87–88).
6   See Osiek, *Philippians*, p. 18.
7   See Jürgen Becker, *Paul: Apostle to the Gentiles* (Louisville: Westminster/John Knox Press, 1993), pp. 309–10.
8   *Ibid.*, p. 311.

thanks at the end of the letter. However, one may be astonished why a redactor would have placed a separate thanksgiving letter in such a strange place.[9] If there was no such redactor, how can it be explained that Paul decided to place his thanks for the gift at the end of a letter? Even though some researchers have considered this placement of the thanks strange, such was not unusual in the Hellenistic world. Loveday Alexander and Craig S. Wansink have presented examples of letters that are stylistically close to Philippians and in which the writer expresses his gratitude for the received support only at the end of the letter.[10]

In the light of what has been presented above, it seems most probable that verses 4.10-20 are in their original place in Philippians. Thus, the following observation can be made. If chapter three is extracted from the original Philippians, the thanksgiving section is in a considerably more natural place than when all of Philippians is supposed to be uniform.[11] The references to Epaphroditus would not be very far from each other and the letter would proceed logically towards the thanksgiving without disrupting the grateful atmosphere.

3. *The Problem of Philippians 3*

A. *Possible Beginnings and Endings of a Supposed Later Letter-fragment of Phil. 3*

At the beginning of chapter three, something significant takes place in the text. Paul's sudden outburst against the evil Jewish-Christian workers in verse 3.2 forces even a researcher who thinks that Philippians is a uniform letter to give some kind of explanation for that hostile attack. Some mitigations and explanations have been presented for Paul's anger, but they are not very convincing.[12]

In the theories based on a rhetorical analysis or a specifically formulated structure of a uniform letter, the sudden change in tone at the beginning of chapter three has been neutralized by looking for factors which refer to the seamless continuity of text throughout Philippians. The

9 This is questioned also for example by Ralph P. Martin, *Philippians* (NCBC; Grand Rapids: Eerdmans, 1976), p. 20.

10 See Loveday Alexander, 'Hellenistic letter-forms and the structure of Philippians', *JSNT* 37 (1989), pp. 81–101 (97–98); Craig S. Wansink, *Chained in Christ: The Experience and Rhetoric of Paul's Imprisonments* (JSNTSup, 130; Sheffield Academic Press, 1996), pp. 129–32.

11 This is quite surprising, because it is just interpretation of chapter three as an independent letter that has led to suspicions that there might be some other originally separate parts in Philippians. Maybe those who see Philippians as a composition of three letters have not examined Philippians as a whole after separating chapter three.

12 See e.g. B.S. Mackay, 'Further thoughts on Philippians', *NTS* 7 (1961), pp. 161–70 (163).

problem with these theories is that the break caused by the change of tone in the text seems understandable only when the reader of the letter has studied the structural or rhetorical theories offered by a contemporary scholar. In my opinion, reading the text of Philippians as it stands in the Bible makes it nearly impossible to ignore an unexpected break at the beginning of chapter three.

It is easily perceived that there is no consensus about the exact location of the later interpolated letter among the researchers who consider Philippians a compilation letter. To find a solution to the question of whether the second letter or part of the second letter has been added to this section of Philippians, one must first determine where the supposed joint is exactly.

Jeffrey T. Reed's thorough analysis of verse 3.1 shows that its two sentences form a whole and belong together with the preceding verses 2.25-30 where Paul writes about Epaphroditus becoming ill and getting well. According to Reed, it is probable that Paul has used in 3.1b his own modification of the so-called *hesitation formula* that was generally used in Hellenistic letters. The verb ὀκνέω (to hesitate) was specifically used in letters when the writer wanted to request the receiver not to hesitate in some matter or when the writer wanted to indicate that he was not hesitating in some matter himself. In Paul's *hesitation formula*, the verb ὀκνέω is replaced by the expression οὐκ ὀκνηρόν. The noun ἀσφαλές in 3.1b is syntactically strongly connected to the expression οὐκ ὀκνηρόν. Writing about the same matters is not οὐκ ὀκνηρόν to Paul, and to the Philippians that is ἀσφαλές. According to Reed's idea of the *hesitation formula*, οὐκ ὀκνηρόν means here that to Paul writing about the same matters will not cause a hesitation. Thus, the most natural translation for the word ἀσφαλές is not *safety* as is often suggested, but rather *consolidation*.[13]

Reed suggests that τὰ αὐτά points to a preceding exhortation to rejoice which is a natural interpretation when the expressions οὐκ ὀκνηρόν and ἀσφαλές are translated in the way presented above. Paul does not hesitate to exhort repeatedly to rejoice and be happy and to the Philippians this is a source of consolidation and strength. Thus the sentences 3.1a and 3.1b belong seamlessly together. The reason for happiness is found in the preceding verses where Paul writes about Epaphroditus who had recovered after being seriously sick. In this context, τὸ λοιπόν should be translated as *from now on* or *henceforth* – not *finally* as sometimes is suggested.[14]

Reed's arguments are convincing. Thus, the only remaining place for a

13   Jeffrey T. Reed, 'Philippians 3.1 and the epistolary hesitation formulas: the integrity of Philippians, again', *JBL* 115 (1995), pp. 63–90 (65, 73–78).
14   *Ibid.*, pp. 79–84.

beginning of an interpolated letter would be verse 3.2.[15] It is possible that all of verse 3.1 was composed by a redactor trying to join two separate letters more naturally by composing an extra verse. However, this would seem a little strange because such an angry warning immediately after a joyful exhortation is a reason to doubt the unity of the letter. On the other hand, the redactor could have used some kind of repetition technique in connecting the letters by repeating right before the added fragment a sentence from where the original text would continue. In Philippians, the next exhortation to joy is found in verse 4.4. However, this kind of a repetition technique usually functions in the opposite way. In fact, a more probable technical-repetition explanation would be to suppose that verse 4.4 was added by a redactor. The most probable place for the beginning of the later added text is verse 3.2.

Where would the supposed interpolated text end? Verse 4.3 is a worthy alternative because the exhortation to joy is repeated in verse 4.4. This choice would require a redactor who had used some kind of repetition technique when attaching the text to the letter. Paul would hardly repeat his exhortation to joy within such a short period.[16] However, the repetition added by the redactor is an unnecessarily complex default.

It has also been suggested that the later added text continues to verse 4.1. The fact that in verse 4.1 Paul refers to the Philippians with the word στέφανος (crown, wreath) supports this solution, if it is thought that it refers to verse 3.14 where Paul runs towards the goal in order to gain the winner's prize. On the other hand, verse 4.1 contains a lexicon which can be considered to connect it rather to other parts of Philippians than to chapter three.[17] When interpreting verse 4.1 as a part of the section beginning with verse 3.2, the exhortation to 'stand firm in the Lord' would refer to the idea of standing firm despite opposition.

Few supporters of a three-letter hypothesis find verses 4.1-9 to belong to

---

15   *Ibid.*, p. 73. In fact, Reed ends up with a slightly different result. Reed namely presents the imperative mood βλέπετε in the verse 3.2 as structurally and thematically connected to the imperative moods in the verses 2.29–3.1a (*Ibid.*, pp. 84–87). Thus Reed's analysis could defend the unity of Philippians. Reed's argumentation on the joining of the 'warning verse' together with the 'hesitation formula' is not as convincing as his other thoughts. In my opinion, when looking at the contents of the verses, verse 4.1, including the imperative mood στήκετε, seems to be the most natural verse to follow verse 3.1. This interpretation would strengthen the assumption that verses 3.2-21 have been added later to Philippians.

16   To me, the exhortation in verse 4.4, 'Rejoice in the Lord always; again I will say, Rejoice', would sound like a too comical repetition right after verse 3.1.

17   The lexicon of verse 4.1 as noticed by David E. Garland: ἀδελφοί (1.12, 3.1, 13, 17), ἀγαπητοί (2.12), ἐπιπόθητοι/ἐπιποθῶ (1.18), χαρά/χαράν (2.2). David E. Garland, 'The composition and unity of Philippians: some neglected literary factors', *NovT* 27 (1985), pp. 141–73 (161–62).

the same later-added text of chapter three.[18] This interpretation would indeed be one of the easiest solutions, and justified if verses 4.10-20 are also interpreted as a separate letter. In that case, the letters C (the warning letter) and A (the thanksgiving letter) included in letter B will be placed consecutively without the material of letter B left in between. The only work of the redactor will have been transferring some final greetings of letter B to the end of the compilation letter. As shown above, there is no need to interpret verses 4.10-20 as a separate letter. Therefore, interpreting verses 4.1-9 as a part of the warning letter does not make partitioning Philippians any easier, as would be the case with a three-letter hypothesis. From now on in this article, the warning letter is called letter B and the rest of Philippians will be letter A. Another point against the interpretation of verses 4.1-9 as a part of the warning letter is that the reference to the gentleness of the Philippians in verse 4.5 does not fit the tone of chapter three. In the section beginning with verse 3.2, the Philippians are not exhorted to be especially gentle. On the contrary, Paul's aim is to make it clear to the Philippians that they have by any means necessary to refuse the heresies of the Jewish-Christian workers.

A more logical and better solution is to think that the last verse of letter B is verse 3.21.[19] If Reed's interpretation of verse 3.1 is accepted, the text would continue most naturally in verse 4.1. Contrary to Reed's claims,[20] the exhortation to joy in verse 3.1 would continue much more logically with the imperative mood στήκετε in verse 4.1 than with the imperative mood βλέπετε (3.2). Thus the phrase οὕτως στήκετε ἐν κυρίῳ (4.1) would mean that the Philippians have to stand firm in the Lord 'this way' – which means rejoicing and being happy. According to Reed, verse 3.1 aims at the consolidation of the Philippians. Thus, the line of thought continues naturally with an exhortation to stand firm in the Lord. Because Paul exhorts the Philippians to rejoice in the Lord in order to confirm them, it is natural that he continues: 'Therefore, my brothers, you whom I love and long for, my joy and wreath of victory, this is how you should

---

18   See B.D. Rahtjen, 'The three Letters of Paul to the Philippians', *NTS* 6 (1960), pp. 167–73 (169); Günther Bornkamm, *Paul* (trans. D.M.G. Stalker; London: Hodder and Stoughton, 1971), pp. 246–47.

19   Surprisingly, there are only a few scholars who define letter B simply to verses 3.2-21. One of those is Becker (Becker, *Paul*, p. 310), who is a supporter of the two-letter hypothesis. The only supporter of the three-letter hypothesis who defines letter B in that way seems to be Müller-Bardorff, whose theory of partitioning looks otherwise like a very complicated 'shredding' of the text (see Garland, 'Composition', p. 155). Darrel J. Doughty suggests also that the verses 3.2-21 are a separated fragment, but he interprets the section as a non-Pauline text (Darrel J. Doughty, 'Citizens of heaven: Philippians 3.2–21', *NTS* 41 [1995], pp. 102–22 [121]).

20   See Reed, 'Hesitation', pp. 84–87.

stand firm in the Lord, dear friends!' When verses 3.2-21 are removed, the text proceeds logically and seamlessly:

προσδέχεσθε οὖν αὐτὸν ἐν κυρίῳ μετὰ πάσης χαρᾶς καὶ τοὺς τοιούτος ἐντίμους ἔχετε, ὅτι διὰ τὸ ἔργον Χριστοῦ μέχρι θανάτου ἤγγισεν παραβολευσάμενος τῇ ψυχῇ, ἵνα ἀναπληρώσῃ τὸ ὑμῶν ὑστέρημα τῆς πρός με λειτουργίας. τὸ λοιπόν, ἀδελφοί μου, χαίρετε ἐν κυρίῳ. τὰ αὐτὰ γράφειν ὑμῖν ἐμοὶ μὲν οὐκ ὀκνηρόν, ὑμῖν δὲ ἀσφαλές. ὥστε, ἀδελφοί μου ἀγαπητοὶ καὶ ἐπιπόθητοι, χαρὰ καὶ στέφανός μου, οὕτως στήκετε ἐν κυρίῳ, ἀγαπητοί.

One needs to be careful when interpreting verses 4.8-9. Verses 4.8-9 have been understood in several division theories to be a loose ending to one of the original letters.[21] In letter B, an actual ending with its final greetings seems to be missing. Verses 4.8-9 would serve as an ending to the letter most naturally, but then one would have to suppose that the redactor has moved the verses to their present place. If verses 4.8-9 are in their original place in 'the canonical' Philippians, one has to suppose both the salutations and the final greetings of the letter B (3.2-21) had been removed by the redactor. The latter default is slightly more well-founded. The salutations and possibly a few other words of the introduction seem to be missing from the beginning of letter B, and there is reason to suppose that the redactor may have omitted a similar amount of text also from the end of letter B. If partitioning Philippians into two separate letters, the question of verses 4.8-9 must be left eventually open.

B. *The Relationship Between Verses 3.2-21 and Other Parts of Philippians*
In T.E. Pollard's interpretation of verse 3.17, the expression συμμιμηταί μου does not mean imitating Paul, but Christ. Thus Pollard tries to connect 'the Christ-hymn (2.5-11)' with chapter three.[22] Even if Pollard was right, it does not prove the unity of the letter. Paul may emphasize the exemplariness of Christ, but that does not have to be a reference to the hymn in chapter two.

According to Pollard, the letter seems uniform because Paul repeatedly writes of the unity of the Philippian congregation. Paul appeals to the examples of Christ and himself when advising the Philippians to have an

---

21   See Eduard Lohse, *Uuden testamentin synty* (trans. Heikki Räisänen; Mänttä: Mäntän kirjapaino Oy, 1986), p. 64; Gerhard Barth, *Der Brief an die Philipper* (ZBK, 9; Zürich: Theologischer Verlag, 1979), pp. 10–11; Becker, *Paul*, p. 310. Helmut Koester leaves the question about verses 4.2-9 and 4.21-23 open in his own three-letter hypothesis (Helmut Koester, 'The purpose of the polemic of a Pauline fragment: Philippians III', *NTS* 8 [1962], pp. 317–32 [317]).
22   See T.E. Pollard, 'The integrity of Philippians', *NTS* 13 (1967), pp. 57–66 (63–64).

attitude that unites the congregation.[23] Pollard suggests that the main subject of Philippians is humility and humbling to keep the Christian congregation united. If Pollard is right, it seems that Paul's own action runs totally against that theme. Paul's angry attack against the Jewish-Christian workers does not fit very well with the ideal of Christian unity.

Finding lexical and thematic parallelism between only 'the Christ-hymn' and verses 3.20-21 is not a very convincing argument for the unity of Philippians. Thus the scholars who defend the unity of the letter have tried to find further parallelism between verses 3.2-21 and other parts of the letter. Some lexical parallels found are: κέρδος (1.21, 3.7), πολιτευ-(-ομαι 1.27, -μα 3.20), ἀπώλεια (1.28, 3.19), σκοπέω (2.4, 3.17), σχῆμα/μετασχηματίζω (2.7/3.21), ταπεινοφροσύνην/ταπείνωσις/ταπεινόω (2.3/3.21/4.12) and ἐπίγειον (2.18, 3.19). Thematic parallels are, for example: *the call for the unity and the agreement* (1.27-28, 3.16), *the sufferings* (1.29-30, 3.10), *the exhortation to imitate* (1.30, 2.11, 3.17), *humility* (2.1-11, 3.1-11) and *the progressing in the Christian life* (2.12-18, 3.12-13).[24]

Do these connections prove that the letter is originally uniform? The supposed letter B (3.2-21) was written only a short time later than the letter that includes 'the Christ-hymn'. If any lexical or thematic connections between these texts could not be found, it would be somewhat strange. In that case, one would have a reason to suppose that chapter three is an interpolated text from a totally different context, perhaps from another Pauline letter that was not addressed to the Philippians. Such an interpretation is made by F.W. Beare.[25] In light of Pollard's observations, Beare's interpretation seems to be very problematic. Finding lexical parallelisms does not make it impossible to see verses 3.2-21 as a later letter sent to Philippi only a short time after 'letter A'. Paul may well have used the vocabulary of the hymn and letter A in his later letter. He may have had the previous letter in mind at least subconsciously when dictating letter B.

Although Paul's aim in letter B is different than in the earlier letter, he can use the same already-mentioned themes when dealing with a new subject. For example, it is natural that, when warning the Philippians of the Jewish-Christian workers, he leans on his own exhortation to stay as a unanimous congregation (1.27-28; 3.16). The verb στοιχέω, in verse 3.16, means *stepping forward in the line*. Thus one can interpret verse 3.16 as if Paul has meant to emphasize the unity and the agreement of the Philippians in their Christian striving. In letter A, Paul clearly supposes

23   *Ibid.*, p. 66.

24   For details and a more specific list of the parallels, see L. Gregory Bloomquist, *The Function of Suffering in Philippians* (JSNTSup, 78; Sheffield Academic Press 1993), pp. 102–3.

25   See F.W. Beare, *A Commentary on the Epistle to the Philippians* (BNTC; London: Adam & Charles Black, 1959), pp. 100–1.

that the Philippians are able to stand united, as he advises. Thus, in the later letter he can refer to that unity when he states that *whereto we have attained, we have to step forward 'as one front'*.

At least one of the lexical connections between the different parts of the letter can be explained by the fact that Paul was writing explicitly to the Philippians. The words πολιτεύεσθαι and πολίτευμα are 'special vocabulary' that Paul especially used when writing to the Philippians. 'Citizen' and 'citizenship' were terms especially understandable to the Philippians because they lived in a city that was a Roman colony (*Colonia Augusta Iulia Philippiensis*). As the inhabitants of a Roman colony, the Philippians will have understood Paul's words on 'the citizenship of the Heaven' in the light of their own idea of citizenship. To the Philippians, the juxtaposition between 'the heavenly and the profane colony (πολίτευμα)' may have been one of the most moving themes in the letter(s) in a very concrete way.[26] It is reasonable to suppose that only a short time later in the 'extra- letter' Paul used the same vocabulary and the same themes as in his earlier letter to the Philippians.

Is Paul referring to the same opponents in verses 1.15-18, 1.28 and 2.15 as in verses 3.2-21? In verses 1.15-18 he clearly refers to the heretic Christians who preached Christ using the wrong motifs when Paul was in prison. The next time the opponents are mentioned is in verse 1.27, when Paul advises the Philippians to conduct themselves *in a manner worthy of the gospel of Christ* (μόνον ἀξίως τοῦ Χριστοῦ πολιτεύεσθε). Paul continues by saying that the Philippians must stand firm in the same spirit and mind, and *not be frightened by the opponents* (καὶ πτυρόμενοι ἐν μηδενὶ ὑπὸ τῶν ἀντικειμένων) (1.28). By interpreting Paul as referring here to the same opponents as in verses 3.2-21, the unity of the letter can be either defended or denied. A point against the unity of the letter is that Paul's attitude towards the opponents seems to change completely within the letter. In verse 1.28 Paul does not have to warn about the opponents, but he seems to suppose that the Philippians do not care about any opponents at all. On the contrary, in verse 3.2 the opponents seem to be a real and serious threat. Some scholars who defend the unity of the letter and base their theories on rhetorical analysis suggest that in verses 1.27-30 Paul introduces the subject which he will deal with later in the same letter. Thus verses 3.2-21 are simply a continuation of his earlier (1.28) reference to the opponents.[27]

---

26 Lilian Portefaix writes similarly about the word πολίτευμα (Lilian Portefaix, *Sisters Rejoice: Paul's Letter to the Philippians and Luke-Acts as Seen by First-century Philippian Women* [ConBNT, 20; Stockholm: Almqvist & Wiksell International, 1988], p. 139).

27 See Watson, 'Rhetorical', pp. 72–76; Jukka Thurén, *Galatalaiskirje, Filippiläiskirje* (Helsinki: SLEY-kirjat, 1993), p. 130.

Alternatively, it is reasonable to suppose that the opponents in verse 1.28 are not the same Jewish-Christian missionaries as in verse 3.2. In verse 1.28 Paul refers to the opponents with the word ἀντικείμενος. In that context, the most natural interpretation of the word ἀντικείμενος is that Paul does not mean the opponents that are against him, but those who are against the Philippians. The Jewish-Christian missionaries were explicitly Paul's opponents. To the Philippians, those missionaries were not the opponents, but nice preachers who tried to win the Philippians over to their cause. The Philippians would not have associated the opponents mentioned in verse 1.28 with those Jewish-Christians who were preaching Christ like Paul, and besides that demanding that Jewish laws be kept. By 'a crooked and perverse generation' in verse 2.15, Paul hardly meant the Jewish-Christian 'nomistics'. It is hard to understand what would be perverse in keeping the Jewish law.

It seems very probable that the opponents mentioned in chapter three do not appear elsewhere in Philippians. This does not mean that Paul's attitude towards the dissidents has not changed inside the letter. In verse 1.18 he is happy about all the preaching of Christ, even if it is done with the wrong motifs. In this light, it seems strange that Paul uses very strong words when he warns the Philippians about the Jewish-Christian preachers. Were those Jewish-Christians not preaching Christ as well?

After all, the theory on the rhetorical structure of Philippians, where verses 1.27-30 are the introduction to the matters dealt with in chapter three, is not very convincing. It is difficult to see the opponents mentioned in verse 1.28 as a reference to the polemic of chapter three.

4. *Two Logical and Coherent Letters*

A. *The Themes and Structures of the Letters to the Philippians*

It has been shown above that Philippians could be a compilation of two originally separate letters A (1.1-3.1; 4.1-23) and B (3.2-21). Appealing to rhetorical or other structural theories involving 'literary critical' questions of the unity and integrity of particular texts is a problematic way to approach them. Because the rhetorical analysis presupposes the integrity of the examined text, it would be hard to arrive at any other conclusion than finding the text to be uniform. Thus, the following examination will not prove that Philippians is a compilation of two letters. However, there is good reason to examine whether the supposed letters A and B function as logical and independent letters that have functional structures and themes of their own.

B. *The Themes and Structure of Letter A*

When interpreting verses 3.2-21 as a separate letter, one can clearly find the two most essential themes in Philippians A (1.1-3.1; 4.1-23): Paul's gratitude towards the Philippians and his wish that the Philippians stand unanimously and in harmony in a manner worthy of the gospel. According to Rafael Gyllenberg, the only purpose of Philippians is that Paul is giving thanks to the Philippians for their gift and explaining why Epaphroditus is already coming back to Philippi instead of assisting Paul for a longer time.[28] If Gyllenberg was right and if verses 3.2-21 were part of the uniform letter to the Philippians, those verses would seem like a totally wrong track in Paul's line of thought.[29] Instead, the two-letter hypothesis would perfectly fit Gyllenberg's interpretation. There is no problem interpreting letter A as a letter whereby Paul wanted to show his gratitude. Giving thanks for the gift may well be the main purpose of letter A, but it is not its only purpose as Gyllenberg suggests. In letter A, Paul also wants to reassure the Philippians so that they are not too worried about his adversities. Paul wants to strengthen the faith of the Philippians by advising them to rejoice and stand unanimously in the Lord. The atmosphere is warm throughout the letter and reflects the close relationship between Paul and the Philippians.

According to Becker, the easily discerned logical structure of letter A is as follows: The epistolary opening (1.1-2) and thanksgiving (1.3-11) are followed by verses 1.12-26, where Paul reports his own situation to the Philippians. The next part (1.27–2.18) tells how the Philippians are expected to live in a manner worthy of the gospel in faith (1.27-30), love (2.1-11) and hope (2.12-18). The long ending of the letter begins with the travel plans (2.19-30), which are followed by the exhortations to unity and to joy for the future (3.1; 4.1-7). The conclusion of the letter continues with the detailed thanksgiving section (4.10-20) and finally ends with greetings and blessing (4.21-23).[30]

There is also an alternate way to outline the structure of letter A. Alexander interprets Philippians as 'a family letter' which fits perfectly letter A. In that case, the main purpose of the letter is to tell the latest news and Paul affirms to the Philippians that – despite the circumstances – everything is all right with him (1.12-26). In addition, according to Alexander, the thanksgiving (4.10-20) at the end of the letter fits with Hellenistic letter-forms. Alexander is forced to explain verses 3.1b-21 as Paul's 'intermediate sermon'.[31] In the light of the two-letter hypothesis, Alexander's idea of 'the family letter' holds nicely when there is not a

---

28 Rafael Gyllenberg, *Uuden testamentin johdanto-oppi* (Helsinki: Otava, 1948), p. 106.
29 Despite this, Gyllenberg does not deny the unity of Philippians.
30 Becker, *Paul*, pp. 310–11.
31 See Alexander, 'Hellenistic', pp. 87–100.

problematic 'intermediate sermon', but an originally separate, later letter
to the Philippians.

Also in the light of the rhetorical analysis, there seems to be a logical
structure in letter A. The patterns of the rhetorical structure of Philippians
presented by Watson and J. Thurén[32] can be applied without problems to
letter A. Verses 1.1-2 and 4.21-23 are the salutations and greetings of the
letter. The first section 1.3-26 is the introduction or the *exordium*. This
section includes the epistolary thanksgiving in verses 1.3-11 and the news
about Paul's situation in verses 1.12-26. Verses 1.27-30 are the *narratio* or
the *propositio*, in which the theme of the letter is introduced. Thus, the
main theme of the letter seems to be Paul's exhortation to act *in a manner
worthy of the gospel*.

Verses 2.1-30 are the main part of the letter. This section may be
interpreted as an advising speech (the *exhortatio*) or as the *probatio*, in
which the claims introduced in the *propositio* are dealt with further. In
either case, verses 2.1-11 deal with the mutual love, unanimity and
spiritual unity of the Philippians. In the second part (2.12-18), Paul
advises the Philippians to be *'blameless and innocent, children of God
without blemish in the midst of a crooked and perverse generation'* (2.15), in
other words, to act in a manner worthy of the gospel, being in *'no way
intimidated by their opponents'* (1.28), as presented in the *propositio*. In the
section that deals with the travel plans (2.19-30), Paul presents Timothy
and Epaphroditus as examples of righteous workers for the gospel.

Verses 3.1 and 4.1 are transitional verses between the main part and the
end part of the letter – the *peroratio*. Those verses belong to the repetition
part of the *peroratio* (3.1; 4.1-9), where Paul revises what is written above
in the letter. In the repetition, the theme or *topos* of joy is essential. In
verses 4.10-20 Paul appeals to the emotions of the recipients by
emphasizing his warm relations to the Philippians, hoping that they will
live *in the manner worthy of the gospel* in the future too.

All these outlines for the structure of letter A prove that letter A is a
rhetorically and thematically functioning whole. Letter A seems to be
easier to outline than the canonical letter to the Philippians. According to
all the theories above, letter A emphasizes the warm relations and the
bonds of friendship between Paul and the Philippians. Paul does not need
to appeal to his authority when advising them to stand firmly together and
act in a manner worthy of the gospel. Letter A gives an impression that
the Philippians have stood firmly and are blameless in the Lord and have
been unanimous (despite Euodia and Syntyche). There do not seem to be
any problems or major threats in the air. Nothing seems to threaten the
warm relationship between Paul and the Philippians. Most of the main
themes of Philippians suggested in the unity theories are the themes of

---

32   Watson, 'Rhetorical', pp. 61–79; J. Thurén, *Filippiläiskirje*, p. 130.

letter A: 'The partnership of the gospel',[33] the friendship,[34] the exhortation to live unanimously and in one spirit,[35] the advice to live in a manner worthy of the gospel and Paul's gratitude towards the Philippians for the gift. All those themes are clearly present in letter A – Paul's warm 'family letter' to the Philippians.

C. *The Theme and Structure of Letter B*

The only theme and purpose of letter B is to warn the Philippians about the heresies preached by the Jewish-Christian missionaries. Paul appeals to his own experience and example when justifying his claim that the only right way to live like a Christian is the way that Paul has taught. It is not self-evident against whom the polemic is directed. Robert Jewett presents some strong arguments for the fact that Paul does not refer to the same group of Jewish-Christian missionaries throughout chapter three.[36] On the other hand, in letter B Paul may be referring also to the opposition that he himself has been struggling with elsewhere, before writing the letters to the Philippians. The reference to the libertines (who 'worship the belly') is easily explained in terms of Paul's exemplary battle against all kinds of heresies.

Paul's struggle with the Jewish-Christian preachers is reflected also in Galatians. According to Becker, letter B is thematically and rhetorically close to Galatians. Both Galatians and letter B resemble the rhetoric of the court speech of antiquity.[37] Galatians seems to have been in Paul's

---

33   See A. Boyd Luter and Michelle V. Lee, 'Philippians as chiasmus: key to the structure, unity and theme questions', *NTS* 41 (1995), pp. 89–101 (97–99); Dalton, 'Integrity', p. 101; Robert C. Swift, 'The theme and structure of Philippians', *BSac* 141 (1984), pp. 234–54 (237).

34   The theme of the friendship is emphasised by for example Ken L. Berry, 'The function of friendship language in Philippians 4.10–20', in J.T. Fitzgerald (ed.), *Friendship, Flattery, and Freakness of Speech: Studies on Friendship in the New Testament World* (NovTSup, 82; Leiden: Brill, 1996), pp. 107–24 (121); Gordon D. Fee, *Paul's Letter to the Philippians* (NICNT; Grand Rapids: Eerdmans, 1995), p. 285; and Abraham J. Malherbe, 'Paul's self-sufficiency (Philippians 4.11)', in J.T. Fitzgerald (ed.), *Friendship*, pp. 125–39 (128).

35   For example Davorin Peterlin, *Paul's Letter to the Philippians in the Light of Disunity in the Church* (NovTSup, 79; Leiden: Brill, 1995), p. 217.

36   See Robert Jewett, 'The epistolary thanksgiving and the integrity of Philippians', *NovT* 12 (1970), pp. 40–53 (48).

37   Becker, *Paul*, p. 311. According to George A. Kennedy, it is a mistake to see Galatians as a court speech. Kennedy states that Galatians is rather an example of *deliberative* rhetoric than *judicial* rhetoric (George A. Kennedy, *New Testament through Rhetorical Criticism* [Chapel Hill: The University of North Carolina Press, 1984], pp. 144–45). That is, Paul's words are not just a defence against the opponents. For the future, more important is his own example: the fact that Paul has been preaching clearly the gospel of Christ, unlike the opponents. Kennedy presents the three estimates of the rhetoric according to the theory of Aristotle (*ibid.*, p. 19). In *judicial* rhetoric, a speaker or a writer tries to get his audience to make a judgement on something that has happened before. *Deliberative* rhetoric

mind when he dictated Philippians B. The introduction or the *exordium* begins with judging the opponents in verses 3.2-3. It is made clear to the Philippians that the opponents are evil. The 'mutilation' is confronted with the real 'spiritual' circumcision. In the same way Paul makes clear the difference between the congregation and the opponents in Gal. 1.6-9. Later in the same letter (Gal. 5.2; 6.12) the opponents are proved to be the Judaisers (or Jewish-Christians) who are demanding circumcision, just as is the case in letter B. Next in verses 3.4-7, Paul describes his former pious Jewish life and in the light of his experience in Christ, he shows that the Judaisers represent the condemnable old ideals. The style of verses 3.4-7 is the historical representation of the problem or the *narratio*. The same kind of *narratio* is to be found also in verses Gal. 1.11-21.[38]

The *probatio*, the argumentative part of letter B, begins in verse 3.8 where Paul proves that the Judaisers are wrong on the basis of righteousness. The corresponding *probatio* is found in Gal. 3.1–5.12. In verses 3.8-11 Paul emphasizes that the new life in Christ is a gift. In verses 3.12-14 the gift is understood to be the power of the progression in Christian striving. Finally, verses 3.15-16 make it clear that the gift of belonging to Christ and the striving by the power of that gift are the only true patterns of the Christian life. The congregation's new life in Christ is the normative theme of Gal. 3.23-29 and 4.1-7. Likewise, the exemplary idea of being a Christian in Philippians B (3.8-11 and 3.12-14) aims at the application of that idea in being a congregation in the verses 3.14-16.[39]

Verses 3.17-21, that correspond to the section beginning in Gal. 6.11, are the ending of the letter or the *peroratio*. The advice to think like Paul (3.15a) is mentioned again in verse 3.17, now advising the Philippians to imitate Paul. The opponents are condemned in verses 3.18-19 as in Gal. 6.12-13. The end of the opponents is juxtaposed with the salvation of the congregation that lives in the Pauline spirit the same way as in Gal. 6.14-16, in which the blessing on the congregation is given after passing a sentence on the opponents.[40]

The above presented outline for a structure of letter B made by Becker proves that Watson is wrong when he claims that one cannot find the rhetorically important parts like the *exodium*, *narratio* or *peroratio* in the

---

aims at advising the audience to particular action in the future. *Epideictic* rhetoric is the case when a writer or a speaker tries to convince his audience that something or someone in the present is good. Kennedy's different rhetorical idea on Galatians does not break the structural correspondence between Philippians B and Galatians that Becker has noticed.

38 Becker, *Paul*, p. 311.

39 *Ibid.*, pp. 311–12.

40 *Ibid.*, pp. 312–13. In addition, Becker suggests that verses 4.8-9 are a perfectly fit ending for the *peroratio* of Phil. B that corresponds to the end of Galatians. As stated above, this interpretation is possible, but not necessary. Verses 4.8-9 seem to fit pretty well also where they stand now.

separate letters of Philippians.[41] Even if Becker's outline was not fully accepted, it proves that letter B is a logical, functioning independent whole with its own rhetorical structure – if it is necessary to think that every occasional letter written by Paul has to have a structure like that.

5. *Conclusions*

The critical analysis above has shown that Philippians is either an originally uniform letter or a compilation of two originally separate letters A (1.1–3.1; 4.1-23) and B (3.2-21). In the latter case, it is possible that verses 4.8-9 belong at the end of letter B. This two-letter hypothesis does not seem to cause any trouble for interpreting Philippians, and thus it can be considered the most probable solution for the unity question of Philippians. If one wants to defend the unity of the letter, one must give a reason for the break in the tone, the contents and the style of the text in the beginning of chapter three. If Philippians is uniform, the best explanation for the break is the difficult circumstances of dictating a letter in prison. The new unity theories, which are based on rhetorical or structural observations, are not more convincing than the old-school division hypotheses. The only 'weak link' in the two-letter hypothesis is the assumption of the redactor, which is a 'lesser evil' in light of how well the two-letter hypothesis can help us to understand Philippians and the background of the letter. Any final solution to the unity question will have to give the best explanation for the problems with the content of Philippians. The best solution is that Philippians is a compilation of two originally separate letters A (1.1–3.1; 4.1-23) and B (3.2-21).

---

41 See Watson, 'Rhetorical', p. 88.

Chapter 9

THE FALSE TEACHING AND ITS SOURCE ACCORDING TO 2 THESS. 2.2:
A PROPOSAL FOR A 'FRESH' READING OF THE OLD CRUX

Kenneth Liljeström

1. *Introduction*

The subject of this study is the eschatological conflict of Deuteropauline[1]
2 Thessalonians, and especially how Paul was connected to it. The life of
the congregation(s) to which 2 Thessalonians was addressed was greatly
disturbed by the claim that the day of the Lord had come (2 Thess. 2.2).
And further, to add to the seriousness of the situation, the teaching of the
present day of the Lord was presented as a true Pauline teaching. This is
the special element in the conflict of 2 Thessalonians that gives it a distinct
character: whether the author of the letter wanted it or not, he was forced
into the midst of the hermeneutical battle over the correct interpretation
of Paul.

Consequently, it would not have sufficed simply to replace one
eschatological scheme by another that constructed the end-time differently. The author of 2 Thessalonians could not argue solely on the level of
eschatology, since his opponents had not done that either. The conflict
revolved from beginning to end around the correct interpretation of Paul.
Hence, the eschatological conflict behind 2 Thessalonians is a conflict
about the true Pauline eschatology. It is about who has the right to claim
to be a faithful follower of Paul and a rightful interpreter of his
theological heritage.

The author of 2 Thessalonians had to battle on two fronts. On the one
hand, he needed to convince his readers that those who proclaimed 'the
day of the Lord has come' (ἐνέστηκεν ἡ ἡμέρα τοῦ κυρίου) lacked the
knowledge of God's end-time plan (2.3-12) which proves that the present
time is still separated from the end by a number of apocalyptic events and
figures. On the other hand, in order to succeed in his argumentation, the

---

1 For the argumentation of this position, see, e.g., William Wrede, *Die Echtheit des
zweiten Thessalonicherbriefes* (TU, 9/2; Leipzig: J.C. Hinrichs, 1903) and Wolfgang Trilling,
Untersuchungen zum zweiten Thessalonicherbrief (ETS, 27; Leipzig: St Benno Verlag, 1972).

author had to win the 'battle over Paul'. He needed to deprive his opponents of Paul's support, and he needed to present his own teaching as being true Pauline eschatology.

At the heart of this article stands the question of how the author of 2 Thessalonians sought to discredit his opponents' teaching by denying its connection to Paul. The way in which the author of 2 Thessalonians argued for his position was not similar to his opponents. While they probably took the existing Pauline material and interpreted it according to their present situation, the author of 2 Thessalonians created new Pauline material. In other words, he argued for his position by using the literary device called 'pseudepigraphy'.

First, before beginning the analysis of the key verse 2 Thess. 2.2, I will briefly examine the phenomenon of ancient pseudepigraphy in order to place 2 Thessalonians in its literary setting. After the main section of my study, in which I introduce an alternative interpretation for v. 2.2, I will again widen the hermeneutical horizon and discuss the implications of the pseudepigraphical nature of 2 Thessalonians and how the letter should be seen in the interpretation and actualization process of Pauline theology in a post-Pauline period.

2.2 Thessalonians as a Pseudepigraph

a) *Ancient Pseudepigraphy*

Pseudepigraphy, both modern and ancient, is a multifaceted and complicated phenomenon. Consequently, even the definitions of this literary device differ considerably from one another. However, for the purposes of the following short introduction, this explication, which closely follows that of Wolfgang Speyer, is useful and broad enough: *a pseudepigraph[2] is any literary work whose author is different from what the title of the work, its content, or the literary transmission of the work claims or leads one to assume.*[3] The definition therefore excludes anonymous and

2 The words 'pseudepigraphon' (singular) and 'pseudepigrapha' (plural) are also used in the literature. In my opinion, however, it is wise to avoid this terminology since the word 'pseudepigrapha' is strongly connected to the study of extra-canonical biblical literature. Hence: a pseudepigraph (singular)/pseudepigraphs (plural).

3 Cf. Wolfgang Speyer, *Die literarische Fälschung im heidnischen und christlichen Altertum: Ein Versuch ihrer Deutung* (München: C.H. Beck'sche Verlagsbuchhandlung, 1971), p. 13. This kind of definition of pseudepigraphy is sometimes criticized because it attributes the label 'pseudepigraph' also to works that initially were not written under a pseudonym. As a result, some scholars prefer, e.g., the term 'secondary pseudonymity' for these kinds of writings and confine the use of the term pseudepigraph to those works which were originally written under a pseudonym. Cf. Raymond F. Collins, *Letters that Paul did not Write: The Epistle to the Hebrews and the Pauline Pseudepigrapha* (Eugene: Wipf & Stock, 2005), p.75.

homonymous works, which, however, could later become pseudepigra-
phical if they are attributed to a different author. Such is the case with the
Gospels, which were initially anonymous but were later attached to Mark,
Matthew, Luke and John[4] respectively.

Within the concept of pseudepigraphy, a distinction should be made
between (a) works which have been accidentally attributed to someone
other than their actual writer and (b) works which are intentionally
written under the cloak of a pseudonym.

The first group contains, for example, works whose pseudonymity
results not from the author of the text but from the later copyist who
accidentally, or against better knowledge, attributed the text to someone
other than its original author.[5] The danger of this was especially close
with the copying of different collections of writings. Occasionally the
copyist attributed the whole collection to a single author, either to the
most famous one of the collection, or to the one whose work was at the
beginning of it.[6] Consider, for example, certain biblical commentaries on
Paul's letters that were written by the famous heretic Pelagius. At some
point in the process of their literary transmission, they had been
mistakenly attributed to the church father Jerome. Jerome, of course,
had fiercely opposed Pelagius during his lifetime and even composed
works (e.g. *Dialogus contra Pelagianos*) against him.[7]

Another, more or less accidental, source of the pseudepigraphs is the
ancient schools of rhetoric. These schools often assigned their pupils the
production of fictitious speeches of renowned Attic speakers. As a result,
some students of rhetoric succeeded in their task so well that their works
were later thought to be authentic speeches of the orator they imitated.[8]
However, some of these pupils who had learned the art of skilful imitation
might also have succumbed to the temptation of intentionally producing
pseudepigraphical works.[9]

The second group of pseudepigraphs, works written intentionally under
a pseudonym, is even more heterogeneous. In it one finds a plethora of
different motives for writing under a pseudonym. Occasionally the hope
of financial gain led to the production of pseudepigraphs. The demand for
literary works increased sharply at the times when the great libraries of

---

4   Jn 21.24 does not reveal the actual author of the Gospel.

5   For more on accidental pseudepigraphs, see Speyer, *Die literarische Fälschung*, pp. 37–
44.

6   See Horst R. Balz, 'Anonymität und Pseudepigraphie im Urchristentum: Überlegungen
zum literarischen und theologischen Problem der urchristlichen und gemeinantiken
Pseudepigraphie', *ZTK* 66 (1969), pp. 403–36 (413).

7   Bruce M. Metzger, 'Literary forgeries and canonical pseudepigrapha', *JBL* 91 (1972),
pp. 3–24 (4).

8   *Ibid.*, pp. 8–9; Speyer, *Die literarische Fälschung*, pp. 32–33.

9   Thus Balz, 'Anonymität', p. 411.

Alexandria and Pergamon were founded. This also prompted the production of pseudonymous works as the libraries sought to acquire the 'classics' and to fill their shelves.[10]

Some works were written under a pseudonym out of modesty and respect. To these belong, for example, many treatises which are attributed to Pythagoras although they were actually written by Neo-pythagoreans several centuries after the death of their revered mystical teacher.[11] Several psalms that are attributed to David might present a 'biblical parallel' for a similar motive of pseudonymity.

Sometimes, pseudepigraphs were written in order to denigrate an opponent. For example Eusebius tells us in his church history of the work called 'Acts of Pilate', which was later exposed as a forgery on the basis of an anachronism (Hist. eccl. 1.9.2-3). It was directed against Christians by the defamation of Jesus (Hist. eccl. 9.5.1.). Rufinus, in turn, tells of a person who erased the words 'Homo Dominicus' from the manuscript which contained Athanasius' work – and then wrote it again on the manuscript. The result was that the words 'Homo Dominicus' looked like a later interpolation in the text and, thus, cast doubt on the authenticity of the work.[12]

There is no simple answer to the question of how one reacted to pseudepigraphy in ancient times. It is said that the issue of literary origin as such was not as important in the early Israelite literature, or in Oriental literature in general, as it was in Greece.[13] Be that as it may, this distinction cannot be maintained in later years when Hellenism had also spread into Judaism. Still, one should note that in certain genres of religious literature it was commonplace to use a pseudonym even in the Hellenistic period. Especially in the Judaeo-Christian literature, pseudonymity was a quite common literary device in prophetic tradition, wisdom literature and apocalyptic writings.[14]

Then again we know of instances where the authority of a Judaeo-Christian work has been called into question with the help of, if not because of, doubts concerning its literary origin.[15] However, the existence of pseudepigraphs in certain genres of literature does not necessarily mean that the readers or listeners of those works knew that they were written

10 Speyer, *Die literarische Fälschung*, pp. 132–34.

11 Metzger, 'Literary forgeries', p. 8.

12 According to Martin Rist, 'Pseudepigraphy and the early Christians', *NovT* 33 (1972), pp. 75–91 (79).

13 So Franz Weißengruber, 'Zum Problem der Pseudepigraphie und des Kanons', SNTU A/13 (1988), pp. 179–91 (180).

14 For more, see David G. Meade, *Pseudonymity and Canon: An Investigation into the Relationship of Authorship and Authority in Jewish and Earliest Christian Tradition* (WUNT, 39; Tübingen: J.C.B. Mohr [Paul Siebeck], 1986), pp. 17–102.

15 See, for example, Tertullian's discussion on the Book of Enoch in De Cultu Fem. 1.3.

under a pseudonym. It could equally well indicate that questions of literary origins and authenticity as such were not the main issues among the groups that read the apocalyptic literature.

However, to balance these examples, one finds a plethora of instances where pseudepigraphy is explicitly condemned and strict measures are taken against it.[16] Not only does the concept of forgery derive from antiquity, but the different collections of highly advanced and modern-seeming criteria for distinguishing authentic works from forgeries do as well. Sometimes even the authors themselves took measures against possible forgeries of their own works. For example, Galen, a Greek physician, wrote a tract where he enumerated and described his own works.[17]

In Christian circles, one also finds multiple cases where pseudepigraphy is at least implicitly condemned. Tertullian for example strictly condemned the presbyter who composed the pseudonymous work called 'Acts of Paul and Thecla' (De Baptismo 17). Although Tertullian's poignant critique is directed mainly at the doctrinal error that the work contained, the fact that it was a pseudepigraph no doubt made the case even worse. He also lets his readers know that the presbyter in question later lost his office because of the forgery, even though he maintained that he had composed it from love of Paul.[18] In general, the whole process of the formation of the New Testament canon bears witness to sensitivity on the issue.[19]

Finally, it should be emphasized that the people of antiquity also had the appreciation of 'geistiges Eigentum', intellectual property, although no modern copyright agreements existed at the time. It is safe to say that the majority of people in antiquity would probably not have been delighted to find out that the scroll they were reading or listening to did not come from the alleged author of the text.

b) *Fictitious and Historical Context of 2 Thessalonians*

2 Thessalonians begins, as do most of the contemporary Graeco-Roman letters, with a tripartite prescript. According to this, Paul, Silvanus and Timothy wrote the letter to the congregation of Thessalonians (1.1). Since

---

16   It is interesting to note, for example, that the early criticism against the Johannine origin of the Book of Revelation sounds quite familiar to a modern reader (cf. Hist. eccl. 7). To be sure, Eusebius does not deny that the author of the Apocalypse was John, only that it was not the same John, the apostle John, who wrote the Johannine epistles and the Gospel of John, cf. Hist. eccl. 7.18-27.

17   Metzger, 'Literary Forgeries', pp. 6.

18   '[C]onvictum atque confessum id se amore Pauli fecisse loco decessisse.'

19   See Bruce Metzger, *Canon of the New Testament: Its Origin, Development, and Significance* (Oxford: Clarendon Press, 1987).

2 Thessalonians is a pseudepigraph, or to use more nuanced terminology, a deuteronymous work,[20] the information pertaining to the letter's historical context should be treated with care. When reading a pseudepigraphical letter, one should differentiate between the letter's intended audience and its alleged audience, for the latter, i.e. the audience that the letter itself names as its addressee, is not necessarily the same as the letter's intended audience.

A pseudepigraph that seeks to address the current situation of its intended audience is bound to live in two different worlds. On the one hand, it needs to be credibly situated in the alleged historical context. Thus, lest a pseudepigraph should fail in its intention, it should not, for example, contain any awkward anachronisms, present a style seemingly different from the alleged author's, or display perplexingly different thought when compared with the thought of the alleged author. On the other hand, a pseudepigraphical writing needs, to some degree, to 'break free' from the fictitious historical settings in order to convey its contemporary message to its intended audience. But it must happen in a very subtle and tactful way. Thus, a pseudepigraphical work seeks to address its intended contemporary audience through a fictional, but yet historically plausible, setting.

How should one, then, decipher the prescript of 2 Thessalonians (1.1-2)? The prescript of 2 Thessalonians links the letter to Paul's so-called second missionary journey. Like 1 Thessalonians, this letter is also written by Paul, Silvanus and Timothy. Like 1 Thessalonians, this letter is also directed to the congregation of Thessalonians; but if the first claim does not hold true, there is a chance that the second claim could also belong to the author's literary fiction. In my opinion, the very fact that we have the letter called 2 Thessalonians is most plausibly explained if one assumes that the letter was directed to some other audience than the Thessalonians. In the following paragraphs I intend to demonstrate this by noting the obvious problems which arise if one assumes that the pseudepigraphical 2 Thessalonians was addressed to Thessalonica.

The ancient Thessalonica[21] lay on the Via Egnatia, which was the main land route for travelling between Asia Minor and the Adriatic Sea. Before

---

20   For the definition of deuteronymity, see Hans-Josef Klauck, *Ancient Letters and the New Testament: A Guide to Context and Exegesis* (trans. and ed. Daniel P. Bailey; Waco: Baylor University Press, 2006), p. 402.

21   By the time of Paul, the city breathed cosmopolitan air and belonged to Greece's most important commercial centres. For more on the city and its history, see Winfried Elliger, *Paulus in Griechenland: Philippi, Thessaloniki, Athen, Korinth* (SBS, 92/93; Stuttgart: Verlag Katholisches Bibelwerk, 1978), pp. 78–116.

their entrance in Thessalonica in ca. 49/50,[22] Paul and his co-workers Silvanus and Timothy had been in Philippi, another important city in the province of Macedonia that lay on Via Egnatia. There they had endured hardships (1 Thess. 2.2) – and eventually the same fate of being forced to flee from the city that awaited them also at Thessalonica (cf. 2.17).[23]

Paul's stay at Thessalonica was successful.[24] 1 Thessalonians, which was penned in Corinth only a few months after, is one of the most heartfelt letters in the Pauline letter collection. It is not clear whether Paul visited Thessalonica again. Nowhere in his letters, or in Acts, is there any mention of a further visit. Nevertheless, according to Acts 19.21, 20.1-3, Paul visited Macedonian congregations during his 'collection journey', but Luke does not mention whether Paul visited Thessalonica or not. Still, although the Corinthian conflict forcefully erupted after the writing of 1 Corinthians, Paul's initial travel plans in 1 Cor. 16 do correspond to his actual route to Corinth – he came to Corinth via Macedonia (cf. 1 Cor. 16.5; 2 Cor. 2.13, 9.4).

This, in brief, is the historical continuum which should be borne in mind when situating 2 Thessalonians. At some point in the last third of the first century AD,[25] a serious eschatological conflict had taken place in the congregation (2.1-2), which had possibly also caused social problems, described in vv. 3.6-13, among the members of the congregation. On top of that, the conflict revolved around the interpretation of Paul's theology. The 'publication' of 2 Thessalonians must have been considered a surprising turn of events: a post-Pauline debate about the correct interpretation of Paul's eschatology received a reaction and a corrective explication from Paul himself!

The situation is not overly problematic in itself. The Corpus Paulinum

22   Udo Schnelle, *Apostle Paul: His Life and Theology* (trans. M. Eugene Boring; Grand Rapids: Baker Academic, 2005), p. 172.

23   The word ἀπορφανίζω in v. 2.17 clearly carries a nuance of an unexpected and untimely departure from Thessalonica.

24   Quite likely, vv. 2.1-12 do not function as Paul's *apologia*, and, thus, Paul is not defending himself against the Thessalonians' accusations. Cf. Karl P. Donfried, 'The epistolary and rhetorical context of 1 Thessalonians 2.1-12' in Karl P. Donfried and Johannes Beutler (eds), *The Thessalonians Debate: Methodological Discord or Methodological Synthesis* (Grand Rapids, Michigan: Eerdmans, 2000), pp. 31–60.

25   Cf. Hans-Josef Klauck, *Ancient Letters*, p. 399; Paul Metzger, *Katechon: II Thess 2,1– 12 im Horizont apokalyptischen Denkens* (WUNT, 135; Berlin/New York: Walter de Gruyter, 2005), p. 90; Maarten J.J. Menken, *2 Thessalonians* (New Testament Readings; London/New York: Routledge, 1994), p. 66; Lars Hartman, 'The eschatology of 2 Thessalonians as included in a communication', in Raymond F. Collins (ed.), *The Thessalonian Correspondence* (Leuven: Leuven University Press, 1990), pp. 470–85 (482); Franz Laub, *1. und 2. Thessalonicherbrief* (NEchtB, 13; Würzburg: Echter Verlag, 1985), p. 40, Wolfgang Trilling, *Der zweite Brief an die Thessalonicher* (MeyerK, 14; Neukirchen-Vluyn: Neukirchener Verlag, 1980), p. 28.

was only evolving during the course of the first century, and at the time of 2 Thessalonians it is probable that different congregations had different, mostly small, collections of Paul's letters. Thus, it would not be a highly improbable situation if the congregation of Thessalonica received a new Pauline letter. What makes this hypothesis suspect is the assumption that 2 Thessalonians was directed to Thessalonica.

It is probable that the memory of Paul's visit to Thessalonica and the apostle's correspondence with them had not vanished from the memory of the Thessalonian believers in the following decades.[26] Thus, how could the members of the congregation be convinced, against all previous knowledge and tradition, that Paul did not write them one letter but two?

Even if it were possible to persuade the audience to believe that for some reason a Pauline congregation had lost the letter sent to them by Paul, the situation that 2 Thessalonians presumes must have still been accessible via the congregation's collective memory.[27] The time gap between Paul's interaction with the congregation and the writing of 2 Thessalonians is not that huge, and Paul was not just any person to the congregation but its founder and also well known thereafter. If the situation that 2 Thessalonians presupposes could not be verified, this newly found letter would have had an immense task ahead of it. Not only is the letter completely unknown to the congregation, but also the historical context it assumes is also unverifiable at best. And the letter seems curiously topical with its references to eschatological fervour among its receivers.

The situation becomes considerably easier to understand if one assumes that the letter was directed to some congregation other than Thessalonica. In this case the formation of Paul's letter collection also supports the theory.

Some of Paul's letters were initially directed to an audience larger than a single house-church (cf. Rom. 1.7; Gal. 1.2; 1 Thess. 5.27). Consequently, it can be stated that the early circulation, albeit small-scale, had begun already during the lifetime of Paul.[28] The author of the Deuteropauline

---

26   If this were not the case, one should assume that Paul was no longer an important figure for the next generation. But why, then, would the author of 2 Thessalonians even bother to write in the name of Paul if he was of no importance for his audience?

27   Here I am not using the term 'collective memory' in any specific or technical meaning. By it I simply refer to the traditions and memories, etc., which are preserved and mediated in a community. I find it very unlikely that Pauline tradition would not have belonged to the traditions which the congregation of Thessalonica kept alive.

28   For more on the subject, see, e.g., Lucetta Mowry, 'The early circulation of Paul's letters', *JBL* 63 (1944), pp. 73–86.

letter to the Colossians, which was written during the 70s or 80s AD,[29] urges his readers to exchange letters with the congregation of Laodicea so that both congregations can read each other's letters (Col. 4.16).[30] Although Colossians is pseudepigraphical, the encouragement to circulate Pauline letters reflects the situation in the author's time: Pauline letters were in circulation. This small-scale circulation of the Pauline epistles led gradually to larger collections in the second century.[31]

Thus, in the first century AD, when there was no exclusive corpus of the Pauline letters, it was theoretically possible to join a new Pauline letter to some already circulating collection. And it should be remembered that such late Deuteropauline letters as the Pastorals, which were written at approximately the beginning of the second century, were eventually also included in the Pauline letter corpus. Therefore, if one grants the existence of Deuteropauline letters in Paul's letter collection, the initial publication and a benign reception of 2 Thessalonians becomes understandable within the context of first-century Pauline Christianity.[32]

Where was 2 Thessalonians directed, if not to Thessalonica? It is notoriously difficult to situate 2 Thessalonians in its historical context.[33] Since the letter is written under Paul's name, it is reasonable to assume that it was directed to an audience to whom Paul was an authoritative figure. Otherwise the author's choice for a pseudonym would have been totally inconceivable, especially since Paul was, and remained, a controversial man even after his death.[34] But whether 2 Thessalonians was directed to a single congregation or to a larger group of believers is difficult to say.[35]

Assuming that the audience of 2 Thessalonians considered Paul as an authoritative figure, it is reasonable to search for the letter's place of origin in the areas where he most likely had an influence even after his death. This criterion leaves us with Paul's main missionary areas, i.e., the provinces of Achaia, Asia, Galatia and Macedonia, or in terms of larger geographical units, Roman Greece or Asia Minor. Usually, the scholars

29   Cf. Outi Leppä, *The Making of Colossians: A Study on the Formation and Purpose of a Deutero-Pauline Letter* (PFES, 86; Helsinki: The Finnish Exegetical Society, 2003), p. 15.

30   Or, alternatively, the author at least wanted to encourage his audience to do this.

31   For more on the subject, see Harry Y. Gamble, *Books and Readers in the Early Church: A History of Early Christian Texts* (New Haven/London: Yale University Press, 1995), pp. 95–100.

32   By Pauline Christianity I refer to the sphere of Christianity which saw Paul as an authoritative figure, and which sought to preserve and actualize his thought.

33   Cf. Wrede's laborious attempts to date the letter in Wrede, *Die Echtheit*, pp. 86–114.

34   Cf. Calvin Roetzel, *Paul: The Man and the Myth* (Studies on Personalities of the New Testament; Minneapolis: Fortress Press, 1999), pp. 152–57.

35   For the sake of clarity, I have decided to speak of a congregation instead of congregations, although it is totally possible that the letter was written to a larger audience than a single congregation.

who consider 2 Thessalonians as a pseudepigraph place the letter in Asia Minor. This option warrants a distance from Thessalonica. Assuming that the verses that speak of the audience's suffering (1.4-7) do reflect the actual situation of the addressees,[36] it is significant that the Book of Revelation, which was composed at the end of the first century AD in Asia Minor,[37] displays many similarities with 2 Thessalonians.[38] Thus, Asia Minor is the most likely candidate, although the question still remains somewhat open because of the letter's pseudepigraphical nature and vagueness concerning historical details.

3.2 Thess. 2.2 – Crux Interpretum

The author relates in v. 2.2 that some people had proclaimed ἐνέστηκεν ἡ ἡμέρα τοῦ κυρίου, 'the day of the Lord has come'. It is beyond the scope of this article to decipher what this phrase exactly means and what kind of eschatology lies behind it, but in the light of the author's response to it in vv. 2.3-12, I am inclined to think that the author opposed an eschatological fervour rather than some spiritualized interpretation of the day of the Lord. Besides, because the letter is a pseudepigraph, one should not proceed from the text to a reality too fast. Since the phrase ἐνέστηκεν ἡ ἡμέρα τοῦ κυρίου is rather distinctive, if not unique at the time, I find it improbable that it was the author's opponent's maxim

---

36   It seems to be the case that 2 Thessalonians was directed to an audience that felt persecuted and afflicted (1.4). How concrete their sufferings were is impossible to say because of the lack of related material. Then again, it should be noted that the identity of a group is often built on a common experience of an outside rejection, or oppression, and the experience of an outside pressure is a subjective interpretative process. Thus, what may be interpreted as hostility and persecution in one community might not be interpreted in the same light in some other community. In any event, that the audience of 2 Thessalonians felt persecuted should not be doubted and labelled as a literary fiction. In the opening thanksgiving section of 2 Thessalonians (1.1-12) the suffering of Thessalonians takes an essential role. Not only does the author thank and encourage his audience for the endurance and faithfulness that they display while suffering, but he also maintains that their sufferings have a theological importance and meaning: they are suffering for the kingdom (1.5), and the sufferings show that God has elected, not abandoned, them (1.6-7).

37   Steven K. Friesen, *Imperial Cults and the Apocalypse of John. Reading Revelation in the Ruins* (Oxford: Oxford University Press), p. 151.

38   The most obvious of them is that in both works eschatology, with different apocalyptic timetables, plays an important role in consoling an audience that has suffered from outside oppression.

verbatim.[39] Rather, it is probable that the author himself has coined the phrase.[40]

The situation behind 2 Thessalonians is curious: both sides of the conflict, the author of 2 Thessalonians and his opponents, claim Paul's support for their view. With the excuse of hyperbole, it could be said that Paul is being made responsible for both the presence and absence of the day of the Lord. When one turns to study how the author deprives his opponents of the right to claim Paul's support for their teaching, a difficult problem emerges. At what cost is the author willing to win the battle of the correct Pauline eschatology? The key verses of the problem are 2.1-2, and they read as follows:

> (2.1) We ask you, brothers, concerning the parousia of our Lord Jesus Christ and our gathering to him (2.2) not to be quickly[41] shaken in your mind or alarmed, either by a spirit, or by a word, or by a letter, ὡς δι' ἡμῶν, that[42] the day of the Lord has come.

---

39   A somewhat corresponding situation can be found, for example, in 2 Tim. 2.17-18 where 'Paul' mentions a certain Hymenaeus and Philetus who have taught that the resurrection had already taken place. Should one really think that some forty years after Paul had died the author of 2 Timothy let Paul argue against the author's own foes by calling them by their real names and repeating their exact claims? If he really wished to maintain the pseudepigraphical fiction, he would not have done this. In general, the pseudonymous author speaks to his own time through literary fiction. All that is needed is that the intended audience be able to identify and interpret the fictitious situation as having importance and counsel for their own situation.

40   Thus, when interpreting the phrase ἐνέστηκεν ἡ ἡμέρα τοῦ κυρίου, one cannot simply assume that it conveys the fulcrum of the author's opponent's proclamation as it was. The more reliable way to decipher what the author opposes is to analyse how he actually argues against it. And this, in my opinion, reveals that he does not argue against some spiritualized interpretation of the day of the Lord but a wrong reading of an 'eschatological timetable'. In the author's opinion, the day of the Lord is still in the future because an apostasy and the Man of Lawlessness have not yet arrived (v. 2.3). And, besides, currently a mystical restraining force (τὸ κατέχον) and a restraining person (ὁ κατέχων) hinder the coming of the Lawless One (v. 2.6-7). These detectable signs prove that the day of the Lord could not have come.

41   Here the adverb ταχέως may also mean 'easily'.

42   There is disagreement among the commentators whether the words ὡς ὅτι are equivalent to a simple conjunction ὅτι (that), or whether the words emphasize the subjective nature of the false claim (as though). This is due to the fact that, in later Greek, the words ὡς ὅτι meant practically the same as the simple conjunction ὅτι. For different views, see Abraham Malherbe, *The Letters to the Thessalonians: A New Translation with Introduction and Commentary* (AB, 32B; New York: Doubleday, 2000), p. 417; Friedrich Blass, Albert Debrunner, and Friedrich Rehkopf, *Grammatik des neutestamentlichen Griechisch* (Göttingen: Vandenhock & Ruprecht, 15th edn, 1979), § 396,2. Although, for the sake of readability, I have translated the sentence 'that the day of the Lord has come' it is possible that the words ὡς ὅτι do emphasize the subjective nature of such a claim.

In the above translation I have left intact the key words ὡς δι' ἡμῶν, which are decisive in deciphering the author's tactic in the hermeneutical battle for Paul's support. The critical element in the phrase is the word ὡς which is used here as a relative adverb.[43] Basically, then, it can be understood in two ways:

1) *As from/by us.* In this case the words refer to a real state of affairs.[44]
2) *As though from/by us.* In this case the words refer to an unreal or imagined state of affairs.[45]

The words δι' ἡμῶν, of course, are ambiguous in Greek. Along with the spatial and temporal, the basic uses of the preposition διά with genitive consist of expressing the means or agency by which something is done.[46] In v. 2.2 the combination διά with genitive probably expresses agency, although it may also have some other nuances within itself. Consequently, a proper translation of the word would then be 'by' or 'through'. However in the translation below, I have also retained the word 'from' as a translation variant since it is widely used in different English translations and commentaries on the letter.

In the research, the words ὡς δι' ἡμῶν are almost without exception taken to refer backwards.[47] In my opinion, there are some weighty reasons for not doing this. Whether it is symptomatic or not, among the scholars who maintain that the words ὡς δι' ἡμῶν refer backwards, there is no general agreement on which word or words this phrase ultimately refers to. If the words ὡς δι' ἡμῶν are taken to refer backwards, three different solutions are grammatically possible: the words refer to the whole triad spirit-word-letter, or to the word and letter, or only to the letter. Each of these options has garnered proponents in the study of 2 Thessalonians.[48]

What is common in all of these options is the fact that, in the end, in each of them the words ὡς δι' ἡμῶν refer to the last member of the triad, the letter. Thus, in the following I will concentrate only on the solutions

---

43   On ὡς as a relative adverb, see Herbert Weir Smyth, *Greek Grammar* (rev. Gordon M. Messing; Harvard: Harvard University Press, 1956), pp. 670–71.

44   On this use of ὡς, see e.g. Walter Bauer, 'ὡς III,1' in *Griechisch-deutsches Wörterbuch zu den Schriften des Neuen Testaments und der übrigen urchristlichen Literatur* (Berlin/New York: Walter de Gruyter, 6th edn., 1988), pp. 1791–92.

45   On this use of ὡς, see, e.g., Bauer, 'ὡς III,3', p. 1792.

46   Cf., e.g., Bauer, 'διά', pp. 359–62; Smyth, *Greek Grammar*, p. 374.

47   To the best of my knowledge, the only scholar who does not do so is Gordon D. Fee. See Gordon D. Fee, 'Pneuma and eschatology in 2 Thessalonians 2.1-2: a proposal about "testing the prophets" and the purpose of 2 Thessalonians', in T.E. Schmidt and M. Silva (eds), *To Tell the Mystery: Essays on the New Testament Eschatology in Honor of Robert H. Gundry* (JSNTSup, 100; Sheffield: JSOT Press, 1994), pp. 196–215.

48   A curious exception is G. Wohlenberg, *Der erste und zweite Thessalonicherbrief* (KNT, 12; Leipzig: Deichert, 1903), p. 139. He claims that the words ὡς δι' ἡμῶν should be taken together with the verbs σαλεύω and θροέω which are at the beginning of the verse.

that connect the words ὡς δι' ἡμῶν to the letter. And since this is also the case in the two other options, spirit-word-letter/word-letter, the critique is equally applicable to them as well. Next, I will go through two different explanations that both derive from the conviction that the words ὡς δι' ἡμῶν refer to the letter. Although I treat 2 Thessalonians as a pseudepigraph, several of the following notions are also applicable if the letter is taken to be authentic. Lastly, as a third option, I introduce an alternative interpretation of v. 2.2, which, in my opinion, has some decisive advantages compared to theories which connect the words ὡς δι' ἡμῶν backwards.

a) *'Paul' Discards Paul's Earlier Letter*

[We ask you]
not to be quickly shaken in your mind or alarmed,
   either by a spirit,
   or by a word,
   or by a letter *as from/by us*
that the day of the Lord has come.

The first theory, as such, does not exactly follow any particular scholar but in the end it is the most logical conclusion if one maintains that the words ὡς δι' ἡμῶν refer to a real state of affairs.

Hence, the author of the letter lets his readers know that the false proclamation of the present day of the Lord was derived from Paul's own letter. The innocence of the author is perplexing. In passing he mentions that the false proclamation, that he so ferociously opposes, might actually derive from his, 'Paul's', own letter. And yet he does not make a single attempt in the whole letter to 'save' his earlier letter, or to explain away such an implication. 'Paul' does not deny that he really wrote thus nor does he try to explain that in the previous letter he really did not mean that. The situation becomes even more absurd in the following verse 2.3 where the author warns his readers 'do not let anyone deceive you in any way'. One is bound to ask does 'Paul' here warn his reader of himself and his letters.

Some commentators[49] have, understandably, tried to avoid this conclusion by maintaining that the author does not refer here to Paul's letter but to a false interpretation of it. This proposal is not without credit, but it does not work very well within the interpretation where the words ὡς δι' ἡμῶν are taken to refer backwards. The situation becomes notably different in this regard if one takes them to refer forwards, as I will suggest below.

---

49   For example Malherbe, *The Letters*, p. 408. Cf. also F.F. Bruce, *1 and 2 Thessalonians* (WBC, 45; Nashville: Thomas Nelson, 1982), p. 164.

In v. 2.2 there is nothing that hints that the author did not actually mean the letter itself but only its incorrect interpretation. Had that been the case, the author would have had no reason to mention the letter as one of the sources of the false proclamation. And besides, the first two members of the triad, spirit and word, both refer to oral communication, whereas the letter most naturally refers to literary communication. Had the problem been only a false interpretation of Paul's letter, it would have sufficed to refer only to the oral mediums. This would have distanced the letter from the debate, and emphasized that the problem was not the letter itself but its interpreters.[50]

Therefore, within this interpretation (a) it is almost inevitable to assume that Paul, or the author writing under his name, has decided to discard Paul's earlier letter. Quietly, but surely, he lets his readers understand that he no longer returns to that earlier letter, neither to defend it, nor to condemn it. It should be left alone and forgotten. The author of 2 Thessalonians wants to start 'afresh'.

As can be seen, this interpretation has some serious flaws in it. To start with, it is difficult to imagine a situation where Paul would simply decide to distance himself from his own letter. And even if it were possible for him, could he really expect that his audience would play along with this 'collective amnesia'? Surely, he would not warn his readers of his letters, and still assume that his audience would take seriously what he writes to them this time. Besides, in v. 2.5 the author implies that what he has written in this letter (i.e. 2 Thessalonians) is nothing new to the congregation since it corresponds to what Paul taught the Thessalonians while he was with them. Still, in v. 2.15 the author, without any reservation, mentions the 'letter' as one of the sources of sound Pauline teaching. While solving certain problems, this interpretation model creates new, even more difficult ones.

b) *2 Thessalonians Trying to Replace 1 Thessalonians?*

[We ask you]
not to be quickly shaken in your mind or alarmed,
   either by a spirit,
   or by a word,
   or by a letter *as though from/by us*
that the day of the Lord has come.

In this option the words ὡς δι' ἡμῶν are taken to refer to an unreal state of affairs. It should be noted in passing that a variant of this theory is the assumption that Paul really suspected that someone had written a letter

---

50 Thus also Ben Witherington III, *1 and 2 Thessalonians: A Socio-Rhetorical Commentary* (Grand Rapids, Michigan: Eerdmans, 2006), p. 214.

under his name. This interpretation has had some followers from the time of the church fathers onward: for example, Origen explained it so.[51] Nevertheless, it is quite improbable that at such an early period as the beginning of the 50s there were pseudepigraphical letters written under Paul's name in circulation.[52] Scholars who consider 2 Thessalonians as Paul's authentic letter often raise this point too.[53]

This theory is more comprehensible if one assumes that 2 Thessalonians is inauthentic. Most often the scholars who are proponents of this theory also assume that the spurious letter to which v. 2.2 refers is 1 Thessalonians.[54] Hence, it is assumed that the intention of the author of 2 Thessalonians was to present his letter as *the* letter to Thessalonica. Consequently, the goal of 2 Thessalonians was to replace 1 Thessalonians because of its erroneous eschatology. Its should be noted, though, that in the first 1700 years of the interpretation of 2 Thessalonians not a single interpreter had come even near to this conclusion. It was not until the nineteenth century that the forgery hypothesis was first proposed, one of its first pioneers being Adolf Hilgenfeld in 1862.[55]

The greatest obstacle for this replacement theory can be found in the letter itself: 2 Thess. 2.15 seems to contradict this theory in a decisive manner. In this verse we read 'so then, brothers, stand firm and hold on to the traditions which you were taught (ἐδιδάχθητε), whether by our mouth or by our letter'. To which letter does the author refer here? Whether or

---

51 According to Adolf Hilgenfeld, 'Die beiden Briefe an die Thessalonicher', *ZWT* 5 (1862), pp. 225–64 (250, n. 1).

52 Cf. also the criticism of Frank Witt Hughes, *Early Christian Rhetoric and 2 Thessalonians* (JSNTSup, 30; Sheffield: Sheffield Academic Press, 1989), pp. 78–79; Andreas Lindemann, 'Zum Abfassungszweck des Zweiten Thessalonicherbriefes', *ZNW* 68 (1977), pp. 3–47 (37–38) and Trilling, *Der zweite Brief*, pp. 75–77.

53 For example Howard I. Marshall, *1 and 2 Thessalonians: A Commentary* (Vancouver: Regent College Publishing, 2002), p. 187.

54 Cf. Hilgenfeld, 'Die beiden Briefe', pp. 249–59; Lindemann, 'Zum Abfassungszweck', pp. 38–40; Willy Marxsen, *Der zweite Thessalonicherbrief* (ZBK, 11,2; Zürich: Theologischer Verlag Zürich, 1982), p. 35.

55 Hilgenfeld, 'Die beiden Briefe', pp. 225–64. This is not to say that because no one in the Early Church or later up to the nineteenth century interpreted v. 2.2 in such a manner, this could not have been the original intention of its author. However, it should make the proponent of the theory aware that he or she is the one who has the burden of proof in this matter. It is true that the author does not always succeed in communicating his message clearly enough to his/her audience, but it should not trivialize the fact that authors usually do want to get their message through and, thus, influence their audience. I think that this is also fair to assume when it comes to the author of 2 Thessalonians and his message in v. 2.2. A part of this assumption, the one concerning the author's use of the phrase ὡς δι' ἡμῶν, is contested by Hanna Roose, '"A letter as by us": intentional ambiguity in 2 Thessalonians 2.2', *JSNT* 29 (2006), pp. 107–24.

not one thinks that 2 Thessalonians is a pseudepigraph, it is extremely difficult to explain 1 Thessalonians away from v. 2.15.[56]

The addressees of the letter read in v. 2.15 that Paul has encouraged the Thessalonians to hold fast to those traditions which they were *taught* by the word and by the letter. To the intended audience of 2 Thessalonians this verse explains that some decades ago Paul had encouraged the Thessalonians to remember what he taught them while he was with them and read the letter that he had sent to them. No other letter could possibly arise in the minds of 2 Thessalonians' later readers than 1 Thessalonians: it was the only known letter besides 2 Thessalonians that was directed to Thessalonica.

Thus, the proponents of the forgery hypothesis are compelled to resort to a forced and awkward assumption: although the author of 2 Thessalonians lets Paul encourage the Thessalonians to hold on to the traditions which they have received either by word or by letter, he has somehow not meant 1 Thessalonians. Although he can let Paul direct the Thessalonians to read the letter by which they were taught, by 'taught' (ἐδιδάχθητε) he does not mean taught in the past (since this would then clearly refer to 1 Thessalonians). This, in turn, is thought to prepare the way for the interpretation that the letter they (the Thessalonians) have already been taught by is none other than the present letter they are reading, 2 Thessalonians.[57] This explanation forces a highly unnatural meaning into the text, and it probably convinces only those already convinced of forgery theory in general. For others, it seems very unlikely.[58]

One further point that makes the forgery hypothesis less likely is the fact that the false proclamation of the day of the Lord, ἐνέστηκεν ἡ ἡμέρα τοῦ κυρίου, should be more or less clearly found in some of Paul's other letters, in this case especially in 1 Thessalonians. For if 1 Thessalonians is clearly beyond the possibility of being 'rescued' from the author's opponents, one would expect to find something in 1 Thessalonians which unambiguously supports the false teaching of the present day of the Lord. Yet, that is just what one does not find in 1 Thessalonians. In none of his letters does Paul say that the day of the Lord is present. He does say that

56 Cf. also the following scholars who see 1 Thessalonians as the letter referred to in v. 2.15: Ernest Best, *The First and Second Epistles to the Thessalonians* (BNTC; London: Black, 1972), p. 215; Ernst von Dobschütz, *Die Thessalonicher-briefe* (MeyerK, 10; Göttingen: Vandenhoeck und Ruprecht, 7th edn, 1909), p. 301; Malherbe, *The Letters*, p. 440.

57 For this kind of interpretation see, for example, Marxsen, *Der zweite*, p. 94.

58 Hence, the argumentation for this position is far from convincing. And, although it is somewhat debatable, should one at least expect that if the author had wanted to refer to 2 Thessalonians, he would have used the article with the 'letter'? That is just what he did in v. 3.14, where the reference is clearly to the letter itself. See also Trilling, *Der zweite Brief*, p. 128.

the day is near (cf. Rom. 13.12; Phil. 4.5), or that it comes unexpectedly (1 Thess. 5.1), but what he does not say is that the day of the Lord has come.

This is a critical point in the interpretation of v. 2.2, since even though the author might have 'corrected' some part of Paul's eschatology, he formulated his words carefully and disguised his critique so that it *seems* that he brings nothing new to what Paul has already said or written. Thus, the forgery/replacement hypothesis has some serious shortcomings and fails to explain both the critical verses 2.2 and 2.15 plausibly.[59]

c) *Paul and His (False) Interpreters*

[We ask you]
not to be quickly shaken in your mind or alarmed,
    either by a spirit,
    or by a word,
    or by a letter
as if [said etc.] by us that the day of the Lord has come.

In this interpretation, the words ὡς δι' ἡμῶν are now taken to refer forwards rather than backwards. As a result, 'Paul' is not distancing himself from the prophetic utterances which have been connected to him (2.2: πνεῦμα), nor is he erasing false memories that some thought he may have spoken about the day of the Lord (2.2: λόγος). And he is definitely not denying the authenticity of his previous letter (2.2: ἐπιστολή). *Thus, what is left is the author's stern denial of Paul's responsibility for the false proclamation itself.*

The critical sentence could then be paraphrased in the following way: 'we have had nothing to do with the false claim that the day of the Lord has come'. No matter the mediums as such – they could be prophetic utterance, spoken word, or a letter – the main point is that Paul is not responsible for the false proclamation about the presence of the day of the Lord. This also coheres well with the words δι' ἡμῶν. As noted above, in Greek the combination διά with genitive could be used in many different ways, but often it is used in expressing mediation, an agency or means by which something is done.[60]

It should also be noted that, as a result of this decision, the triad spirit-word-letter becomes perfectly balanced, since none of its members is

---

59   In addition, I would like to point out that v. 3.17 is not relevant to this discussion since in that verse the author's main point is to convince his audience of the authenticity of 2 Thessalonians, not of the inauthenticity of 1 Thessalonians. In fact, 2 Thess. 3.17 is the only verse in Paul's letter collection in which Paul's personal handwriting is explicitly used as authentication of the letter's genuineness. It is also relevant that besides 1 Thess. one does not find an explicit mention of Paul's own handwriting in Rom., 2 Cor., and Phil. If v. 3.17 was meant to function as a criterion for detecting forgeries, these letters also would be in danger.

60   See Bauer, 'διά', pp. 359–62; Smyth, *Greek Grammar*, p. 374.

burdened with the words 'as if by us'. Therefore, if the repetition of ὡς seems to make the rest of v. 2.2 quite heavy (ὡς δι' ἡμῶν ὡς ὅτι ἐνέστηκεν ἡ ἡμέρα τοῦ κυρίου), it should be noticed that connecting the first ὡς to the last member of the preceding triad also harms the balance of the sentence (μήτε διὰ πνεύματος μήτε διὰ λόγου μήτε δι' ἐπιστολῆς ὡς δι' ἡμῶν). And whether one connects the first ὡς backwards or forwards in v. 2.2, it does not change the fact that the first and the second ὡς are nonetheless unnecessarily near to each other. And besides, already the very next verse 2.3 is anacoluthon: the author starts with the protasis ὅτι ἐὰν μὴ ἔλθῃ, which lacks the apodosis. Thus the decision to connect the words ὡς δι' ἡμῶν forwards is not more susceptible to grammatical and stylistic counter-arguments than the solution where they are connected backwards.[61]

However, it should be emphasized that connecting the words ὡς δι' ἡμῶν forwards does not mean that the triad and its members are unconnected to the conflict. On the contrary, it is quite clear that the author's opponents had leant on Paul in their teaching. From their perspective, Paul was on their side. It could have been that the first two members of the triad, the 'spirit' and 'word', refer to their means of promoting their message in the gatherings of believers. Those means could be, in turn, linked to Paul by the third member of the triad, the 'letter'. Possibly, while acquainting themselves with some Pauline letters, or letter, they found support for their message. If a Pauline letter was a substitute for Paul's physical presence in a congregation even during his lifetime, all the more was this so after his death. Hence, had they found something useful for their proclamation in Paul's letters, there would have been no need to hide it.

Therefore, if the words ὡς δι' ἡμῶν are taken to refer forwards to the false eschatological claim rather than to the preceding triad or to some of its member(s) in v. 2.2, many pieces come together quite smoothly not only textually but also in the larger historical context of the letter. Of course, the lack of previous scholarly support, Fee being the only one I know of who has suggested this kind of grammatical solution,[62] may at first be interpreted as a sort of counter-argument against this solution. But the lack of a pedigree in scholarship is not as overwhelming a problem as it first seems.

First, the ancient text should always be given the chance to be heard and preserve the right to have its say at any given time or place. Occasionally, some explanations or possibilities are not discussed because they have not been on the 'agenda' of contemporary biblical research. For example, one can only marvel at the new aspects and proposals that the

61 Cf., e.g., Prov. 8.15, 16 (LXX); Dan.-Theod. 4.6; Jn 10.9; 2 Tim. 4.17.
62 Fee, 'Pneuma and eschatology', pp. 196–215.

so-called 'new perspective on Paul' has brought to Pauline studies. If such major issues as 'the law' and 'grace' are hotly disputed in scholarship, it is small wonder if the last word in some less dramatic detail, still important for the correct understanding of the post-Pauline literature, in the short text 2 Thessalonians is yet to be said.

Second, in many studies on 2 Thessalonians a curious and telling contradiction surfaces: a scholar chooses explicitly to link the words ὡς δι' ἡμῶν backwards, but in the actual interpretation of the words the same scholar treats them as if they referred onward. Consider, for example, the following statements:

> In writing ὡς δι' ἡμῶν, Paul does not deny that he has used such instruments [i.e. the triad spirit-word-letter], or that he has expressed himself in reference to times and seasons; he disclaims simply all responsibility for the statement: 'the day of the Lord is present'. (James Everett Frame).[63]

> It is more likely that the phrase goes with all three nouns, and that it refers not to whether the sources of teaching were truly Pauline but to whether the message attributed to Paul was a faithful representation of his teaching. (Howard I. Marshall).[64]

> But he is making quite clear that he accepts no responsibility whatever for the report [i.e. the proclamation that the day of the Lord has come]. However it had come, and however it had been attributed to him, he had had nothing to do with it. (Leon Morris).[65]

This inner disagreement is quickly solved when one also admits on the grammatical level that the words ὡς δι' ἡμῶν are concerned with Paul's responsibility for the false claim about the day of the Lord, and thus should be seen in connection with the false claim itself, not with its mediums.

Conclusion

The ethical questions belong to the hermeneutics of pseudepigraphy, but because of their subjective nature they are not, as such, useful categories for research. Pseudepigraphs should not be simply arranged into the neat categories of moral and immoral, or acceptable and condemnable. In many instances different motives overlap to such a degree that it is impossible to decipher which motive is predominant and which one is

63	James Everett Frame, *The Epistles of St. Paul to the Thessalonians* (ICC; Edinburgh: T&T Clark, 1912), p. 247.

64	Marshall, *1 and 2*, p. 187.

65	Leon Morris, *The First and Second Epistles to the Thessalonians* (NICNT; Grand Rapids, Michigan: Eerdmans, 1991), pp. 215–16.

subsidiary. In some cases the honourable motive of modesty and respect could very easily couple with the less honourable motive of a need to gain more attention and authority for one's own message.

Without doubt, the authors of Deuteropauline letters revered Paul highly. They belonged to the Pauline tradition and sought to preserve their master's theological heritage in the time after his death. Yet, at the same time, they were not only the preservers of the tradition but also its interpreters. In order to keep their master's voice alive, they needed to actualize his message in the midst of the discussions of their own time. They faced the questions that Paul never did. And, as a result, they were forced to give the answers that Paul never gave. It is a matter of individual taste, perhaps coupled with the interpreter's underlying theological stance, how one sees their primary motivation: does Paul speak through them, or do they speak through Paul?

Although it is a matter of definition, the author of 2 Thessalonians no doubt saw himself as a defender of correct Pauline tradition, a true Paulinist in a sense. However, it is curious to note in what way the author chose to battle against his foes. To him, Paul seemingly was not a 'dogmatic' authority whose theology and thought could only be found from his surviving letters. He, instead, saw it as possible to *create* Pauline theology, when the material was either lacking, or too ambiguous – or, perhaps, was in disagreement with the thought of the author.

That the author created new Pauline material ultimately raises the question of why he chose to do so instead of being just another interpreter of Paul's thought. Perhaps the answer lies in the fact that his position was not strong enough. Maybe he had tried to wrestle hermeneutically with his opponents and/or their followers, and did not succeed. It is doubtful that writing a pseudepigraph was the writer's first attempt to resolve the conflict. So, it could be that the author's opponents really had some entitlement to claim Paul's support for their message. It could be that they had connected, for example, Paul's teaching about the unexpected coming of the day of the Lord (1 Thess. 5) with some contemporary event which they interpreted eschatologically.

The author chose not to engage in a battle of hermeneutics with his opponents when writing 2 Thessalonians. He set himself above the debate by letting Paul interfere in the conflict and ultimately settle it down. There would be no need to argue whether one could find some support for his proclamation in Paul's letter, when Paul himself castigates and dismisses such an interpretation. Surely, no one is in a better position to explicate his texts than the one who had written them. Such is the case with 2 Thessalonians. Very likely the author's opponents found useful material, say in 1 Thessalonians, and he was forced to counter them with nothing less than the real 'voice' of Paul. No matter who maintains it, no matter what evidence he brings to the table, Paul is not to be connected to the claim that the day of the Lord has come, for he himself says that claim does not come from him.

Was his answer Pauline? Again, there is no simple answer to this. In matters of eschatology, his position was not unquestionably Pauline if one sees Paul's eschatology in terms of what is to be found in his surviving letters. The author seems to have had a different eschatological time structure. For Paul, the end of this era was not far away (cf. Rom. 13.11; Phil. 4.5) and the remaining time had no specific predictable structure as such. It is probable that Paul thought that the present evil age (cf. Gal. 1.4; 1 Cor. 7.26) was not getting any better by any human endeavour: quite the contrary, it was becoming worse. But in Paul's undisputed letters one does not find such an eschatological timetable with different supernatural end-time characters and powers, which are so prominent in vv. 2.3-12. In the end, for Paul, there was no reason per se why the Lord could not come. For the author of 2 Thessalonians, there were plenty of reasons why the Lord could not come.

Then again it is not fair to compare the texts themselves and to consider them as static entities. Every work is impacted by its historical context, socio-cultural settings, and by a plethora of other different variables. Could one then simply compare two texts coming from different situations, and decide to what degree the later is faithful to the meaning of the earlier? Such a supposition also makes Paul a static and dogmatic figure whose thinking and theology were timeless and unaffected by all the 'fuss' surrounding him. It reduces Paul's thinking to a historical vacuum. Thus, the difference in eschatology exists mainly on the textual level but it says little about the different setting, new challenges and new generation striving to keep Paul 'alive' in their time.

Hence, in a certain sense the author of 2 Thessalonians was a faithful follower of Paul despite his different eschatological concepts. He sought to actualize Pauline tradition in his own time, since without actualization no tradition is able to survive and remain meaningful for the communities which inherit it from the previous generations.

PART IV

Chapter 10

FIGHTING AGAINST STRAW MEN: DERHETORIZING THEOLOGY AND
HISTORY IN PAUL

Lauri Thurén

Source criticism is crucial for the study of Pauline theology and history. I
do not thereby refer to isagogical questions, but to the nature of the
Pauline corpus per se. The discovery of rhetorical criticism has changed
our approach to our primary sources: Paul's texts were addressed to an
audience, and worded to influence their way of life, values and behaviour.
He did not dictate his epistles simply in order to present theories. His goal
was persuasion. Consequently, all the reasoning and historical data in his
texts are delivered through heavy rhetoric. This imposes specific requirements on modern scholars seeking theological and historical data in these
documents.

The neglect of source criticism has had an unwanted impact on Pauline
studies. Thus the promising research on the 'New Paul' is about to reach
the point of retardation, if not stagnation.[1] It is my claim that this is due
to an ill-considered view of the nature of the research material. Even
scholars with a critical attitude towards the traditional view of Paul are
inclined to read his texts as neutral information about his or his
opponents' thinking. The basic nature of our sources is thereby forgotten,
and the documents are misinterpreted. Scholars have found sophisticated
theological structures with little relevance to the actual text, or grave
inconsistencies generated by their own unnatural approach.

The persuasive nature of the Pauline documents by no means excludes
theology or history. But awareness of the nature of the New Testament
texts calls for greater diligence when we attempt to retrieve theological or
historical information from them. Not until we take into account the
effect of this persuasive goal on the way in which the apostle's or his
antagonists' ideas are presented in these documents, can we discern a true

---

1   The quantity of research is still growing, as M. Bird's informative web page illustrates:
http://www.thepaulpage.com/Bibliography.html. This, however, does not indicate the
growth of essential and inspiring innovations or a consensus among scholars.

picture of their theology and their historical setting. I maintain that in this way the research of the 'New Paul' can be revitalized.

I shall illuminate my thesis with three examples: the question of Paul's theology, the Damascus road incident, and Paul's portrayal of his antagonists.

A. *From Breakthrough to Stagnation*

After the Holocaust, New Testament scholars were encouraged to see Jesus in the light of his Jewish background, not just as an ideological figure. A similar change of paradigm meant increasing awareness of Paul's thorough Jewishness. Scholars wanted to be rid of the anachronistic pictures of the great theologian of all Christian churches and reach the original thinking of the apostle beyond all pious but harmonizing explanations. Paul's texts were no longer read as solid presentations, which served as raw material for timeless dogmatics. For such dogmatics tend to reflect the scholar's own religious convictions. The backbone of church doctrine was about to evolve into flesh and blood, perhaps also spirit. Paul was seen against a distinct Jewish background, and as a pastor counselling his congregations, whose texts ought to be read without any latter-day doctrinal ballast.[2]

The change of perspective was liberating and necessary, even if not wholly new. Yet it was not until the last decades of the past millennium that it really began to transform Pauline studies. The point of departure of the New Paul was not, however, always carefully considered. There were some oversimplifications, which now, in my opinion, hamper the progress of our new approach to Paul.

According to one typical view, the fact that Paul writes in certain contexts, in a dialogical process with his recipients, means that he was not an 'abstract thinker', but a 'situational or contextualist theologian'.[3] This is however a *non sequitur*. We cannot directly conclude from what Paul or anybody else *writes* what he *is*.[4] Not even a world-view or a possible theoretical doctrinal structure can be easily visualized, if the nature of the texts is very goal-oriented. This description is well suited to all the Pauline epistles.

A more sophisticated, yet corresponding simplification arises, even if one avoids assessing Paul's personality or essence. Then 'Paul's writings are not products of theological reflection, and can thus not be interpreted

---

2 For my more detailed description of this change of paradigm, see L. Thurén, *Derhetorizing Paul: A Dynamic Perspective on Pauline Theology and the Law* (WUNT, 124; Tübingen: Mohr, 2000), pp. 5–13.

3 W.G. Doty, *Letters in Primitive Christianity* (Philadelphia: Fortress, 1973), p. 37.

4 For more about this topic, see Thurén, *Derhetorizing*, pp. 12–18.

theologically... They are written out of fundamental religious/pastoral concerns.'[5] This idea, which among some scholars has become axiomatic, includes an untenable premiss, according to which theoretical reasoning cannot be expressed in rhetorical terms, and behind religious proclamation there cannot be any coherent thought.

To be sure, not all researchers assess Paul's thinking in such a simplistic way. Even many 'New Paul' scholars argue that he had some kind of theology, albeit lacking in consistency.[6] But to move from an extreme position to a more moderate one does not solve the principal problem: conclusions are reached on the basis of text material without a proper assessment of its qualities. Source criticism is neglected.

In my opinion, this defect has caused major problems for perception of the thinking of the 'New Paul'. The scholarship has failed to follow through. The old statue of the apostle is broken down, but sitting among the splinters does not do justice to the documents and the man behind them. It has become evident that these documents were not originally intended to define certain doctrinal systems, but what then was their purpose? And how could we describe the thinking *behind* them? Can we ever penetrate it?[7]

B. *Proclamation or Theology?*

It is an easy solution to label Paul's letters as mere practical guidance to congregations. In that case theology would remain a minor point or at least a loose, labile system without any sharp contours. Paul's opinions would eventually find an explanation in pragmatic needs. Conscious or unconscious logical fallacies and inconsistencies would serve his practical aims.

Ineptitudes or not, it is difficult to think that Galatians, for example, is a merely practical document, so heavily theological is Paul's approach to

---

5 H. Boers, *The Justification of the Gentiles* (Peabody: Hendrickson, 1982), p. 195. According to him, it is not meaningful to search for any theological integrity in Pauline documents or even an implicit theological system behind them, for the apostle's thinking was mythical. The latter claim has later proven untenable. Paul's 'logic' can well be studied with modern tools of argumentation analysis. See M. Hietanen, *Paul's Argumentation in Galatians: A Pragma-Dialectical Analysis* (ESCO; LNTS, 344; London: T&T Clark, 2007).

6 H. Räisänen, *Paul and the Law* (WUNT, 29; Tübingen: Mohr, 2nd edn, 1987), p. 264ff.

7 J.S. Vos, 'Theologie als Rhetorik', in C. Breytenbach and J. Frey (eds), *Aufgabe und Durchführung einer Theologie des Neuen Testaments* (WUNT, 205; Tübingen: Mohr, 2007), pp. 247–71 (252–54) regards my theory of a theology behind the author's rhetoric as almost Platonic. Yet the opposite model, in which the way an author expresses himself in any given situation completely and in a balanced way represents his thinking seems difficult to accept. At least such a speaker would be a poor rhetorician indeed.

the defect he has found among his recipients, even if the problem, at least from a modern perspective, seems rather trivial and practical.

From an outsider's point of view it is even hard to perceive aright the alleged theological tension in the Galatian congregations. If somebody urged believers to follow a few Jewish rituals, this does not seem to be so catastrophic from a theoretical and doctrinal point of view, that Paul therefore had to lose his temper.[8] Yet for him, the principle seems to be extremely important on the high abstract level, although even he admits that the practical issue as such is insignificant. The new demands are nothing but 'little yeast', Gal 5.9. They are perceived as a great theological issue by Paul himself, as he claims that they in fact 'leaven the whole batch of dough'.

Why such exaggeration? The reason may be connected to Paul's desire of social power, or, as is more traditionally thought, to his theology. Or it may be a combination of the two.[9] Perhaps Paul attempted by dramatic theologization to prop up his own authority, or he really felt that his theological system was about to collapse in the congregation, due to these ritual details. Nevertheless, it is not crucial to determine which of the options is the more plausible. It is more important to focus on the means by which Paul attempts to resolve the situation. When he is free to choose the weapons, he chooses theological ones. Thus, he saw himself as a theologian.

Yet both Doty and Boers, whom I have criticized above, are right: Scholars must take into account the fact that Paul's epistles were written 'out of fundamental religious/pastoral concerns', or that they were basically persuasive, not demonstrative texts. But this ought to lead to a correct conclusion: the theoretical thinking behind the text, or the lack thereof, its strengths and weaknesses, are more difficult to assess than previously was thought. In other words, the way the utterances in the text describe the author's and particularly his antagonists' thinking and identities, as well as different historical events and circumstances, must be critically scrutinized.

It is my claim that Pauline studies can progress only if we ponder the ways in which the text's purpose of influencing its recipients' thinking, values, attitudes and behaviour to a maximal extent colours the information contained therein. Not until the texts' rhetorical nature and persuasive goals are identified, and the sometimes misleading technique of

8 According to Paul, the antagonists tried to 'pervert the gospel of Christ'. He is ready to curse them, and simultaneously almost curses himself, if not the Divinity as well: Gal. 1.7-9. The addressees are 'turning away from Christ', 1.6, they are 'bewitched', 3.1, and so on.

9 See A. du Toit, 'Alienation and re-identification as tools of persuasion in Galatians', *Neot* 26 (1992), pp. 279–95 (279–80); L. Thurén, 'Paul had no antagonists', in A. Mustakallio (ed.), *Lux Humana, Lux Aeterna* (Festschrift L. Aejmelaeus; PFES, 89; Helsinki: Finnish Exegetical Society, 2005), pp. 268–88 (72).

argumentation is analysed,[10] can we accurately observe and examine the doctrinal data behind them. This makes it easier to discover whether and what kinds of permanent ideological structures can be identified behind the Pauline texts.[11] By 'rhetoric' I do not refer to a battery of Greek and Roman rhetorical techniques. Rhetorical criticism seeks to study the conventions of human communication and interaction on a higher abstract level.[12] Perhaps most important is the above-mentioned search for a realistic source-critical vision, viz. recognition of the persuasive character of the text. We read early Christian documents in a different perspective from that for which they were originally created, and this must be taken fully into account.

Summing up, we can state that Paul's primary aim with his texts was to influence his audience, and this goal dictates his mode of presentation. Assessing his and his alleged opponents' doctrinal opinions leads inevitably to biased results if the communicative, interactive function of the expressions occurring in his texts is neglected.

Naturally, the perception of this function makes our search for historical or theological data more difficult. Thus, the rhetorical perspective can be rejected by *reductio ad absurdum*: If Paul does not mean what he says, then what is the point of studying his texts at all? This objection is however untenable. A modicum of communicative colour by no means prevents the text from conveying the thoughts of its author – on the contrary. But as we strive for more accurate information about historical and theological issues, the increased demands of source criticism, set by

---

10   Hietanen, *Argumentation*, pp. 185–93.

11   In a corresponding way, Karris argues that the polemical character of the Pastoral epistles needs to be recognized in order to gain reliable information: R.J. Karris, 'The background and significance of the polemic of the Pastoral epistles', *JBL* 92 (1973), pp. 549–64. For more on the same topic, see Thurén, *Derhetorizing*, pp. 23–35. Derhetorizing is not of course free from fallacies either. In my opinion, the most perilous pitfall is the temptation to label unpleasant expressions in the material as 'mere rhetoric'. A good example of such a purposeful derhetorization is provided by the classical solution to the problem of *ego* in Rom. 7 by W.G. Kümmel, *Römer 7 und das Bild des Menschen im Neuen Testament* (TBü, 53; München: Kaiser, 1974), pp. 119–32. A minimum requirement is that the author could presume that his audience was capable of perceiving his rhetorical devices as he intended, viz. that the device utilized was commonly known. For more on this topic, see Thurén, *Derhetorizing*, pp. 117–26, and L. Thurén, 'Motivation as the core of paraenesis: remarks on Peter and Paul as persuaders', in J. Starr and Troels Engberg-Pedersen (eds), *Early Christian Paraenesis in Context* (BZNW, 125; Berlin: de Gruyter, 2004), pp. 353–71 (368, n. 44).

12   See L. Thurén, *The Rhetorical Strategy of 1 Peter With Special Regard to Ambiguous Expressions* (Åbo: Åbo Academy, 1990), pp. 52–57; Thurén, *Derhetorizing*, pp. 27–28. It is arguable to what degree Paul was influenced by contemporary rhetorical culture, see, e.g., S. Porter, *The Paul of Acts: Essays on Literary Criticism, Rhetoric and Theology* (WUNT, 115; Tübingen: Mohr, 1999), pp. 101–9.

rhetorical criticism, cannot but be welcome, even if this makes the job of a Biblical scholar more arduous.

I proposed a new opening for Pauline studies, especially regarding his relationship to the Torah, in the monograph *Derhetorizing Paul*. The principle is as follows: when we take into account the rhetoric used by Paul, we can find a rather well-thought-out view of the Mosaic law in the new situation. Such an attempt to derhetorize his texts can of course lead to different results as well. It is essential to admit, however, that as the international community of Biblical scholars becomes increasingly aware of the rhetorical nature of early Christian texts, we cannot sustain a romantic faith according to which these documents could be used without amendment as raw material for objective theological or historical research.

The question of the Mosaic law is not the only phenomenon which requires a rhetorical perspective. When seeking any doctrinal positions, the roles of the expressions and possible rhetorical strategies need to be identified, as we are using the text for another purpose than that for which it was originally composed. Another good example is Paul's teaching about spiritual gifts in First Corinthians. The highly diverse opinions of scholars and churches on this question can be traced back to different ways of understanding Paul's rhetorical strategies.[13]

C. *Romans 9–11 as a Case Study*

Heikki Räisänen's article on Paul's desperate tightrope walk in Romans 9–11 in this volume offers a telling example of how difficult it is to focus on the theological content of a persuasive text. The presentation does not pay sufficient attention to the fact that the aim of the text was not to share information about Paul's ideological structure, but to influence its implied recipients, viz. the congregations in Rome.

But is not Rom. 9–11 Paul's attempt to present his theological view of Israel? Yes, but not in the way we as scholars would like. Instead of clear definitions and structures, his presentation consists of examples and similes: Abraham, Isaac, Jacob, Moses, Pharaoh, the potter, Sodom and Gomorrah, the olive tree, etc. Note all the details in a parable can be taken into account; there is no exact match. When, for example, predestination is not included in the picture of an olive tree, this tells us only that a complete dogmatic system cannot be fitted into a single image.

Moreover, as Rom. 9–11 is intended to influence its audience, the text is

---

13 See further L. Thurén, 'Paavali ja armolahjat Ensimmäisen Korinttilais- ja Galatalaiskirjeen valossa', in A. Laato (ed.), *Karismaattisuuden haaste kirkolle* (Studier I exegetik och judaistik utgivna av Teologiska fakulteten vid Åbo Akademi, 4; Åbo: Åbo Akademi, 2007), pp. 79–91.

not to be dissected into arbitrary sections, but must be studied as a whole. When Paul at the beginning presents a problem, this does not mean that he is content with the situation. Not until the end does he 'reveal a secret', viz. the solution to the problem. The audience is kept in thrall until the end. In academic treatises such a technique is seldom used, but per se it does not indicate any inconsistency.

Every minor section within these chapters cannot and should not contain a balanced system of thought. It does not take long to read through these chapters. Paul must have counted on his audience's ability to remember what he said a few moments ago, and their inability to see the big picture until he has arrived at the end. It would be exceptional if Paul's own thinking would radically change from one sentence to another. Every speaker's presentation can be made absurd if arbitrary sections are cut out.

As an analogy, we may consider 1 Cor. 13. When Paul there proclaims that love is more important than faith, scholars do not usually see this as an inconsistent deviation from Paul's general theology, where faith is central. Our natural sense of style helps us to understand that he has something else in mind in this poetic presentation.

It would be unprecedented in all ancient literature if we perceive in this text the author's desperate search, a trial of several solutions which he must reject. The ancient process of producing texts was too slow for such a modern presentation.[14] Indeed, Paul probably knew very well what he was doing and how he intended to influence the people for whom he was writing. Whether or not he succeeded in solving the problem in an acceptable and reasonable way is another issue.

Although when reading Rom. 9–11 as a whole I find a coherent definition of Israel's theological position, my main criticism of Räisänen's approach is methodological. I do not suggest that Paul's texts and thinking there do not contain any inconsistencies or, even worse, unfair argumentation. However, it is not acceptable to study such possibilities by neglecting the persuasive and literary function of the documents, let alone by 'revealing' other scholars' secret religious motives – a rhetorical device known from Galatians. We need a modern analysis of argumentation, which penetrates the structures of Paul's persuasive logic in a neutral and controllable way.[15]

---

14 In a similar way, Räisänen's thesis that Paul was so furious when dictating Galatians that he happened to reveal that his 'mind was divided' (Räisänen, *Law*, pp. 132–33) is anachronic; see Thurén, *Derhetorizing*, pp. 59–64.

15 Good methods are offered in the rapidly growing field of modern academic argumentation analysis; see L. Thurén, 'Is there biblical argumentation?', in A. Eriksson, T.H. Olbricht, and W. Übelacker (eds), *Rhetorical Argumentation in Biblical Texts* (Harrisburg: Trinity Press International, 2002), pp. 77–92 and Hietanen, *Argumentation*.

D. *Historical Studies Require Derhetorization*

The requirement of rhetorical source criticism also applies to the study of the historical dimension of Paul's texts. Historical signals in the texts have often been interpreted without due consideration of their function vis-à-vis their implied audience. Thus the claims I made above about studying Pauline theology are relevant also to the scrutiny of historical information in his texts.

The eventual goal of Paul's letters was hardly to describe his own life or the 'antagonists' mentioned in these texts. Expressions connected to these issues must not be regarded either as data intended to be historically accurate or as reliable facts. *Narratio*, viz. a goal-oriented description of what has happened, was and still is one of the most efficient devices of rhetorical argumentation.[16] *Vituperatio*, viz. denigration of the opposition, and the creation of a soft opponent or straw man, also belong to the standard, even if unfair, means of rhetoric.[17] Paul was by no means free from these 'vices'.

What happens when we realize that the historical information provided by Paul is basically rhetorical? In other words, how does our view of his context(s) alter when we admit that the primary purpose of the narrative sections of his epistles is not to present reliable data about what happened, but to influence the recipients' behaviour, values and attitudes, just like all other discourse?

Again it must be stated that the rhetorical perspective does not assess the text as empty jargon, nor does it seek extraordinary persuasive techniques. The purpose is to discover what the author originally had in mind. For example, I claim that Paul's experience on the road to Damascus and its impact on the formation of his theology must be reassessed. Likewise, the classical picture of Paul's antagonists will appear in a new light. These historical descriptions have suffered from the same problem as the description of Paul's theology.

A balanced view is necessary. As was the case with the study of Pauline theology, even now it is inadvisable to assess the historical claims in Pauline texts automatically either as facts or as wholly unreliable. Instead, we need a more critical attitude when seeking historical data. Even propaganda can include facts, but to strain them from the material is not simple. It is essential to know at least how the propaganda works and how it colours the narration.

---

16 See J.D. O'Banion, 'Narration and argumentation: Quintilian on narratio as the Heart of Rhetorical Thinking', *Rhetorica* 5 (1987), pp. 325–51.

17 On the use of these devices in Gal., see A. du Toit, 'Vilification as a pragmatic device in Early Christian epistolography', *Bib* 75 (1994), pp. 403–12, and Thurén, 'No antagonists'.

E. *On the Road to Damascus*

Paul's conversion is a typical topic where theological and historical dimensions are intertwined. Traditionally, the incident has been interpreted as a sudden and surprising experience, which completely changed Paul's theology, especially his assessment of Jesus' identity and the meaning of his death on the cross. Irrespective of how his theology developed *ex eventu*, it is seen as the starting point of this process. At least implicitly his new theology was created in that situation.[18] Moreover, the narrative of the incident has been seen as a rich autobiographical source.[19]

The description of the incident in the Acts (9.3-19) and especially in Gal. (1.15-17) raises questions. The divine aspect of the revelation cannot be examined by an academic approach, and even the phenomenological dimension remains outside the scope of this study. Nor do I here compare the interesting tensions between these two narratives. For me, it is essential to ask what purpose these narratives, especially Paul's own version, serve.

The narration resembles old-fashioned historiography, where changes in world history were illustrated through great heroes and sensational events. According to the creator of the 'Great Man' theory, philosopher Thomas Carlyle, 'the history of the world is but the biography of great men'.[20] This narrative technique may be pedagogically effective, but reality is thereby simplified at the cost of historical accuracy and reliability. Dramatic turning points in great men's lives hardly explain everything in history, not even in the development of their thinking.

The account of the Damascus road incident, especially in Galatians, has a clear rhetorical function, which is recognized by several commentators. In the structure of the text, it belongs to the *narratio*,[21] and is therefore especially questionable as an historical source.

In the account Paul emphasizes his independence from the theological authority of Jerusalem: he has received his theology directly from the Risen Lord.[22] The impact of this tendency is difficult to overestimate. It is

---

18 F.F. Bruce, *Epistle to the Galatians* (NIGTC; Grand Rapids: Eerdmans, 1982), p. 93; R. Longenecker, *Galatians* (WBC, 41; Waco: Word, 1990), p. 32.

19 See e.g. N.T. Wright, 'Paul, Arabia, and Elijah (Galatians 1.17)', *JBL* 115 (1996), pp. 683–92.

20 T. Carlyle, *Heroes and Hero-Worship* (Lincoln: University of Nebraska, 1966). For more on this theory and for good examples, see http://en.wikipedia.org/wiki/Great_Man

21 H.D. Betz, *Galatians: A Commentary on Paul's Letter to the Churches in Galatia* (Hermeneia; Philadelphia: Fortress, 1979), pp. 16–17, 58–62. For the function of this device, see above.

22 This function of the account is commonly acknowledged. See, e.g., B. Holmberg, *Paul and Power: The Structure of Authority in the Primitive Church as Reflected in the Pauline Epistles* (Philadelphia: Fortress, 1980), p. 15; Longenecker, *Galatians*, p. 35. Its effect on the historical reliability is however seldom discussed.

significant that when Paul's goal is the opposite, when he wants to emphasize himself as a scrupulous mediator of Early Christian traditions (1 Cor. 15.1-3) the message is completely different: Paul argues that he proclaims verbatim (τίνι λόγῳ) the heritage of the first congregation.

Hardly anybody denies that the role of the first congregation and of other Christian tradition in the formation of Pauline theology is far greater than he allows us to perceive in the beginning of Galatians. Simultaneously, however, we should presume that Paul's own theological meditation, which preceded the conversion experience, has an important role. It seems natural to describe the impact of the Damascus road incident on Paul's theological thinking with the verb 'trigger'.[23] The incident was the culmination of long theological pondering rather than its *terminus a quo* or *ad quem*.[24]

For example, Paul's view on the Torah was hardly unproblematic before the incident, even if the 'Lutheran' idea of him struggling against sin and bad conscience is anachronistic. The carefree young theologian described in Philippians 3.4-6 does not tell the whole truth. I have suggested several 'pre-Damascan' reasons which could explain at least partly Paul's special relationship with the Mosaic Law.[25]

In the future, we should study more carefully the narratives in Acts and Galatians about the Damascus road incident from the point of view of their rhetorical function.[26] It should be clarified what implications for historical relevance and the reliability of the seemingly objective narration arise from the way in which the narrative attempts to influence the recipients' thinking and attitudes in completely different matters. Then the account's impact on the development of Pauline theology is of special interest.

F. *Difficulties in Characterizing Paul's Antagonists*

The persuasive nature of Paul's texts has moreover a major impact on the way his opposition and their theological thinking are described in his texts. To assess their historicity is an interesting and important task indeed.

23 Thurén, *Derhetorizing*, p. 164.

24 Correspondingly, when Paul's conversion is explained with social or psychological factors, even these have their roots in the time before the Damascus road incident. They indeed offer interesting insights on the incident, but by no means exclude the theological perspective.

25 A possible problem with the Torah could have been, e.g., the internal Jewish tension between universalism and particularism, which cast doubt on monotheism. Moreover, boasting as a theological theme, or Paul's own black-and-white thinking, could have caused difficulties. See further Thurén, *Derhetorizing*, pp. 138–78.

26 Although Betz (*Galatians*, pp. 64–66) sees the tension between the stories, he does not study enough the impact of their rhetorical character.

The 'antagonists' in the New Testament, particularly Paul's opponents, appear problematic in current research. Scarce, stereotypical utterances have been used for maximal and biased characterizations, which prove untenable.[27] The critical attitude, typical of studies of the historical Jesus, is not evident in the description of these individuals. Correspondingly, the characterization of Gnostic groups has been more critical. Although they were accused of, e.g., immorality, this is not taken at face value, as we possess some Gnostic documents as well. Concerning the antagonists in the New Testament the situation is worse, since their own voice cannot be heard.

Some epistles can contain so many and contradictory signals that a commonly accepted characterization of the antagonists is impossible to attain. For example, the descriptions in modern research of the heresy in Colossae contain an incredible number of different ancient religious and philosophical movements. Most of them have support in the epistle itself![28] The spectrum of hypotheses concerning the situation in Corinth or Galatia is almost as wide. We cannot speak of any consensus of scholars.

Behind the symptoms, a reason must be found. Scholars' wild imagination or carelessness should not be blamed. Instead, the problem is caused by the basic character of the documents, as I have argued above. Several scholars have already criticized the technique of 'mirror-reading'. For example Karris, Berger, Barclay, Vorster, Johnson, du Toit, Lyons and Mitternacht voiced serious theoretical doubts over this approach.[29]

According to the critics, 'mirror-reading' inevitably means the unconscious incorporation of extra information into the text. It is however virtually impossible to know which claims about the opponents are true and which are invented by the author.[30] Moreover, the approach often seems to presume an omniscient author and is built on several other axiomatic presuppositions as well.[31]

---

27 I have discussed this problem-area in more detail in L. Thurén, 'The antagonists: rhetorically marginalized identities in the New Testament' (paper presented at the Nordic New Testament Conference in Helsingborg, 19 August 2007; forthcoming. The volume will be: L. Thurén; 'The Antagonists-Rhetorically Marginalized Identities in the New Testament', in *Identity Formation in the New Testament*. Paper from the Nordic New Testament Conference in Lund, August 2007. Ed. by Beugt Holmberg and Mikael Wanninge (WUNT 2). Tübirgen: Mohr Siebeck.).

28 See e.g. P.T. O'Brien, *Colossians and Philemon* (WBC, 44; Dallas: Word, 1982), xxx–xxxviii.

29 See Thurén, 'No Antagonists', pp. 271–73.

30 G. Lyons, *Pauline Autobiography: Toward a New Understanding* (SBLDS, 73; Atlanta: Scholars, 1985), p. 97, 104; J.M.G. Barclay, 'Mirror-reading a polemical letter: Galatians as a test case', *JSNT* 31 (1987), pp. 73–93.

31 J. Vorster, 'The context of the Letter to the Romans: a critique on the present state of research', *Neot* 28 (1994), pp. 127–45.

G. *Blaming the Antagonists Was Stereotypical*

Concerning some texts, the problem of identifying the opponents does not ensue from too many attributes. On the contrary, we gain next to no specific information. Most explicit and implicit accusations stay on the general level; they are stereotypical.

Concerning the Catholic epistles, analyses of the historical situation and the antagonists' identity, behaviour and doctrinal thinking are typically based on educated guesses. Signals in the text are used as raw material, but they have not been compared with contemporary epistolary and rhetorical conventions. Thus, for example, wide-ranging yet untenable assumptions about the situation of the letter of Jude have been presented, based on the conventional opening phraseology.[32] Moreover, the antagonists are described in the document 'by the book', viz. in accordance with general conventions of stereotypical *vituperatio*. Corresponding labelling can be found in other New Testament epistles as well as in other Greek and Jewish sources. Even in modern propaganda, several forms of *vituperatio* are known. Historical characterizations based on such claims are untenable.[33]

It is symptomatic of *vituperatio* that both the sender and the recipients recognized the rhetorical technique. After all, people known to everybody are described. Thus, this technique is not particularly misleading in its original context. Correspondingly, in modern political language vilifying labels are seldom meant to be taken literally. The goal is simply to label specific individuals as *non gratae* by stereotypical language. A certain analogy is established by pejorative slang utterances. The vilifying expressions create problems for interpreters, whose perception of the context is lacking. This is especially true when studying the world of the New Testament.

In an article on the opponents of Galatians I assume that Paul's 'antagonists' were astonished when the epistle was read aloud for the first time.[34] Most of the accusations against them, too, can be explained by stereotypical *vituperatio*.

Whereas the censure usually stays on the general level, some identifiable individuals have been victimized and marginalized by rhetorical vilification. Diotrephes (3 Jn.), Hymenaios and Philetos (2 Tim.) are such persons. It is difficult to assess whether they were scapegoats when the author has emphasized his own views and position.

---

32   L. Thurén, 'Hey Jude! Asking for the original situation and message of a Catholic epistle', *NTS* 43 (1997), pp. 451–65 (451–53, 456–62).

33   Thurén, 'Jude', pp. 457–59.

34   See also G. Howard, *Paul's Crisis in Galatia* (SNTSMS, 35; Cambridge: Cambridge University Press, 1979).

Of Paul's great letters, First Corinthians offers interesting material for the study of the antagonists. A critical rhetorical assessment of the putative heresies is necessary. Modern scholarship has indeed begun to question the traditional views of these individuals and their ideologies.[35]

The heresies in Colossae are problematic not because of stereotypical vilification, but because the flood of theological accusations and corrections is so copious that a unified characterization of the antagonists is impossible of attainment. One should ponder the possibility that the author was not omniscient, but opposed all the possible heresies just in case.[36]

For our exegetical research, it is not essential to know who the 'antagonists' present in the documents actually were and what they thought about the issues, for which Paul and other authors so vehemently criticize them. A detailed, reliable picture of them is unlikely to emerge. Yet it is even more important to ask how the accusations were expected to be perceived by the original recipients. What kind of response was envisaged, what kind of reaction did the author hope to elicit, and for what purpose?

H. *Straw Men?*

One explanation of the prominence of 'antagonists', especially in Pauline texts, even in Romans, is his own polemical vocabulary. I have argued that Paul actually needed antagonists in order clearly to convey his own message.[37] Strong language was typical of him. Thus the opponents in Galatia were distanced from their historical context and transformed into ideological figures. In Romans, where no real opponents were manifest, Paul had to invent one. The questions of this 'puppet' proved especially intriguing for him.[38]

In Galatians and Romans, nobody actually represented the antagonists' views, at least to the degree and in the way Paul describes them. Such a technique of using a soft opponent is known throughout history.[39] The acknowledgment thereof ought to impinge on the search for the opposition's historical profile, but also on the perception of Paul's own theology, since the opponents serve as its dark background.

35 See further Thurén, *Derhetorizing*, p. 102, especially footnote 102.

36 The axiom of an omniscient author in the New Testament has been criticized especially by Vorster, 'Context', pp. 137–38.

37 Thurén, 'No antagonists', pp. 280–85.

38 A certain analogy is provided by Mr Kratzinger, Gerd Theissen's fictive opponent in G. Theissen, *Im Schatten des Galiläers* (Gütersloh: Gütersloher, 5th edn, 2007).

39 See T.E. Damer, *Attacking Faulty Reasoning: A Practical Guide to Fallacy-Free Arguments* (Belmont: Wadswort, 3rd edn, 1995), pp. 157–59.

To be sure, the concept of the *straw man* does not indicate a non-historical figure – on the contrary. In political propaganda, real people are needed if the description is to be convincing. In academic discussion such a technique is of course a fallacy. A scholar who is criticized should be willing to accept the ideas which are put into his mouth. In political and religious discussion such a requirement of fair play is not always even desirable.

At least to a certain degree both the *interlocutor* in Romans and the antagonists of Galatians are soft opponents defined by Paul himself. They offer a good contrast for his own theological ideas and theories. To what degree we can find real, historical, people and thoughts remains to be seen.[40]

Conclusion

The new wave of Pauline studies stands in need of realizing that Paul's primary goal with his texts was to influence his original audience. To reconstruct a structured ideological system or to achieve reliable historical data based on these documents requires knowledge of the rhetoric utilized, and its impact on the contents of the texts. Thereby our research can explain better than before what Paul really thought about spiritual gifts, Mosaic law, or many other issues which interest modern theologians and religious communities.

The use of New Testament documents as historical sources also requires rhetorical source criticism, as the case of the Damascus road incident demonstrates. Moreover, the historical and theological dimensions are combined in an interesting way in the question of the antagonists. They have lost the information war, but their voice can at least partly be heard, if the New Testament authors' language, style and rhetorical techniques are correctly interpreted. In some cases, these individuals may however prove mere straw men, soft opponents created by the authors. Thus, their voice can sound like a 'straw epistle' indeed.

---

40 To an article dealing with the hyperbolic nature of the antagonists, I gave a corresponding hyperbolic title 'Paul had no antagonists' (Thurén, 'No antagonists'). For the reader, the title may cause corresponding difficulties despite a better knowledge of the context.

Chapter 11

TOWARDS A COMPREHENSIVE ANALYSIS OF PAUL'S ARGUMENTATION

Mika Hietanen

1. *Analysis of Argumentation and Rhetoric*

a. *Argumentation, Rhetoric and Logic*

One aspect rarely addressed in rhetorical analyses of Pauline texts is that the emphasis on rhetorical features tends to exclude dialectical aspects such as the layout of arguments and their soundness.[1] However, these are equally important aspects alongside the rhetorical ones when assessing argumentation from an overall perspective.

I suggest that when analysing Paul's argumentation it is useful to unite dialectical and rhetorical perspectives. Such a balanced view is important when reaching for a theology of Paul. To this end the Pragma-Dialectical approach (the so-called Amsterdam school of argumentation analysis) provides the exegete with a set of sophisticated tools.

In many rhetorical analyses of Pauline texts, the terms 'rhetoric' and 'argumentation' are used more or less synonymously. To argue persuasively is to make use of rhetoric, and to use persuasive rhetoric requires clear argumentation. For the purposes of making a point I will here make a distinction between these two concepts and illustrate how a comprehensive analysis requires us to take both perspectives into account.

The dictionary defines 'argumentation' as 'the action or process of reasoning systematically in support of an idea, action, or theory', whereas 'rhetoric' is defined as 'the art of effective or persuasive speaking or writing, especially the exploitation of figures of speech and other

---

1 I here understand dialectic to refer to reasoning by justifying or refuting expressed opinions in a discussion. See Frans H. van Eemeren *et al.*, *Fundamentals of Argumentation Theory: A Handbook of Historical Backgrounds and Contemporary Developments* (Mahwah, NJ: Lawrence Erlbaum Associates, 1996), pp. 37–42; and Frans H. van Eemeren and Rob Grootendorst, *Speech Acts in Argumentative Discussions: A Theoretical Model for the Analysis of Discussion Directed towards Solving Conflicts of Opinion* (PDA, 1; Dordrecht, The Netherlands and Cinnaminson, NJ: Foris Publications, 1984), pp. 15–18.

compositional techniques'.[2] Although such definitions point in the right direction, they are incomplete. Is not, on the one hand, a 'systematic support of an idea' also important for 'persuasive speaking or writing'? And are not, on the other hand, 'compositional techniques' involved in the 'process of reasoning systematically'? In other words, the one concept can at least to some extent be incorporated into the other and vice versa.[3]

A further clarification is in order. Argumentation theory differs substantially from formal logic where the interest is focused on how conclusions are derived from premises. In formal logic, the arguments are de-contextualized so that valid and invalid argument forms can be distinguished more easily. Argumentation analysis, on the other hand, is focused on arguments in context. Pragmatic factors are adequately dealt with, which is not the case in formal logic.[4] Further, the aims of argumentation analysts are much more far-reaching than those of formal logicians: 'The general objective of the study of argumentation is to develop criteria for determining the validity of argumentation in view of its points of departure and presentational layout and to implement the application of these criteria in the production, analysis and evaluation of argumentative discourse.'[5]

When setting out to analyse a text we first need to decide what features we are interested in. If our main interest lies in how topical potential, auditorial demand or presentational devices are used in order to persuade, then a rhetorical analysis is called for. If our interest, on the other hand, lies in the arguments as such, in how standpoints are defended, in fallacies or in argument schemes or argumentation structures, then a basic argumentation analysis is needed. For an overall view we need both.

Among the many studies of Paul's rhetoric one often finds comments not only relating to rhetorical aspects, but to all facets of argumentation. The problem that often presents itself in such cases is that rhetorical approaches do not provide instruments for careful analysis of the dialectical make-up of arguments. In addition, the use of theory from the classical handbooks presents its own problems.[6] Unless the historical connections to classical theories are specifically the issue, modern methods provide better instruments. Knowledge of historical and sociological

2   Judy Pearsall (ed.), *The New Oxford Dictionary of English* (Oxford: Oxford University Press, 2001).

3   For different perspectives on these two concepts, see Frans H. van Eemeren and Peter Houtlosser (eds), *Dialectic and Rhetoric: The Warp and Woof of Argumentation Analysis* (Argumentation Library, 6; Dordrecht: Kluwer Academic Publishers, 2002).

4   Van Eemeren *et al.*, *Fundamentals*, pp. 5–12.

5   *Ibid.*, p. 22.

6   See Philip H. Kern, *Rhetoric and Galatians: Assessing an Approach to Paul's Epistle* (SNTSMS, 101; Cambridge: Cambridge University Press, 1998) and R.D. Anderson Jr, *Ancient Rhetorical Theory and Paul* (CBET, 18; Kampen: Kok Pharos, 1996).

circumstances, including classical rhetorical conventions, should of course be taken into account in the analysis whenever necessary. Several approaches are available that provide sophisticated tools.[7] Here I make use of the Pragma-Dialectical method.

b. *Analysis of Paul's Argumentation*

Turning now to Paul, the existence of problems in Paul's argumentation has been acknowledged ever since his letters first appeared (cf. 2 Pet. 3.16-17). How we interpret these difficult arguments plays an important role in many issues, as is clearly exemplified by the debate about Paul and the law.[8] It is interesting to note that help has rarely been sought from argumentation theory even when Pauline argumentation has explicitly been the issue.

Although historical, semantic, grammatical and other such information is important for a correct understanding of an argumentative text, an approach that is satisfied with this type of information is not sufficient. Many traditional exegeses contain quite detailed analyses that aim towards disentangling and understanding the arguments in a text,[9] but traditional exegesis simply does not provide the necessary tools for a systematic and detailed argumentation analysis.

Among exegetes, *rhetorical* analyses abound from the 1980s onward.[10] There are many types of such an approach, but they have in common a focus on arrangement, style, rhetorical effectiveness and, in more recent studies, invention as well.[11] Another perspective is the argumentation analytical one where one studies how arguments are construed and argued in view of the relationship between claims and premises, argument schemes and argumentation structures, soundness and fallaciousness. These aspects are secondary in rhetorical analyses, if included at all.

Studies which set out specifically to study Paul's argumentation (from a mainly non-rhetorical perspective) are few in number. In 1985, Siegert noted that the history of argumentation analysis in New Testament exegesis has been widely neglected and that it is 'now completely forgotten'.[12] There are a number of older works that consider Paul's

---

7   For an overview of different approaches I refer to van Eemeren et al., *Fundamentals*.

8   See, e.g., Heikki Räisänen, *Paul and the Law* (WUNT, 29; Tübingen: J.C.B. Mohr [Paul Siebeck], 2nd edn, 1987).

9   A feature traditionally prominent in German commentaries, such as Heinrich Schlier, *Der Brief an die Galater* (MeyerK, 7; Göttingen: Vandenhoeck & Ruprecht, 6th edn, 1989).

10   See Duane F. Watson and Alan J. Hauser, *Rhetorical Criticism of the Bible: A Comprehensive Bibliography with Notes on History and Method* (BIS, 4; Leiden: Brill, 1994).

11   Anders Eriksson, *Traditions as Rhetorical Proof: Pauline Argumentation in 1 Corinthians* (ConBNT, 29; Stockholm: Almqvist & Wiksell International, 1998), pp. 7–10.

12   Folker Siegert, *Argumentation bei Paulus gezeigt an Röm 9–11* (WUNT, 34; Tübingen: J.C.B. Mohr [Paul Siebeck], 1985), p. 5.

212 The Nordic Paul

argumentation but these often limit their analysis to aspects of style, for example the use of *parallelisms, antitheses,* or *tropes.*[13]

The formation of modern theories for the analysis of rhetoric and argumentation in the 1950s resulted in implementations in Pauline exegesis in the 1970s. The plethora of *rhetorical* studies that were published in the 1980s and 1990s present a wide variety of analyses. Quite a few of the early explorations present implausible analyses, typically including long discussions on rhetorical genera and sometimes 'proving' that Paul's argumentation strictly follows ancient rhetorical practices as laid out in handbooks of the time.

Among modern works, the first thorough description of Paul's argumentation from the perspective of argumentation analysis is Folker Siegert's *Argumentation bei Paulus.* Siegert makes use of *The New Rhetoric,* originally published in 1958,[14] a work that has been characterized as a rediscovery of classical rhetoric.[15] In addition, it incorporates dialectical features and caused a new interest in argumentation analysis generally.[16] Another method, which has raised some interest among exegetes, is the one devised by Stephen Toulmin, in the same year as *The New Rhetoric.*[17] Other approaches have been tested but none has become widely used within exegesis.[18]

Since Betz' pioneering work in 1975 and 1979,[19] Galatians especially has been again and again subjected to new analyses. In 2005 alone, five

---

13   Cf. the following two works: Ed. König, *Stilistik, Rhetorik, Poetik in Bezug auf die Biblische Literatur Komparativisch Dargestellt* (Leipzig: Dieterich'sche Verlagsbuchhandlung Theodor Weicher, 1900) and E.W. Bullinger, *Figures of Speech Used in the Bible Explained and Illustrated* (London: Messrs Eyre and Spottiswoode, 1898). See also David E. Aune, *The Westminster Dictionary of New Testament and Early Christian Literature and Rhetoric* (Louisville: Westminster John Knox Press, 2003), which provides an extensive bibliography. For an overview of this research history, see Siegert, *Argumentation,* pp. 5–12.

14   Ch. Perelman and L. Olbrechts-Tyteca, *The New Rhetoric: A Treatise on Argumentation* (trans. John Wilkinson and Purcell Weaver; Notre Dame: University of Notre Dame Press, 1971).

15   Burton L. Mack, *Rhetoric and the New Testament* (Minneapolis: Fortress Press, 1990), p. 16.

16   See van Eemeren *et al., Fundamentals,* pp. 93–97.

17   Stephen Toulmin, *The Uses of Argument* (Cambridge: Cambridge University Press, updated edn, 2003). The first application of the method in a monograph within New Testament studies is: Lauri Thurén, *Argument and Theology in 1 Peter: The Origins of Christian Paraenesis* (JSNTSup, 114; Sheffield: Sheffield Academic Press, 1995).

18   Cf. Mika Hietanen, *Paul's Argumentation in Galatians: A Pragma-Dialectical Analysis* (LNTS; ESCO, 344; London: T&T Clark, 2007), pp. 23–39.

19   Hans Dieter Betz, 'The literary composition and function of Paul's Letter to the Galatians', *NTS* 21 (1975), pp. 353–79; and *Galatians: A Commentary on Paul's Letter to the Churches in Galatia* (Philadelphia: Fortress Press, 1988).

scholarly monographs were published with analyses of Paul's rhetoric and argumentation in Galatians.[20]

c. *The Pragma-Dialectical Method*

Within the field of argumentation analysis, there are different methods to choose from. However, many methods are designed for the analysis of a specific kind of discourse such as everyday argumentation, spoken argumentation judicial argumentation and political argumentation.[21] Other methods are very limited in scope; some approach the topic from a specific point of view while others focus on some specific discourse or argumentation phenomenon.[22]

Van Eemeren and Grootendorst's Pragma-Dialectical method is one of the most comprehensive methods for argumentation analysis. It has a firm base in advances within pragmatics and argumentation theory. The method has been developed in Amsterdam by the same group of scholars who took the initiative with the conferences of the International Society for the Study of Argumentation (ISSA) and the journal *Argumentation*.

The Pragma-Dialectical approach provides a methodological framework and useful instruments. It also provides a framework for understanding and evaluating argumentation in the context of a dialogue, such as between Paul and his addressees. The short definition of argumentation as it is understood from a Pragma-Dialectical perspective reads as follows: 'Argumentation is a verbal, social, and rational activity aimed at convincing a reasonable critic of the acceptability of a standpoint by putting forward a constellation of one or more propositions to justify this standpoint.'[23]

The extended version of the Pragma-Dialectic theory also takes account of rhetorical features of an argument through an analysis of what is called *strategic manoeuvring*. An analysis of the strategic manoeuvring in an

---

20 Hietanen, *Paul's Argumentation* (rev. diss. 2005); Moisés Mayordomo-Marín, *Argumentiert Paulus logisch? Eine Analyse vor dem Hintergrund antiker Logik* (WUNT, 188; Tübingen: Mohr Siebeck, 2005); Susanne Schewe, *Die Galater zurückgewinnen. Paulinische Strategien in Galater 5 und 6* (FRLANT, 208; Göttingen: Vandenhoeck & Ruprecht, 2005); D. François Tolmie, *Persuading the Galatians: A Text-Centred Rhetorical Analysis of a Pauline Letter* (WUNT, 2/190; Tübingen: Mohr Siebeck, 2005); Sam Tsang, *From Slaves to Sons: A New Rhetoric Analysis of Paul's Slave Metaphors in His Letter to the Galatians* (Studies in Biblical Literature, 81; New York: Peter Lang, 2005).

21 See van Eemeren *et al.*, *Fundamentals*, pp. 353–55.

22 For an overview of different methods, see van Eemeren *et al.*, *Fundamentals*, and the four volumes of Teun A. van Dijk (ed.), *Handbook of Discourse Analysis* (London: Academic Press, 1985).

23 Frans H. van Eemeren, Rob Grootendorst and Francisca Snoeck Henkemans, *Argumentation: Analysis, Evaluation, Presentation* (Mahwah, NJ: Lawrence Erlbaum Associates, 2002), p. xii.

argumentation reveals how 'the opportunities available in a certain dialectical situation are used to complete a particular discussion stage most favourably for the speaker or writer'.[24] The options available at each stage refer to topical potential, auditorial demand and presentational devices.[25] Although these three aspects can be distinguished analytically, in actual practice they usually work together. As van Eemeren and Houtlosser note, these aspects run parallel with important classical areas of interest: topics, audience-orientation and stylistics.[26]

If the strategic manoeuvring is consistently implemented, there is reason to talk about a rhetorical strategy. In such a case the speaker consistently tries to influence the outcome to his own advantage. It is 'manoeuvring' since the speaker manoeuvres between what follows the dialectical ideal and that which is rhetorically most persuasive.[27] To put it in other words, an argument needs to be solid as an argument but it also needs to be chosen carefully, adapted to the audience, and presented in the best way.

A traditional historical-critical exegesis typically focuses on historical, grammatical and semantic aspects. In contrast, many rhetorical analyses after 1979 focus mainly on aspects relating to *dispositio* and *elocutio*, and any elements relating to the persuasiveness of the text. But, as van Eemeren and Houtlosser note, even a very rhetorical text has dialectical substance:

> The alleged rhetorical pervasion of argumentative discourse does not mean that the parties involved are interested exclusively in getting things their way. Even when they try their best to have their point of view accepted, they have to maintain the image of people who play the resolution game by the rules: they may be considered committed to what they have said, assumed or implicated. If a given move is not successful, they cannot escape from their dialectical responsibility by simply saying, 'I was only being rhetorical'. As a rule, they will therefore at least have to pretend to be interested primarily in having the difference of opinion resolved.[28]

From a Pragma-Dialectical perspective it is argued that rhetorical moves can best be explained within a dialectical framework since an arguer's aim is seldom solely to win a discussion, but also to conduct it in a reasonable

24 Frans H. van Eemeren and Peter Houtlosser, 'Delivering the goods in critical discussion', in van Eemeren and Houtlosser (eds), *Proceedings of the Fourth International Conference of the International Society for the Study of Argumentation* (Sic Sat, 7; Amsterdam: Sic Sat, 1999), pp. 163–67 (165).

25 Van Eemeren and Houtlosser, 'Delivering the goods', pp. 165–66.

26 Frans H. van Eemeren and Peter Houtlosser, 'Strategic maneuvering: maintaining a delicate balance', in van Eemeren and Houtlosser (eds), *Warp and Woof*, pp. 131–59.

27 Frans H. van Eemeren and Peter Houtlosser, 'Strategic manoeuvring in argumentative discourse', *Discourse Studies* 1(4) (1999), pp. 479–97 (485–86).

28 *Ibid.* p. 481.

way. Consequently, rhetorical moves can be viewed against the dialectical objective of the discussion stage under analysis.[29]

2. *Analysis of Galatians 3.6-9: Abraham's Faith*

a. *Analysis*

In the following I will illustrate an argumentation analysis with a passage in Gal. 3 often recognized as containing an enthymeme:[30] vv. 6–9.[31] The pericope is traditionally recognized as a part of the argumentative section of Galatians, chs 3–4, and does as such call for an argumentation analysis. The text reads as follows:

> 3.6 Just as Abraham 'believed God, and this was reckoned to him as righteousness', 3.7 recognize, therefore, that those who are of faith, these are sons of Abraham. 3.8 And the Scripture, foreseeing that God would justify the Gentiles by faith, proclaimed the Promise beforehand to Abraham, saying, 'All the Gentiles shall be blessed in you.' 3.9 Therefore, those who are of faith are blessed with Abraham who believed.[32]

Betz describes 3.6 as the 'proof text for the entire argument in 3.6-14'.[33] The Old Testament quotation is used as grounds for the claim in 3.7 'those who believe are the descendants of Abraham'. Setting the argument in a form with premises followed by conclusion and separated by a line, it reads as in Fig. 1.

Abraham believed God.
Abraham's faith was reckoned to him as righteousness.

Those who believe are the descendants of Abraham.

Fig. 1: The text of Gal. 3.6-7 in Standard Form

---

29   Frans H. van Eemeren and Peter Houtlosser, 'Strategic maneuvering with the burden of proof', in Frans H. van Eemeren (ed.), *Advances in Pragma-Dialectics* (Sic Sat; Amsterdam: Sic Sat, 2002), pp. 13–28.

30   Basically, an enthymeme is a syllogism with one of the elements (usually the so-called minor premiss) left implicit. One can distinguish between logical enthymemes, where the focus is on validity, and rhetorical enthymemes, where the focus is on persuading a certain audience. See Frans H. van Eemeren (ed.), *Crucial Concepts in Argumentation Theory* (Amsterdam: Amsterdam University Press, 2001), p. 53.

31   The analysis follows Hietanen, *Paul's Argumentation*, pp. 100–21.

32   *The New Revised Standard Version Bible* (Oxford: Oxford University Press, 1995, anglicised edn; Copyright 1989, 1995, Division of Christian Education of the National Council of the Churches of Christ in the United States. Used by permission. All rights reserved). The translation is slightly adjusted.

33   Betz, *Galatians*, p. 138.

This presentation shows an imbalance in the argument. Mußner notes that we would rather have expected another conclusion, namely: 'Erkennt also, daß der Mensch aus Glauben gerechtfertigt wird und nicht aus Gesetzeswerken.'[34] Hansen recognizes that '[v]erses 6 and 7 taken together form an argument by enthymeme', and notes that '[t]he conclusion ... in v. 7 is derived from the implicit premiss that as God dealt with Abraham, so he will deal with all men'.[35] The enthymeme suggested by Hansen then reads as in Fig. 2:

Abraham believed God, and it was reckoned to him as righteousness. [As God dealt with Abraham, so he will deal with all men.]

Those who believe are the descendants of Abraham.

Fig. 2: Hansen's Understanding of Gal. 3.6-7

Hansen does not display the enthymeme schematically and the figure shows his description to be unbalanced as well, since the premisses do not directly support the conclusion. For a modern argumentation analytical approach this is not a problem since one does not have to assume that a certain classical or other specific form of argument is followed. The problem is solved by seeing that two different arguments have been mixed in vv. 6–7: one about Abraham, one about faith and works. Paul has shortened the argument by leaving out two premisses. Logically, the first unexpressed premiss is: 'Faith is reckoned to one as righteousness.' That this is the premiss that is implied is clear from the statement in v. 8 that 'God would justify the Gentiles by faith' (it is also clear from the whole section of vv. 6–14, which focuses on faith). The second unexpressed premiss has to do with the thought that those who share the same faith and righteousness as Abraham are the (spiritual, true) descendants of Abraham. In other words, to be a descendant of Abraham is to be one that is justified by faith like him. Paul simply omits some of the intermediate stages of the argument. By using the schematical notation of Pragma-Dialectics,[36] the argument can be explicated as in Fig. 3.

---

34   Frans Mußner, *Der Galaterbrief* (HTKNT, 11; Freiburg: Herder, 4th edn, 1981), p. 216.

35   G. Walter Hansen, *Abraham in Galatians: Epistolary and Rhetorical Contexts* (JSNTSup, 29; Sheffield: JSOT Press, 1989), p. 112.

36   The figures are quite self-explanatory. It is important to note, however, that unexpressed elements are indicated by a prime,', and put in brackets, [ ]. An unexpressed premiss is linked to an explicit premiss with an ampersand, &. Premisses in coordinatively compound arguments are connected with an overbrace. For further details, see Frans H. van Eemeren and Rob Grootendorst, *Argumentation, Communication, and Fallacies* (Hillsdale, NJ: Lawrence Erlbaum Associates, 1992), pp. 73–89.

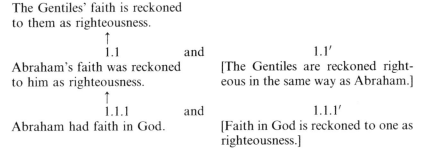

Fig. 3: Gal. 3.6-9: Part 1/2, Abraham's and Gentiles' Faith

In order to analyse an argument we need to specify the relationship between standpoint and premises. The way in which these are related is important for the function of an argument as a defence or refutation. The relation can be symptomatic, analogous or causal.[37] Argument schemes describe the relation between the expressed premiss and the standpoint in a single argument. In assessing the scheme used, the primary interest is not in the logical validity but in the way in which the scheme advances the argument. The use of particular argument schemes is closely connected with the argumentative strategy chosen. It is more a question of rhetoric than of logic. In a certain type of argument, certain types of speech acts presented in a certain way are more likely to be accepted than others.

The argument scheme in argument 1.1→1 (Fig. 3) is *analogous*:[38] just as Abraham's faith was reckoned to him as righteousness, so also the Gentiles' faith is reckoned to them as righteousness.

Pragma-Dialectics enables us to evaluate the use of argument schemes by understanding how the elements relate to each other. The general argument scheme for an argumentation based on a relation of analogy is: Y is true of X *because* Y is true of Z *and* Z is comparable to X. The most important critical question to ask about argumentation based on analogy is: 'Are there any significant differences between Z and X?' The similarities should be evaluated on an abstract level (unlike in the case of a literal comparison): 'By which general principle are the two connected and does this principle indeed apply?'[39] Illustrating how the scheme works, we substitute the appropriate variables in this particular argumentation as follows:

37   Van Eemeren *et al.*, *Argumentation*, pp. 96–104; ch. 4 in van Eemeren (ed.), *Crucial Concepts*.

38   In an analogous relation 'a standpoint is defended by showing that something referred to in the standpoint is similar to something that is cited in the argumentation'. Van Eemeren *et al.*, *Argumentation*, p. 99.

39   *Ibid.*, p. 100.

- 'reckoned as righteousness' is true of 'the Gentiles' faith';
- *because*: 'reckoned as righteousness' is true of 'Abraham's faith';
- *and*: 'Abraham's faith' is comparable to 'the Gentiles' faith'.

The analogy is well chosen since Abraham's example seems to lend support to Paul's argument. It is a good choice among the topical potential since it has the potential of adding scriptural authority to Paul's argument. In order to examine if it is correctly applied we ask the critical question: are there any significant differences between Abraham's faith and the Gentiles' faith? Or: by which general principle are the two connected? The principle is here expressed by the implicit premiss in the underlying argument, 1.1.1', 'Faith in God is reckoned to one as righteousness.' For the argument scheme to be correctly applied one needs to agree with Paul that Abraham's faith and the Gentiles' faith are comparable, a comparison which is not unproblematic.

In the second argument, 1.1.1→1.1 (Fig. 3), the argument scheme is *causal*.[40] The general argument scheme for an argumentation based on a causal relation is: Y is true of X *because* Z is true of X *and* Z leads to Y. The most important critical question to ask about argumentation based on causality is: 'Does Z always lead to Y?' Again, substituting the variables from our argument, we get the following:

- 'reckoned righteous' is true of 'Abraham';
- *because*: 'faith in God' is true of 'Abraham';
- *and*: 'faith in God' leads to 'reckoned righteous'.

The critical question is then: does 'faith in God' always lead to 'reckoned righteous'? Could 'reckoned righteous' have been caused by something else (something other than 'faith in God')? Could, for instance, God have reckoned Abraham righteous because of some of his deeds or was it specifically his faith that led God to reckon him righteous? These are difficult questions, but in Paul's argument they are simple: it was Abraham's faith. But is Paul here doing justice to the Old Testament passage on which the argument is built or is the causal argument scheme more of a presentational device which leads the addressees to a conclusion that is not well founded?

The unexpressed premiss 1.1.1', 'faith in God is reckoned to one as righteousness', is not the only possible interpretation of Gen. 15.6, but Paul's argumentation shows that here this is his interpretation. Paul makes Abraham's experience a general rule and makes this interpretation seem like a fact of the argument (a rhetorical move): the faith of those who believe is reckoned to them as righteousness. The problem is that in the argument, it seems that it was Abraham's faith specifically – or even only

40   In a causal relation 'a standpoint is defended by making a causal connection between the argument and the standpoint'. *Ibid.*, p. 100.

– that led to righteousness. This is not the point of Gen. 15.6 so the application of the argument scheme is not without its problems. However, Paul needs to use a causal scheme in order to arrive at standpoint 1 (Fig. 3): the Gentiles' faith is reckoned to them as righteousness.

1

Christian Gentiles are sons of Abraham, spiritually.

↑

1.1a – – – – – – – –1.1b		and	1.1(a–b)'
Abraham's faith was reckoned to him as righteousness.	The Gentiles' faith is reckoned to them as righteousness.		[To have a faith which is reckoned to one as righteousness is to be a son of Abraham, spiritually.]

Fig. 4: Gal. 3.6-9: Part 2/2, The Gentiles are Abraham's Sons

Elements 1 and 1.1(a–b)' in Fig. 4 represent my interpretation of what Paul meant by being 'a descendant of Abraham'. Since there can be no question of a physical descent on behalf of the Gentiles, Paul must have had a spiritual lineage in mind. What is meant by 'those who believe' in 3.9 are Gentile Christians and Jewish Christians who believe in God and because of their faith are reckoned righteous. Verses 8 and 14 indicate that Paul has the Gentiles especially in mind. If we explicate this, the argument can be presented as in Fig. 4. Standpoint 1 means, in biblical language, that 'Christian Gentiles are descendants of Abraham' or 'Christian Gentiles are sons of Abraham'. Jewish Christians are then clearly included at the end of the pericope, in the 'we' of v. 14.

The argument scheme here is *symptomatic.*[41] The general argument scheme for an argumentation based on a symptomatic relation is: Y is true of X *because* Z is true of X *and* Z is symptomatic of Y. The most important critical questions to ask about argumentation based on a symptomatic relation are: 'Are there not also other non-Ys that have the characteristic Z?' and 'Are there not also other Ys that do not have the characteristic Z?' In this argument we have the following:

- 'sons of Abraham' is true of 'the Gentiles';
- *because*: 'faith reckoned to one as righteousness' is true of 'the Gentiles';

---

41 In a symptomatic relation 'a standpoint is defended by citing in the argument a certain sign, symptom, or distinguishing mark of what is claimed in the standpoint'. *Ibid.,* pp. 96–97.

   – *and*: 'faith reckoned to one as righteousness' is symptomatic of 'sons
     of Abraham'.

The critical questions are: are there not also other non-sons of Abraham
whose faith is reckoned to them as righteousness? And: are there not also
other sons of Abraham whose faith is not reckoned to them as
righteousness? The problem is here the same as above: is it only those
who exhibit a faith of the kind Abraham had that should be counted as
Abraham's sons or should some other criteria in addition to faith be
fulfilled, such as being a Jew or obeying the law? Of course, this problem is
not solved by the use of a certain argument scheme, but Paul's choice of a
symptomatic argument scheme shows that he considers the Gentiles'
position *vis-à-vis* righteousness to be essentially the same as that of
Abraham (a rhetorical move): faith is reckoned to both as righteousness.
Again, it can be discussed whether the argument scheme is correctly
applied or not.
   It is here worth noting that the acceptability of starting points,
premisses and standpoints must be evaluated from the perspective of the
discussants. What they both accept is acceptable. The Pragma-Dialectical
method offers normative rules only for what in a discussion is unacceptable with regard to potential obstacles to resolving a difference of opinion.
The acceptability of starting points depends on the context in question.

Regarding the rhetorical strategy, a complete analysis cannot be made
based just on a short excerpt of Galatians, but the whole letter needs to be
taken into account. Suffice it to say here that in Gal. 3 we find examples of
strategic manoeuvring and the letter as a whole indicates the presence of a
rhetorical strategy.[42] Here just a few further observations have to suffice.
   As noted above, the analogy of Abraham has much dissimilarity, which
reduces its argumentative value. This indicates that the appeals to the
authority of Abraham and the implied tradition of righteousness by faith
may be rhetorical moves (*argument by appeal to tradition and to authority*).
For instance, the reference to Abraham can be argued not to be
evidentially relevant; it is, however, *topic relevant* since it does deal with the
key concepts of faith and righteousness. Abraham as an example of a faith
not based on works of the law seems to be a clever argumentative
construction created in order to support Paul's thesis of a righteousness
based on faith alone.
   The same holds true for the many quotations from Scripture: they add
authority to Paul's argument, especially through the quotations centred
on Abraham. At the same time they make good use of the auditorial
demand since the Scriptures, the law and Abraham were certainly

---

42   Cf. Hietanen, *Paul's Argumentation*.

discussed among the Galatians generally and among Paul's antagonists especially.

It is possible that the Old Testament quotations which Paul makes use of are suggested by some earlier stage in the argumentation, either between Paul and his addressees or within the Galatian congregations. By making claims that seem conclusive and are based on a tradition that is traced all the way back to Abraham, Paul can give the impression that the tradition he represents is firmly attested to in the Scriptures and therefore authoritative also for the Galatians.

b. *Evaluation*

Already in the analysis above, some evaluation was included, namely about the acceptability of premises and the correct use of argument schemes. In addition, the pragmatic validity of the arguments can be put into the larger context to check if the different arguments and sub-arguments are consistent with each other. Without going into detail here, I note that Gal. 3.6-9 is consistent with the rest of the argument in Galatians.[43] The argument that faith is the basis for righteousness supports Paul's standpoint that the Galatians should not give into circumcision and other forms of law-abiding.

Although not necessary for understanding the argument, an evaluation is useful if we want to characterize Paul's argumentation. By mirroring it against an ideal, both strengths and weaknesses are easier to spot and describe precisely.

A crucial part of an argumentation analysis is the identification of fallacies. The traditional definition of a fallacy is an argument that seems to be valid, but is not.[44] This definition is problematic and is abandoned in Pragma-Dialectic theory. Instead, fallacies are seen as such moves in a discussion that hinder the resolution of a dispute. By providing a code of conduct for critical discussion, Pragma-Dialectics enable the analyst to mirror an argumentation against a normative set of discussion rules.[45] Van Eemeren *et al.* theorise that argumentation follows certain conventions and they present ten 'rules' based on theoretical and analytical assumptions. When these 'rules' or ideal conditions are fulfilled, the chances for a successful resolution of a debate are high. The more the discussants depart from or directly offend against these rules, the less the chances of a resolution.

The set of ten rules, then, function as a 'heuristic, analytical and critical

---

43 Cf. *ibid.*

44 See C.L. Hamblin, *Fallacies* (London: Methuen, 1970), p. 12.

45 This code of conduct is first presented in van Eemeren and Grootendorst, *Speech Acts*, pp. 151–75.

framework' for dealing with argumentative discourse.[46] In *Reconstructing Argumentative Discourse* the usefulness of this ideal model is described as follows:

> The model does not prevent our seeing what argumentative practice is actually like. This fact should be evident from the empirical analyses presented throughout, in which observed arguments are set up in contrast to what the model portrays as ideal. It is precisely in the contrast that some of the most interesting observations are to be made. The model's function is thus to help us to notice what is, from a certain point of view, most important about argumentative practice.[47]

It should be pointed out that argumentative shortcomings do not automatically reduce the persuasive effect of a discourse. But if one embarks upon an argumentation that, for example, relies on premises that turn out to be poor as support for the argument made, the credibility of the argumentation (and of the arguer) may suffer, and thereby also lessen the persuasive effect. In the following I give a few examples of possible violations in Gal. 3 against the discussion rules.

We do not know exactly what possible standpoints have been advanced among the Galatians, and which Paul now attacks. It is not even certain that the Galatians perceived their situation as problematic before they received Paul's letter. In that case we have a violation against *The Standpoint Rule* (Rule 3), which states that a party's attack on a standpoint must relate to the standpoint that has indeed been advanced by the other party. Even if the Galatians experienced some internal theological conflict, it is not certain that they conceived such problems in the same way as Paul did. The idea that permeates the whole passage, the dichotomy between law and faith, may not have been a relevant formulation of the problem from a Galatian perspective. Law and faith need not be as mutually exclusive as Paul asserts.

In the beginning of the passage, in 3.6, Paul indicates as a fact that it was Abraham's faith that was reckoned to him as righteousness. This statement is then used as a premiss for the following arguments. There is reason to believe that this premiss was not an accepted starting point between Paul and the other party. Similarly, the statement in 3.10 may not have been agreed upon. An indication of this is the space in the passage Paul allocates to defending these two ideas. As noted in the analysis above, several crucial premises are such that they may have been in dispute. Still, Paul presents them as facts. To presuppose the justificatory power of an argument can lead to the fallacy of *petitio principii* (begging

---

46   Van Eemeren *et al.*, *Fundamentals*, p. 283.

47   Frans H. van Eemeren *et al.*, *Reconstructing Argumentative Discourse* (Studies in Rhetoric and Communication; Tuscaloosa: University of Alabama Press, 1993), pp. 177–78.

the question). If this is so, we here have violations against Rule 6, *The Starting-Point Rule*: a party may not falsely present a premiss as an accepted starting-point nor deny a premiss representing an accepted starting-point.

One could raise the question as to whether the analogy with Abraham is a *false analogy*: (1) Abraham's faith was not faith in Christ; and (2) the righteousness reckoned to Abraham is not identical with the righteousness reckoned to those who believe in Christ; and, most importantly, (3) in Gen. 15 the intention is not to contrast Abraham's faith with his deeds. Based on the original context, Abraham's faith cannot as easily be separated from his deeds as it is in Paul's argument. This means that the connection that Paul makes in v. 7 ('those who believe are the descendants of Abraham') is easy to contest: Abraham does not represent such a division between faith and deeds as wanted by Paul.[48]

Rule 7, *The Argument Scheme Rule*, states that a party may not regard a standpoint as conclusively defended if the defence does not take place by means of an appropriate argument scheme that is correctly applied. The argument schemes in Galatians are generally appropriate, but they are in several cases not correctly applied. Many of the premisses can be contested which renders the arguments problematical. For instance, is it really so that Christian Gentiles are spiritually sons of Abraham? (Fig. 4). Many of the conclusions are formulated in a more conclusive way than is warranted by the premisses. The tactic of trying to make a standpoint appear to be a statement of fact, and the argumentation merely an explanation, creates the impression that the standpoint needs no defence. Paul does seem to regard several claims as conclusively defended. But almost all of Paul's standpoints can be contested by someone who does not share his conviction about the relationship between faith and works of the law. In both Figs 3 and 4 we find such problems, and consequently we here seem to have violations against Rules 6 and 7.

Rule 10, *The Usage Rule*, states that a party must not use formulations that are insufficiently clear or confusingly ambiguous and he must interpret the other party's formulations as carefully and accurately as possible. However, the opening premiss, 3.6, is not clear in the sense Paul presents it. How is Abraham's faith comparable with the faith of the Galatians? How is Abraham's righteousness comparable with that of the Galatians? However, it is precisely this ambiguity with the Old Testament quotations that makes it possible for Paul to use them in a sense that fits his argumentation. In some cases, the quotations fit his arguments better, in other cases they are easy to contest. The use of ambiguous texts seems

---

48   Cf. Mußner on vv. 6–9: 'Ein Jude kann der "Logik" des Apostels kaum zustimmen. Warum soll allein der Weg des Glaubens zur Rechtfertigung führen und nicht die von Gott selbst verordneten Werke des Gesetzes?' Mußner, *Galaterbrief*, p. 223.

deliberate on Paul's part – an ambiguous text is easier to incorporate as a premiss than an exact and precise one.

In addition to the above, Rule 1, *The Freedom Rule*, states that parties must not prevent each other from advancing standpoints or casting doubt on standpoints and Rule 2, *The Burden-of-Proof Rule*, that a party that advances a standpoint is obliged to defend it if the other party asks him to do so. *The Relevance Rule* (Rule 4) states that a party may defend his standpoint only by advancing argumentation relating to that standpoint and Rule 8, *The Validity Rule*, that in his argumentation a party may only use arguments that are logically valid or capable of being validated by making explicit one or more unexpressed premisses. Finally, Rule 9, *The Closure Rule*, states that a failed defence of a standpoint must result in the party that put forward the standpoint retracting it and a conclusive defence in the other party retracting his doubt about the standpoint.

c. *Summary*

The analysis of the beginning of the section, vv. 6–7, is an example of the benefits of the use of a proper method of argumentation analysis. The analysis shows that the argument should not be explained as an enthymeme, as in Figs 1 and 2.[49] Instead, the analysis indicates that two arguments have been combined and two premisses left implicit. The analysis shows that Paul includes his own interpretation in the argument in such a way that the argument seems at first glance to be based on fact, not on opinion. A compact mode of argumentation favours such an approach since (a majority of) the addressees do not necessarily have the time or ability to scrutinize unexpressed premisses.

The analysis shows that Paul makes maximal use of the selected Old Testament quotations to support his argument about Abraham's faith and the promise of salvation through faith for the Gentiles. On closer inspection, the quoted passages do not necessarily support all of Paul's conclusions. The arguments analysed here are probably not in themselves enough to persuade anyone, which indicates that Paul's strategy is one of cumulative 'evidence': that by stacking in the letter small, more or less convincing arguments, the cumulative effect would be in favour of his argument. This is a rhetorical presentational technique.

Another tendentious use of Scripture is found in v. 8: Paul's interpretation that the blessing of the Gentiles in Abraham can only mean that the Gentiles will be justified specifically and only because of their faith is not warranted in the quotation of Gen. 12.3, as has been noted in earlier studies.[50] Based on this interpretation, Paul deduces that

---

49 *Contra* Mußner, *ibid.*, p. 216 and Hansen, *Abraham*, p. 112.
50 E.g. Betz, *Galatians* and Hansen, *Abraham*.

the promise to Abraham must have been the gospel, which then in turn must include the Gentiles. The whole chain of argument is rather loose at some points.

In the above-analysed passage we find the rhetorical move of appeal to tradition and to authority. Most important is the dominant use of Old Testament passages in support of the argument. Since the quotations rarely support the argumentation clearly – and certainly not conclusively – their use can be seen as rhetorical moves; in other words they are convincing by seemingly supporting an argument.

3. *The Use of Argumentation Analysis*

No single method can bring out all aspects of a text. What is more, an analysis from a very specific perspective runs the danger of distorting aspects to which another method would have done better justice. These two considerations lead us towards using comprehensive methods, such as the standard historical-critical approach. When analysing aspects that relate to argumentation, we need a method that does not focus only on one feature, such as presentation, topics, or audience, nor only on argument schemes, validity, or structures. In argumentation all of these come together forming a whole, which is then more or less sound, from a dialectical perspective, and more or less persuasive, from a rhetorical perspective.

A good argumentation analysis establishes what the different standpoints are and how they are organized with respect to the overall argument. Even if the interest of an analyst would be on rhetorical features, it is valuable to know if the arguments can be seen as convincing from a *logos*-perspective. Concerning Galatians, the *logos*-element is clearly not indifferent – otherwise Paul would not dedicate such a great part of the letter to arguments in favour of his position, arguments which at some points are very difficult and which must have required careful consideration also on Paul's part.

The Pragma-Dialectical approach also allows us to analyse how *logos*, *ethos* and *pathos* function in the argumentation as part of strategic manoeuvring. In Galatians we find a wide variety of topical potential, including arguments from Scripture, from tradition, from experience and from common practice. Galatians also includes a variety of presentational devices, including intimidation, teaching, irony, personal appeal, allegory and vilification. There is indeed a clear use of strategic manoeuvring. Pragma-Dialectics enable us to evaluate Paul's argumentation from a normative perspective. Mirroring Paul's argumentation against the ten rules of argumentation clarifies the qualities of the argumentation in a very specific way. Even if some such violations can be explained as strategic manoeuvres, it is helpful to be able to describe the shortcomings exactly. A rhetorical analysis does not enable us to do this. Neither would a purely descriptive argumentation analysis of some sort show us why certain features are problematic.

Further work is needed in order to gain a comprehensive description of Paul's argumentation. Recent advances within the field of argumentation theory aid the exegete in this endeavour. An accurate understanding of the strengths and weaknesses of Paul's argumentation will help us understand the apostle and his message better.

Chapter 12

THE VERY FIRST AUDIENCES OF PAUL'S LETTERS: THE IMPLICATIONS OF END GREETINGS

Antti Mustakallio

Among the main questions in Romans research is the composition of the letter audience: has the letter been addressed to Jewish Christians, Gentile Christians, or both? It is virtually certain that the first option is incorrect, for in 11.13 Paul addresses explicitly Gentile Christians: 'I am speaking to you Gentiles.'[1] Thus the audience included Gentile Christians. However, scholars are divided over whether the audience consisted *solely* of Gentile Christians or whether it was a mix of Gentile and Jewish Christians. The latter view has been clearly held by the majority of scholars,[2] but lately the alternative option has gained ground.[3]

---

1 Strained attempts at explanation by those who advocate a solely Jewish Christian audience confirm this conclusion. For example, according to Steve Mason, '"For I am not ashamed of the Gospel" (Rom. 1.16): The Gospel and the first readers of Romans', in L. Ann Jervis and Peter Richardson (eds), *Gospel in Paul: Studies in Corinthians, Galatians and Romans* (Festschrift Richard Longenecker; JSNTSup, 108; Sheffield: Sheffield Academy Press, 1994), pp. 254–87 (273–74) 'The context requires that the Gentiles in question are not those of any particular locale but ... the fruits of his Gentile mission. ... He addresses them directly here, in imaginary convocation, for obvious rhetorical effect.'

2 Thus, all the major commentators. A helpful list is provided by Runar M. Thorsteinsson, *Paul's Interlocutor in Romans 2: Function and Identity in the Context of Ancient Epistolography* (ConBNT, 40; Stockholm: Almqvist & Wiksell Intenational, 2003), p. 88 n. 5.

3 James C. Miller, 'The Romans debate: 1991–2001', *CRBS* 9 (2001), pp. 306–49 (327). The view is most thoroughly argued for by Angelika Reichert, *Der Römerbrief als Gratwanderung: Eine Untersuchung zur Abfassungsproblematik* (FRLANT, 194; Göttingen: Vandenhoeck & Ruprecht, 2001), pp. 101–46 and Thorsteinsson, *Interlocutor*, pp. 37–39, 87–122. Other scholars who favour it include Neil Elliott, *Rhetoric of Romans: Argumentative Constraint and Strategy and Paul's Dialogue with Judaism* (JSNTSup, 45; Sheffield: JSOT, 1990), p. 96, pp. 290–292; L. Ann Jervis, *The Purpose of Romans: A Comparative Letter Structure Investigation* (JSNTSup, 55; Sheffield: JSOT Press, 1991), p. 77, pp. 158–164; Stanley K. Stowers, *A Rereading of Romans: Justice, Jews, and Gentiles* (New Haven: Yale University Press, 1994) pp. 21–33; Mark D. Nanos, *The Mystery of Romans: The Jewish Context of Paul's Letter* (Minneapolis: Fortress, 1996), pp. 78–84 (also 'The Jewish context of the Gentile audience addressed in Paul's Letter to the Romans', *CBQ* 91 [1999], pp. 283–304);

Paul's greetings in ch. 16 are commonly considered to indicate the composition of the audience; since many Jewish Christians are greeted (16.3-15), the audience of Romans is considered to be a mix of Gentile and Jewish Christians. But what do the end greetings indicate in the event? In this article, I will examine the end greetings in ancient Greek letters, Romans and other Pauline letters. How do they contribute to our understanding of the audiences and delivery processes of Pauline letters?

1. *The Form of Greetings in Romans*

Terence Mullins classifies the types of greetings that occur in ancient Greek letters as follows:[4]

> As a literary form, the greeting appears in three types, corresponding to the three persons of the verb.
>
> 1. In the first-person type of greeting, it is the writer of the letter who greets someone; in P. Tebt. 415, for example:
>
> ἀσπάζομαι πολλὰ τὸν πατέρα σου καὶ τοὺς ἐνοίκους πάντας.
>
> 2. In the second-person type of greeting, the writer tells the addressee to greet someone for him; in P. Tebt. 412, for example:
>
> ἀσπάζου τὴν μητέρα σου καὶ τὸν πατέρα σου.
>
> 3. In the third-person type of greeting the writer relays to the addressee the information that a third party greets someone – either the addressee or a fourth party; for example, P. Oxy. 300:
>
> ἀσπάζεται ὑμᾶς Λογγεῖνος.
>
> and P. Oxy. 114:
>
> ἀσπάζεται Ἀίαν Ξάνθιλλα καὶ πάντας τοὺς αὐτῆς. [5]

Paul uses the same verb, ἀσπάζομαι, to send greetings at the end of his letters. In Romans, we are able to find all three kinds of greetings. There is one *first-person* type of greeting in ch. 16, which at the same time happens

---

John G. Gager, *Reinventing Paul* (New York: Oxford University Press, 2000), pp. 101–2; Lloyd Gaston, 'Reading the text and digging the past: the first audience of Romans', in Stephen G. Wilson and Michel Desjardins (eds), *Text and Artifact in the Religions of Mediterranean Antiquity* (Festschrift Peter Richardson; ESCJ, 9; Waterloo: Wilfrid Laurier University Press, 2000), pp. 35–44 (39); and Troels Engberg-Pedersen, *Paul and the Stoics* (Louisville: Westminster John Knox Press, 2000), pp. 185–86.

4 'Greeting as a New Testament form', *JBL* 87 (1968), pp. 418–26. The article has not received much attention, especially given its importance. An exception is Thorsteinsson, *Interlocutor*, p. 1, 63, 98.

5 Mullins, 'Greeting', p. 418.

to be the only occurrence of its type in the NT: in 16.22 Paul's secretary Tertius greets the addressees. The verb ἀσπάζομαι is used four times in the *third-person* type of greetings in 16.16b, 21–23. The *second-person* type of greeting is even more common. The verb ἀσπάζομαι can be found 16 times in vv. 3–15, in which the second-person type of greetings occur. In those verses Paul mentions twenty-six individuals and an undefined number of other people. Because the second-person type is the most relevant to the question of audience, it will be examined more closely.

As private papyrus letters are usually conversations between two individuals, second-person type of greetings occur much more often in singular than in plural. Both present (ἀσπάζου) and aorist tenses (ἄσπασαι) can be found. In some letters, the greeting serves to maintain warm relations particularly between a sender and an addressee. Such is the case when the addressee is asked in a formulaic manner to give the sender's regards to his family. For example, in P. Oxy. 67.4624 gymnasiarch Dius ends his business letter to Sarapion by writing ἀσπάζου το[ὺ]ς σοὺς [πάντας.] ἔρρωσο ('Greetings to all your family. Farewell.').[6] A nearly identical greeting, in which only the tense of the verb differs, occurs at the end of a short business note: ἄσπασαι τοὺς <σ>οὺς πάντας. ἔρρως[ο] (P. Oxy. 2.269.2).[7]

Sometimes salutations to an addressee's family are more specific. This implies that a sender is at least acquainted with the persons greeted. For example, Sarapion asks Justus to greet his brothers: ἀσπάζου τοὺς ἀδελφούς σου (P. Oxy. 36.2786). Calocaerus asks his sister Euphrosyne to greet Thaisus, his other sister: ἀσπάζου Θαϊσοῦν τὴν ἀδελφήν (P. Oxy. 59.3994).[8] Aelius Theon, a suitor, sends greetings to his bride-to-be and her mother via Herminus, his prospective father-in-law: ἀσπάζ[ου] οὖν αὐτὴν καὶ τὴν μητέρα αὐτῆς (P. Oxy. 59.3992). In a short note (P. Oxy. 33.2679), Onesimus sends greetings to the addressee's son: ἀσπάζου τὸν ἀβάσκαντον υἱὸν καὶ πάντας τοὺς ἐν οἴκῳ ('Give my best wishes to your son, whom the evil eye shall not touch, and to everyone in the house.').

Greetings are also addressed to people outside a family. For example, Demas asks his friend Agathodaemon to greet Demetrius the guard and his children: ἄσπασαι Δημήτριον τὸν φύλακα καὶ τὰ [π]αι[δ]ία αὐτοῦ (P. Oxy. 55.3808). Flavius Herculanus ends his sentimental letter (P. Oxy.

---

6   All English translations of Oxyrhynchus papyri are taken from volumes of the series *The Oxyrhynchus Papyri* published by the Egypt Exploration Society. The first number after the abbreviation P. Oxy. marks the volume number.

7   A formulaic request does not necessarily imply distant relations between a sender and persons to be greeted. This is the case when a sender asks an addressee to give his love to his own family. For example, Serenus writes to his mother Tapsais, and asks to be remembered to the rest of the family: [ἄσ]πασαι τοὺς ἡμῶν πάντας (P. Oxy. 59.3996).

8   It is possible, however, that the letter exhibits the free use of the terms related to family relations, in which case Euphrosyne and Thaisus are actually not Calocaerus's sisters.

14.1676) to his emancipated slave Aplonarion with a short request: 'Salute all your friends' (ἄσπασαι τοὺς [φιλοῦ]ντάς σε πάντας). Horeis asks his brother Horion to greet Claudia and all his friends: ἄσπασαι Κλα[υ]δίαν τὴν ἀγαθοτάτην καὶ τοὺς φιλοῦντάς σε πάντας (P. Oxy. 14.1757). Sattos asks his sister Euphrosyne to convey his greetings to Stratus, Stratonice and their children: ἀσπάζου Στρᾳτ[ο]ν καὶ Στρατονείκην καὶ τὰ πεδ[ία] ὑῷ (P. Oxy. 12.1489).

Since the greetings in Romans which we focus on are in the plural form, those few second-person type of greetings in papyri that occur in plural are of particular interest. In a letter from Apion to his son Apion and son's friend Horion, the father mentions various members of his family by name and asks the addressees to greet them: ἀσπάσασθε Στατίαν τὴν θυγατέρα μου καὶ Ἡρ[α]κλείδην καὶ Ἀπίωνα τοὺς υἱούς μου. ἀσπάσασθε τὸν μικρὸν Σερῆνον καὶ Κοπρέα καὶ το[ὺ]ς ἡμῶν πάντας κατ᾽ ὄνομα (P. Oxy. 3.533). The Papyrus sherd O. Claud. 1.152 contains a fragment of a letter in which an unidentifiable sender asks Heras and other, unidentifiable, addressees to greet 'Sarapias through (?) Isidora': ἀσπάζεσθε Σαραπιάδα διὰ Ἰσίδωρας.[9] P. Harr. 1.102 contains a letter of formal greeting, in which the unidentifiable sender requests the addressee Ptolemaeus and his wife to salute 'Diogenes, and Ptolemaeus, and all your people by name': ἀ<σ>πάσασθε καὶ Διογένην καὶ Πτολεμαῖον καὶ τοὺς ὑμῶν πάντας κατ᾽ ὄνομα.[10]

These and other greetings of the same type in other letters[11] show that the second-person type of greeting is an indirect salutation. This holds true for greetings in singular as well as those in plural. Mullins puts forth the following description (italics mine):

> The writer of the letter indicates that the addressee is to greet someone for him. In this way, the writer of the letter becomes the principal agent in establishing a communication with a third party who is *not intended to be among the immediate readership of the letter*.[12]

9 English translation from Jean Bingen et al. (eds), *Mons Claudianus: Ostraca Graeca et Latina (O. Claud. 1 à 190)*, vol. 1 (Documents de fouilles, 29, Le Caire: Institut Français d'Archéologie Orientale du Caire, 1992), p. 152.

10 English translation from *The Rendel Harris Papyri of Woodbrooke College, Birmingham* (ed. and trans. J. Enoch Powell; Cambridge: Cambridge University Press, 1936), p. 86.

11 Second-person type of greetings in plural occur also in P. Iand. 6.111, P. Kell. 1.66, P. Mich. 15.752, P. Oxy. 14. 1681, PSI 8.899, 12.1247, SB 6.9017.13 and 6.9017.36. P. Oxy. 9.1216 also contains one, but this occurrence is a misspelling of ἀσπάσασθαι.

12 Mullins, 'Greeting', p. 420. The last observation seems to be the rule. I have found only one, rather curious, instance, in which the person greeted might have been present when the letter was read for the first time. At the end of his letter (P. Oxy. 59.3997), Heracles asks the addressee, Cerdon, to greet 'Chenamun, the old lady, and her children, and *the man who reads you the letter*' (italics mine): ἀσπάζου Χεγαμοῦν τὴν γραῖαν καὶ τὰ τέκνα αὐτῆς καὶ τὸν

The consequences of the above observations prove to be interesting for Romans. Mullins has not failed to notice this and he remarks acutely: 'The relationship between Paul and the congregation at Rome seems to be other than scholars have assumed, and no simple readjustment of our old notions is likely to bring it into focus.'[13]

Besides Mullins, Runar M. Thorsteinsson is one of the few scholars who has taken the implications of the second-person type greetings in 16.3-15 seriously.[14] He notices, 'It is commonly thought that the identity of the persons greeted in Romans 16.3-15 may be illustrative both of the composition of "Roman Christianity" and of Paul's intended audience.' He criticizes the latter assumption by appealing to the type of greeting Paul applies: 'If Paul's choice of salutatory form is to be taken seriously it must be concluded that, instead of being descriptive of the letter's audience, these greetings suggest that the persons meant to be greeted should *not* be counted among those to whom Paul wrote the letter' (italics original).[15]

If Paul did not send the letter to those whom he greets, who could the recipients then be? If the persons greeted were not among the *first*

ἀναγιγνώσκοντα. If τὸν ἀναγιγνώσκοντα refers to the man who read the letter to the addressee, he certainly attended the first reading event. In the context of the correspondence, however, the Greek word might have stood for something else, and in this case particularly one should consider this option seriously. After all, it does seem odd that the sender would ask the addressee to give the sender's regards to the one who reads the request to him!

13 Mullins, 'Greeting', p. 426.

14 To be sure, the verb form in Paul's greetings has not been left unnoticed, but its consequences have not been taken seriously. Jeffrey A.D. Weima, *Neglected Endings: The Significance of the Pauline Letter Closings* (JSNTSup, 101; Sheffield: Sheffield Academic Press, 1994), p. 108, cannot accept the idea that many persons greeted in ch. 16 would not have been among the recipients. He contends that 'a second-person greeting functions almost as a surrogate for a first-person greeting', but he fails to rationalize this view. Harry Gamble, *Textual History of the Letter to the Romans: A Study in Textual and Literary Criticism* (Studies and Documents, 42; Grand Rapids: Eerdmans, 1977), p. 92, states emphatically: 'There can be no question here, any more than in the case of the kiss-greeting, of the imperative forms meaning that the greetings are addressed to persons outside the actual readership.' But Gamble also fails to offer a sufficient rationale for his conclusion. He is followed by Jerome Murphy-O'Connor, *Paul the Letter-Writer: His World, His Options, His Skills* (GNS, 41; Collegeville: The Liturgical Press, 1995), p. 105. It is true that in every kiss-greeting in Paul's letters (1 Cor. 16.20b, 2 Cor. 13.12; Rom. 16.16), except one (1 Thess. 5.26), Paul clearly urges the addressees with imperative ἀσπάσασθε to greet *each other* with the holy kiss (φίλημα ἅγιον). But in those cases the verb is modified by ἀλλήλους, which leaves no doubt about the meaning. However, in 1 Thess. 5.26 there is τοὺς ἀδελφοὺς πάντας instead of ἀλλήλους. Gamble simply calls this 'a variant' and without explanation considers its meaning identical to the reciprocal pronoun (p. 75, 92 n. 162). This remains questionable, however. Moreover, Gamble fails to take the textual context into account. See below n. 32.

15 Thorsteinsson, *Interlocutor*, pp. 98–99. After writing this article, I noticed that also A. Andrew Das has taken the implications of the end greetings into account in his recent study *Solving the Romans Debate* (Minneapolis: Fortress Press, 2007), pp. 101–3.

audience, could they still have been among the *second* audience, that is, did Paul address the letter to them, after all, but via mediator(s)? On these questions, 1 Thess., Phil. and Col. can shed some light.

2. *Second-person Type of Greetings in 1 Thess. and Phil.*

In 1 Thess. 5.26-27 Paul sends his final greetings: 'Greet [ἀσπάσασθε] all the brothers with a holy kiss. I adjure you by the Lord that the letter be read to all the brothers.' These words have aroused some confusion among commentators. As Abraham Malherbe notes, 'It is not clear what situation Paul visualizes.'[16] Ernest Best gets to the point in asking: 'Who is to greet whom?'[17] In all likelihood, 'all the brothers' (τοὺς ἀδελφοὺς πάντας) refers to all the believers in the Thessalonian church.[18] The trickier challenge is to discover who are asked to greet 'all the brothers' and urged to take care of the reading of the letter to them. There is a real possibility that Paul addresses the leaders of the Thessalonian church.[19] Paul's greeting in v. 26 is of the second-person type, which means that he did not assume 'all the brothers' to be present when the letter was read to its first listeners. Also, the fact that Paul does not urge the addressees to greet one another (ἀλλήλους) – which is typical of him (Rom. 16.16; 1 Cor. 16.20; 2 Cor. 13.12; cf. 1 Pet. 5.14) – but to greet 'all the brothers' suggests that these 'brothers' were not among the first listeners. This conclusion is supported by the next verse (v. 27), in which Paul uses the second person plural (ὑμᾶς) and urges the addressees to read the letter to 'all the brothers'.[20] Hence, it seems that at first the letter was not read to the whole congregation but to a much smaller group of people, which is asked to send Paul's greetings to 'all the brothers' and take care of the reading of the letter.[21] If Paul addressed the leaders, it does not have to

16   Abraham J. Malherbe, *The Letters to the Thessalonians: A New Translation with Introduction and Commentary* (AB, 32B; New York: Doubleday, 2000), p. 341.

17   Ernest Best, *A Commentary on the First and Second Epistles to the Thessalonians* (BNTC; London: Black, 1972), p. 245.

18   This is the conclusion to which almost every commentator – Best included – comes.

19   Thus Charles Masson, *Les deux Épitres de Saint Paul aux Thessaloniciens* (CNT, 11a; Neuchâtel: Delachaux & Niestlé, 1957), p. 79.

20   Many scholars are of the opinion that in v. 26 τοὺς ἀδελφοὺς πάντας is equivalent to ἀλλήλους. (So, e.g., Gamble, *Textual History*, p. 75, who, however, does not give any rationale for his conclusion.) But this is an insufficient solution, for it ignores the evident question of why Paul then did not dictate ἀλλήλους. Neither does the context suggest such an interpretation, for, as Malherbe, *Thessalonians*, p. 341 points out, 'It is unlikely … that the phrase "all the brethren" is equivalent to "each other," for it is immediately repeated in v 27, where it could not mean "each other".'

21   Similarly Malherbe, *Thessalonians*, p. 341: 'The natural way to understand Paul's command is that "all the brethren" has in view Christians beyond the primary recipients of the letter.'

mean that there is a division between the leaders and the people.[22] It is quite conceivable that he ordered the letter carriers to read the letter and clarify its potentially unclear features to the leaders, who would then be equipped to read it to 'all the believers'.

Some commentators have not even considered this possibility,[23] whereas many reject it.[24] To be sure, this is not the only imaginable scenario,[25] although in my opinion it makes the best sense of the data. Most importantly, however, we are reminded that at the end of the day hard evidence of the events surrounding the first reading(s) of Paul's letters is very scarce.[26]

Another example comes from the end of Paul's letter to the Philippians (4.21a): 'Greet every saint in Christ Jesus.' We may ask together with F. W. Beare: 'Who is to convey the greetings? Who may we take to be the subject of the imperative greet?' He concludes: 'A trifle such as this makes us realize how little we know about organization and procedure in these early churches.'[27] The greeting is again of the second-person type (ἀσπάσασθε), which means that Paul assumed those to be greeted, 'every saint' (πάντα ἅγιον), to be absent when the letter was read. The suggestion

---

22   *Pace* Masson, *Thessaloniciens*, p. 89. Also Best, *Thessalonians*, p. 245, who criticizes the idea that the leaders are addressed, seems to think (wrongly) that this view necessarily assumes a division within the church.

23   E.g., A.L. Moore (ed.), *1 and 2 Thessalonians* (NCBC; London: Nelson, 1969), p. 87; Leon Morris, *The First and Second Epistles to the Thessalonians* (NICNT; Grand Rapids, Mich.: Eerdmans, rev. edn, 1991), p. 185; and I. Howard Marshall, *1 and 2 Thessalonians* (NCBC; Grand Rapids, Mich.: Eerdmans, 1983), pp. 165–66. In commenting on v. 27, Marshall does seem to imply that not all the Thessalonian believers were in attendance when the letter was being read for the first time. However, he fails to explicate the consequences of this matter.

24   E.g., James E. Frame, *A Critical and Exegetical Commentary on the Epistles of St. Paul to the Thessalonians* (ICC; Edinburgh: T&T Clark, 1979), p. 216; F.F. Bruce, *1 & 2 Thessalonians* (WBC, 45; Waco: Word Books, 1982), p. 134; Best, *Thessalonians*, pp. 245–46; and Malherbe, *Thessalonians*, pp. 341–42, who, despite his view that 'all the brethren' differs from the primary recipients, does not see any reason why 'Paul's injunction to greet should not be seen as directed to the entire church, as the rest of the letter is' (p. 341). But can we be so sure that 'the rest of the letter' was sent *directly* to 'the entire church' without any intermediaries such as church leaders?

25   See the discussion in Malherbe, *Thessalonians*, p. 200, pp. 340–46. Malherbe himself regards 'all the brethren' as 'those persons in the environs of Thessalonica who had been converted by Paul's converts after he had left the city but whom Paul included in his care' (pp. 341–42).

26   Best, *Thessalonians*, p. 245 rejects the possibility that in 1 Thess. 5.26-27 Paul is instructing the leaders of the community by arguing 'if the instruction was restricted to a few then we should expect them to be clearly identified'. I ask, why? There is no reason to expect that the letters would contain exact information of details concerning the first reading event.

27   F.W. Beare, *A Commentary on the Epistle to the Philippians* (BNTC; London: Black, 1959), p. 157.

that the Philippians are to greet each other[28] is not satisfactory.[29] In my opinion, Gerald Hawthorne's proposal is the most likely:

> [P]aul calls upon the leaders, the overseers of the church, to pass along his greetings to the Christian fellowship. Surely, in spite of the wording of the opening address (1.1), this letter would not have been handed over by Epaphroditus to the church as a whole, but to the responsible officials of the church who would then read it aloud to the assembled congregation.[30]

There is also another feature – a minor one, however – which can be explained through this kind of hypothesis concerning the first readers of Philippians. In 4.2-3a it reads: 'I urge Euodia and I urge Syntyche to be of the same mind in the Lord. Yes, and I ask you also, my loyal companion, help these women.' Why does Paul suddenly ask somebody a favour in a vocative case (ναὶ ἐρωτῶ καὶ σέ, γνήσιε σύζυγε)? Who is this man to whom Paul directs his words? Predictably, during the history of biblical exposition these words have inspired much guesswork and received a variety of imaginative explanations.[31] Whatever the identity of this person is, the sudden address seems to call for certain assumptions on Paul's part of a situation in which the letter is read and an audience which was to be present. It is easy to envision that in a small group of people listening to the letter everyone understands to whom Paul refers when they hear the

28   Thus, e.g., Ralph P. Martin, *Philippians: Based on the Revised Standard Version* (NCBC; Grand Rapids, Mich.: Eerdmans, 1980), p. 169.

29   Gerald F. Hawthorne, *Philippians* (WBC, 43; Waco: Word Books, 1983), p. 214. Hawthorne rightly remarks that had Paul wanted to convey such a message he would have chosen to dictate ἀλλήλους.

30   Hawthorne, *Philippians*, p. 214. Similarly Beare, *Philippians*, p. 157 and Marvin R. Vincent, *A Critical and Exegetical Commentary on the Epistles to the Philippians and to Philemon* (ICC; Edinburgh: T & T Clark, 1985), p. 153. Gordon D. Fee, *Paul's Letter to the Philippians* (NICNT; Grand Rapids, Mich.: Eerdmans, 1995), p. 457 n. 6, however, disagrees, being of the opinion that the whole question pertaining to the verb (ἀσπάσασθε) is raised because of 'our own sociology (sense of logic?) and need for precision that both raises and answers the question in this way'. According to him, 'the greeting is from Paul to the whole church, not from Paul through others to the rest'. But how can Fee be so sure that Paul did not intend the letter to be read first to the leaders of the church?

31   Hawthorne, *Philippians*, pp. 179–83 lists the following suggestions: Lydia as Paul's wife (Clement of Alexandria), the husband or brother of Euodia or Syntyche (Chrysostom), Epaphroditus (Lightfoot), Timothy (Collange), Silas (Delling), Luke (Manson), the chief Bishop at Philippi (Ellicott), Christ (ναί introducing a prayer) (Wiesler), and a person named Σύζυγος (Michael, Müller). Hawthorne himself subscribes to none of these views, but considers that Paul addresses the congregation collectively. This sounds far-fetched, however, and it is much safer to simply conclude with Beare, *Philippians*, p. 145 that 'the words point to some man of tact and influence, who can intervene to help the two women resolve their differences'. This 'man of tact and influence' might have been Paul's itinerant co-worker (so Fee, *Philippians*, p. 393) or a local church leader.

designation a 'loyal companion'. In a larger meeting of a community, that kind of a sudden exhortation to an individual whose name remains unmentioned might cause some confusion. Therefore, Paul's mysterious address seems to fit better with the idea of a limited audience composed of leaders of the church than a large meeting with dozens of believers present. At least, as the address presumes a particular setting, it is certainly inapt for different audiences in various house-churches.

If the suggestion that those greeted in Rom 16.3-16a would not have been within the immediate audience sounded somewhat peculiar at first, this should not be the case any more after a look at 1 Thess. and Phil.[32] The natural impression one gets from 1 Thess. 5.26-27 is that not 'all the brothers' of the Thessalonian church were present when the letter was read for the first time. Similarly, according to Phil. 4.21a 'every saint' was to be greeted, and thus those saints were not among the very first audience. A proposal that the intended first audience of the letter to Philippians would have been composed of 'responsible officials of the church' is in line with Phil. 4.2-3a, which suggests a restricted audience group. Also, in the case of 1 Thess., it is fully conceivable that the very first audience consisted of leaders of the church.

The evidence related to the greetings shows that the delivery process was two-staged: the first audience was probably composed of church leaders, but the second audience was much larger, the ordinary believers in the church. This is evident in both 1 Thess. and Phil.

Just like Rom., Phil. contains an all-inclusive address at the beginning of the letter (1.1): Paul (and Timothy) addresses it 'to all the saints in Christ Jesus who are in Philippi, with the bishops and deacons' (πᾶσιν τοῖς ἁγίοις ἐν Χριστῷ Ἰησοῦ τοῖς οὖσιν ἐν Φιλίπποις σὺν ἐπισκόποις καὶ

---

32   *Contra* Gamble, *Textual History*, p. 92 n. 162 who appeals to reversed logic: 'The kiss-greeting is to be exchanged *among* the readership (certainly not to be given by *the* reader to the congregation!), which is the sense of the reciprocal ἀλλήλους. Likewise, in Phil 4.21 "every saint" means simply "every member of the community." Thus we must assume that the recipients of the second person imperative greeting in Rom 16 are members of the community, and therefore also are among the addressees of the letter' (italics original). There are many problems with this line of thought. Firstly, while mentioning kiss-greetings Gamble forgets 1 Thess. 5.26, in which there is τοὺς ἀδελφοὺς πάντας instead of ἀλλήλους. (However, he treats that verse elsewhere. On the assessment of his view, see above n. 14.) Secondly, Gamble is certainly right that in Phil. 4.21 'every saint' means 'every member of the community', but it is another thing to say that 'every saint' is urged to greet *one another*. If this is what Gamble wants to convey, it is by no means 'simple'. (See above n. 20.) Thirdly, it is true that 'the recipients of the second person imperative greeting in Rom 16', i.e., those to be greeted, 'are members of the community', but it does not follow from this that they are 'among the addressees of the letter'. I assume that Gamble means that those persons whom Paul greets in Rom. 16 by using the second-person type of greeting belong to the intended audience. This conclusion he tries to back up by his view on Phil. 4.21 and kiss-greetings in Paul's letters. However, as I have demonstrated, Gamble's argument is shaky.

διακόνοις). It seems implausible that the second-person type of greeting in 4.21a would exclude 'every saint in Christ Jesus' from the letter audience, because in that case only the very limited audience of leaders would hear the letter. That would contradict the all-inclusive address in 1.1.

In 1 Thess. 1.1 Paul wishes grace and peace to 'the church of the Thessalonians in God the Father and the Lord Jesus Christ'. As we noticed, 1 Thess. 5.26-27 suggests a limited first audience. However, there will be a second, much larger, audience; Paul explicitly commands, 'I adjure you by the Lord that the letter be read to all the brothers.' This is a clear indication that the second-person type of greeting does not exclude 'all the brothers' from the audience. On the contrary, Paul insists that they must both be greeted and hear the letter.

This is confirmed by an additional example from the New Testament letters; in Col. 4.15 Paul asks the addressees to convey his greetings to 'the brothers and sisters in Laodicea, and to Nympha and the church in her house'. It is obvious that Laodicean 'brothers and sisters' are not among the first audience. Despite that fact, this does not preclude them from hearing the letter, for in the next verse Paul requests, 'when this letter has been read among you, have it read also in the church of the Laodiceans'.[33]

3. *Conclusions*

For some reason, when readers of Pauline letters visualize the very first reading of a letter, they usually tend to assume a rather stereotypical situation. A usual idea may be that were the letter addressed to all the believers in a given congregation, they were all gathered to hear it when it was read for the first time. But it must be admitted that we have very limited knowledge of what really happened after Paul ended his dictation. Very likely Paul and a letter carrier (or carriers) looked the finished letter through together, and Paul gave instructions pertaining to the contents and public presentation. The carrier was instructed on how to act when he or she arrived at the target church. Paul probably told him or her whom he or she must meet first and what kind of oral message he or she must give them. Maybe Paul wanted the leaders of the local church to hear the letter before it was presented to a wider audience.

In the cases of both 1 Thess. and Phil., scholars have rightly wondered what kind of situation Paul had been visualizing. According to the present study, the end greetings and the inclusive addresses in the letters suggest a two-staged delivery process. The first audience was composed of a limited number of persons, probably church leaders. They had a responsibility to transmit Paul's message to the second audience, the believers in the

33 These observations are valid even if Colossians is inauthentic.

congregation. Thus, second-person type of greetings in Paul's letters do *not* imply that the persons to be greeted would not eventually hear the letter. In Phil. and Col., Paul asks the addressees to send greetings to certain groups of people *and* read the letter to the same people as well.

As regards Romans, the second-person type of greetings in ch. 16 suggest that no person mentioned in the greetings belonged to the circle of first hearers of the letter. The first audience was probably composed of leaders of some house-churches who were commonly held in repute and got along with many Roman believers; thus they were able to convey Paul's greetings and realize his appeal concerning Phoebe (16.1-2).

The second-person type of greetings do not reveal the composition of the second audience, the larger group of believers.[34] It is possible that Paul intended the letter to be read to every believer he mentions in the greetings. On the other hand, maybe he wanted the message of the letter to be transmitted only to some of them. Be that as it may, the answer must be sought in other places in the letter, whereupon we will face the old notorious problems: on the one hand, 'all' in 1.7 suggests that eventually every Christian in Rome was intended to hear the letter, but, on the other hand, the first chapter in particular, with its heavy emphasis on Gentiles, implies a Gentile readership.

34 Following Mullins and Thorsteinsson, Das, *Solving*, pp. 101–3 concludes in a similar way: '[T]he second-person greetings of Rom 16.1–16 do not provide any evidence for the ethnic composition of Paul's audience' (p. 103).

INDEX OF REFERENCES

INDEX OF AUTHORS

Mack, B.L.   212
Mackay, B.S.   159
MacMullen, R.   75
Malherbe, A.J.   169, 182, 184, 187,
    232–3
Malina, B.J.   21
Mannermaa, T.   98, 104
Marion, J.-L.   102
Marshall, I.H.   186, 190, 233
Martin, D.B.   80, 84–5
Martin, R.P.   55, 234, 140, 159
Martyn, J.L.   25
Marxsen, W.   186–7
Mason, S.   227
Masson, C.   232–3
Meade, D.G.   175
Menken, M.J.J.   178
Metzger, B.M.   174–6
Metzger, P.   178
Michel, O.   82, 88
Miller, J.C.   227
Mitchell, M.   21
Mitternacht, D.   23
Montefiore, C.G.   8
Moo, D.J.   38–9, 52
Moore, A.L.   233
Morris, L.   44, 54, 62, 190, 233
Mowry, L.   179
Mullins, T.   228, 230–1, 237
Murphy-O'Connor, J.   231
Murray, J.   47–8, 50, 54
Mußner, F.   216, 223–4

Nanos, M.D.   22, 27, 31–2, 227
Neyrey, J.H.   21
Nissinen, M.   82–5
Nygren, A.   52

O'Banion, J.D.   202
O'Brien, P.T.   42, 74, 205
O'Neill, J.C.   28
Olbrechts-Tyteca, L.   212
Oldfather, W.A.   74, 78
Osiek, C.   157–8

Pannenberg, W.   98
Patte, D.   22
Pearsall, J.   210
Pearson, B.A.   31
Perelman, C.   212
Pesch, O.H.   98
Peterlin, D.   169
Peters, A.   98
Peura, S.   98, 104

Pfleiderer, O.   37
Piper, J.   50–3, 60
Plank, K.A.   76
Pohlenz, M.   75, 81–2
Pöhlmann, W.   87
Pollard, T.E.   163
Portefaix, L.   165
Porter, S.   199

Rahtjen, B.D.   162
Räisänen, H.   4–7, 12, 19–20, 25, 27,
    33, 37–8, 52, 74–6, 81, 86, 88, 90, 197,
    200–1, 211
Raunio, A.   100–2, 105
Reasoner, M.   21, 23
Reed, J.T.   160–2
Reese, J.M.   75
Rehkopf, F.   182
Reichert, A.   227
Rendtorff, R.   46
Rengstorf, K.H.   77
Riddle, D.W.   33
Riekkinen, V.   87–9
Rist, J.M.   78, 175
Ritschl, A.   97
Robiglio, A.   110
Roetzel, C.   180
Roose, H.   186
Ruether, R.   33–4

Saarinen, R.   90, 96–7, 102, 104,
    109–10
Sanders, E.P.   3–4, 6–9, 12–14, 19–20,
    22, 24, 31, 33–4, 36, 38–43, 69, 74, 81,
    92–4, 96, 132
Sandmel, S.   75
Sänger, D.   29, 32–3
Schewe, S.   213
Schlier, H.   49, 211
Schmeller, T.   84
Schneider, T.   104
Schnelle, U.   21, 30–1, 34, 151–2, 178
Schoeps H.-J.   37
Schrage, W.   56, 76, 80
Schreiner, T.R.   43, 52
Schweitzer, A.   65, 68, 97
Seeberg, R.   97–8
Seifrid, M.   42, 46, 62, 65–7, 74, 95–6
Siegert, F.   211–12
Smyth, H.W.   138, 140, 183, 188
Sorabji, R.   84
Spanje, T. van   22
Spanneut, M.   75
Speyer, W.   173–5

Stendahl, K.   12, 91–2, 94
Stott, J.   71
Stowers, S.K.   22, 227
Strecker, G.   32
Strobel, A.   89
Strüder, C.W.   120
Stuhlmacher, P.   57, 60, 65–6, 87
Swift, R.C.   169

Theissen, G.   23, 34, 205
Thesleff, H.   82
Thorsteinsson, R.M.   227–8, 231, 237
Thrall, M.E.   125, 127–9
Thurén, J.   54, 165, 168
Thurén, L.   10–13, 157, 196, 198–202, 204–8, 212
Tolmie, D.F.   213
Toulmin, S.   212
Trilling, W.   172, 178, 187
Tsang, S.   213
Työrinoja, R.   105

Unnik, W.M.   89

Vincent, M.R.   135–7, 146–7, 150, 234
Vogelsang, E.   97
Vollenweider, S.   80–1
Vorster, J.   205, 207
Vos, J.S.   197

Walter, N.   32, 34

Wansink, C.S.   159
Watson, D.F.   148, 158, 165, 168, 171, 211
Watson, F.   22
Way, D.   60
Weima, J.A.D.   231
Weinel, H.   37
Weißengruber, F.   175
Wengert, T.   105
Wenz, G.   104
Westerholm, S.   3, 19–21, 40–2, 68, 74, 90–5, 99–101, 106
Wicke-Reuter, U.   75
Wilckens, U.   32, 59, 88
Winter, B.W.   141
Wisløff, C.F.   72
Witherington III, B.   185
Witte, J.   100
Wöhle, A.   100, 105–6
Wohlenberg, G.   183
Wolf, E.   98
Wolff, C.   76
Wrede, W.   68, 172, 180
Wright, N.T.   23, 26–7, 31, 93, 203

Yeago, D.   105

Zahl, P.F.M.   60–2
Zeller, D.   24